DATE DUE

COINAGE IN THE BALKANS
820-1355

COINAGE
IN THE
BALKANS
820-1355

by
D. M. Metcalf

INSTITUTE FOR BALKAN STUDIES

ARGONAUT   PUBLISHERS
CHICAGO   MCMLXVI

Library of Congress Catalog Card Number 66-20439

First Printing 1965
Second Printing 1966

Printed in the United States of America

CONTENTS

PART 1.

INTRODUCTION

PART 2.

THE LOCAL DEVELOPMENT OF MONETARY ECONOMY

PART 3.

INTEGRATION INTO THE EUROPEAN ECONOMIC SYSTEMS

MAPS AND TABLES

MAPS

ACKNOWLEDGEMENTS

I am largely indebted to Mr Philip Grierson, Reader in Medieval Numismatics in the University of Cambridge, under whose stimulating and kindly guidance I began to work on Balkan monetary history. It gives me much pleasure to mention the friendly good-will and help, and the generous hospitality, of colleagues in Greece, Bulgaria, Jugoslavia, and Romania, especially Mrs E. Varoukha-Khristodhoulopoulou, until recently Keeper of the National Numismatic Museum at Athens, and Mr R. Stroud, formerly Secretary of the American School of Classical Studies there; the late Dr R. Marić, Keeper of the Numismatic Collection in the National Museum, and Dr. S. Dimitrijević, of Belgrade; Mr O. Iliescu, Keeper of the Coin Cabinet of the Romanian Academy, and Mr B. Mitrea, of the Institute of Archeology, in Budapest; Dr D. Pinterović, formerly Director, and Mr E. Spajić, Director of the Slavonian Museum, Osijek; Mr A. Jeločnik, Keeper of the Numismatic Cabinet, the National Museum, and Mr E. Pegan, at Ljubljana; Dr T. Gerasimov, Keeper of the Coin Cabinet in the Archaeological Institute and Museum, Sofia; Professor Basil Laourdas, Director of the Institute for Balkan Studies, Thessaloniki; Miss L. Kojić, Director of the Zavićajni Museum, Trebinje; and Mrs I. Degmedžić and Dr Z. Vinski, of the Archaeological Museum, Zagreb.

I am required, or wish, to acknowledge financial assistance from the tenure of a Strathcona Research Exhibition at St. John's College, Cambridge; a scholarship of the Jugoslavian Commission for Cultural Relations; the School Studentship, 1958-59, of the British School of Archaelogy at Athens; a travel grant from the Cyril Foster Fund at Oxford; and a research award from the British Academy.

ABBREVIATIONS

1. Titles of periodical publications

ABSAthens	*Annual of the British School of Archaeology at Athens*, London.
BASDalmat.	*Bulletino di Archeologia e Storia Dalmata*, Split (continued as *VAHDalmat.*)
BCH	*Bulletin de Correspondance Hellénique*, Athens-Paris.
Dacia	*Dacia, Revue d'Archéologie et d'Histoire Ancienne*, Bucarest.
GZMBH, GZMS	*Glasnik Zemaljskog Muzeja u Bosni i Hercegovini*, subsequently *Glasnik Zemaljskog Muzeja u Sarajevu*, Sarajevo.
HBN	*Hamburger Beiträge zur Numismatik*, Hamburg.
Hesperia	*Hesperia, Journal of the American School of Classical Studies at Athens*, Baltimore.
IAI	See *IBAD*.
IBAD, IBAI, IAI	*Izvestiya na Bŭlgarskoto Arkheologichesko Druzhestvo*, continued as *Izvestiya na Bŭlgarskiya Arkheologicheski Institut*, continued as *Izvestiya na Arkheologicheskiya Institut*, Sofia.
JIAN	*Journal International d'Archéologie Numismatique*, Athens.
NC	*The Numismatic Chronicle and Journal of the Royal Numismatic Society*, London.
NK	*Numizmatikai Közlöny*, Budapest.
NLOB	*Numismatische Literatur Osteuropas und des Balkans*, Graz.
NV	*Numizmatičke Vijesti, Izdaje Numizmatičko Društvo u Zagrebu*, Zagreb.
NZ	*Numismatische Zeitschrift*, Vienna.

RN	*Revue Numismatique*, Paris.
SCN	*Studii şi Cercetări de Numismatică*, Bucarest.
Starinar	*Starinar Srpskog Arheološkog Društva*, (continued under other similar titles, now) *Starinar, Organ Arheološkog Institut*, Belgrade.
VAHDalmat.	*Vjesnik za Arheologiju i Historiju Dalmatinsku*, Split.
VHrvat.AD	*Viestnik Hrvatskoga Arheološkoga Družtva*, subsequently *Vjesnik Hrvatskoga Arheološkoga Društva*, subsequently *Vjesnik Arheološkog Muzeja u Zagrebu*, Zagreb.
WMBH	*Wissenschaftliche Mittheilungen aus Bosnien und der Hercegovina*, Vienna.

2. Writings (Sources and major studies for monetary history)

Ahrweiler-Glykatzi "Le Tétartèron"	H. Ahrweiler-Glykatzi, "Nouvelle hypothèse sur le tétartèron d'or et la politique monétaire de Nicéphore Phocas", *Zbornik Radova Vizantološkog Instituta* viii/i (=Mélanges Georges Ostrogorsky, vol. I) (1963), 1-9
Aleksova, "Naodi"	B. Aleksova, "Naodi na Srednovekovni Pari, 1921-1954", *Vesnik na Muzejsko - Konzervatorskoto Društvo na N.R. Makedonija* iii (1955), 17-22
Băncilă, "Unor Tezaure"	I. Băncilă, "Note asupra unor Tezaure de Monede Bizantine", *SCN* i (1957), 425 - 38
Baumgartner, "Die Blütezeit"	E. Baumgartner, "Die Blütezeit der friesacher Pfennige. Ein Beitrag zur Geschichte des innerösterreichischen Münzwesens im 13. Jahrhundert", *NZ* lxxiii (1949), 75-106, lxxviii (1959), 14-57, and lxxix (1961), 28-63
Bellinger, *Anonymous Byzantine Bronze*	A. R. Bellinger, *The Anonymous Byzantine Bronze Coinage* (Numismatic Notes and Monographs, 35), New York, 1928

Bellinger, *Corinth*, 1925   A. R. Bellinger, *Catalogue of the Coins Found at Corinth*, 1925, New Haven, 1930

Bellinger, "Three Hoards"   A. R. Bellinger, "Three Hoards of Byzantine Bronze Coins", *Greek and Byzantine Studies* i (1958), 163-71

Bertelè, *L'Imperatore Alato*   T. Bertelè, *L'Imperatore Alato nella Numismatica Bizantina*, Rome, 1951

Bertelè, "L'Iperpero"   T. Bertelè, "L'Iperpero Bizantino dal 1261 al 1453", *Rivista Italiana di Numismatica* lix (1957), 70-89

Brunšmid, "Našašća Novaca"   J. Brunšmid, "Nekoliko Našašća Novaca na Skupu u Hrvatskoj i Slavoniji", *VHrvat. AD* NS i (1895), 96-119 (I-IV); ii (1896), 42-103 (V-VII); iv (1898), 81-155 (V, VIII-XI); v (1900), 235-43 (XII-XV); vi (1901-02), 167-84 (V, XVI-XVII); viii (1905), 176-192 (V, XVIII-XXV); ix (1906-07), 210-40 (XXVI-XXVII); x (1908-09), 223-30 (XXVIII - XXXII); xi (1910-11), 241-77 (XXXIII); xii (1912), 260-86 (XXXIV-XXXVI); xiii (1914), 269-306 (XXXVII-XL)

CN Italicorum   *Corpus Nummorum Italicorum*, Rome,1910-.

Dimian, "Cîteva Descoperiri"   E. I. Dimian, "Cîteva Descoperiri Monetare pe Teritoriul R. P. R.", *SCN* i (1957), 189-216

Dimitrijević, "Bakarni Novac"   S. Dimitrijević, "Srpski Srednjovekovni Bakarni Novac", *Istoriski Časopis* viii (1959), 27-45

Dimitrijević, "Hronologija"   S. Dimitrijević, "Hronologija Dušanovog Carskog Novca", *Istoriski Glasnik* ix - x (1959), 113-138

Dimitrijević, "Problemi"   S. Dimitrijević, "Problemi Srpske Srednjovekovne Numizmatike", *Istoriski Glasnik* 1957, 1-2, 69-99; 3-4, 104-30

Dölger, *Regesten*   F. Dölger, *Regesten der Kaiserurkunden des oströmischen Reiches von* 565 - 1453, Munich, 1924, 1925, 1932, 1960

Edwards, *Corinth*, 1896-1929   K. M. Edwards, *Coins*, 1896 - 1929 (Corinth Reports, VI), Cambridge, Mass., 1932

Edwards, "Corinth, 1930 - 35"   K. M. Edwards, "Report on the Coins Found in the Excavations at Corinth During the Years 1930-1935", *Hesperia* vi (1937), 241-56

Filov, "Novootkriti Starini"   B. Filov, "Novootkriti Starini", *IBAD* i (1910), 222ff.; iii (1912-13), 328-39; iv (1914), 278-93

Gerasimov, "Andronic II et Andronic III"   T. D. Gerasimov, "Les Hyperpères d'Andronic II et d'Andronic III et leur Circulation en Bulgarie", *Byzantinobulgarica* i (1962), 213-36

Gerasimov, "Bŭlgarski Moneti"   T. D. Gerasimov, "Nekoliko Neizdadeni Bŭlgarski Moneti", *Godishnik na Narodniya Muzei* vi (1932-34), 1936, 223-42

Gerasimov, "Kolektivni Nakhodki"   T. D. Gerasimov, "Kolektivni Nakhodki na Moneti prez 1933 i 1934 G.", *IBAI* viii (1934), 467-73; *ibid.*, 1934-36, *IBAI* xi/I (1937), 315-24; ibid., 1937-38, *IBAI* xii (1938), 450-57; *ibid.* 1939, *IBAI* xiii(1939), 341-45; *ibid.*, 1940, *IBAI* xiv (1940-42), 282-85; *ibid.*, 1941-45, *IBAI* xv (1946), 235-44; *ibid.*, 1946-48, *IAI* xvii (1950), 316-26; *ibid.*, 1949-51, *IAI* xviii (1952), 400-404; *ibid.*, 1951-54, *IAI* xx (1955), 602-611; *ibid.*, 1955, *IAI* xxi (1957), 323-27; *ibid.*, 1956-57, *IAI* xxii (1959), 356-66

Gerasimov, "Monetni Sŭkrovishta"   T. D. Gerasimov, "Monetni Sŭkrovishta Namereni v Bŭlgariya prez 1958 i 1959 G.", *IAI* xxv (1962), 225-37; *ibid.*, 1960-61, *IAI* xxvi (1963), 257-70

Gerasimov, "Neizdadeni Moneti"   T. D. Gerasimov, "Neizdadeni Moneti ot Paleolozite", *Razkopki i Prouchvaniya* iv (1950), 23-44

Gerasimov, "Solun"   T. D. Gerasimov, "Prinos kŭm Numizmatika na Solunskata Imperiya", *Izsledvaniya v chest na Marich S. Drinov*, Sofia, 1960, pp. 381-98

Grierson, "Coinage and Money"   P. Grierson, "Coinage and Money in the Byzantine Empire, 498-c. 1090", *Moneta*

| | *e Scambi nell'Alto Medioevo* (Settimane di Studio del Centro Italiano di Studi sull' Alto Medioevo, VIII), Spoleto, 1961, pp. 411-53 |

Grierson, "Debasement" — P. Grierson, "The Debasement of the Bezant in the Eleventh Century", *Byzantinische Zeitschrift* xlvii (1954), 379-94

Grierson, "Fineness" — P. Grierson, "Notes on the Fineness of the Byzantine Solidus", *Byzantinische Zeitschrift* liv (1961), 91-97

Grierson, "Nicéphore Phocas" — P. Grierson, "Nomisma, Tetartèron et Dinar: un Plaidoyer pour Nicéphore Phocas", *Revue Belge de Numismatique* c (1954), 75-84

Harris, "Corinth, 1936-39" — J. M. Harris, "Coins Found at Corinth. I. Report on the Coins Found in the Excavations at Corinth during the Years 1936 - 1939", *Hesperia* x (1941), 143-55

Hóman, "Szlavon Denárok" — B. Hóman, "II. András- es IV. Béla-kori Szlavon Denárok", *NK* xviii-xix (1919-20), 33-42

Jeločnik, "Dve Najdbi" — A. Jeločnik, "Dve Najdbi Srednjeveškïh Novcev", *Zgodovinski Časopis* vi - vii (1952 -53), 443-72

Klemenc, "Nalazi Novaca" — J. Klemenc, "Nalazi Novaca u Jugoslaviji, 1910-1936", *Numizmatika* ii - iv (1934-36), 124ff

Lishev, *Paritsa* — S. Lishev, *Za Pronikvaneto i Rolyata na Parite v Feodalna Bŭlgariya*, Sofia, 1958

Ljubić, *Opis* — S. Ljubić, *Opis Jugoslavenskih Novaca*, Zagreb, 1875

Longuet, "Une Trouvaille" — H. Longuet, "Une Trouvaille de Monnaies des Paléologues", *Revue Belge de Numismatique* cvi (1960), 243-66

Luschin, "Friesacher Pfennige" — A. Luschin von Ebengreuth, "Friesacher Pfennige, Beiträge zu ihrer Münzgeschichte und zur Kenntnis ihrer Gepräge", *NZ* lv (1922), 89-118; lvi (1923), 33-144

Luschin, "Steierische Münzfunde" — A. Luschin von Ebengreuth, "Steierische Münzfunde", *Jahrbuch der k. k. Zentral-*

kommission iv (1906), 162-99; *Jahrbuch für Altertumskunde* i (1907), 137-84 and ii (1908), 161-215

Marić, "Ostave" — R. Marić, "Ostave Starog Novca u Numizmatičkoj Zbirci Narodnog Muzeja u Beogradu", *Konzervatorski i Ispitivački Radovi* (Saopštenja Zadova za Zaštitu i Naučno Proučavanje Spomenika Kulture Narodne Republike Srbije, vol. I), Belgrade, 1956, pp. 179-81

Marić, *Studije* — R. Marić, *Studije iz Srpske Numizmatike* (Srpska Akademija Nauka, Posebna Izdanja, vol. CCLIX), Belgrade, 1956

Metcalf, "Alexius I Comnenus" — D. M. Metcalf, "The Reformed Gold Coinage of Alexius I Comnenus", *HBN* v (1962), 271-84

Metcalf, "*Deniers Tournois* in Frankish Greece" — D. M. Metcalf, "The Currency of Deniers *Tournois* in Frankish Greece", *ABSAthens* lv (1960), 38-59

Metcalf, "East Mediterranean World" — D. M. Metcalf, "The Byzantine Bronze Coinage in the East Mediterranean World", *Congresso Internazionale di Numismatica, Roma, 11-16 Settembre* 1961, vol. II, Rome, 1965

Metcalf, "John Vatatzes" — D. M. Metcalf, "John Vatatzes and John Comnenus: Questions of Style and Detail in Byzantine Numismatics", *Greek, Roman and Byzantine Studies* iii (1960), 203-14

Metcalf, "Provincial Issues" — D. M. Metcalf, "Provincial Issues among the Byzantine Bronze Coinage of the Eleventh Century", *HBN* v (1962), 25-32

Metcalf, "Scyphate Bronze Coinage in Greece" — D. M. Metcalf, "Byzantine Scyphate Bronze Coinage in Greece", *ABSAthens* lvi (1961), 42-63

Metcalf, "Syrmia and Slavonia" — D. M. Metcalf, "The Currency of Byzantine Coins in Syrmia and Slavonia", *HBN* iv (1960), 429-444

Metcalf, "Theophilus" — D. M. Metcalf, "The New Bronze Coinage of Theophilus and the Growth of the Balkan Themes", *American Numismatic Society Museum Notes* x (1962), 81-98

Mosser, *Byzantine Coin Hoards* — S. McA. Mosser, *A Bibliography of Byzantine Coin Hoards* (Numismatic Notes and Monographs, 67), New York, 1935

Mushmov, Kolektivni Nakhodki" — N. A. Mushmov, "Kolektivni Nakhodki na Moneti prez 1891-1914 G.", *IBAD* iv (1914), 270ff.; *ibid.*, 1915-18, *IBAD* vi (1916-18), 161ff.; *ibid.*, 1919-20, *IBAD* vii (1919-20), 124ff.; *ibid.*, 1921-22, *IBAI* i (1921-22), 239-43; *ibid.*, 1923, *IBAI* ii (1923-24), 229-31; *ibid.*, 1924, *IBAI* iii (1925), 254f.; *ibid.*, 1925-26, *IBAI* iv (1926-27), 321-26; *ibid.*, 1927-28, IBIA v (1928-29), 328-36; *ibid.*, 1929-30, *IBAI* vi (1930-31), 314-18; *ibid.*, 1931-32, *IBAI* vii (1932-33), 423-25.

Mushmov, *Monetite* — N. A. Mushmov, *Monetite i Pechatite na Bŭlgarskite Tsare*, Sofia, 1924

Mushmov, "Neizdadeni Moneti" — N. A. Mushmov, "Neizdadeni Bŭlgarski Moneti", *IBAI* vi (1930-31), 221-40

Nuber, "Slavonische Münzen" — C. F. Nuber, "Beitrag zur Chronologie slavonischer Münzen", *WMBH* vi (1899), 467 - 77. (Also in Serbo-Croat as "Prinos Kronologiji Slavonskih Banovaca", *GZMS* ix [1897], 169-80)

Ostrogorsky, *Byzantine State* — G. Ostrogorsky, *History of the Byzantine State*, translated by J. M. Hussey, Oxford, 1956

Panchenko "Pechati i Monety" — B. A. Panchenko, "Vizantiiskiya Pechati i Monety", *Izvestiya Russkago Arkheologicheskago Instituta v Konstantinopolie* x (1905), Sofia, 291-300, and *Al'bom' k' X Tomu Izvestu,* Vienna, 1905, plate LVIII

Ratto, *Monnaies Byzantines* — R. Ratto, *Monnaies Byzantines et d'Autres Pays Contemporaines à l'Epoque Byzantine* (sale-catalogue of 9 December 1930, Lugano), reprinted Amsterdam, 1959

Rengjeo, *Corpus* I. Rengjeo, *Corpus der mittelaterlichen Münzen von Kroatien, Slavonien, Dalmatien, und Bosnien,* Graz, 1959

Rešetar, *Dubrovačka Numizmatika* M. Rešetar, *Dubrovačka Numizmatika* (Srpska Kraljevska Akademija Nauk i Umetnosti, Posebna Izdanja, vols. XLVIII and LIX), Sremski Karlovac, 1924, and Belgrade, 1925

Réthy and Zimmermann, *CNHungariae* L. Réthy, *Corpus Nummorum Hungariae,* revised edition introduced and translated by G. Probszt, with an additional section by L. Zimmermann, Graz, 1959

Sabatier, *Description Générale* P. J. Sabatier, *Description Générale des Monnaies Byzantines,* 2 vols., Paris, 1862

Saria, "Altserbische Münzwesen" B. Saria, "Die Entwicklung des altserbischen Münzwesens", *Südost-Forschungen* xiii (1954), 22-61

Schlumberger, *L'Orient Latin* G. Schlumberger, *Numismatique de l'Orient Latin,* Paris, 1878; *Supplément,* 1882

Shear, "Analytical Table" J. P. Shear, "[Excavations in the Athenian Agora] Analytical Table of Coins", *Hesperia v* (1936), 123ff

Stockert, *Spalato* K. Stockert, *Le Monete del Comune di Spalato,* Split, 1919 (supplement to *BAS Dalmat.* xxxviii (1917-19)

Svoronos, "Ekthesis" I. N. Σβορῶνος, "Ἔκθεσις περὶ τοῦ Ἐθνικοῦ Νομισματικοῦ Μουσείου καὶ τῆς ἰδιαιτέρας νομισματικῆς συλλογῆς τοῦ Ἐθνικοῦ Πανεπιστημίου μετὰ περιγραφικοῦ καταλόγου τῶν προσκτημάτων κατὰ τὸ ἀκαδημαϊκὸν ἔτος 1905 -1906", *JIAN* ix (1906), 245-334; and with similar titles, for 1906-07, *JIAN* x (1907), 163-268; for 1907-08, *JIAN* xi (1908), 249-328 and xii (1909-10), 1-80; for 1908 -09, *JIAN* xiii (1911), 33-112 (by Svoronos and K. M. Κωνσταντόπουλος); for 1909 -10, *JIAN* xv (1913), 33-74. Earlier(brief) reports: for 1903-04 (with a summary from 1890 onwards), *JIAN* vii (1904), 317-90; for 1904-05, *JIAN* viii (1905), 251-56.

Thompson, *Coins*

M. Thompson, *Coins from the Roman through the Venetian Period* (The Athenian Agora, vol. II), Princeton, 1954

Truhelka, "Die slav-onische Banaldenare"

Ć. Truhelka, "Die slavonische Banaldenare. Ein Beitrag zur croatischen Numismatik", *WMBH* vi (1899), 328-466 (Also in Serbo-Croat as "Slavonski Banovci. [Prinos Hrvatskoj Numismatici]" *GZMS* ix [1897], 1-160)

Truhelka, "Verzeichnis"

Ć. Truhelka, "Verzeichnis der bosnischen, serbischen und bulgarischen Münzen des Landesmuseum in Sarajevo", *WMBH* iv (1896), 303ff

Varoukha-Khristodhoulo-poulou, "Acquisitions"

E. Varoukha-Khristodhoulopoulou, Acquisitions du Musée Numismatique d'Athènes", *BCH* lxxxiv (1960), 485-503; lxxxvi (1962), 417-27

Varoukha-Khristodhoulo-poulou,

Ε. Βαρούχα-Χριστοδουλοπούλου, "Εὕρημα βυζαντινῶν νομισμάτων Πάρου", Ἀρχαιολογικὸν Δελτιον xiv (1931-32), 78-83

Wroth, *BMC(Byz.)*, I, II, III

W. Wroth, *Catalogue of the Imperial Byzantine Coins in the British Museum*, 2 vols. (but consecutively paginated), London, 1908; *ibid.*, *Catalogue of the Coins of the Vandals, Ostrogoths and Lombards, and of the Empires of Thessalonica, Nicaea, and Trebizond, in the British Museum*, London, 1911

Zakythinos, *Crise Monétaire*

D. Zakythinos, *Crise Monétaire et Crise Economique à Byzance du XIII au XV Siècle*, Athens, 1948.

PART 1
INTRODUCTION

CHAPTER I

THREE QUESTIONS

In their twenty-second plenary session, in 1903, the Historical Commission for Baden passed a resolution to admit into their programme the preparation of a "numismatic and monetary history of the regions united in the Grand Duchy of Baden." It was planned that the work should be of use "equally to numismatic and to economic history.The two disciplines", it was said, "although closely related, have until now to too great an extent gone their own ways. ...The economic section will deal with: the privilege of striking coins; the monetary policy of the issuing authorities; when, to meet what needs, and in what quantities coins were struck;" and so on, through a score of categories of information. The proposals laid before the Historical Commission were doubtless influenced—how could they have failed to be?—by the achievements and fruits of the *Monumenta Germaniae Historica.* The list of topics which was set out was comprehensive, and, through Cahn's early monographs [1] in particular, was destined to guide subsequent writing by German scholars on the numismatics of the Franconian and Hohenstaufen period to such an extent that one can speak of the German school of medieval "*Münz- und Geldgeschichte*". Much work of great distinction has been accomplished in its tradition. Looking back, one can see that if there has been a fault, it is that what has been written has sometimes been not very much more than "*Münz- und Geldarchiv*", and that not sufficiently strenuous efforts have been made to answer three small, but difficult, questions from among those proposed by the Historical Commission for Baden, namely, when, to meet what needs, in what quantities. Sixty years later, the gulf between economic history and numismatics is almost as great as it was, and there is still no way of bridging it except through an answer to the same three questions.

The methods that have been characteristic of *Münz und Geldgeschichte* are exceptionally well suited to central Europe in the age of

---

[1] J. Cahn, *Münz-und Geldgeschichte von Konstanz und des Bodenseegebietes im Mittelalter,* Heidelberg, 1911.

localized currency, when monetary organization and monetary policy were on the whole simple and rather passive, but they are less suitable when applied to the territory of a powerful state with a tradition of centralized administration and complex policies, such as the Byzantine Empire was during a part at least of the period with which this study is concerned. The subject-matter of Byzantine numismatics compels the researcher to distinguish between numismatic history and monetary history and to apply different techniques to each of them. One could say that the central task in numismatic history is to trace out, usually by means of a reconstruction of the work of individual mints and the detailed chronology of the coinage, the policies that were pursued by the government and the administrative machinery through which they were implemented. The central task in monetary history, which must rely heavily on the interpretation of coin-finds, is to depict the use of coinage as money, as it came about in practice. The two projects, obviously, go on side by side and help each other, but the former is apt to range more widely in time, in order to examine the continuity, and development, of policy, while the latter may take as its unit a region which is the object of the policies of several states.

There is a more striking contrast between numismatic history and monetary history. The former proceeds from the particular towards the general, the latter, from the general towards the particular. Unless the issues of coinage can be very closely dated, say, to within two years, on reasonably independent evidence, then the association between monetary policies and other governmental policies or historical events (of which the dates are accurately known) will generally involve a large element of conjecture. Numismatic history therefore has to make its advances at scattered points, where the chances of the evidence enable it to do so. It may be less obvious, but the point is fundamental, that monetary history must normally take its start from generalities. This is especially true in a region such as the Balkan peninsula. The two kinds of evidence which, apart from the parallel study of numismatic history, contribute most to its monetary history are, first, hoards, and, secondly, stray coins discovered in archaeological excavations. What conclusions can properly be drawn from the evidence of coins that have been found in the soil? If we had only one hoard of coins, there would be very little that could be deduced from it about the monetary affairs of the period to which it belonged, since there is not, and cannot be, any way of knowing which out of a great variety of possible circumstances occasioned its deposit. Similarly, if we had the stray-finds from only one archaeological site, there would be no way of knowing whether the pattern they revealed was purely local or whether it was of wider relevance. Fortunately, however, we have several hundred hoards of medieval coins from the Balkans, and two superb series of stray-finds from the excavations at Corinth and Athens. [2] The number of hoards is still being added to year by year, and we may look forward to being able one day to study a third very important series of site-finds, from Thasos. By comparing many hoards with each other, we can form an opinion about their character: this one is perhaps a savings-hoard, that one was almost certainly concealed in haste, a third consisting of foreign coins is unlike any from the same region and undoubtedly represents a sum of money carried there by a traveller. Again: if we discover that the overall character of the finds in this region is different from that, we shall be able to conclude that there were differences in monetary affairs. By applying comparative methods to a large enough body of information we can make the unknown particularities discount each other, and we can thus be quite sure (provided we have delimited the regions with reasonably good sense) that we are studying reliable evidence, even if its precise interpretation remains a matter for debate; but the validity of the conclusions subsists in the comparisons, and it cannot be detached from them. The whole argument depends upon the randomness of the evidence, and the hoards are random only in certain respects. To take an obvious, and very simplified, example, two hoards concealed in haste in face of the same threat may be random in respect of the age-composition of the currency, if their owners hid whatever cash they happened to have in hand, but they will be far from random in respect of their date and place of deposit. Site-finds are as different as could be from hoards concealed in haste, for they are usually casual losses of coins of small value, but comparative methods must equally be applied to them. It is certain that their evidence is in itself highly reliable,[3] and that the differences between the finds at two sites, however they are to be interpreted, reflect differences in the composition of the currency in the two cities; but the evidence must be studied in terms of the differences.

Even when he writes, or thinks, in a shorthand which omits them, the numismatist's arguments from hoards and site-finds depend on

---

[2] Edwards, *Corinth*, 1896-1929; Edwards, "Corinth, 1930-35"; Harris, "Corinth, 1936-39"; a continuation for the years 1940-1960 is under preparation by R. Stroud; Shear, "Analytical Table"; Thompson, *Coins*.

[3] Metcalf, "Provincial Issues".

comparisons. Such comparisons frequently involve the *minutiae* of the coins themselves; and almost always they have to be made on the basis of fewer hoards or finds than one could wish were available. For both these reasons it is constantly necessary to re-examine old evidence — both because it was not published with attention to details of which the importance has since become apparent, and because the degree of confidence that is to be attached to each conclusion is a matter for a complex judgement of probabilities. Thus, the numismatist can never relegate to a scholarly limbo the coins that he has tried to interpret; hence the need for a hand-book with a rather full bibliographical apparatus.

For the purposes of monetary history it is desirable to be able to date coins to within two or three years. A surprisingly large proportion of the issues that circulated in the medieval Balkans cannot yet be dated more closely than within twenty or thirty years. The coins of a prince whose reign was short, and who did not share the name of his successor or predecessor, will present little or no difficulty. The sole reign of Andronicus Comnenus, for example, lasted only from 1183 to 1185. Manuel Comnenus, on the other hand, reigned from 1143 to 1180, and the numismatist has at present virtually no secure foothold among the numerous different coinages struck in his name. There is a strong probability that various hoards from Corinth were concealed at the time of the Norman raid of 1147, but the many types that were not represented in those hoards might, on the present evidence, belong virtually anywhere in a period of 33 years, or indeed 37 years, for the argument *a silentio* would not necessarily be correct. It is a matter of luck whether there is available a hoard or group of hoards, of which the deposit can be associated fairly firmly with some historical event, to break up the period of a long reign and to give a first clue to the sequence of the coinage within it. The study of a newly-discovered hoard will sometimes permit a whole series of adjustments in the dating of other hoards and of the coins in them, if they have been published in sufficient detail. Since the precise date of a coin, if it is of a type that was issued for many years, may, even after that, have to be determined from its style, the only form of publication which is certain to be sufficiently detailed for future needs is photographic illustration of a quality which enables dies to be searched for "near-duplicate" features. The term "near-duplicate" indicates that the obverses or reverses (or both) of two coins are so extremely similar to each other that one has to look at them very closely, and perhaps compare the alignment of a number of different details, in order to make sure that they are not in fact struck from the same die. An experienced workman could make a pair of dies very quickly, say, in half a morning. The existence of "near-duplicate" dies implies that, through habits and foibles which grew up with the constant repetition of his task, he produced dies that were very much alike in the same way that specimens of a personal signature are alike. It is reasonable to assume that "near-duplicate" dies were manufactured within at most two or three months of each other. Only by constructing stylistic sequences based on die-similarity can issues which continued unchanged for a long time be dated more accurately. The task is difficult and extremely laborious, but until it has been undertaken the answer to the first of the three questions proposed by the Historical Commission for Baden will, in many cases, be so imprecise as to be relatively useless. For the Balkan coinages little has yet been done, and there are numerous opportunities for research.

Just the same is true about another of the questions, "in what quantities". In the general histories, one sometimes finds statements such as, "his coinage was plentiful, if we are to judge from the number of specimens that has survived to our own day". From whichever point one views it, such a judgement is worthless. If one wishes to know how many million coins were struck, it does not give even a vague idea. If one is interested in comparing one period with another, it is totally untrustworthy. The coins of Manuel Comnenus (1143-1180), for example, are many times more plentiful in collectors' cabinets and dealers' trays today than those of John II Comnenus (1118-1143), but there is no good reason to say that they were many times more plentiful originally. John's reign was notably peaceful, and only a few hoards concealed during it have come to light. There are not many hoards from Manuel's reign either, but his coins are still to be found in large quantities in hoards from the last fifteen years of the twelfth century and the first decades of the thirteenth, when John's coins were no longer in circulation. It is possible to make an accurate estimate of the actual quantities in which coins were struck by means of a statistical sampling technique applied to die-varieties. Given a random sample of surviving coins, the number of pairs of die-duplicates shows how many dies there were altogether in the "population" from which the sample was drawn. The fewer the dies that were used, the more frequently are duplicates likely to occur. The remaining step in the argument is to multiply the number of dies by the average number of coins struck from each die. The figure is almost entirely speculative, and there seems to be no way in which it can be recovered; 7,500 is probably a conservative estimate, while 15,000 may be too high. This step in the argument introduces a factor of error which might be as large as 2, but even with this limitation, the result can be extremely useful.

First, let us postulate a coinage struck from x dies, and assume that an equal number of coins was struck from each die. Since dies are ordinarily used until they are worn out this assumption should not introduce much error. Next, we make a random sample of y coins. Unless the sample includes a hoard of coins that had left the mint not long before, one can assume that it is random in respect of the dies; the sample can be checked from this point of view by common sense. Taking the first coin from the sample (y), the probability that it will be from some one particular die among the total (x) is $\dfrac{1}{x}$. In the whole sample, the probability that one coin will be from some one particular die is roughly $\dfrac{y}{x}$ (provided that $\dfrac{y}{x}$ is less than about 0.2, which is discovered by making the calculation; more precisely $\dfrac{y}{x}$ should be replaced by $\left[1-(\dfrac{x-1}{x})y\right]$, but $\dfrac{y}{x}$ is often good enough for the monetary historian's purposes) and the probability that two coins will be from some one particular die is, using the same approximation, $\dfrac{y\,(y-1)}{2\,.\,x^2}$. The factor of 2 is introduced to avoid counting the pair twice, in the list of configurations. Finally, we wish to know the probability of a pair, not from some one particular die, but from any die, it does not matter which. That probability is x times as great as for one particular die, $\dfrac{y(y-1)}{2x}$. This is the derivation of the formula

$$p = \frac{y(y-1)}{2x}$$

or $\qquad x = \dfrac{y(y-1)}{2p}$ where p is the number of pairs

y is the sample

x is the total of dies. [4]

---

[4] The formula was used by I. D. Brown, in "Some Notes on the Coinage of Elizabeth I with Special Reference to Her Hammered Silver", *British Numismatic Journal* xxviii (1955-57), 568-603, at p. 580. I am indebted to Dr Virgil Barnes for discussing it with me, and to Mr C. S. S. Lyon for valuable critical comments.

An example: if there are 5 pairs of dies in a sample of 150 coins, the total number of dies is calculated as follows:

$$5 = \frac{150.149}{2x}$$

$$x = \frac{22350}{10} = 2235$$

We check to see that $\frac{y}{x}$ is tolerably small: it is 0.07. Another random sample of 150 coins from the same source might easily yield 6 pairs, or 4 pairs, and the values obtained for x would then be 1879 or 2794. The figure 2235 is, in other words, only an estimate, and is subject to variation in the same way as the random sample. It needs, therefore, to be accompanied by some indication of the possible margins of error. The setting of the margins is a matter of discretion: one can be cautious to whatever degree one chooses. One's choice will depend on the nature of the problem, the nature of the evidence, and, above all, on the purpose for which the answer is required. The larger the number of pairs the smaller (relatively) the margins for any given degree of probability. The same is true of the size of the sample, but in practice the number of pairs is the major source of random error, and one can reasonably calculate the margins as $x \pm (\frac{\sqrt{p}}{p})$ %, e.g.

$$2235 \pm (\frac{\sqrt{5}}{5})$$

$$= 2235 \pm \quad 45\%$$

$$= 2235 \pm 1006$$

This is a cautious estimate; but obviously, a sample which yields as few as 4 or 5 pairs is not in itself large enough to be very accurate.

For the whole of medieval monetary history, except for the few restricted areas and periods from which complete mint-records have survived, quantitative estimates of the numbers of coins struck are still of great interest, as little work of this kind has been done. For the end of the European and East Mediterranean *Völkerwanderungszeit,* and for all studies of the early stages of the growth or spread of monetary economy, such estimates are of a fundamental importance which is so obvious that comment would be superfluous. For a general theory of Balkan monetary history in the ninth and tenth centuries it is, perhaps, the key question, which affects the formulation of all the others. The formula $x = \frac{y(y-1)}{2p}$ should be as much a part of the numismatist's everyday equipment as his magnifying glass or balance. The preliminaries to its use are the same as those which go towards answering the question "when", namely the arrangement of a large number of specimens into stylistic sequences on the basis of die-linkages and "near-duplicates". In the practical application of the formula, the most important thing is to ensure that there is no error in the total number of instances of die-duplication, since an error even of only one may make a considerable difference to the final answer.

It remains to point out that the estimates of quantity are not perfectly satisfactory because they do not measure the effectiveness of the currency. If a fixed quantity of coinage circulating within a city or a region changes hands twice as frequently, it is, for the purposes of commodity exchange, just as effective as twice as much coinage changing hands less frequently. Coins which have been hoarded are already at one remove their proper state, for they have, of course, been withdrawn from circulation. Even so, it is occasionally possible to discover something about the velocity of circulation from a related group of hoards, if their dates of deposit are clear, by analysing the mint-structure against the age-structure. The only Balkan coinage for which this has yet been attempted even at a simple level is the series of Frankish *deniers tournois*.

The question "to meet what needs", unlike the other two, cannot receive an exact or quantitative answer. The phrase itself, "circulation of coinage", is a reminder that the same coin met a different need on successive occasions when it changed hands. The workman to whom it was given in payment for a glass bottle spent it, perhaps, to buy fish, and the fisherman used it to buy a piece of rope. The best answer that one could hope to give, therefore, would define the sector of the economy within which monetary transactions were normal, and would discuss any unusual features of monetary economy in particular regions or at particular periods. The difficulty lies in finding any direct evidence.

One argument, which is simple but which stands up to careful consideration, is that if the smallest coin in use was, say, a silver grosso with quite a large purchasing power, the currency was not accommodated to everyday use in the market-place. A plentiful supply of petty currency, on the other hand, suggests that coinage was used in a wide sector of the economy. It is instructive that the Byzantine coinage of the ninth, tenth, and eleventh centuries consisted largely of a single denomination in bronze, together with gold solidi; half-folles, miliaresia, and tremisses were, generally speaking, absent. The scyphate bronze coins of the twelfth century, known as stamena, which were intermediate between folles and solidi although still of a rather low value, seem to have been essentially a "trade coin", used by merchants.

A second argument, of more general scope, in that the extent of the region in which a particular type of coinage was used, and the distribution of coin-finds within that region provide clues about the main needs that the currency met. For the period extending from the twelfth to the fourteenth century, when coinage was being used widely throughout the area of the Balkans, the geographical analysis of distribution - patterns is as much a standard method for answering the question "to meet what needs" as the use of statistical formulae is standard in estimating the quantities of coins struck. Even for the earlier period, when a monetary economy was less widepread, the reasoning is very much geographical, as will be seen below. Also, it draws its strength from being comparative.

The broad results yielded by these two arguments are an emphasis on the contrast between the economic life of the "Mediterranean" coastlands and the rest of the peninsula, and an indication that the circulation of coinage into the interior was compartmented into a number of separate regions, distributed around the edges of the peninsula, and shaped by the routes leading inland. Thus, the two main themes of Balkan monetary history are the petty currencies of the coastal settlements, and the trade coinages of which the use was connected with the economic penetration of the peninsula, not least by foreign merchants. [5]

The value of the Venetian grosso in present-day prices may be roughly estimated at two to two and a half dollars. Although there is little to be gained by comparisons of prices in very different societies, an approximate figure can at least usefully give an idea of the kind of transactions in which a grosso might, and could not, have been used.[6]

---

[5] K. Dieterich, "Zur Kulturgeographie und Kulturgeschichte des Byzantinischen Balkanhandels", *Byzantinische Zeitschrift* xxxi (1931), 35-57 and 334-49, insists upon the predominant part played by the Byzantine merchants, I am not sure with what justification.

[6] The value of silver at various dates is set out in an appendix in C. Clark, *The Conditions of Economic Progress*, 1951.

A stable and pure coinage is not automatically an excellent thing; and conversely a coin of very debased silver is by no means necessarily a bad coin, if it is adapted to the needs of the people for whose use it was struck. There are, even, arguments in justification of progressive debasement of the coinage. Cipolla has published figures to illustrate the persistent secular fall in the silver-content of the denarius, throughout Europe and throughout the Middle Ages. In Venice, 240 denarii in about the year 800 contained *ca.*390 grammes of pure silver; by 1250 this had fallen to 20 grammes, and by 1500 to 6 grammes. Except for brief periods, the purchasing power of silver, he claims, went on increasing throughout the Middle Ages. Cipolla analyses the "causes" of the debasement, and concludes that the policy was usually seen as the most expedient way of dealing with one or other of a number of problems, of which the four most important were:

a) the long-term increase in the demand for money, resulting from the long-term growth of population and | or of income and | or of the "monetization" of the economy;

b) the growth of government expenditure and deficits;

c) the pressure of social groups in the direction of profit-inflation;

d) disequilibrium in the balance of payments.[7]

In light of this analysis, the progressive debasement of the Serbian coinage in the fourteenth century takes on great interest.[8]

The population of the medieval Balkans, which is, obviously, the basic statistical series that the monetary historian would like to be able to consult in working out his answer to the question, "to meet what needs", is a topic about which desperately little information is available. At the end of the nineteenth century, there was a population of ɛ¾ million in Bulgaria, 2½ million in Serbia, 2½ million in Greece, 2½ million in Croatia and Slavonia, 1½ million in Bosnia, the Hercegovina, and Novi Pazar, just over 1 million in Istanbul, ¾ of a million in Dalmatia and Istria. Russell estimated that in 1500 there were 1½ million in Greece and another 3 million in the rest of the Balkans; he has recently revised this estimate slightly on the basis that there were a little over 5 millions in the Balkans as a whole excluding Istanbul in the early sixteenth

---

[7] C. M. Cipolla, "Currency Depreciation in Medieval Europe", *Economic History Review* 2nd. Ser., xv (1962-63), 413-422. This analysis appears to me to be so instructive for the numismatist that I have taken the liberty to quote part of the summary *verbatim*.

[8] See below.

century. [9] Much the same figure as in 1500 may already have been reached before the middle of the fourteenth century; but in the early ninth century, the total must surely have been far less. The view, which has for a long time been current, that the population of Constantinople in the ninth to fourteenth centuries was generally within the range $\frac{1}{2}$ a million to 1 million has been questioned by Jacoby, who would put the total much lower. [10]

[9] J. C. Russell, "Late Medieval Balkan and Asia Minor Population", *Journal of Economic and Social History of the Orient* iii (1960), 265-274 and references cited there.

[10] D. Jacoby, "La Population de Constantinople à l'Epoque Byzantine: un Problème de Démographie Urbaine", *Byzantion* xxxi (1961), 81-109, suggesting a total of not more than 375,000 before the plague of 541; but cf. *Byzantinische Zeitschrift* 1960, 322.

PART 2

THE LOCAL DEVELOPMENT OF MONETARY ECONOMY

CHAPTER II

THE TRAFFIC OF THE AEGEAN AND THE BLACK SEA:
820-1025

There is nothing that would lead one to suppose that either the Bulgarians or the Slavonic tribal groupings of the Balkan peninsula had by the early ninth century adopted the use of coinage for the purposes of the everyday exchange of commodities. It appears extremely unlikely, notwithstanding the negative character of the evidence, that they regularly struck coins of their own.[1] The Byzantine Empire, on the other hand, had a viable system of coinage in gold, silver, and copper for use in the eastern parts of the Empire, not to speak of other issues that were struck for use in Italy and Sicily. The coinage of the main system supplied the needs of Asia Minor and Constantinople as well as the Balkan provinces. Such detailed connexions as there may be between the numismatic history of the late eight and early ninth centuries and the monetary affairs of any one of these three major economic-geogra-

---

[1] There is a large and difficult literature on the history of the central and western parts of the Balkan peninsula in the seventh to tenth centuries. Without entering upon it, I draw attention to a few recent contributions, where references to earlier writings will be found: S. P. Kyriakides, *The Northern Ethnological Boundaries of Hellenism*, Thessaloniki, 1955, and *Ibid.*, "The Northern Boundaries of Hellenism in the 7th and 8th Centuries", *Balkan Studies* i (1960), 57-64. G. Ostrogorsky, "The Byzantine Empire in the World of the Seventh Century", *Dumbarton Oaks Papers* xiii (1959), 1-21. P. Charanis, "Ethnic Changes in the Byzantine Empire in the Seventh Century", *Ibid.*, 23-44. G. Cankova-Petkova, "Bulgarians and Byzantium during the First Decades after the Foundation of the Bulgarian State", *Byzantinoslavica* xxiv (1963), 41-53. R. J. H. Jenkins, *Byzantium and Byzantinism* (Lectures in Memory of Louise Taft Semple), University of Cincinnati, 1963. G. Arnakis, "Byzantium and Greece", *Balkan Studies* 4, 2.

Cf. I. Duichev, "Kŭm Vŭprosa za Poyavata na Parite v Nasheto Narodno Stopanstvo", *Izvestiya* iii-iv (1951), 87-112.

See also Lishev, *Paritsa*, pp. 80ff., emphasizing the use of coinage for non-monetary purposes or for unilateral payments outside the scope of normal exchange, e.g. for the payment of fines, for "prestige" gifts, for personal adornment, hoarding, etc. Lishev also suggests that coinage would mostly have been carried inland as payments outside the scope of normal exchange, e.g. as tribute, ransom-money, or donatives (pp. 59ff.).

phical regions tends therefore to be "blanketed" and obscured. In the years following the peace treaty of 816 the monetary situation in the Balkans, we may surmise, was that the imperial copper coinage was in use in a few cities of the Aegean coastlands, and that the same coinage was being carried inland and used in Bulgaria and among the Slavs only to a very limited extent, if at all.

To detect the small beginnings of a movement is always difficult. Obviously, the period from the middle of the eight century to the middle of the eleventh century witnessed a very large growth in the Byzantine monetary economy in the provinces; but it is less obvious how far development was concentrated into the early part of those three centuries, and how uniformly or otherwise the development went forward in different places. The site-finds from Athens and Corinth are the *locus classicus* for evidence that, after its first hey-day in the age of Justinian, the volume of circulation of petty coinage in the Balkans dwindled to a minute fraction of what it had been, from about the middle of the seventh to at least the middle of the eighth.[2] The same pattern is repeated in other, smaller find-series from excavations in Greece, such as that from Argos, so one may conclude that the statistics from Athens and Corinth are a quantitative, and probably an accurate, reflection of the petty currency, not merely as it was in those two cities, but over wide areas. The seventh-century decline can be seen at Caričin Grad, and at a number of sites at the mouths of the Danube.

A very solid and valuable piece of evidence for the currency of the Balkan provinces in the "dark ages", which is of some general relevance to the monetary history of the ninth century, is that among 31 better - preserved coins of Philippicus (711-713) from the excavations of the Athenian Agora, only 6 obverse dies were represented.[3] The correct con-

---

[2] S. Vryonis, "An Attic Hoard of Byzantine Gold Coins (668-741) from the Thomas Whittemore Collection and the Numismatic Evidence for the Urban History of Byzantium", *Zbornik Radova Vizantološkog Instituta* viii /1 (= *Mélanges Georges Ostrogorsky*, vol. I), 1963, 291-300 fires a mixed salvo at an extensive target. The conclusion that the hoard from Attica "shows how capricious the numismatic evidence is" rests upon a deplorable series of arguments by analogy and *non sequitur*, e.g. it remains to be shown that the hoard is not a traveller's hoard before such important conclusions should be drawn from it.

[3] M. Thompson, "Some Unpublished Bronze Money of the Early Eighth Century", *Hesperia* ix (1940), 358-80. P. Charanis, "The Significance of Coins as Evidence for the History of Athens and Corinth in the Seventh and Eighth Centuries", *Historia* iv (1955), 163-72. Such evidence as there is suggests that, in the "dark ages",

clusions to be drawn from this are, first, that the finds suggest an original total of the order of 50,000 to 200,000 coins, and, secondly, that there has been a quite exceptionally high rate of survival. The 61 coins attributed to Philippicus were all found singly, and came from many different sections of the Agora excavations, with a concentration, which is usual in other reigns as well, along the Panathenaic Way. There is nothing in the distribution or context of the finds to indicate special circumstances for the loss of the coins. The only special event that ought to be noted as a possible explanation is the Plague of 747. Otherwise the rate of loss should be seen as a factor of the velocity of circulation and also the length of time for which the coins of Philippicus remained in use—presumably for many decades; but this in itself could hardly be a sufficient explanation: accepting the conclusion of Miss Thompson that they were a local issue, their use would seem to have been concentrated to a great extent within the urban area itself, and not much spread over the neighbouring countryside. Certainly, these coins of Philippicus did not circulate as far afield as Corinth. To say that there is no evidence for special circumstances in the loss of the coins does not imply that there were none in their issue or use. Athens may have been an important administrative centre for a time. (Only half a century earlier, Constans II had temporarily made it his capital.) In Athens, then—but apparently not in Corinth—an effective petty currency was in use for much or all of the eighth century; the lowest ebb of the city's monetary affairs seems not to have come until the first half of the ninth century.

The information about the Athenian currency of Philippicus is exceptionally good. No other estimates of quantities of folles struck in the eighth century have yet been made; but the excavation coins may turn out to have an important and independent contribution to make to the interpretation of such estimates, if it should appear that the statistics reflect not merely the total numbers of petty coins but also their velocity of circulation.

Questions of the quantity of gold coins, and their velocity of circulation, have so far attracted less study. Vryonis has argued that the Byzantine Empire, during the period of supposed economic recession, possessed a vital urban society and a money economy, and that the cash payment of the army put large amounts of gold coinage into circula-

---

copper coins continued in circulation usually for many decades after their issue, and that an effective re-call and re-minting of the currency at the beginning of a new reign was not usual; calculations of the number of "finds per year" separately for a series of short reigns are therefore often quite misleading.

tion. Two instances drawn from the reign of Nicephorus I (802-11) show that the military pay chest of a theme might easily contain 75,000 solidi; and Theophanes mentions rich tax revenues in gold from Thrace at the same date. One of the pay-chests was from the theme of Strymon. That and the evidence from Thrace are particularly relevant to Balkan monetary history. Other references, such as those in law codes, may have applied much more to the metropolitan region and to one or two large cities than to the Balkan provinces generally. A solidus probably had either a very short or a very long "life": the length of time between its issue as a soldier's pay and its return to the treasury as tax may have been measured in months; alternatively, it may have been put aside for use as, e.g. a marriage-dot and remained as savings for a generation or more. The total number of gold coins in circulation in the Balkan provinces, measured against the size of the population, seems likely to have been small.

The reign of Michael II (820-29) has been selected as a starting-point for the examination of the numismatic evidence because it was he who reformed the bronze coinage in the eastern parts of the Empire, introducing a new, large follis of about $7\frac{1}{2}$ grammes that seems to be connected with the first appreciable signs of revival in provincial monetary affairs. An estimate from the occurrence of die-duplication suggests that it was struck from something of the order of 600 pairs of dies, and that the issue was therefore something of the order of 6 million folles. It should not be forgotten that this estimate is subject to wide margins of random error, but with that caveat it hints that Michael's folles were struck for everyday use as petty coinage. His reign was too short for it to be probable that the folles represent more than one monetary issue. The surviving specimens can be arranged on the basis of style into three main groupings, which are likely to have been the work of three different mints, although there is no formal difference in their design, let alone any mint-mark. The argument for dividing the coins among three mints, and not merely, for example, among three officinae of the Constantinople mint, or three different workmen, is that the same sort of stylistic range is to be seen again in the immediately following reign, that of Theophilus, for which the localization of some at least of the stylistic varieties is perfectly clearly attested. In the absence of provenances, one might conjecture that of the three groups, one large group in good style is Constantinopolitan, and a second, smaller group also in very good style but struck to a heavier weight-standard is the product of a separate mint, perhaps in Asia Minor. The third (large) group, which includes a high proportion of coins in crude style, with tall crosses on the crowns worn by the emperor and by Theophilus, is problematic, and better evidence in the shape of provenances is much to be desired.

The only specimen of the reformed follis from the Corinth excavations is of the third group, but there is one other in the Corinth museum, the circumstances of discovery of which are not recorded, which is likely to have been found at or near Corinth; it is of the "Constantinopolitan" variety. There are three reformed folles from the Athens excavations, of which only one is in a very legible condition. It is of the first group. The one further specimen to which a Balkan provenance attaches was bought in Istanbul by Tolstoy.There is one other coin (not from the Balkans) of which the stylistic variety is recorded: a coin of the third group was bought, again by Tolstoy, in Trebizond.

The smaller folles of Michael II, which are certainly Italian, include a few, rather larger and bolder than the rest. There was one among the Corinth finds, and one from Athens.

Thus, the evidence of provenances for localization is not by any means clear-cut. This fact is, in itself, of interest for monetary history, for it reflects an early and rather tentative phase in the development of regional monetary economy. The same character is to be seen in the Romanian hoards of Cleja and Urluia. [4]

One can hardly argue from the absence of finds in the interior of the peninsula that Michael's folles did not circulate there, when virtually no finds have been recorded from the coastlands either. Their use may have been in great part confined within the walls of a few cities, especially Constantinople, far more than was the case with the folles of, say, the eleventh century, but this is conjectural. On a broader view, one can say that the folles of the ninth and tenth centuries are more plentiful on the coastlands than in the interior, but one must renounce altogether the attempt to distinguish the pattern for any particular reign in those two centuries by an analysis of the geographical pattern of findspots. Arguments that relate specifically to the second and third decades of the ninth century must be sought in other directions.

---

[4] For the classification of the coinage of Michael II, see Metcalf, (work in progress). For the Istanbul and Trebizond finds, see Tolstoy, *Vizantiisky Monety*, *ad loc*. For the medium-sized coins, which are decidedly scarce in general collections, cf. Wroth, *BMC (Byz.)*, plate xlviii, 11. A follis of Michael II with Theophilus was found in the excavation of the Agora on Santorin: for the reference, see p.28 below. For Cleja and Urluia, see p. 23 below.

Duichev has discussed a documentary record that when Nicephorus I captured and burned Pliska, in 811, he opened Krum's treasury, and distributed the rich treasure he found there, including *inter alia* copper coins. Duichev's argument is that the word χαλκὸς can, in its context in the document, be interpreted only to mean copper coins.[5] From the existence of copper coins in Krum's treasury to their use for purposes of commerce in his territories is, of course, another argument entirely (as is the conjecture that they might have been coins struck in Krum's own name). The absence of eighth—or ninth—century coins from the excavations at Aboba must be regarded as very weighty evidence, in view of the long architectural history of the "palatine chapel", where the earliest find-series was obtained, and of the undoubtedly early dates of many of the levels that have since been dug on the outskirts of the place. The lack of any coins earlier than one of Basil I from the excavations around the Golden Church at Preslav is less conclusive. But it can be accepted that there was little if any petty currency in the main centers of the Bulgarian Empire in the ninth century.[6]

The Romanian finds suggest that already before the treaty of 816 coinage was being carried along the routes by which the transhumant pastoralists led their beasts down from the Carpathian mountains across the Danube to sell them at the fairs, or perhaps to take them across the Dobruja to the Black Sea coasts.[7] The circumstances of deposit of the finds from Berezeni, in Moldavia, and Mediaş and Voila, in central Transylvania, are necessarily speculative, but the coins of Leo IV from Con-

---

[5] Duichev, *op. cit.*

[6] Coins from Aboba - Pliska are described in Panchenko, "Pechati i Monety", and S. Stanchev, "Materiali ot Dvortsoviya Tsentŭr v Pliska", *IAI* xxiii (1960), 23 - 65. Those from Preslav are described in Mushmov, "Kolektivni Nakhodki, 1929 - 30". Among the general excavation reports and studies should be mentioned S. Mikhailov, "Arkheologicheski Materiali ot Pliska", *IAI* xx (1955), 49-181 and "Dvortsovata Tsŭrkva v Pliska", *ibid.*, 229-64. For the general importance of these centres in the history of the First Bulgarian Empire, see S. Stanchev, "Pliska und Preslav, ihre archäologischen Denkmäler und deren Erforschung", in *Antike und Mittelalter in Bulgarien*, edited by V. Beshevliev and J. Irmscher (Berliner Byzantinische Arbeiten, XXI), Berlin, 1960, pp. 219-264; but on the question of the identification of Aboba as Pliska, see V. Beshevliev, "Iz Kŭsnoantichnata i Srednovekovnata Geografiya na Severoiztochna Bŭlgariya", *IAI* xxv (1962), 1-81. For a recent note on the archaeological programme, see G. Cankova-Petkova, "Contemporary Research at Pliska and Preslav (North-eastern Bulgaria)", *Byzantinoslavica* xxiv (1963), 167-8.

[7] V. Mihăilescu, R. Vulpe, S. Manuila, and A. P. Arbore, *La Dobroudja* (Académie Roumaine, Connaissance de la Terre et de la Pensée Roumaines, IV), 1938.

stantsa and Țichileşti and the later Rasova and Urluia hoards[8] are fairly obviously to be associated with the route into the hinterland. The little Rasova find consisted of only 3 coins of Theophilus. The intriguing Urluia deposit falls into two parts, one belonging to the first half of the tenth century, the other (and larger) part consisting of silver as well as bronze essentially of the last quarter of the eighth century. The exact circumstances of discovery are not available, and so one cannot be certain whether one or two hoards are in fact involved (although it seems improbable that the coins should be stray finds); if a single deposit, is the Urluia find a "hoard within a hoard", or does its age-structure reflect the composition of the currency in the Dobruja, and hint at an intermission in the arrival of new coins in the region in the time of Krum? The existence of the Rasova hoard and of a find of a follis of Theophilus from Isperikh [9] perhaps speak against such an intermission lasting for most of the ninth century, and therefore in favour of the "hoard within a hoard" theory. Nothing definite can be said about the Urluia deposit without some more hoards from the Dobruja from the ninth and tenth centuries with which to compare it. Even so, the numismatic evidence is that petty coinage was being used in the Black Sea coastlands in the ninth century, apparently in connexion with an inter-regional trade of which we may conjecture that the purpose was the provisioning of Constantinople. [10]

When we turn to the coastlands of the Aegean Sea, there is unfortunately no similar direct evidence. The historical background is that of the growth of the system of themes, and of the establishment or re-establishment of cities. Mrs. Glykatzi-Ahrweiler has recently discussed the character of the decentralization of government, and has gathered up the references to the themes in the earlier period, among them those of Thessaloniki-Strymon-Boleron (Thettalia), Macedonia-Thrace, Hellas-Peloponnesus (κατωτικὰ μέρη), Bulgaria (Paristrion), the Aegean (the Cycladic theme), and Dyrrachium. [11] It is clear that new episcopal sees were founded in considerable numbers in the Balkans in the eighth and ninth centuries, from the varying lists of signatories to the records of the Councils of 692 and 787, the anti-Photian assembly of

---

[8] Dimian, "Cîteva Descoperiri".

[9] Metcalf, "Theophilus".

[10] On the general question, see J. L. Teall, "The Grain Supply of the Byzantine Empire, 330-1025", *Dumbarton Oaks Papers* xiii (1959), 87-139.

[11] H. Glykatzi-Ahrweiler, "Recherches sur l'Administration de l'Empire Byzantin aux IXe-XIe Siècles", *BCH* lxxxiv (1960), 1ff.

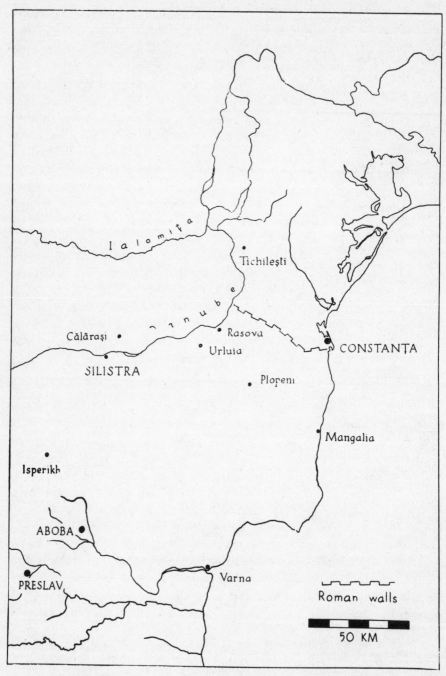

Map I. The Dobruja and north-eastern Bulgaria, IX—X centuries.

869, and the Photian Synod of 879. One may fairly suppose that the place-names that appear for the first time reflect not merely an intensive Christian mission to the Slavs but also a phase of political consolidation and urban growth[12]. Not all the places named can be located. The lists nevertheless give a most valuable impression of what must have been the framework of monetary affairs in the ninth and tenth centuries. New names appearing in the list of 787 include, for example, Monemvasia, Troezen, and the island of Aegina, all in the metropolitan province of Corinth, and Oreos and Porthmos (both in Euboea) in the province of Athens. In 879 Patrai appears as a new metropolitan see, with Methone in its province. One wonders how far the geographical extension of metropolitan provinces—and of the themes—was along the same lines as the extension of commercial contacts. The new names of 787, and 879 as well, are heavily concentrated in eastern Thrace, the lower basin of the river Maritsa, and the Rhodope, and it may be that there is a whole topic of monetary history there which awaits attention.[13] From the coasts of Greece and from the islands there is, with the exception of the Santorin hoard, mentioned below, and of the few coins from Athens and Corinth, nothing to record.[14] If even only a few stray finds could be collected, they would almost certainly repay study in the context of the conciliar lists.

The reigns of Theophilus (829-42) and Michael III (842-67) witnessed a large increase in monetary circulation in the Aegean coastlands, especially at Corinth and, it would seem, Thessaloniki. Theophilus continued and extended the reform of the bronze coinage in the eastern parts of the Empire; it was his substantive issue which firmly marked out the characteristics of the currency in the Aegean region that were to continue with little change for more than two hundred years. The mark of value M was replaced, on the reverse of the follis, by an inscription in four lines. The reformed folles have been divided into seven stylistic

---

[12] For a general discussion and for the lists of place-names, see G. Ostrogorsky, "Byzantine Cities in the Early Middle Ages", *Dumbarton Oaks Papers* xiii (1959), 45-66.

[13] Dr. Gerasimov has kindly informed me, in a letter of January 1962, that coins of the eighth and ninth centuries are rarely found in Bulgaria, but occur on the Black Sea coasts, and also in the region of Plovdiv.

[14] Of a slightly earlier date, there is one follis of Leo V and Constantine VII (Sabatier, *Description Générale* xlii, 13 = Wroth, *BMC (Byz.)*, II, lxix, 2) found at the Byzantine church of Theotokou, Thessaly, in 1907. The find-spot was only some 50 or 100 metres from the sea-shore; *ABSAthens* xiii (1906-07), 312.

groups, and, although it is still possible that some of the groups should be put together as the work of a single mint (there are few provenances by which they can be localized), it seems certain that Groups Ϛ and Z belong to central Greece, that Groups A and B belong to the metropolitan region, and that coins of Group Δ are not, as had long been supposed, half-folles, but the product of a provincial mint. Groups Γ and E are both very small; the former is comparable, in its fine style, large flans, and metrology, with the least plentiful variety of folles of Michael II. The mint-attribution of Group E is still entirely speculative, but Patrai seems to be an interesting possibility.

The case for attributing Group Δ to Thessaloniki is, on the evidence available, not finally proved. The arguments are, first, that the issues are so different from the rest in fabric and metrology that they should be given to a region of the Empire at some distance from both the metropolitan region and from central Greece; secondly, that they are so numerous that they would seem to belong to an important city; thirdly, that the secret-marks on the emperor's head-dress are quite different in scheme from those on the other stylistic groups, therefore to a city that had its own well-developed administration; fourthly, that the occurrence of mechanical, uncomprehending die-cutting suggests that the local workmen were not closely in touch with the culture of the capital. [15] The most plausible attributions are Thessaloniki or Trebizond, and the third and fourth arguments perhaps favour the former. There were no folles of Theophilus among Tolstoy's purchases at Trebizond: Schlumberger, on the other hand, had a very fine run of coins of Group Δ. Two of the four folles of Theophilus in the Sofia cabinet are of that Group. Bronze of unspecified varieties has been brought to light at Kazichene, in the region of Sofia, [16] at Thessaloniki, in 1933, and on the island of Delos. [17]

---

[15] See Metcalf, "Theophilus".

[16] Filov, "Novootkriti Starini, 1912-13".

[17] There was also a single coin from Istanbul, found in 1910 or shortly before; see Mosser, *Byzantine Coin Hoards*, p. 20. A (typically) small hoard from the Chersonese in 1926 contained one reformed coin of Theophilus, 24 mm. in diameter (but this is not a sufficient reason to assume a coin of Group Δ, especially as the reference cited was Tolstoy, lxxi, 26, 27) and a second, 28 mm. in diameter. The deposit is, however, almost certainly to be dated by a local issue of Basil I; L. N. Belova - Kud' "Khronologicheskoe Opisanie Monet, Naidennikh v Khersonese pri Raskopkakh 1926 Goda", *Khersonesskiy Sbornik* (Gosudarstvenny Khersonesskiy Muzey) ii (1927), 289 - 93, nos. 33-34 and 53, from Square III/6/2, 15 July 1926. For Thessaloniki, see *BCH* lviii (1934), 236. For Delos, see Svoronos and Konstantinopoulos, "Ekthesis, 1908-09" p. 82; the coin was 30mm. in diameter, so it cannot have been of Group Δ.

The curious pattern, then, is that folles on three different weight-standards were issued in three regions of the Empire. The heaviest coinage belonged to the metropolitan region, a somewhat lighter issue to central Greece, and the small variety probably to northern Greece. The issues of Theophilus continued to meet the needs of the Aegean coastlands for petty currency for several decades, since Michael III struck very little bronze. The predominance of Groups Ϛ and Z at Corinth is all the more weighty evidence for the localized use of the coins, when the varieties had so long to become intermingled. It is worth remarking that no fewer than three of Michael's rare IMPERATOR / REX coins have been found in the Corinth excavations, and one at Athens. [18]

The gold coinage of Theophilus, but of no other emperor of the eighth to tenth centuries, has been found in a good many localities in the west Balkans; there must have been some special circumstances to account for this fact. The systematic occupation of Sicily by the Arabs in the early ninth century led to a severe setback in Byzantine influence on the Adriatic coast and in the Slav territories of the hinterland. Constantine, *De Administrando Imperio* records that the Dalmatian cities and islands paid tribute to the Slavonic tribes, and the numismatic evidence reveals how large that tribute must, for a time, have been. [19] Like the gold coins of Romanus III, discussed below, those of Theophilus seem to be essentially finds from the interior. The only coastal find of gold from the Adriatic in this period is a Beneventan piece discovered at Trogir, near Split, in 1937. [20]

---

[18] Wroth, *BMC (Byz.)*, plate L, 2; Edwards, *Corinth*, 1896 - 1929; Thompson, *Coins*. On the iconography of the issue, see Grierson, "Coinage and Money", at pp. 440f. Finlay had one of these pieces, bought at Rhodes: MS "List of Antiquities" in the library of the British School at Athens, ref. S. 9. 3 (b).

[19] See Ostrogorsky, *Byzantine State*, pp. 183 and 209-10; I. Marović, "Zlatnici Cara Theofila u Numizmatičkoj Zbirci Areološkog Muzeja u Splitu", *VAH Dalmat.* lv (1953), 213-216 — the light weight of some of the coins is intriguing, and indicates a need for the most detailed stylistic examination of them; M. Vego, in *Glasnik Zemaljskog Muzeja u Sarajevu*, NS vii (1952), 410-11; for a find at Sisak, Metcalf, "Syrmia and Slavonia"; for a find in the region of Skopje, M. Grbić, "Iz Numizmatičke Zbirke Istorijsko-Arheološkog Muzeja u Skoplju", *Glasnik Skopskog Naučnog Društva* v (1929), 51-58; Miss L. Kojić, Director of the Zavičajni Museum, Trebinje has kindly shown me a cast of a coin found in that region. See also Ratto 2490.

[20] For the coins of Romanus, see below. The Trogir find is as Wroth, *BMC (Byz.)*, III, plate xxii, 2. I am indebted to the authorities of the Split Archaeological Museum, where the coin now is, for information about it. A hoard of 50 gold Byzantine coins, of unspecified date, came to light at Gardun, near Split, ca. 1843:

Nor is there much silver or copper coinage recorded from the west Balkans, which would seem to have been without a monetary economy during the ninth and tenth centuries. The Vučemilović collection, which was built up from local finds in central Dalmatia, included very few medieval coins, and only one from this period, a denier of Louis I (814 - 40). [21]

From the Aegean, the Santorin find of 1900 consisted of 29 silver coins of Theophilus and one gold coin attributed to Michael III, and dated after 856. The year 864 was suggested as a possible date for the deposit of the hoard. [22] One cannot, however, altogether rule out the possibility of a date of deposit *ca.* 830. The reasons for suspecting some confusion in the account are, first, that all the silver is of the same type, in the name of Theophilus alone; secondly, that the solidus was originally described simply as "a gold coin of *Michael Basileus*" (Michael III, *BMC* 5 reads *Basile,* and is a scarce type: could the gold coin not have belonged to Michael II?); and thirdly, that the stray finds from the same excavations were "a coin of an emperor Michael" and "another copper coin attributed to Michael II with Theophilus". The first reason is the weighty one, but the others go to show that the identifications were rather vague.

The general association of the silver miliaresion, struck from the middle of the eight century, with the monetary economy of the Arab world has recently been underlined by the publication of twenty milia-

J. G. Seidl, "Beiträge zu einer Chronik der archäologischen Funde in der österreichischen Monarchie", *Archiv für Kunde österreichischer Geschichts-Quellen* iii (1849), 159-202, at 193.

[21] The coin-collection was formed in the first half of the nineteenth century by M. Vučemilović, largely from finds from Imoski (Runović-Ad Novas) or from Duvno Polje. It was shared out, and supplemented, by his three sons, who lived at Sinj, near Imoski, and at Vrlika. The collections were subsequently re-combined, and were acquired by the Sarajevo museum. See C. Hörrmann, "Erwerbung einer numismatischen Sammlung für das bosn.-herceg. Landesmuseum", *WBMH* i (1893), 339-40; C. Patsch, "Archäologisch-epigraphische Untersuchungen zur Geschichte der römischen Provinz Dalmatien, V Theil", *WMBH* viii (1901), 61 - 130 at 83.

[22] F. Hiller von Gaertringen and P. Wilski, *Stadtgeschichte von Thera* (Thera, Untersuchungen, Vermessungen und Ausgrabungen in den Jahren 1895 - 1902, vol. III), Berlin, 1904, pp. 13 and 200. For the chronology of Theophilus's reign and coinage, see A. R. Bellinger, "The Emperor Theophilus and the Lagbe Hoard", *Berytus* viii (1943-44), 102-06.

resia actually overstruck on dirhems. [23] The most important evidence for the Aegean coastlands, however, lies in the fact that miliaresia have been discovered among the site-finds at Corinth and Athens. At Athens, there was one of Constantine V with Leo IV, one of Basil I with Constantine, and one of John I; at Corinth, there was one of Theophilus. Although the numbers may not appear very significant, one must remember that the miliaresion was worth 24 folles, and that coins of a large face-value are very rare in site-finds, for the reason that people took more trouble not to lose them. [24] The few finds that there are therefore probably indicate a plentiful currency of silver. Along with them may be mentioned the Thessaloniki hoard of 1891, which included 7 or 8 of the extremely rare miliaresia of Artavasdes (742-43). The other coins from the hoard were not recorded: its date of deposit may have been well into the second half of the century, for some of the pieces of Artavasdes were of low weight. [25]

On the Black Sea coasts, too, silver was probably quite plentiful. As well as the Tichileşti and Urluia finds, mentioned above, there is the Călăraşi hoard of 1947, which consisted of 5 silver pieces of John I, again from the route leading inland towards the mountains. [26] An extremely rare silver coin of Alexander (912-13) has a presumed Bulgarian provenance, and may well have been from the coastlands. [27]

Varied and extensive issues of folles were made in the reign of Basil I (867-886). Like those of Theophilus, they are without any mint-marks, but can be arranged into groups on stylistic grounds. There is, in addition, the evidence of overstriking; the flans of Theophilus's coins were re-used, and the workmanship is often so poor that the stylistic variety of the under-type can be made out. On this basis, on their generally provincial style, and on the evidence of the Corinth site-finds, a number of the varieties of Basil's folles can be attributed to central Greece. Corinth was still a rather isolated centre of monetary affairs,

---

[23] G. C. Miles, "Byzantine Miliaresion and Arab Dirhem: Some Notes on their Relationship", *American Numismatic Society Museum Notes* ix (1960), 189-218.

[24] Statistics are adduced in Grierson, "Coinage and Money".

[25] A. Szemiothowa, "Les Rares Monnaies Antiques du Musée National de Varsovie", *Polish Numismatic News*, 1961 *(Wiadomosci Numizmatyczne* v [1961]), 85-90.

[26] Dimian, "Cîteva Descoperiri".

[27] N. A. Mushmov, "Une Monnaie d'Argent de l'Empéreur Alexandre", *Byzantion* vi (1931), 99-100.

but the monetary economy at Athens had already expanded about two - fold relatively to Corinth, and perhaps three-or four fold in all, if the statistics from the site-finds in the two cities are a guide. [28] The stylistic classification of the coins that appear to belong to central Greece suggests that there were two mints there; and the preponderance of the "First Three Busts, III" variety in the Corinth finds is the reason for assigning it to the local mint, and accordingly for assuming that the "First Three Busts, II" variety belongs to another mint. The attribution of coins to Thessaloniki rests essentially on the metrology of the variety concerned: the smaller "Two Busts" type is on a weight-standard only a little heavier than the Theophilan folles of Group Δ. It is the most plentiful variety, of any of Basil's folles, in the Athens site finds, acounting for half the specimens. This certainly raises the question whether it should be attributed to a mint as far away from central Greece as Thessaloniki. The form of the argument, and the kind of uncertainty involved, are precisely the same as for the folles of Theophilus, discussed above. There is, however, no more possibility of associating the smaller "Two Busts" folles with the sequences of varieties that have been provisionally assigned to Corinth and (?) Thebes than there is of amalgamating Groups Δ with Ϛ and Z of Theophilus's folles; the stylistic groupings appear to be quite separate in each case. It seems preferable to envisage consignment as the explanation for the "Two Busts" coins found at Athens. The problem is paralleled by that of the folles of Class Al at Athens, discussed below.

There is a heavy concentration of the finds of Basil's folles in a small area within the Agora, on either side of a particular section of the Panathenaic Way. Moreover, the varieties assigned to Greek mints are mostly from that area, whereas the non-Greek varieties are mostly from other parts of the Agora, such as the south-western corner of the excavations. This pattern of localization is not repeated in the coins of Leo VI.

The classification of Basil's folles summarized in Table 1, together with a brief description of the details by which the varieties can be distinguished from each other, is the simplest arrangement that takes adequate account of the evidence at present available.

---

[28] See below. For the classification of Basil's folles, see Metcalf, work in progress.

	Proposed mint-attribution	Variety	Characteristics
1	CONSTANTINOPLE	"Two Seated Figures, I"	Fine style; rev. inscription begins BASILO,; obv. ends AYGST, (usually); ends of loroi fall outwards and have 2 rows of dots.
2		"First Three Busts, I" Basil's hand not raised)	Fine style. (i) with AYG (ii) with * and AYGG
3		"Second Three Busts, I" (Basil's hand raised to his breast)	Fine style; x Basil's hand is held high; his face is broad and somewhat triangular; x the hair-style is elaborate;x the arch of the crown is quite flat; x the jewels at the bottom of the loros are sometimes exaggerated; x characteristic S in + BASIL. x
4		"Seated Figure, II"	Very fine style; 5 vertical or nearly vertical rows of dots on emperor's chest; end of loros, with 3, later 2, rows of dots, falls to right and is not fringed; the emperor's kness are not prominent; the throne is wide and without a footstool; the forefinger of the raised hand is exaggerated.
5	(?) ASIA MINOR	"Two Seated Figures, II"	Finest style. Rev. begins BASILIO,; obv. ends BASILIS; ends of loroi fall inwards and are fringed, and have 3 rows of jewels
6		"Second Three Busts, IV"	Rare; uncertain attribution
7		"Seated Figure, I"	Finest style. Loros draped diagonally across chest; end of loros, with 2 rows of dots, falls to left and is fringed; the emperor's kness are shown in high relief; the throne is narrow.
8	(?) THEBES	"Missing Type"	(Two busts and labarum, but the figure on the left wears a loros; cf. BMC (Byz.), II, plate L, 10.) Known only as an undertype.
9		"First Three Busts, II"	Reversed loros. (i) with AY, (ii) with * and AYGG
10		"Second Three Busts, II"	Intermediate style. Basil's hand is held lower than on I; his hair is shown sometimes with, but usually without, curls that are rounded outwards; x the line of

	Proposed mint-attribution	Variety	Characteristics
			his fringe intersects the lower arch of the crown, cf. III; the neck-line of the loros is wide and shallow, cf. III; the panels of the loros are often diamond-shaped; the O of the rev. inscription is round,[x] cf. III.
11	CORINTH	"Two Busts, large"	Large module; 6½ gramme standard.
12		"Two Seated Figures, III"	Inferior style. Rev. begins BASILIO or BASILO; obv. ends BASL or BASIL; ends of loroi variable, often fall the same way, and have 1 row of dots.
13		"First Three Busts, III"	"Theophilan" loros; (i) with AY, (ii) with + and AYGG.
14		"Second Three Busts, III"	Poor style. Basil's hand is held low. His hair is shown with prominent curls;[x] the line of the fringe is curved and meets the ends of the lower arch of the crown, cf. II; Basil's face, and those of Leo and Constantine, are often long and narrow, cf. II; the O of the rev. inscription is lemon-shaped,[x] cf. II.
15	THESSALONIKI	"Two Busts, small"	Small module; 5 - 5½ gramme standard
16		"Two Seated Figures, IV"	(Irregular; rare; uncertain attribution)
17		"First Three Busts, IV"	(Irregular; rare; uncertain attribution.)

Table 1. Provisional scheme of mint-attributions for the folles of Basil I.

The very plentiful "Second Three Busts" issue (on which Basil's hand is shown raised to his breast) is the most difficult to divide up into stylistic groups; but many of the details noted in the list above correspond with the "First Three Busts" varieties. These details are marked[x] in Table 1. There may well have been some overlapping of the issues, but with that reservation, it appears that the "Two Busts" and "Two Seated Figures" issues will belong to the year 869 (except at Thessaloniki) and that the bulk of both the "Three Busts" issues may belong to a period as short as two or three years, beginning January 870. There was, in other words, an intensive recoinage of folles early in Basil's reign. As a very rough guide to the relative output of the various mints, the number of surviving specimens from Constantinople (in a survey of museum collections) is the greatest, with Corinth only a short way behind; Thessaloniki and (?) Thebes each account for about half as many coins as Corinth; and (?) Asia Minor is a small mint. From a study of die-linkage, it appears that the total output of folles from all mints was very roughly of the order of 15 to 50 million. This figure is much the same as that from the reign of Theophilus, and yet there are twice as many finds at Corinth of coins of the later emperor. The number of years for which each coinage remained in use was probably similar, so that one might have expected similar numbers of finds, or a larger estimate of the total for Basil. A factor of two is not reliable evidence, because the statistical (random) errors in the sampling of die-duplication might easily combine to give a final error of that order of magnitude. When much better estimates of the total quantities of coinage struck are available, however, it should be possible to see clearly whether the statistics of site-finds are reflecting the velocity of circulation as well as the quantities of coinage.

Balkan provenances from the reign of Basil are lacking, except for the Corinth and Athens finds, and one coin from the excavations on the site of the Golden Church, at Preslav. [29] There are, indeed, extremely few hoards of later date either which include Basil's coins, and from the Balkans, only the Urluia hoard, in which there was one coin of Basil, and the Corinth hoard of November, 1937, also with one coin. [30]

The provisional attribution of the smaller "Two Busts" variety to Thessaloniki prompts some speculation. In the scheme set out in Table 1, it is the first and the only substantive issue at the mint, the others being very rare even if they are correctly attributed. Leo and Alexander continued the same type, in the same small module; the inference is that it remained current at Thessaloniki throughout Basil's reign and into that of Leo. Why should one provincial mint have been allowed to continue with the type, when it had been abandoned everywhere else? Fortunately, this question can be considered in the light of parallel instances from the mint-history of the sixth and seventh centu-

---

[29] N. A. Mushmov, in *IBIA* vi (1930-31), 314f.

[30] For the Urluia hoard, see p. 23 above. For the Corinth hoard, which may have been brought to the city shortly before its concealment, probably from somewhere further south in the Peloponnesus, see below, and note the presence of a coin of Leo VI alsos: see p. 35.

ries. Then, Thessaloniki was several times permitted to lag behind the mints of the metropolitan region in the implementation of new policies; the general reason seems to have been a local unwillingness to do away with a trade-coin which had become well-known and acceptable in Macedonia or further to the north or north-east. [31] In the sixth century, too, Thessaloniki had a persistent preference, which was indulged by the central authorities, for smaller bronze coins than were being used elsewhere. One may suspect, then, that the "Two Busts" folles won some special favour locally. The city's monetary affairs were probably seriously interrupted by the Arab raid of 904, which may have caused the issue of the small "Two Busts" folles to dwindle or cease.

A slender but tough thread of evidence for the monetary organization and policies of Basil's reign comes from Sardis. Only two of his folles were found during the excavations there in 1910-14. [32] They came to light separately. Both were of the "First Three Busts, III" variety, and both had a blundered reverse inscription reading bAIL, for bASIL. Short of supposing that Group III was struck at more than one mint, which would be very implausible on stylistic grounds, the only explanation for the Sardis finds is that they were coins from the same or closely similar dies and that they had reached the city as a consignment. Elaborately co-ordinated policies of consignment had been normal from the time of the Anastasian reform until at least the latter part of Justinian's reign. The currency needs of different cities (such as Athens and Corinth) were separately supplied, often from distant mints, at irregular intervals of, for example, three or four years. The folles tended to remain very much within the region where they had been issued - even within the walls of the particular city where they had been issued - so much so that the pattern of localization might still be clear after half a century of use. [33] If consignment was a part of Basil's monetary policies, one is entitled to expect to discover equally clear localization. There are signs of it in the composition of the Cleja and Taranto hoards, and in the differences between them; but more finds are needed.

Consignment perhaps rose to greater importance under Leo VI (886-912). There is far more stylistic uniformity among his folles, and they

---

[31] Metcalf, "East Mediterranean World".

[32] H. W. Bell, *Coins, Part I*, 1910-14 (Sardis, Publications of the American Society for the Excavation of Sardis, XI), Leiden, 1916.

[33] D. M. Metcalf, "Organization of the Constantinople Mint for the Follis of the Anastasian Reforms", *NC* 7. i (1961), 131-43.

are rather more widely scattered in their provenances, although not in the Balkans. Little detailed numismatic study has yet been devoted to them, so that any theory of widespread consignment rests only on a general impression, and not on the collation of die-varieties. For the monetary historian, the implication of consignment at the end of the ninth century and the beginning of the tenth would be that the number of cities in the Balkans which were flourishing centres of monetary affairs could no longer be counted on the fingers, and that the need for petty currency was becoming more widespread in the provinces.

Balkan provenances are however still extremely few. There is the little Bratimir hoard of 11 coins, from the region of Silistra on the lower Danube, in which Leo's "Seated Figure" type, as well as the more usual "Bust" type, occurred. [34] The Corinth and Athens excavations have yielded just over a thousand specimens; there are a few from Thasos; and there is one stray find from Osijek. Since finds outside central Greece are so scarce, particular interest attaches to the presence of coins of Leo in the Sparta hoard of 1924 - 25 and in the Corinth hoard of November 1937 which, it is suggested, may have been carried to the city from somewhere further south in the Peloponnesus shortly before its concealment. [35]

The Book of the Eparch, with which Leo's name is associated, contains several references to money. [36] For a variety of reasons, there is disappointingly little to be discovered from them about coinage and currency; but the diversity of organized trades and occupations in the capital clearly implies that a monetary economy for everyday transactions, and an ample petty currency, were normal there. They had probably been so even in the eighth century.

Copper coins of the Arab Amirs of Crete have been found in small numbers in central Greece. They date from the second half of the ninth into the second quarter of the tenth centuries. The Corinth excavations yielded 8 specimens, and there were 3 from Athens. Miles reports two more, seen in shops in Athens, and comments, "one can hint at least at

---

[34] Gerasimov, "Kolektivni Nakhodki, 1956-57".

[35] For Corinth and Athens, see Edwards, *Corinth*, 1896 - 1929; Thompson, *Coins;* and Table 2 below. For Osijek, see Metcalf, "Syrmia and Slavonia"; For Sparta, see *ABSAthens* xxvi (1925), 157f.

[36] W. Kubitschek, "Zum 'Επαρχικὸν Βιβλίον", *NZ* xliv (1911), 185-201; cf. Ostrogorsky, *Byzantine State*, pp. 191-2 and 224.

the possibility of commerce of some sort between Arab-occupied Crete and the mainland of Greece". If the figures are compared with the totals of Byzantine coins of 829-912 from Corinth and Athens (see Fig. 2), the Arab coins are seen to be relatively much more plentiful at Athens, although the numbers are of course so tiny that they must be treated with caution. Nevertheless, this reverses the normal pattern, according to which "strays" from other regions are relatively much more plentiful at Corinth, so abruptly that there must be some special explanation for the Athens finds. The Arab mosque there gives a likely clue. [37]

The statistics of the site-finds from the two cities reveal the steady growth of the monetary economy at Athens, relative to Corinth, during the ninth, tenth, and early eleventh centuries. Since the circulation of coinage was almost certainly increasing at Corinth as well, the ten - fold increase in two hundred years implied by the index-figures in column (h) of Table 2 will be an under-estimate — perhaps seriously so. The general interpretation of the statistics is that Athens, which at the beginning of the ninth century still belonged to the hinterland, was thereafter drawn increasingly into the economic orbit of the Aegean coasts.

The Argos site-finds are of value for the support they give to the thesis that the revival of the monetary economy began on the coasts and spread inland only slowly. The total number of coins found is trifling in comparison with the number from Corinth (in spite of the extent of the areas excavated), and indeed too small altogether for precise conclusions, but with that reservation the evidence points to a substantial recovery in monetary circulation at Argos as early as the recovery at Corinth and certainly earlier than at Athens. There are coins of Theophilus and of Leo VI from the site. [38]

The statistics from Athens and Corinth are of considerable theoretical interest not merely because they relate to such large totals, and to two sites not very far apart, at both of which the workmen were rewarded for all the coins they found, but because the publication of totals

---

[37] G. C. Miles, *The Islamic Coins* (The Athenian Agora, vol. IX), Princeton, 1962, p. 21; *ibid.*, "The Arab Mosque in Athens", *Hesperia* xxv (1956), 329 - 44.

[38] Svoronos and Konstantopoulos, "Ekthesis, 1909-10"; J. Bingen in *BCH* lxxvii (1953), 257f., lxxviii (1954), 183-89, and lxxix (1955), 329-31, where the find-spots of the coins are particularized. I must express my thanks to Professor Daux, Director of the French School, and to Dr T. Hackens, for allowing me to see these and the more recent finds.

stage by stage permits an estimate of their degree of internal consistency. A comparison of columns (a), (b), and (d) in Table 2 suggests that there was more variability in the ninth and tenth centuries than in the eleventh, the figures for which have been discussed elsewhere. [39] The overall quantities of coins found at Corinth were much larger in 1936-39 (column (c)) because that period covered the excavation of the Agora. [40]

	CORINTH					ATHENS		RATIO (COR-INTH=100)
	a	b	c	d	e	f	g	h
Theophilus	23	38	96	(32)	157	0	4	3
Michael III	4	4	12	(4)	20	0	1	5
Basil I	50	37	193	(64)	280	2	17	6
Leo VI	158	173	626	(209)	957	20	81	8
Constantine VII:								
BMC 1 - 6 (913 - 19)	10		30	(10)			6	12
BMC 11 - 13 (919 - 21?)	4		—	—			—	
BMC 14 - 29 (931 - 44?)	357		568	(189)			59	5
BMC 45 - 57 (945 - 59?)	150		544	(181)			164	18
BMC 70 - 76 (945 - 59?)	23		101	(34)			28	18
Total	544	497	1243	(414)	2284	48	257	11
Nicephorus II	37	38	133	(44)	208	15	46	16
Rex Regnantium folles:								
Class A (970 - 1028?)	825	650	1910	(637)	3385	125	623	18
Class B (1028 - 34?)	154	146	381	(127)	681	39	218	32
Class C (1034 - 41?)	96	103	284	(95)	483	36	154	32
Totals	1891	1686	4878	(1626)	8455	285	1400	

Table 2. Statistics of the site-finds from Athens and Corinth, 829-1041.

(Column a, 1895-1929; b, 1930-35; c, 1936-39; d,=c divided by 3; e, total; f, 1931-35; g, 1931-49.)

The bronze coinages of the period of Constantine VII and Nicephorus II have not yet received much serious attention, although there is reason to suspect that more than one mint was at work. The bulk of the issues of Constantine (BMC 14-29 and 45-57) may have comprised a re-coinage in the 940's. [41] There is more than one hoard from the

---

[39] Metcalf, "Provincial Issues".

[40] Further valuable information should be available shortly, in a synopsis of the coins found during the years 1940-1960.

[41] Following the recoinage, as it should perhaps be interpreted, by Leo VI, the date of which may possibly have been some time in the first decade of the tenth century.

Corinth excavations consisting exclusively of folles in the name of Romanus I *(BMC* 14-29); and the Stimanga hoard, found near-by in 1955, consisted of 66 folles of Romanus. [42]

A stray find of a follis of Nicephorus II is reported from Mangalia, and others of Romanus I from Aboba, and from Megalopolis in Arcadia. [43]

A small hoard of gold coins from Byala, in the Yantra valley north of Tŭrnovo, included three pieces in the names of Romanus I and Christopher, and one, of the same design, of Constantine VII and Romanus. The provenance is of exceptional interest, in a period in which there are hardly any hoards from the interior, because the issue of Romanus and Christopher has been associated, on grounds of iconography, with the marriage of Christopher's daughter Maria to Peter, king of the Bulgarians, in 927. The hoard does something to confirm the association, even if it does not clarify it. There is a nomisma of a related type from Aboba. [44]

Nicephorus II is credited with the introduction of the tetarteron, or light-weight nomisma, which was to be struck regularly almost throughout the eleventh century, alongside the ordinary nomisma. [45] Grierson has argued that its introduction was not a financial expedient but "a laudable attempt to meet the local needs of the provinces reconquered from the Arabs by providing the inhabitants with a coin equivalent in value to the dinar to which they were accustomed and in which all their accounts were reckoned". [46] The hoard-evidence from the Balkans suggests that this is in any event not the complete situation: the Garvăn (Dinogetia) hoards of 1939 and 1954, both deposited two decades

---

[42] Mosser, *Byzantine Coin Hoards*. There is a more recent hoard, which is to be published shortly. For Stimanga, see *BCH* lxxx (1956), 256.

[43] *BMC* Type 2. [O. Iliescu, "Însemnari Privitoare la Descoperiri Monetare (II)", *SCN* ii (1958), 447-463; Panchenko, "Pechati i Monety" *(BMC* 14-29); J. G. Milne in *NC* 6. ix (1949), 83-92.

[44] Cf. the article by Friedlaender referred to in Wroth, *BMC*, *(Byz.)*, p. 458 note 2. Gerasimov, "Kolektivni Nakhodki, 1951 - 54". The hoard was found in 1954. There were 3 coins as *BMC* plate liii, 1, and one as lii, 5, and one other, among those examined out of a total of ten. Panchenko, "Pechati i Monety".

[45] R. S. Lopez, "La Crise du Besant au Xe. Siècle et la Date du Livre du Préfet", *Mélanges Henri Grégoire* II (= *Annuaire de l'Institut de Philologie et d'Histoire Orientales et Slaves* x) (1950), 403-18.

[46] Grierson, "Nicéphore Phocas"; Grierson, "Debasement".

or more after the death of Basil, both contained so far as is known coins of Basil and Constantine of only one variety, *BMC* 5-6, which Grierson has identified as a tetarteron. [47] The weights of the coins in the two hoards fully confirm that *BMC* 5-6 is a light issue, but the provenances do not seem to fit in with the "Islamic" theory of the origins of the tetarteron. *BMC* 5-6 is not an especially common coin in the sale-room, yet the finds make it appear probable that the issues of Basil in the lower Danube region were largely if not exclusively of that variety. Such a pattern might be the result of consignment, or, alternatively, a provincial mint may have been set up in the region of the lower Danube, perhaps in connexion with Basil's Bulgarian campaigns.

Mme. Ahrweiler-Glykatzi reads Zonaras's account of the new gold coin as follows: Nicephorus invented the tetarteron, and used it for official disbursements, while insisting that his revenues should be paid in coins of full weight. Further, he gave his own issues a preferential rate of exchange against those of earlier emperors, which was contrary to tradition. These statements by Zonaras imply that Nicephorus was undertaking the essentially simple operation of reducing the weight of the nomisma and calling the old currency back into the treasury. His objective, no doubt, had to do with the use of the nomisma in the Empire's external trade and its circulation in competition with the Islamic dinar, which was slightly lighter than the traditional *nomisma hexagion*. The scheme was brought to failure by popular misunderstanding and hostility towards the temporary hardship it caused, and by the early death of Nicephorus. Mme. Ahrweiler-Glykatzi suggests that the military policies of Nicephorus, and more particularly the needs resulting from the maintenance of the paid army of the *tagmata,* may explain the creation of the new light-weight coin. One can readily imagine that succeeding emperors would have succumbed to the temptation to continue an established precedent of paying their mercenaries in tetartera; and such a view fits in well with the hoard-evidence. But it certainly seems advisable to formulate the problems separately

---

[47] See further below. P. Grierson, "Tetarteron or Counterfeit? A Note on Mr Uzman's Coin", *Numismatic Circular* lxx (1962), 53. In Grierson, "Debasement", it is suggested that the three types of nomismata of Basil and Constantine, in chronological order of issue, are 1. with patriarchal cross *(BMC*, plate lvi, 1-2); 2. with patriarchal cross-crosslet *(BMC*, plate lvi, 4-7); 3. with plain cross *(BMC*, plate lvi, 8). One may suspect, however, that this series is more complicated, and that, for example, *BMC* nos. 1, 2, and 4 are tetartera.

Map II. The western Aegean, IX—X centuries.

for the reign of Nicephorus and for later periods, especially where there is the added complication of debasement. [48]

The important Édhessa hoard will belong early in Nicephorus's reign. A gold coin of Nicephorus II occurred in the Voden hoard of 1934, from the region of Elkhovo, but the variety was not noted. [49] From A-boba there is a nomisma of Basil, but again, the variety is not clearly identified; [50] gold of Nicephorus II is reported by Lishev from Kuma-rovo and Maritsa.

On the folles of John I and of his successors to 1028 or thereabouts the portrait of the emperor is replaced by that of the heavenly King, and his name on the reverse is replaced by the four-line inscription, in a mixture of Greek and Latin letters, IhSЧS XRISTЧS ЬASILEЧ, ЬASILE,, Jesus Christ, Βασιλεὺς τῶν Βασιλευόντων, King of Those who Rule. [51] After 1028 the reverse design of the Rex Regnatium folles was changed at quite short intervals, but they were still anonymous. They are refered to, by numismatists, as Class A, Class B, and so on, according to a classification published by Miss Thompson, in its currently revised form, on the basis of overstruck coins from the Athenian Agora excavations. [52] The Rex Regnantium folles of Class A are extremely numerous in the finds at Corinth and Athens, where, altogether, more than four thousand specimens have been brought to light, mostly one by one. In estimating their significance for monetary history, it should be remembered that they were current for a period of about 60 years on their own, and continued in use alongside Classes B and C, and that the quantities of site-finds are proportional *inter alia* to the length of time for which coins remained in circulation. The relative increase in the quantities from Constantine VII to Rex Regnantium A is less than that from Leo VI to Constantine VII, and perhaps less still when it has been adjusted to take account of the length of time for which the coins were in circulation: the expansion of the monetary economy at Corinth was beginning to slow down (see Table 2).

---

[48] Ahrweiler-Glykatzi, "Le Tétartèron".

[49] *BCH* lx (1936), 454. Gerasimov, "Kolektivni Nakhodki, 1934-36".

[50] Panchenko, "Pechati i Monety".

[51] The iconography of the coins and its political significance are eludated in an extremely interesting monograph, J. D. Breckenridge, *The Numismatic Iconography of Justinian II (*685-695, 705-711 A. D.) (Numismatic Notes and Monographs, 144), New York, 1959.

[52] Thompson, *Coins;* cf. Bellinger, *Anonymous Byzantine Bronze.*

More important for monetary history is the almost complete range
of varieties represented in the Corinth site-finds, and the very wide
range at Athens, among the coins of Class A. They show that there was
a considerable flux between the petty currencies of different regions of
the Empire. The force of this argument will be more exactly assessed
when the secret-marks on the folles of Class A are better understood.
The study of them must rest on strictly numismatic techniques, above
all the discovery of die-similarities, and the results for the monetary
history of the Balkans will have to await the application of those techniques, in a task where almost everything still remains to be done. The
scheme of the secret-marks — there is variation in three places in the
design of the coins, namely in the ornament of the Book that Christ
holds, in the nimbus cruciger, and on the reverse — may turn out to be
partly chronological and partly according to mints. (Dimian has submitted [53] that the small coins without secret-marks on the reverse,
Class Al, are later than Class A2, but his argument is merely by analogy,
and is unacceptable. The correct explanation of the coins of Class Al
might be that they are provincial — witness their absence from the
Antioch finds. [54] But here, as at every other point, a definitive answer
must wait upon stylistic analyses). Bellinger's list of varieties, to which
three or four more could be added, is reproduced in Table 3. [55] The system
is evidently so complicated that many hoards will have to be analysed
before it can be reconstructed at all fully.

Nevertheless, it is already clear that the common secret - marks
to be associated with central Greece are those with a dot, or a group
of four dots, above or below the reverse inscription. This group of varieties, all in the same general style (Bellinger 3, 4, 5, 8, and 20, to which
might also be added 7 and 9, often in inferior style) is dominant in the
Athens finds, where it accounts for some 360 out of a total of 583
identified coins of Class A, or 62%.[56] At Corinth the proportion would
seem to be much the same — as nearly as one can judge, 65%.[57] Among

[53] E. I. Dimian, "Cu Privire la Cronologia şi Atribuirea Monedelor Anonime
Bizantine de Bronz", *SCN* iii (1960), 197-221.

[54] D. M. Waage, *Greek, Roman, Byzantine, and Crusaders' Coins* (Antioch-on
-the-Orontes, vol. IV, part 2), Princeton, 1952.

[55] Bellinger, *Anonymous Byzantine Bronze;* H. Longuet, "Die unedierten byzantinischen Münzen des Wiener Kabinettes", *NZ* lxxxvii (1957), 28-57, nos. 225,
-238.

[56] For the Athens finds of Class A, see Metcalf, (work in progress).

[57] Many of the Corinth finds were listed as uncertain, and not classified by varieties. Experience gained in handling the Athens finds suggests that the varieties most

the Corinth finds, Class Al was not properly distinguished, but it seems that there may have been about 60 among 660 identified specimens, that is, a significantly smaller proportion than at Athens, where the figure is within a little of 16%.

At Athens there are 32 coins with the "vine - scroll" secret - mark on the reverse, nearly all of them of the variety of intermediate size, and 15 with the "flower" secret-mark that includes the other variety of Class A2 noted by Bellinger as being of intermediate size. Varieties 24, 33, 39, and 40 are a compact stylistic group, and doubtless come from the same mint. At Corinth the figures are closely comparable.

No other variety is plentiful at either site. At Corinth, there are twos and threes of rather more varieties. This slightly larger proportion of strays is a quite usual difference between the Corinth and Athens finds, and the remarkable thing, as regards the coins of Class A, is that it is not more pronounced. The distribution among the varieties is, in a word, essentially the same at the two places except that B. 5 is relatively more plentiful at Corinth while B.3 and B.20 are relatively more plentiful at Athens. The primary conclusion to be drawn is that in the first half of the eleventh century these cities were participating fairly equally in the monetary economy of the Aegean world.

The excavations of the Athenian Agora have explored a compact area of about 25 acres, or just over 10 hectares, and within that area, corresponding with a suburb of the medieval city, different varieties of the Rex Regnantium folles of Class A are relatively localized in their occurrence. Class Al, for example, is to some extent concentrated in one part of the Agora area, variety B.5 in another, and so on. The only plausible explanation that comes to mind is that different trades or occupations were concentrated in certain streets or districts, and that the stray losses, of coins from mints in various parts of Greece or further afield in the Empire, reflect trading contacts. Specialized trading districts were, of course, a normal feature of medieval and early modern levantine cities. The localization within the Agora area of coins of Basil I from different mints has already been mentioned.

An extremely useful piece of evidence for the study of Class A comes from the Sparta find of 1949. Among 19 folles concealed *ca.* 1080 there

---

likely to be put aside as uncertain are those with a dot above or below the reverse inscription; some trace at least of the more elaborate secret-marks usually remains. Bellinger, *Corinth*, 1925, where the classification is more complete, gives a guide.

Bellinger no.	Reverse	Nimbus	Book	Bellinger no.	Reverse	Nimbus	Book
1	⌐⌐⌐ (wavy)	.	:	29	— ◇	. .	☼
2	nothing	. .	.	30	— · ∩ · —	. . .	.
3	nothing/·	. .	.	31	· ↑ ·	+	.
4	· /nothing	. .	.	32	+	+	+
5	· / ·	. .	.	33	⊙∞	∴	:
6	·—	: . .	.	34	— ✳ —	∷	(?)
7	— · —	. .	.	35	— ◇ —	∷	.
8	∴	. .	.	36	— Γ —	∷	.
9	— ∴	. .	.	37	-o-/-r-	∷	(?)
10	+++	. .	.	38	—)x(—	∷	(?)
11	∴—∴—∴	. .	.	39	∾✳∾	∷	:
12	—✳—	. .	.	40	∾✳∾	∷	∷
13	—∷—	. .	(?)·	41	— ◇ —	※	
14	— ◇ —	. .	.	42	— △ —	※	(?)
15	— · A · —	. .	.	43	— C —	⋊	⊙
16	— ∧ —	. .	.	44	□	(?) ×	∷
17	— h —	. .	.	45	— ⌂ —	⌣	(?)
18	— R —	. .	.	46	— Y —	⌣	∷
19	— p —	. .	?	47	□	□	∷
20	nothing/·	.	:	48	— · : · —	⊔∷⊔	.
21	—✳—	. .	:	49	— · : · —	⊔∷⊔	.
22	— ◇ —	. .	:	50	— ᴄᴐ —	⊔∪⊔	.
23	— ⊙ —	. .	:	51	— + —	(?)	(?)
24	⊙∞	. .	:				
25	— · : · —	. .	⊙				
26	• · : · •	. .	⊙				
27	• · : · •	. .	⊙				
28	• · : · •	. .	⊙				

Table 3. Rex Regnantium Folies, Class A: list of secret-marks.

were 2 of that issue and 8 of Class B. The Class A coins were of Bellinger's varieties 41 and 47, and 3 of the Class B coins were restruck on identifiable varieties of Class A - Bellinger 47; 47 or 44; and 42 or 45.[58] Taken at face value this is strongly suggestive of localization of the secret - marks, for all these varieties together account for only about 3 per cent. of the finds at Athens or Corinth; and it even hints that the striking of Class B was local. The varieties 41-2, 44-5 and 47 are among those that one might have guessed to belong late in the issue of Class A. A late date for them would offer an alternative explanation for the Sparta hoard, but not one that commends itself at the present.

The impression that the varieties were localized is strengthened by a hoard found at Drosaton (Eupalion), on the Corinthian Gulf, in 1960 - 61. Among 34 folles, of which the latest was of John II, there were half -a-dozen of Rex Regnantium Class A2, of varieties 24, 40 (2), 41 (2), and 47, and a worn coin possibly of Class Al.[59] Even with such a small sample, it is really quite remarkable that B. 3, 4, 5, 7, 8, 9, and 20, the varieties which are so plentiful at Athens and Corinth, should be unrepresented, especially as the coins of Class A had been in circulation for upwards of a century when the Drosaton hoard was concealed.

From the Dobruja, there is the Plopeni hoard, which included 44 folles of Class A. Half of them were of the varieties B. 24 and B. 39 [or (?) 40], and there were 6 specimens of B. 41, and 4 of B. 5. If one were obliged to make a guess at the mint that struck the two varieties of intermediate size, B.24 and 40, Thessaloniki would be the first choice, especially as those or similar varieties made up a little hoard found at Mitrovica, in Syrmia.[60] Does the Plopeni hoard put a Thessalonican attribution out of court?— the answer must, as so often, take the form of a series of alternative propositions; and it points to the need for detailed stylistic analyses of these particular varieties. The occurrence of Thessalonican petty coins in finds from the Black Sea coastlands would not be by any means unparalleled. Until better evidence comes to light, one could at least say that B. 24 and 40 seem likely to belong to the northern parts of the Balkan peninsula.

From the more widely scattered provenances of coins of Class A, one may conjecture that there was an increase in the scope of the circula-

---

[58] J. M. Cook and R. V. Nicholls, "Laconia", *ABSAthens* xlv (1950), 261-98.

[59] Varoukha-Khristodhoulopoulou, "Acquisitions, 1962". I am indebted to Mrs. Varoukha-Khristodhoulopoulou for permission to study the coins.

[60] Metcalf, "Syrmia and Slavonia".

tion of petty coinage in the early decades of the eleventh century. Hoards have been found at Plovdiv and Khisara, and, further east, at Lŭdzhene, near Lovech. The Dobrotitsa hoard, consisting of 16 folles, came from half-way between Preslav and Tŭrnovo. Stray-finds have been reported from Kazichene, Asun, and Madara in Bulgaria, [61] from Demir Kapija and Sisak in Jugoslavia, [62] from Durrës in Albania, [63] and from Megalopolis and Orchomenos in Arcadia, [64] as well as from more obvious places such as Preslav and Aboba; Constantsa, Canlia, and Galita in the Dobruja; and Thasos. [65] The Preslav, Aboba, and Megalopolis find-series contain one or two coins earlier than 970, but there is a sharp increase in the numbers with the introduction of the Rex Regnantium folles.

An unusual hoard, discovered at Zlataritsa in north-central Bulgaria, brought to light 15 kilogrammes of copies of Class A folles. They were only about 20 mm. in diameter, and 0.5 mm. thick, and were cast, not struck; they weighed around 1½ grammes. They ranged in style from pieces on which the four-line inscription was quite adequately copied, through more and more barbarous attempts, to coins on which

---

[61] For the Plovdiv (ul. Basil Kolarov) find of 1954, containing 6 folles of Class A, and for the Khisara (Plovdiv) hoard of 1942, containing 3 kilogrammes of Rex Regnantium folles, attributed to John I, see D. Tsonchev, "Kolektivni Nakhodki na Moneti", *Godishnik na Narodnaya Arkheologicheski Muzei Plovdiv* iv (1960), 206-14. For the Ludzhene hoard of 100 folles, see Gerasimov, "Kolektivni Nakhodki, 1934-36", and for Dobrotitsa, Gerasimov, "Kolektivni Nakhodki, 1955". For Kazichene, Filov, "Novootkriti Starini", *IBAD* iii (1912-13); For Asun, D. Tsonchev and S. Stoilev, "La Forteresse d'Asen", ⁋ *Byzantinoslavica* xxii (1961), 20-54; for Madara, T. D. Gerasimov, "Monetite, Namereni v Dvete Rimski Postroiki pri s. Madara", *Izvestiya na Narodniya Muzei, Kolarovgrad* i (1960), 55-65 (no. 35).

[62] B. Aleksova, *Demir Kapija, Izlozba* 31 *Maj*-16 *Juni* 1959, *Skopje* (Sovet za Kultura na NR Makedonija-Arheološki Muzej, Skopje), where the reverse of a coin, of B.41 or a related variety, is illustrated. For Sisak, Metcalf, "Syrmia and Slavonia". Note also a find of a coin of Class B at Senj, on the Adriatic coast; *Archiv für Kunde Osterreichischer Geschichts-Quellen* xxix, 336.

[63] Two coins were found in 1924 between Pazarit and Tomoritsa Streets at 4 metres under some houses destroyed in the war: *Albania* 1925, 28f.

[64] J. G. Milne, "The Currency of Arcadia", *NC* 6. ix (1949), 83-92; A. Plassart, in *BCH*, xxxix (1915) 120-220.

[65] Mushmov, "Kolektivni Nakhodki, 1929-30"; Panchenko, "Pechati i Monety; S. Stanchŭhev, "Materiali ot Dvortsoviya Tsentur v Pliska", *IAI* xxiii (1960), 23-65; E. I. Dimian, *op. cit.;* B. Mitrea, "Découvertes Récentes et Plus Anciennes de Monnaies Antiques et Byzantines en Roumanie", *Dacia NS* v (1961), 583 - 93; *BCH* lxxviii (1954), 205. *Pace* Stanchev, the Roman and early Byzantine coins from Aboba may well have been current in the eleventh century, having been found accidentally in the soil.

the letters of the prototype were represented merely by rectangles or dots. The same kind of coinage, of the better varieties, has been found in north-eastern Bulgaria. [66] Its significance for the monetary historian is obscure, except that the Zlataritsa hoard was so large that the copies must surely have been made for use as money; and that the stylistic range suggests that their manufacture was continued for some time.

Modern forgery (and not some contemporary expendiency) is suggested by Gerasimov as the true explanation of two gold pieces originally published by Schlumberger and attributed by him to the Bulgarian defender of Sirmium in 1018. [67]

There is, finally, the question of the changing purchasing - power of the coinage. Andréadès has made a critical examination of the few documentary references to the price of wheat and barley. One may guess that there was a four- or five-fold decline in the quantity of grain that could be bought for a nomisma, between the middle of the eighth century and the latter part of the eleventh, and that the rate of decline was greatest in the period up to the middle of the tenth century. If this is so, it is of cardinal interest for the question, "to meet what needs", especially in the light of Cipolla's analysis of the forces behind depreciation, which has been summarized above; but the texts are so few and their interpretation is subject to so much uncertainty (as Andréadès made clear) that there is no obvious prospect of relating them to the detailed study of the currency in the Balkan provinces. [68]

---

[66] T. D. Gerasimov, "Starinni Falshifikati na Moneti ot Iv. Tsimiskhii", *IAI* xvii (1950), 313-15.

[67] T. D. Gerasimov, "Mnimite Zlatni Moneti na Bŭlgarskiya Voenachalnik Sermon", *IAI* xxiv (1961), 97-101, citing I. Duichev, "Posledniyat Zashtitnik na Srem v 1018 G.", *Izvestiya* viii (1959), 315-21.

[68] A. Andréadès, "De la Monnaie et de la Puissance d'Achat des Métaux Précieux dans l'Empire Byzantin", *Byzantion* i (1924), 75-115, and p.12 above.For the general background of agrarian history, see P. Lemerle, "Esquisse pour une Histoire Agraire de Byzance: les Sources et les Problèmes", *Revue Historique* ccxix (1958), 32-74 and 254-84, and ccxx (1959), 43-94.

CHAPTER III

MOVEMENTS TOWARDS POLITICAL AUTONOMY: 1025-1097

The death of Basil II in 1025 revealed the extent to which Byzantine control, in the Balkans and elsewhere, had depended on his personal abilities and exertions. The rest of the eleventh century was a period of disastrous weakness for the Empire. The strategic situation of the western Balkans was changed by the growing strength of Hungary and of Sicily; Croatia and Zeta, securing an advantage from the hostility between Rome and Constantinople, obtained western recognition as independent kingdoms, and there were other, less successful movements towards autonomy. The manoeuvres of rival claimants to the Byzantine throne, and, even more, Hungarian raids and the incursions of the Patzinaks and Uzes brought troubled times to the Balkans.

Basil's policy of upholding the peasants and small-holders was reversed, and, under Michael IV, John Orphanotrophos, his chief minister of state, required the payment of taxes in money instead of in kind, in regions which had been exempted from monetary payment. He imposed such severe exactions that he provoked rebellion among the Slavs and Bulgars. Stefan Voislav of Zeta refused to pay tribute from *ca.* 1035. In 1040-41 he again openly defied the Empire, in an incident which has left records for the numismatist: ten *centenaria* of gold which were, apparently, being sent to the emperor at Thessaloniki, were lost in a shipwreck on the Illyrian coast. Stefan Voislav appropriated the treasure and ignored a letter from the emperor threatening war if the gold were not returned. An expedition against Stefan, led by the *strategus* of Dyrrachium, met with a severe defeat. The gold coins of Romanus III that have frequently been found in the uplands of central Dalmatia, for example in small hoards at Gornje Ogorje in 1895 and at Sinjskopolje in 1912, and as single finds from Dugopolje, from the Poljica, and from the island of Biševo, are, it has been suggested, relics of the shipwrecked treasure. From further to the south-east of Sprit, there are finds from Zagvozd, and, in the Neretva and Trebizat valleys, from Klobuk and the site of Narona. A find from near Vitina in 1890, and a much larger hoard which came to light in at Dreznica in 1867, and which was said to have contained upwards of 300 coins together with two rings, help to define further the area over which the coins of Romanus were spread.(See Map III). The Grabovnika (Vitina) hoard included

Map III. The central Adriatic coastlands.

nine coins, concealed in a leaden box, of which 6 of the 7 that were available for study were of Romanus, while the seventh was a nomisma of Theodora (1055-56). [1]

The maintenance of the established order in the early 1040's was extremely precarious. In 1041 Peter Deljan was proclaimed emperor in Belgrade; the revolt was suppressed. In 1043 the general Maniaces, after remarkable victories in Italy, landed at Dyrrachium as a pre-

---

[1] D. M. Metcalf, "A Shipwreck on the Dalmatian Coast and some Gold Coins of Romanus III Argyrus", *Greek, Roman, and Byzantine Studies* iii (1960), 101 - 06. It is not clear why the ship was sailing in the Adriatic (my mention of Rome was a nonsense), but it seems quite clear that that is where the shipwreck was. I am indebted to Mrs M. Wenzel for a correction to the list of provenances: Dugopolje, she suggests, is probably the polje south-east of Duvno Polje. For both the Drežnica and the Vitina hoards, see K. Patsch, "Nahogjaji Novaca", *GZMBH* xii (1900), 543-73. The original latin inscription of the coins in the Drežnica hoard leavs no real doubt about their attribution. The weights of the coins from Vitina were: Romanus, 4.39, 4.36, 4.33, 4.32, 4.28, 4.31; Theodora, 4.16. A nomisma of Romanus III is recorded among the finds from Aboba: Panchenko, "Pechati i Monety".

tender to the throne, and began his ill-fated campaign in the Balkans. In 1047 Constantinople was besieged and nearly fell to Leo Tornices. In 1048 the Patzinaks crossed the Danube and established themselves in Bulgarian territory. The second half of the century witnessed as many troubles. In 1064 the Hungarians occupied Belgrade; and in the autumn of the same year hordes of Uzes poured into the Balkans. Their ravages in Bulgaria, Macedonia, Thrace, and even Greece were terminated by a severe outbreak of the plague.

There was a considerable expansion in the frontiers of the Croatian state, under Peter Cresimir (1058-74), and in its influence on the Adriatic coast. In an unsuccessful Slavonic revolt in 1072 Constantine Bodin was crowned as emperor in Prizren; his father Michael, prince of Zeta, received a royal crown from Rome in 1077. Nicephorus Bryennius, who, as *dux* of Dyrrachium, had suppressed the revolt of 1072, in 1077 entered Adrianople as rival emperor. In 1081 Robert Guiscard captured Dyrrachium; the Norman armies passed through Macedonia, Epirus and Thessaly, and even besieged Larisa. For some years it seemed as though the Sicilians might establish a permanent foothold in the west Balkans. Constantine Bodin, now king of Zeta, was able to extend his power to Rascia and Bosnia.

In 1090-91 Constantinople was again besieged. The victory against the Patzinaks at Mount Levunion, and the lifting of the siege, marked the beginning of a period of greater stability. [2]

Given that hundreds of medieval coin-hoards have been recorded from the Balkans, it is a reasonable proposition that, if coinage had been circulating extensively in the peninsula, the years 1025-1097, during which there were such widespread disturbances, might have been expected to yield a good number of treasures. In fact there are very few. The lack of finds from almost all parts of the Balkans indicates that the development of monetary affairs had still not gone very far, except in central Greece and the region of the lower Danube. Before describing the find-series, however, we must examine the most obvious result for monetary history of the eleventh-century political decline.

The debasement of the gold coinage, which for so many centuries

---

[2] For the historical background, see Ostrogorsky, *Byzantine State*, pp. 283-310. See also a recent study, G. Vernadsky, "The Russo-Byzantine War of 1043", *Byzantinisch-Neugriechische Jahrbücher* xviii (1945-49), Athens, 1960, 123-43.

had maintained the same weight and the same high standard of fineness, began under Michael IV (1034-41) and progressed to its worst point under Nicephorus III (1078-81), when the nomisma, instead of being of a nominal 24 carats, was no more than 8 carats fine. The reform of the gold coinage by Alexius I was not undertaken until, perhaps, 1097. From the reign of Nicephorus II, and throughout the eleventh century, two denominations in gold were issued side by side, the nomisma and the tetarteron. The system has been elucidated in recent years by Grierson's researches on the fineness of the coinage. [3] He has been able to revise certain of the attributions of Wroth and earlier scholars, and, where several types are to be attributed to a single reign, to place them into their chronological order. The sequences that he has proposed, together with the finenesses (which still rest on a limited amount of evidence for some reigns), are summarized in Table 4.

The Rex Regnantium folles of the middle period (Classes B to G) have been placed into a sequence on the basis of overstrikings, [4] but the evidence is in places tenuous and perhaps misleading, and the two underlying assumptions of the hitherto accepted schemes, namely that the coins ought to belong in a single chronological sequence, and that the volume of the coinages ought to turn out to be roughly proportional to the length of the reigns to which they are assigned, are still open to doubt. (It is, of course, no more than an assumption that the period of issue of each Rex Regnantium Class should coincide with a reign). There is singularly little hoard evidence, nor have stylistic studies yet been carried far enough for it to be certain whether Classes C and D, as seems probable, each include the work of more than one mint.

The bulk of Classes E and F may tentatively be assigned to Thessaloniki, F being regarded as a variant, perhaps just an early variant, of Class D. [6] A hoard of 74 coins exclusively of Class D from the Corinth excavations contained 44 specimens with the secret-marks — + — and — ∪ — above and below the reverse inscription, 24 with — + — and — ∪ —, 2 with — ⚓ — and — ∪ —, and 4 of which the variety was uncertain. [7] The variety — + —, — ∪ — is over-represented in the hoard by comparison with the site - finds. Another hoard composed

---

[3] Grierson, "Debasement"; Grierson, "Fineness".

[4] Thompson, *Coins*.

[5] Vacat.   [6] Metcalf, (work in progress).

[7] Edwards, *Corinth*, 1896-1929.

Emperor	Nomisma (Broad flans)	Carats	Tetarteron (Thick fabric)	Carats
Constantine VIII (1025–28)			Type 1, no. 1 (lvii, 6)	23
	Type 2, nos. 3–5 (lvii, 8)	24	Type 2, no. 2 (lvii, 7)	24
Romanus III (1028–34)	Type 1, nos. 1–3 (lvii, 13)	24	Type 3 of Romanus IV (lxii, 1)	
Michael IV (1034–41)	Type 1, nos. 1–5 (lviii, 1, 2)			
Michael V (1041–42)	Type 2 of Michael VI = Sabatier, plate xliv, 16			
Constantine IX (1042–55)	1. Type 4, nos. 8–11 (lviii, 11–12)	24	1. Type 1, nos. 1–3 (lviii, 6–7)	21
	2. Type 5, nos. 12–15 (lix, 1–2)	21½	2. Type 2, nos. 4–5 (lviii, 8)	18 or less
	3. Type 3 of Constantine VIII (lvii, 9–10)	20½		
	4. Type 3, nos. 6–7 (lviii, 9–10)	19 or 18		
	5. Sabatier, plate xlix, 7			
Theodora (1055–56)	Type 2, nos. 4–5 (lx, 3–4)	18	Type 1, nos. 1–3 [(lx, 1–2)	?17
Michael VI (1056–57)	No. 1 of Michael V (lviii, 5)	18	Type 1, 1–2 (lx, 9)	?17
Isaac I (1057–59)	Type 2, nos. 2–3 (lx, 12)	18	Type 1, no. 1 (lx, 11)	?17
	Type 3, no. 4 (lx, 13)	18		
Constantine X (1059–67)	Type 1, nos. 1–3 (lxi, 1)	18	Type 3, no. 8 (lxi, 4)	?17
	Type 2, nos. 4–7 (lxi, 2–3)	18		
Eudocia as regent (1067)	Nos. 1–2 (lxi, 10)	17½		
Romanus IV (1067–71)	Type 1, nos. 1–4 (lxi, 11–12)	18–16	Type 2, nos. 5–6 (lxi, 13–14)	
Michael VII (1071–78)	Type 1, no. 1 (lxii, 7)	16	1. No nimbus; plain cross. BMC–	15-14
	Type 2, nos. 2–10 (lxii, 8–9)	16	2. No nimbus; X on cross (lxii, 10)	15-14
			3. Nimbus; crescent on cross (lxii, 11)	11 or less
Nicephorus III (1078–81)	Type 3, nos. 7–8 (lxiii, 6)	8		
	Type 2, nos. 5–6 (lxiii, 5)	8		
	Type 1, nos. 1–4 (lxiii, 4)	8		
Alexius I (1081–1118)	Type 6, no. 23 (lxiv, 11)		(Types 1–5 probably include tetartera)	
	Type 3, nos. 12–13 (lxiv, 6–7)			

Table 4. Byzantine gold coinages, 1025 — *ca* 1097. References are to Wroth, *BMC* Types, catalogue numbers, and plates. The coinages which are presumably Alexius's pre-reform issues have been added to the list.

exclusively of Class D turned up in a shop in Athens in 1959. There were two or three dozen coins, all with a thin clay-incrustation and all extremely similar in fabric and style. They were of the characteristic variety deeply struck on flans larger than the dies, and all appeared to be in very fresh condition. There were obvious traces of Class C as an undertype on most or all of them. [8] Possibly these two hoards should be assigned to the years 1040 - 41, and the introduction of Class D moved back a little earlier than the accepted date of 1042.

Classes E and F as well as D were absent from the Plopeni hoard of 1934, from near Constantsa in the Dobruja; it consisted of 88 folles, of which 44 were of Class A, 24 of Class B, 15 of Class C, and 4 of Class G with one specimen apparently of Class K. [9] Although it is tempting to try to do so, there are obstacles in the way of amalgamating Classes G and K into a single issue, and the hoard should therefore be assigned to a date in the reign of Alexius I.

There is a variety of other stray finds of folles from the Dobruja, of which several are from Mangalia, on the coast some miles south of Constantsa. [10] From Constantsa itself, Dimian has gathered a series of stray finds which includes specimens of Classes B and D. [11]

The Garvăn (Dinogetia) hoard of 100 folles, described as of the period of Theodora, [12] is, one imagines, of Class C. The remaining hoards of bronze from the Balkans attributable to the years before 1097 show a remarkable concentration in the Dobruja and in central Greece. There is the Comuna 23 August find, in which Classes E and F are again absent; and two little deposits of Classes H, I, J, from Limanu, and, further north in the Dobruja, Tulcea. [13] From Athens, there is a hoard of 20 folles of Nicephorus III, discovered in 1956. From Corinth, there is

---

[8] Metcalf, (work in progress).

[9] Dimian, "Cîteva Descoperiri".

[10] Dimian, *op. cit.*, for a coin of Romanus IV; O. Iliescu, "Însemnari Privitoare la Descoperiri Monetare (II)", *SCN* ii (1958), 447-63, for a coin of Class C, and one of Constantine X with Eudocia, stray finds from 1890; a coin of Class D; and a silver coin of Romanus IV, of the very scarce *BMC* Type 2.

[11] I. Dimian, "Cu Privire la Cronologia şi Atribuirea Mondelor Anonime Bizantine de Bronz", *SCN* iii (1960), 197 - 221.

[12] E. Comşa and G. Bichir, "O Nouă Descoperire de Monede şi Obiecte de Podoabă din Secolele X-XI în Aşezarea de la Garvăn (Dobrogea)", *SCN* iii (1960), 223 - 244 at p. 241.

[13] Dimian, "Cîteva Descoperiri".

a quite large hoard of folles of the time of Alexius I, discovered in 1959. The Corinth and Athens excavations have yielded a number of little parcels of the time of Alexius I, some of which may have been concealed before 1097. From Argos there is a small hoard of coins of Class G; and from Tanagra, a hoard of Rex Regnantium folles of unspecified types. [14]

The military expeditions in support of counter-claims to the imperial throne, several of which have been mentioned above, are the general background to the suggestion, by Grierson, that a very rare type of follis of the later eleventh century may belong to Nicephorus Bryennius. There was one in the Sparta hoard of 1949, which is dated by a coin of Class K. Particularly because of the stylistic variation among the surviving specimens, it seems advisable to keep open the possibility that they are initial issues of Nicephorus III, struck before specific instructions had reached the provincial mints. [15]

Outside the two traditional areas of monetary activity in the Balkan provinces, there is little to report. There are some folles from Thasos; and the Olynthus excavations of 1928 yielded some folles which are potentially of much interest for the monetary history of Thessaloniki. [16] Inland, there are a few site-finds from Preslav, and others from Aboba; and from Arcadia there are finds from Megalopolis and from Orchomenus. [17] There is little from Bulgaria apart from the Silistra hoard of 1948 and the doubtful case of the Sadovets discoveries of 1936. The Silistra hoard consisted of 1 follis of Class B, 9 divided among Class D and the two signed types of Constantine X, 4 of Class G, 2 of the initialled coins of Romanus IV, and 1 of Michael VII. [18] The Sadovets find, from near Lukovit in north-central Bulgaria, consisted of 7 folles of Class A, of more than one variety, and 11 of Class B, apparently in as-

[14] Metcalf, (work in progress); for the Argos hoard, Svoronos and Konstantopoulos, "Ekthesis, 1909-10", pp. 48f., find no. 93; for Tanagra, G. P. Oikonomos, in BCH xlviii (1924), 451.

[15] J. M. Cook and R. V. Nicholls, "Laconia", ABSAthens xlv (1950), 261 - 98; P. Grierson, "A Follis of Nicephorus Bryennius (?)", NC 6. x (1950), 305-11.

[16] BCH lxxvii (1953), 279; D. M. Robinson, The Coins Found at Olynthus, Part III), Baltimore, 1931, p. 119. The coins are illustrated.

[17] Mushmov, "Kolektivni Nakhodki, 1929-30"; Panchenko, "Pechati i Monety"; S. Stanchev, "Materiali ot Dvortsoviya Tsentŭr v Pliska", IAI xxiii (1960), 23 - 65, mentioning coins of Michael IV, Theodora, and Constantine X, but without adequate description; J. G. Milne, in NC 6. ix (1949), 83-92; A. Plassart, in BCH xxxix (1915), 20, 120-22.

[18] Gerasimov, "Kolektivni Nakhodki, 1946-48".

sociation with scyphate bronze of Manuel I and Alexius III Comnenus. [19]

In Syrmia, a coin of Class E has been found at Vukovar; and two pieces of Classes H, I, J are noted from Novi Banovci. [20]

The series of hoards of gold and silver from the years 1025 - 1097 is, again, dominated by finds from the Dobruja and the lower Danube region. The first of them is from Giren, near Nikopol: in 1948 were found 2 silver coins, one being of John I and the other of Constantine IX. These types are scarce enough for the deposit to be of especial interest. It may well have been concealed at the time of the Patzinak incursions of 1048, along with a second hoard of 23 scyphate coins of Constantine IX of the same design but in copper or billon. They were said to have been found in 1952. A similar billon coin came to light at Sinoe, in the region of Constantsa. [21]

The Garvăn (Dinogetia) hoard of 1939 has a peculiar age-structure. There were 103 gold pieces of Basil and Constantine, of a variety that has been identified as a tetarteron, 1 nomisma of Romanus III, one nomisma which was published as being of Constantine VIII but was in fact of Constantine IX, and another nomisma of the latter ruler. The coins of Constantine IX (1042-55) are of the types which Grierson places second and third in the chronological sequence of five, so that it is possible (but still speculative) that this accumulation of gold may originally have been concealed at the time of the Patzinak incursions too. [22]

The Garvăn hoard of 1954, consisting of 7 gold coins of Basil and Constantine of the same kind as those in the earlier hoard, together with 4 miliaresia, of which 1 was of Theodora (1055-56) and 3 were of

[19] *Ibid.*, 1934-36. Dr Gerasimov has kindly informed me that the coins were as *BMC* plate lv, 1-8 (4), lvii, 2, 3 (3), and lviii, 3 (11).

[20] Metcalf, (work in progress), and p. below.

[21] Gerasimov, "Kolektivni Nakhodki, 1946-48", and *ibid.*, 1951-54; Dimian, "Cîteva Descoperiri".

[22] G. Stefan, "Dinogetia. I. Risultati della Prima Campagna di Scavi (1939)", *Dacia* vii-viii (1937-40), 401-25. Cf. V. Laurent, "Bulletin de Numismatique Byzantine (1940-49)", *Revue des Etudes Byzantines* ix (1951), 192ff., reporting that the hoard contained 17 folles, ranging from Justin I to Alexius I. See also Comşa and Bichir, *op. cit.* The coin published as of Constantine VIII was of *BMC* nos. 6 - 9 (cf. Table 2 above).

[23] Comşa and Bichir, *op. cit.*

[24] I. Barnea, "Alt Tezaur de Monede Bizantine de la Dinogetia", *SCN* iii (1960), 245-54.

Isaac I (1057-59), was dated by Comșa and Bichir to 1065. [23] The silver
of this period is sufficiently rare for one to be able to say, even with so
few coins, that the age-structure points to an earlier date for the withdrawal of the coins from currency; but this does not altogether rule out
the suggested date of deposit.

The third Garvăn hoard, discovered in 1959, consisted of 15 gold
pieces, of Romanus IV and Michael VII. It is suggested to have been
concealed either during the revolt of 1073-74 or possibly at some later
date, in the reign of Alexius I. [24] The close age-structure speaks in favour of the earlier date.

Two tetartera were found at Kirilovo, near Preslav, in 1947. One
was apparently of Theodora and the other was of the second issue of
Michael VII.

The Gyurgendzhik hoard of 1911 contained 22 gold coins, along
with gold and silver ornaments. All but one of the coins were nomismata
of Michael VII, and the exception was a tetarteron of his third issue.
Again, the age-structure is close, but the exact date of deposit is not
certain. [25]

The Belene treasure of 1914, from the south bank of the Danube
a little below Nikopol, consisted of one gold coin of Nicephorus III, together with gold objects. [26] Another small hoard of gold of Nicephorus
III is recorded by two coins with Mitrovica as their provenance. [27]

The Kalipetrovo hoard, from near Silistra, discovered in 1928, consisted of 31 gold coins of which the latest was of Alexius I. [28] It was of
a more extended age-structure than the others that have been mentioned.

A miliaresion of Constantine X and Eudocia (1059-67) found near
Prilep, which is of importance to the numismatist on account of the

---

[25] For Kirilovo, Gerasimov, "Kolektivni Nakhodki, 1946-48", and for Gyurgendzhik, Filov, "Novootkriti Starini", *IBAD* ii (1911).

[26] *IBAD* v (1915), 226.

[27] Metcalf, "Syrmia and Slavonia".

[28] See V. Laurent, *op. cit.*, mentioning coins of Basil II (4), Constantine IX (6),
Isaac I (1), Constantine X (4), Romanus IV, etc., (4), Michael VII (6), and Alexius
I (1).

rarity of its type, is of potential interest to the historian too because it is a scrap of evidence from Macedonia which at the moment stands by itself. [29]

Finally, there are a few coins of Alexius I from the Adriatic coast and hinterland. Some pieces from the island of Korčula [30] probably reflect a hoard from his reign; there is a find from Trebinje;[31] and a "silver" coin of Alexius I was said to have been included in a fourteenth-century hoard from Durrës (Dyrrachium), the struggle for which between the Normans and the Byzantines may be the explanation for all three provenances. [32]

---

[29] R. Marić, "Iz Numizmatičke Zbirke", *Zbornik Radova Narodnog Muzeja iii* (1962), 17-30.

[30] See below.

[31] Zagreb Muscm accession-registers.

[32] The Durrës hoard is noted by Ipen in *Monatsblatt der numismatischen Gesellschaft in Wien*, v, 242; see below.

PART 3

INTEGRATION INTO THE EUROPEAN ECONOMIC SYSTEMS

CHAPTER IV

TOWN AND ROUTE, THE FRAMEWORK

Throughout much of Europe in the High Middle Ages the coinage-system, which had been so widely regularized in Carolingian times, and which was again to assume an international character in the fourteenth century, broke down into a multiplicity of local currencies. Numerous mints struck silver coins, which circulated, commonly, only fifty or a hundred miles around the town where their use was concentrated. There were broader groupings of these circulation-areas, stretching for five hundred miles or more, within which coinages of similar fabric and style were used, although their circulation was not necessarily intermingled to any significant extent. Such groupings are referred to as coinage-provinces. The age of the regional coinages offers an exceptional opportunity to discover the geographical patterns of the circulation of coinage, and even to formulate something which begins to approach a quantitative theory of the movement of coin from hand to hand. When a powerful state was able to impose a uniform currency on its territories, or when economic forces of an international character ensured the widespread circulation of a particular issue of coinage, the short-distance movements of coins (which still, no doubt, were statistically dominant) could leave no traces for the monetary historian to assemble and interpret. Thus, eleventh- and twelfth-century numismatics are of significance for the whole of the middle ages; the identification of circulation-areas, and the larger coinage-provinces, permits a study of the framework of monetary affairs, a framework which is likely to have been similar in other periods also. [1]

On the map of Europe, the overall pattern is clear enough; but the evidence for one particular circulation-area may be slender— the mint-

_____

[1] Cf. W. Hävernick, "Welches Material kann die Numismatik zur Feststellung der Verkehrsgebiete in Deutschland im 12. und 13. Jahrhundert liefern?", *Transactions of the International Numismatic Congress*, 1936, London, 1938, pp. 305-07. I am doubtful of the force of the argument from coinage circulation-areas or provinces to trading-regions; but the general conception is seminal.

town, half-a-dozen hoards, perhaps certain obvious route-ways around which the area is articulated, and, if the terrain is mountainous or otherwise fragmented (as it generally is in the Balkan coinage-provinces), recognizable boundaries. The circulation-area, in its continued existence, is a generalized concept of which the basis is, first, the quasi-organic "life" of the currency, centred around the towns, [2] and secondly, the limitation of the evidence to the static aspects of the circulation system. [3] It has little to say about the growing or declining strength of a coinage, its increasing or decreasing ability to meet the needs of the region, or about chronology generally. Obviously, however, the question, "to meet what needs", must be considered in the context of circulation-areas.

Coinage-provinces comprising a number of circulation-areas seem often to have had their origin in an early phase of the development of monetary economy, when the coinage of one particular town or locality, which was in a strong situation economically or commercially, was in widespread use as the currency of a region which initially had no good money: independent rulers sought to establish their own mints, striking coins modelled closely on those that had become well-known and acceptable; and, if the scheme was viable, [4] new circulation-areas grew up within the coinage-province at the expense of the extent of the original one. This theory of the origins of coinage-provinces can all too often not be put to the test. The question of Venetian grossi and the Serbian copies of them illustrates clearly what is frequently the case: from the critical decades there are hardly any hoards, therefore the cha-

---

[2] One may guess that in a typical circulation-area, something of the order of half the total currency was, at any particular moment, concentrated in the towns, and that the number of actual coins which "returned" to a town at intervals was equivalent to a great part of the total. A simile which I think is not misleading compares the coinage circulating in and around a town with bees and their hive—"qualis apes aestate nova per florea rura exercet sub sole labor". For a more complete theoretical discussion, see D. M. Metcalf, *The Coinage of South Germany in the Thirteenth Century*, London, 1961, Chapters III, IV and V. I should now wish to modify the emphasis of the discussion somewhat, to make it clear that a coinage-province can persist for a long time even though there is no significant degree of intermingling of coinages of the various circulation-areas.

[3] See above.

[4] Sometimes it was not, and the scarce coins that survive then appear to us to have a political character; of these, a few may in fact represent merely a mis-judgement of the economic possibilities, or bad luck.

racter of any particular one is uncertain, and also the hoards cannot be dated more closely than to within a bracket of about a decade.

The first of the dozen coinages to be described, that of the Byzantine Empire and its successor-states, was the largest, the most complex, and the most important of the whole number. In the ninth century it included the whole of the peninsula south of the Danube, besides other areas with which this study is not concerned. In Venice, the gold of the emperor Theophilus met the silver of the emperor Louis. [5] Most or all of the Byzantine gold in the Balkans was from Constantinople, and there is no easy way of discovering the rate of interchange between the currency of different places. The bronze coinage, on the other hand, was struck at several mints. In the time of Theophilus, Michael III, and probably Basil I, there seem to have been three main circulation-areas, with a fair amount of intermingling of their currencies. Central Greece, the metropolitan region, and, apparently, Thessaloniki were the places where the coinage was concentrated. There was only a limited penetration of the hinterland, the currency of the metropolitan region circulating into the Black Sea coastlands, and that of Thessaloniki being carried to the north and north - east. The pattern of circulation of gold coinage was doubtless along much the same lines, although particular coins perhaps travelled more widely. The general shape of the coinage - province seems to have remained the same throughout the tenth, eleventh, and twelfth centuries, but mint-attributions for much of the period are so uncertain that an analysis can be no more than speculative. After the introduction of the scyphate bronze stamena, the circulation of folles apparently became more localized. In the second half of the twelfth century, the circulation of stamena certainly fell broadly into two areas, namely Greece and the islands, and Constantinople and Bulgaria; unfortunately it is not equally certain how the issues in "Greek" styles should be divided between mints in central and southern Greece on the one hand and at Thessaloniki and in Macedonia on the other. It follows that the degree of compartmentation between northern and southern Greece, and the composition of the currency in Macedonia are still open questions. The position is little better in the thirteenth century, in spite of the autonomy of Thessaloniki, because so many of the issues are of debateable attribution, and because they occur in only trifling quantities. Even the plentiful gold coinage attributed to John

---

[5] Note the Venice hoard, consisting mainly of gold of Theophilus: *Revue Numismatique* 1956, 122 and references.

III of Nicaea, which might have been expected to define a circulation
-area of much interest, will not help until it has been intensively studied, for it appears on stylistic grounds and on the evidence of the hoards
to have been struck at one if not two Balkan mints, as well as at Nicaea.

The boundaries of the Byzantine coinage-province were pushed
back, even before 1204, as other monetary systems grew up. The Friesacher, which were first struck about 1125-1135, rose rapidly to importance after the middle of the twelfth century, and became the currency first of Istria, then of Slovenia, and, in the early thirteenth century, of Slavonia, Syria, and north Serbia. On the western coasts of the
Balkans, in Albania and Greece, the Byzantine currency may not have
had a strong hold: abortive attemps to introduce Italian types of coinage indicate the economic links that would have been natural for that
part of the peninsula if the Byzantine state had not, for obvious political and military reasons, prevented them. [6]

The capture of Constantinople meant that the Byzantine monetary
system was deprived of its central authority. The functions of government, including the issue of coinage, were quickly taken up in Nicaea,
but control of the outlying provinces fell to other cities, particularly
Thessaloniki and (in Asia Minor) Trebizond. Both the Bulgarian and
the Serbian rulers made some endeavours to continue the issue of scyphate coinage in the Byzantine style. In Constantinople, the Latins apparently continued to use the coinage that they had found already
there, [7] and the same was almost certainly true in central Greece.
Nevertheless, the events of 1204 were a mortal blow to the Byzantine
coinage as a currency for most of the Balkans, especially when they
were followed by the introduction of new types of coinage in Greece,
which had been a key area in the older coinage-province. Grote, in 1857,
wrote with sharp insight about other changes in Balkan monetary affairs
that resulted from the changed political balance:- "Mit der Eroberung
Constantinopels und der Inseln des Archipelagus durch die Venetianer
am Anfange des XIII Jahrhunderts beginnt für Venedig eine reiche
Münzperiode, und gleichzeitig werden auch in den nächstbelegenden
Theilen von Deutschland Münzstätten thätig, aus denen bis dahin wenig
oder gar nichts Vorscheine gekommen war." [8] With the restoration of

---

[6] See below.
[7] See below.
[8] H. Grote, *Münzstudien*, Vol. I, 1857.

1261, when the new situation in south-eastern Europe had become more stable, the imperial coinage-province was much smaller in extent and different in character.

Only one other beside the Byzantine coinage-province included territory in the Balkan peninsula as early as the eleventh century, namely that of the Hungarian regal coinage. Syrmia then lay within its orbit, and remained so throughout the period under review. The coins were silver pence, which must in the eleventh century have had quite a large purchasing power, but which had declined, before the end of the twelfth, into a petty coinage. [9] Mitrovica, and other settlements at crossing-points of the Danube and Sava, seem to have had a monetary economy largely because of their part in a specialized trade, the supply of salt from Tuzla, in Bosnia, northwards into Hungary. There is no evidence of Hungarian coins being carried south along the route to Thessaloniki, nor did their use extend westwards to include Slavonia, either before or after the time when a local coinage was struck there, or to include the Adriatic coast, except possibly for the town of Zadar. Syrmia may well turn out to have been a separate circulation-area within the Hungarian coinage-province, supplied to some extent by the issues of the Mitrovica mint.

Thirdly, from about the middle of the twelfth century, the coinage-province of the Friesacher played a part in Balkan monetary affairs. Its coinage consisted of silver Pfennige, and, in much smaller quantities, their halves. The Pfennige were coins of good silver, with quite a high purchasing power. Although the early issues of the Friesach and St. Veit mints occur in Balkan hoards, they probably did not circulate eastwards when they were new; the first extension of their currency-area was southwards to the head of the Adriatic, along the routes leading to Aquileia, and it may not have been until the fourth quarter of the twelfth century that the Friesacher began to be used in Slovenia. They were then also being carried along the coasts of the northern Adriatic, probably by traders from Aquileia or its region. By that time, the weight of the Friesacher had been reduced, to bring it more closely into line with the Bavarian coinage. In the course of a century, the weight declined from 1.22 grammes to 0.8 grammes; in the same period, the issue and circulation of the coins reached their greatest extent.[10] Mainly in the

---

[9] For an exhaustive study of the metrology of the various issues, see B. Homan, *Magyar Pénztörténet*, 1000-1325, Budapest, 1916.

[10] For the metrology, see Luschin, "Die friesacher Pfennige".

decades 1210-1240, a number of mints in Slovenia struck coins of the Friesacher type, and chiefly in the same period but also for another fifty years, both the Carinthian and the Slovenian coins circulated far to the east, into Slavonia, Syrmia, central Hungary, and occasionally Bosnia and north Serbia.[11] It seems likely, from the limited evidence available, that Slovenia was a partly separate circulation-area, in which the local issues were dominant. The age-structure of the currency, as revealed by hoards, and the occurrence of halves suggest a more "normal" economic background to the use of coinage than was the case further to the east.

The boundaries of the province of the Friesacher, having been pushed forward hundreds of miles in the decades around 1200, were again altered by the monetary reforms of Béla IV (ca. 1237) and by the Mongol incursions of 1241. A new coinage-province was established in Slavonia, and Hungary's traffic with Germany shifted to more northerly routes. The large stocks of Friesacher in Hungary continued in circulation, and Syrmia shared in their use in the second half of the thirteenth century. By the beginning of the fourteenth century, the "Blütezeit" of the Friesacher was over. The coinage of Aquileia and its associated mints of Trieste and Gorizia had become dominant along the Krka valley route, and was spreading into southern Slovenia. The Friesacher coinage-province contracted to include only northern Slovenia out of all its former Balkan territory.

Fourthly, the coins of the town of Split were current in central Dalmatia from 1196 or a few years later. It is difficult to say whether the spalatini replaced any effective petty currency, nor is there much evidence other than that of documents for the circulation of Byzantine coins of higher value, in the twelfth century or before. The extent of the province was quite limited, including the town of Split, the coastal strip to the north, the central group of Dalmatian islands, and perhaps the hinterland around Sinj. Its boundaries were, to the east, the high and arid *planine* of the Dinaric Alps, and, to north and south, the economic watersheds separating the area influenced by Split from those within the orbit of Krk and Senj on the one hand and Dubrovnik on the other.

The currency issued for Slavonia from the time of Béla IV onwards was the coinage of a fifth province. These small silver banovci, as they

---

[11] See below.

are called, were struck in large numbers from ca. 1237 to ca. 1290, and in smaller quantities for another four or five decades. The key-area of their circulation was Zagreb and western Slavonia, but they were current also in Syrmia, alongside the Hungarian coins which have already been mentioned. Syrmia can be distinguished as a separate circulation-area, for certain varieties of banovci seem to have been issued there, and not at Zagreb as was usual. The coinage-province was the first to be established in the Balkans with its key-area inland (apart from the Hungarian coinage in Syrmia, for which a special explanation has been offered). From Slavonia, banovci were carried into the Una basin and into the lower Bosna valley, and also along the routes leading to the Adriatic coast; but virtually no finds have been recorded from south of the Sava which are earlier than the fourteenth century, so that it seems that the boundaries of the province were extended from about the time of Karl Robert. Northwards they reached beyond the Drava and Danube into Pannonia and even towards Transylvania. The total absence of banovci from Slovenian hoards draws attention to the trade-routes around which the coinage-province was articulated: their general trend was from north-east to south-west.

Turning to the south of the Balkan peninsula, we find a sixth coinage province which grew up at about the same time as that of the banovac, and like it flourished mainly in the thirteenth century, but continued into the fourteenth. The petty currency of feudal Greece, which at first included copper coins of very small nominal value but which was subsequently mainly of billon deniers modelled closely on the French "tournois" coinage, may have begun to replace the Byzantine petty currency of folles as early as 1240. It served the commercial life of Corinth and Attica, just as the folles had done, but its key-area extended further to the west to include Patrai and the shores of the Gulf of Corinth, and the north-western Peloponnese. There were two recognizable circulation-areas, supplied by the mints of Corinth (later moved to Clarentzia) and Thebes respectively. A quantitative assessment of the degree of intermingling of the two currencies is possible. The changes which took place in the extent and character of the coinage-province after the fall of Athens to the Grand Catalan Company, in 1311, are comparable with the changes in the Byzantine coinage-province after 1204: several new mints were set up on what had been the periphery of the province; but the disorganization in the key-area was such that the coinage-system as a whole was no longer viable, and the new mints were able to operate only on a small scale. To the north, the Pindus mountains and the sparsely-settled plains of Thessaly were the boundaries of the province.

The coins of the three mints of Aquileia, Trieste, and Gorizia were closely related in style and value, and were quite different from the other north Italian coinages. Their circulation was intermingled, and formed a coinage-province in the march-lands at the head of the Adriatic. The earliest issues were copies of the early Friesacher, with which they circulated, but, not long after 1200, the Friulian coins departed from the Carinthian ones in style, drove them out of north Italy, and became the currency of a separate province. This affords a very clear example of one coinage-province splitting into two. During most of its life, the extent of the Aquileian province was limited to the Italian hinterland, but for a few decades at the end of the thirteenth century and the beginning of the fourteenth, its boundaries advanced to include the Krka valley route-way and southern Slovenia. In this, its history is obviously similar to that of the Friesacher province. When the currency of banovci in western Slavonia fell into decline, the Aquileian coins may have found their way even as far as Zagreb. As with the Friesacher, coins as much as fifty years old are regularly found in the Balkan hoards.

The monetary system of Venice played far less part in the coinage of the Balkans than one might have guessed from its political and economic importance in the peninsula. However, from time to time it had its circulation-areas there. They were largely coastal, and fragmented, in character, being based on the maritime trading-routes of the republic. Such evidence as there is shows Venetian coins in Lika in the thirteenth century, and more generally in Dalmatia in the middle of the fourteenth, at which time they were plentiful also in Greece. In the first half of the fourteenth century, they seem to have been increasingly common in Slovenia, and to have found their way into western Bulgaria. Venetian grossi did not circulate alongside the copies of them in Serbia to any great extent, unless for a short period which is undocumented by the available hoards. Similarly, the denari piccoli of Venice and Verona appear from documents to have been in general use in Dalmatia in the second half of the twelfth century, but no finds have yet been published. In short, until 1300 Venetian coins are known to have been common from unambiguous evidence only in the hinterland of Senj.

Ninthly, the 1260s or 1270s saw the rise of the Serbian coinage - province. The imitations of the Venetian grossi were soon circulating plentifully not only in Dubrovnik, where for a time they enjoyed immunity from the embargo under which they were placed by Venice, but also in the Morava basin, and in north Italy. North Serbia was always the key-area of the province. From there, the coins were carried into Bosnia, where they may have been the chief element in a limited currency until the local issues were struck in quantity. The upper Vardar basin was a second circulation-area within the province. It may have been from there that Serbian grossi were carried, in the years around 1300, to the coastlands of Thrace, Macedonia, and central Greece.

The Bosnian coinage-province, like the Serbian, had a key-area in the interior, and an extension on the Dalmatian coast and along the routes which led to it. The key-area was the Bosna valley, and the point on the coast at which the coins were brought down from the hinterland was probably the Una valley route and Knin. As the recorded find - spots of early Bosnian coins, however, can be counted almost on the fingers of one hand, it is not possible to define the boundaries or even the extent of the coinage-province at all precisely.

The coinage of the restored Byzantine Empire has already been mentioned. It may be considered as the currency of a separate province, since there was an interval during which very little imperial coinage was circulating in the Balkans. Thrace and north-eastern Bulgaria were the extent of the province.

Finally, the coinage-province of the Bulgarian silver grosh rose to importance in the last two decades of the period under review, to drive the failing supplies of Byzantine coins from the eastern Balkans. The crudely-engraved pieces issued in such quantities by Ivan Aleksandŭr and Mikhail (ca. 1350) seem to reflect a sudden flowering in the monetary affairs of Bulgaria, possibly supported by trade across the Black Sea. Hoards of such groshi have been found throughout the area of modern Bulgaria.

Such, then, was the pattern of the dozen coinage-provinces which existed in the Balkan peninsula in the High Middle Ages. Monetary systems grew up, extended their boundaries at each other's expense, and later disappeared. Each system occupied a region independently of its neighbours, and was separated from them, usually by zones where there was apparently little monetary activity. There was some overlapping of the provinces, for example in Syrmia, but not a great deal.

There were two main areas in the peninsula which seem to have been persistently without coinage. Between the Una and the Bosna rivers, there are wide tracts in Bosnia, extending northwards into eastern Slovenia, that form a region from which very few finds have been recorded. Secondly, apart from one or two finds on the shores of the Gulf of Volos, there is a wide area in Thessaly, the Pindus mountains, and Epirus in which virtually no coinage has been found.

Mountain ranges were sometimes economic watersheds, and the boundaries of coinage-provinces, but sometimes they were crossed by routes which merchants followed. There are half-a-dozen routes across the mountains which run parallel to the Adriatic coast, and the same coinages can be found on both sides of the range. The Balkan mountains were never an effective boundary in monetary circulation, either in central Bulgaria, or between the Krain and north-eastern Serbia.

Also, there were two periods when there seems to have been little monetary activity in the peninsula. First, the interior, apart from Syrmia, seems to have been without any regular currency until about 1175, although the boundaries of the negative zone were perhaps being pushed back from about 1125. Secondly, in the period *ca.* 1240-1260, monetary affairs had come almost to a standstill widely throughout the peninsula. The Byzantine monetary system, fatally attacked in 1204, was almost extinct forty years later, while the Mongol raids of 1241 disrupted the German and Hungarian currencies in the north-west. Around the middle of the century, on a broad view, the old order was giving place to a new one, which was more dispersed; central Dalmatia and, very probably, Frankish Greece already had an established petty currency; but the Slavonian, Aquileian, Serbian, and Paleologan coinage-provinces in the Balkans all had their beginnings within a period of about twenty-five years.

The connexions between the coinage-provinces and the economic life of the peninsula deserve careful consideration. The dominant impression which might be gained from historical sources other than numismatics is of the organization of capital and entrepreneurial effort in a few major cities, above all Constantinople and Venice, next, Pisa, Genoa, Ragusa; of a network of regional markets, such as Thessaloniki, Thebes, Rodosto, Mesembria, and many others; and of individual merchants on long itineraries, equipped with considerable sums in capital, conducting the exchange, and to some extent the transport, of commodities. From this impression one might have deduced by guesswork that the monetary affairs of the Balkans, as revealed by coin-finds, would be a kaleidoscopic scattering of the currencies of the large cities from which the commercial exploitation of the Balkans was undertaken, and that the pattern most obviously revealed would be that of the network formed by routeways and market-towns. [12] Such an analysis of monetary affairs would, however, obviously be leaving out of account whatever it was that caused their organization into the regions that are revealed through the coinage-provinces —some powerful group of factors dictating localization on a scale of, say, two hundred to five hundred miles. Coinage-provinces of this kind are a European phenomenon of a particular age, and a full understanding of them therefore needs to be on several levels.

The travellers' hoards (for example, of French coins) which fall outside the pattern of the coinage-provinces form only a trifling proportion of the whole find-assemblage.

One might expect that a petty coinage, such as the copper or very base billon spalatini, would be restricted in its circulation to a small area around the town where it could be redeemed, but that trade-coins of good silver would pass from hand to hand without restriction. This, again, would be too simplified an analysis: witness the currency of Venetian and Veronese denari on the Adriatic coast, and the use of spalatini in packets of a dozen; [13] or witness the scarcity of any but the early Serbian coins in hoards deposited outside Serbia.

A theoretical model of the factors dictating localization, of the kind that might satisfy an economist, seems a remote possibility even if the very laborious preliminary studies of die-occurrence could be completed. One may be able to make some fairly confident guesses when more is known about the total quantities of coinage that were circulating. The best prospect seems to be that one might correlate changes in the volume of the currency, over periods of one, two, or three decades, with changes in the geographical patterns of circulation.

For the present, guesses can rest only on broad impressions of the monetary affairs of the Balkans, and the theory must be of a limited

---

[12] That is the general impression given by K. Dieterich in his study, "Zur Kulturgeographie und Kulturgeschichte des Byzantinischen Balkanshandels", *Byzantinische Zeitschrift* xxxi (1931), 35-57 and 334-49.

[13] See below.

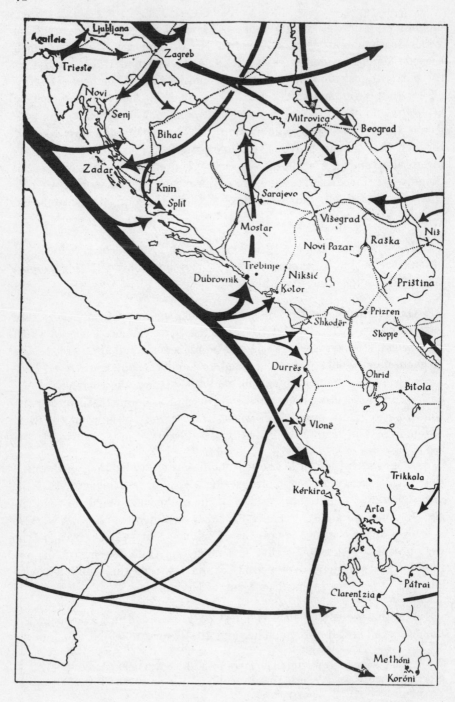

Map IV. Coinage-provinces

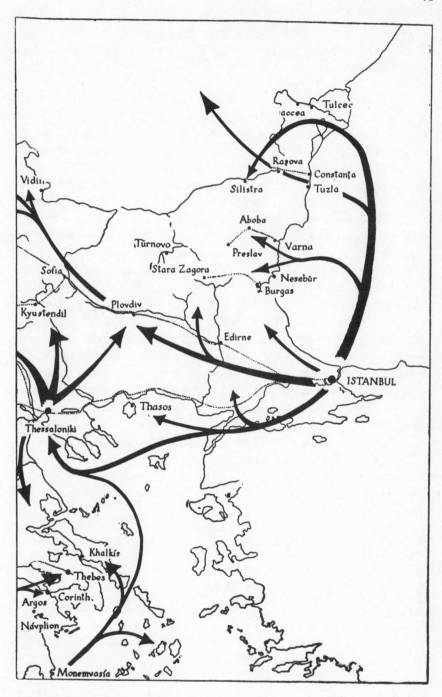

and trade-routes in the Balkans.

scope and in very general terms. Here, then, is a sketch of the view-point from which one might attempt an interpretation of the evidence of the coinage-provinces:

The peninsula was, in comparison with the size and build of a viable state of the time, a very large and a geographically fragmented area. No trade-route of European importance passed through it, and the region's economic history was largely influenced from the surrounding countries. In the coastlands of the western Aegean, Byzantine and Slavonic cultures co-existed for several centuries. [14] On the Adriatic seaboard, easy communications with Italy, and a favourable and familiar environment made possible an influx of settlers: in the little towns of Dalmatia, Slav and Latin lived side by side. [15] In the plains and valleys all round the borders of the area, the same sort of infiltration and mixing took place. Thus, a few Germans settled in south-Slav lands in Slovenia, Franks occupied Byzantine territory in the Peloponnese, and so on. Ethnic mixing seems to have taken place on a larger scale between Magyars and Slavs around the southern edges of the Hungarian Plain. [16] The interior, on the other hand, was by the twelfth century under-developed in comparison with much of western Europe, and the best chance for each part to increase its prosperity lay in an economy of primary production linked by trade with the commerce and industry of the larger European cities. The overland movement of commodities was difficult as well as expensive, so that each region tended to look towards the nearest part of the coast. [17] There were, perhaps, three serious competitors, [18] at any rate from the second half of the eleventh century onwards, for what seemed to be one of the three major areas of outlet for the expanding economy of western Europe. (The other two areas were the

---

[14] See A. Bon, *Le Peloponnèse Byzantin jusqu'en* 1204, 1953, pp. 55ff. M. Vasmer, *Die Slaven in Griechenland*, Berlin, 1941, is a useful work of reference, since the place-name evidence is there set out district by district.

[15] See V. Novak, "The Slavonic-Latin Symbiosis in Dalmatia during the Middle Ages", *Slavonic and East European Review*, xxxii (1954), 1ff.

[16] For the archaeologist's "Bijelo Brdo Culture", see the summary by Z. Váňa, "Mad'aři a Slované ve Světle Archeologickych Nálezu X.-XII. Stoletì", *Slovenská Archeologia Časopis*, ii (1954).

[17] In military campaigns, and in the journeys of rulers and legates, expediency overrode considerations of expense, so that political history commonly does not give a proper picture of the limits normally imposed on merchants and ordinary people.

[18] The balance had eventually tipped against Baghdad, which would be counted among the four great cities of the east Mediterranean world.

"German east" and the "Latin east"; in the former, settlement, and in the latter, military control played a more important role than in the Balkans). Constantinople, Venice, and Palermo had, or hoped they had, the necessary advantages of proximity, military or naval power, and a large urban market. The relations between Byzantium and the Normans, and Byzantium and Venice, in the eleventh and twelfth centuries reflected a struggle for empire, from which Venice, in 1082 and again in 1204, emerged with great advantage. Others besides these three tried to secure a share in the peninsula: the German "drive towards the east" of the later middle ages extended from Styria and Carinthia into the basins of the Drava and Sava; the Italians of Aquileia and its hinterland made their way into Slovenia. In these movements, similarly, we may discern, as one factor, the expansionism of the trade of the growing cities of middle Europe.

The interested powers had differing philosophies of empire. The Byzantines were inclined to rely upon the wisdom of ruling and taxing, the Venetians upon the pursuit of trade and profit, the Germans upon establishing towns with markets, the Franks upon feudal tenure, and the Hungarians upon the strategic defence of their own territory. [19] The different policies to some extent influenced the monetary affairs of the regions they controlled.

The Crusades, from the point of view of Balkan monetary history, were a series of military expeditions which marched through the area on their way to their destination; they were not in the peninsula for any length of time, and they probably had less effect on its economic life, excepting the temporary confusion and unsettlement which their passing caused, than has been claimed. [20] The indirect effects of the Crusades were, however, out of all proportion greater. The capture of Constantinople broke up the whole economic and political life of a large centralized state, and was followed by half a century of chaos which involved much of the Balkan peninsula. The Crusaders themselves set up a

---

[19] Hungary was not particularly successful in deriving advantage from its strong position in Balkan politics. Basically, this seems to have been because Hungary was itself a region of primary production. The military threats which were a preoccupation of Hungarian policy could not be effectively controlled by marcher-territories in the north Balkans.

[20] The view that they stimulated a revival of monetary affair in southern Hungary (Luschin, "Die ungarischen Friesacher") certainly lacks numismatic evidence, as does the similar thesis of I. Sakŭzov, *Bulgarische Wirtschaftsgeschichte*, 1929.

number of the successor-states with which an attempt was made to fill the political vacuum. The events of 1204 preceded important changes in the monetary affairs of the east and the south of the peninsula.

The map of the Balkans showed a number of coastal cities at points where penetration into the hinterland was easier than elsewhere. Thessaloniki, for example, at the foot of the Vardar basin, was a regional centre of government, but its importance and prosperity as a city came chiefly because it stood as a middleman and drew off some of the profits, through its great fairs, in the inter-regional trade of Macedonia with Constantinople and with the north Italian cities. The economic situation of Dubrovnik, as the outlet of the Neretva valley route, was similar; its citizens took the initiative of putting its natural advantages to use, by trading independently.

The pattern of trade to and from the Balkan hinterlands was, again, that appropriate to an under-developed area. The list of exports, so far as it can be reconstructed from documentary evidence, was short. They range through the classic stages of development of primary production. The yield of forests and mines in the remoter parts—timber from Dalmatia, furs from Slavonia, wax and honey from Bulgaria, silver and copper from Serbia and Bosnia—was increasingly supplemented by agricultural exports in the thirteenth and later centuries—cheese from Dalmatia, salt pork from Serbia, cattle and horses from Thrace and Bulgaria, grain from the same regions and, probably, over a good many other short routes. Dubrovnik, for example, imported grain from Arta, Clarentzia, Corfu, Patrai, and other parts of the west coast. From central Greece, of which the economic and monetary history is in such marked contrast with that of most parts of the peninsula, came the silk of Thebes and of Clarentzia, and the purple of Patrai. We have very little information about what was imported into the Balkans, but no doubt the list of commodities was longer and more varied, and included woollen and linen textiles of everyday quality, salt, oil, and metalwork. [21]

---

[21] See W. G. East, *An Historical Geography of Europe* (3rd. edition, 1948), p. 181; and I. Sakŭzov, *op. cit.* pp. 134 and 140. There is a great deal of solidly buttressed evidence in B. Krekić, *Dubrovnik (Raguse) et le Levant au Moyen Age* (Documents et Recherches sur l'Economie des Pays Byzantins, Islamiques et Slaves et leurs Relations Commerciales au Moyen Age, vol. V), Paris, 1961, pp. 89-123, and F. Thiriet, *La Romanie Vénitienne au Moyen Age, Le Développement et l'Exploitation du Domaine Colonial Vénitien (XIIe-XVe Siècles)* (Bibliothèque des Ecoles Françaises d'Athènes et de Rome, vol. 193), Paris, 1959, pp. 40-49.

The exploitation of the silver-mines of the medieval Balkans was of especial importance for the history of the coinage, above all in Serbia. Not only does the silver-mining explain the volume of the Serbian currency, but it seems likely that the political strength and the rich culture of the Serbian kingdom at the end of the thirteenth and for most of the fourteenth centuries rested in no small measure on the wealth derived from the silver-mines. Dubrovnik (and, in a smaller way, Bosnia and Bulgaria), shared in the profit which accrued, originally, from the migration of the "Saxon" miners: mineral exploitation and commerce were closely linked. [22]

One theme in the political geography of the various Balkan states which grew up at the expense of the Byzantine Empire was their aim to unite two complementary economic regions, by controlling the coastal settlements which gave them a trading outlet from their centres of population in the interior. For example, the strength of the Subić rule seems to have lain in successfully uniting their coastal town of Knin with its north Bosnian hinterland by way of the Krka - Una route and Bihać. Thus also, the importance to Serbia of Kotor and of good relations with Dubrovnik; the failure to control either the latter town or Thessaloniki was a major strategic weakness of the Serbian kingdom. The coastal towns were, in fact, the key to the Balkan trade, so that, for example, Hungary sought to retain control of the Dalmatian towns, and Venice after the Fourth Crusade chose to occupy effectively only a few places, such as Rodosto, which was an outlet for the agricultural products of eastern Thrace. From the point of view of the coastal towns, on the other hand, the most favourable political arrangement, provided they were well-situated to resist attack, was to be independent.

One of the most interesting problems for the monetary historian, and certainly one of the most difficult, is to trace the stimulus of foreign trade in local economic expansion, and to work out the implications for monetary affairs of the growth of the inland towns, such as Prizren, Skopje, Sofia, or Plovdiv, from being essentially fortresses, or stages on trade-routes, to becoming regional centres. [23] One may imagine that in the more naturally favoured areas within the peninsula, the volume

---

[22] Cf. M. Dinić and others, "Novo Brdo", *Starinar* NS v-vi (1954-55), 247ff. For a more general discussion, urging the continuity of mining during the Middle Ages, see S. Vryonis, "The Question of the Byzantine Mines", *Speculum, a Journal of Mediaeval Studies* xxxvii (1962), 1-17.

[23] See Sakŭzov, *op. cit.*, pp. 115ff.

and proportion of short-distance trade increased, until the commerce of such areas was predominantly local, and thus independent. Should one see a reflection of this change in monetary affairs, in the gradual evolution of coinages unrelated to the standards of the foreign money on which they were originally based? For example, is the divergence of the Serbian groši from their Venetian prototype, first in weight and then in design, to be connected with the declining importance as a factor in Serbian monetary policy of their acceptability in north Italy and on the Adriatic coasts?

It may be helpful, as a very generalized concept, to think of five links in the economic chain of Balkan trade. They will be (i) the industrial market of the powerful state, (ii) the sea-route, (iii) the coastal town at the point of entry, (iv) the land-route, and (v) the hinterland, often with a developing town as an inland regional centre. The best example of such a chain is Constantinople; the Aegean; Thessaloniki; the Vardar valley; and Macedonia, with Skopje. With variations, it is repeated half-a-dozen times elsewhere. Sometimes one or more links of the chain can be supplied only by conjecture. Thus, the chain which began with Venice; the Adriatic; Dubrovnik; and the Neretva valley, must, one imagines, have had southern Bosnia as its hinterland, and Vrhbosna as its inland town. Ljubljana may have owed its growth partly to its position at the end of the chain from Aquileia, through the Pear Tree Pass, to Slovenia. In Bulgaria, the same sort of economic chains may have stretched from Constantinople by way of the Black Sea ports to Preslav and its region, and through the Dobruja to the cities of the lower Danube.

The focal areas of the coinage-provinces that have been described, and their geographical arrangement around the peninsula, reflected the economic penetration of the Balkans from the edges by a number of foreign states. The various different types of money which were used in them were, generally, those that the exploiting or occupying people introduced, and the framework on which the provinces were aligned would seem often to have been the routes by which trade reached the hinterland. If only a single coinage-province were studied, the evidence might not warrant the conclusion that the use of money was especially connected with certain forms of economic activity. A comparative survey, however, brings out more clearly the significance of the numismatic detail. [24]

---

[24] For a similar interpretation of the use of coinage, see a note by F. Babinger, "Südosteuropäische Handelsmünzen am Ausgang des Mittelalters", *Vierteljahrsch-*

Such, very briefly, are the main features and patterns of the economic and political life of the medieval Balkans in the High Middle Ages, or rather, they are the main features which concern the problems of monetary history. Other important themes have not been mentioned: a systematic study of Balkan economic history would have to devote considerable attention to transhumant pastoralism, which was very widespread even if it has not left many records. [25] The monetary historian may well be curious to know details of how cheeses or animals were used as money in transactions at the periodic fairs of northern Greece, but speculation on such topics would be out of place in a study based on numismatics.

In the Middle Ages, it was characteristically the agriculture of a region which supported its life, and it was particularly when a current of trade began to flow through the region, adding to its basic wealth, that towns were able to grow to importance. As the Balkan peninsula was integrated more fully into the system of inter-regional trade which drew its force, in the later Middle Ages, from the economy of western Europe, so its prosperity increased. For the time being, the student of monetary history must be content to have in mind trends as broad as these, excessively generalized and vague though they are: better to have a rather elementary theory than to study coins with no purposeful thought for how their evidence might make a contribution to historical knowledge.

rift für Sozial- und Wirtschaftsgeschichte xliv (1957), 352ff. Cf. also Gerasimov, "Andronic II et Andronic III".

[25] See J. Dedijer, "La Transhumance dans le Pays Dinaric", Annales de Géographie xxv (1912), and A. J. B. Wace and M. S. Thompson, Nomads of the Balkans: an Account of the Life and Customs of the Vlachs of Northern Pindus, 1914.

CHAPTER V

THE BYZANTINE COINAGE-PROVINCE AND
ITS SUCCESSORS

The preliminary, and the key, to the reform of the gold coinage carried out by Alexius I, very probably in ca. 1097—and indeed to the whole pattern of Byzantine monetary affairs in the twelfth century—was the treaty of May 1082 by which the emperor granted enormous trading privileges to the Venetians, in recompense for their aid against the Normans in the struggle for Dyrrachium. They were to be allowed unrestricted trade in any kind of merchandise, with exemption from all customs dues throughout the Empire, including Constantinople itself. Venice was given warehouses and quays in the capital. Thus the Venetians were placed in a far more favourable position than the native Byzantine merchants; and the commercial system of the Byzantine state was radically affected. Increasingly large amounts of Venetian capital were applied to the economic exploitation of the Adriatic islands and coasts, Macedonia, Attica, the Peloponnesus, Thessaly, and Thrace.

In the years between the treaty and the arrival of Peter the Hermit and his unruly Crusaders, the political situation of the Empire in the Balkans had been much strengthened by the eventual expulsion of the Normans from the western districts of the peninsula, and by the extermination of the Patzinaks at the battle of Mt. Levunion. The siege of Constantinople in 1090-91 by Tzachas, emir of Smyrna, had depended on Patzinak support; Alexius was able to neutralize the threat to his capital from the Seljuqs of western Asia Minor. Thereafter he turned stronger forces against Vukan, the Župan of Rascia, and brought his border warfare to a pause. Finally, he succeeded in destroying the leadership of the Cuman hordes in the north-east. [1]

Even so, Byzantine control over the Balkans in 1097 was preca-

---

[1] See Ostrogorsky, *Byzantine State*, pp. 315-322.

rious. From the point of view of monetary affairs, it would seem that only Constantinople itself, central Greece and the Peloponnesus, and Thessaloniki and its region had a settled and prosperous economy. The geographical pattern was thus essentially the same as it had been from the ninth century onwards: the further isolation of Greece through the insecurity of the Aegean coastlands from 1071 to 1097—a whole generation—had, together with the grave financial difficulties of those years, probably damaged the fabric of the region's economic life.

For that reason, perhaps, the mint which struck the reformed gold coinage of Alexius in Greece did not begin work at the same time as the other three, which are likely to have been located in Constantinople, Nicaea, and Trebizond. It was presumably in either Corinth or Thebes, and a date of ca. 1105 has been suggested for its earliest issues, on the evidence of stylistic parallels with the coins from Constantinople and Nicaea: 1106 is the final date for the activity of the latter mint. The gold of each of the four mints was of the same design, but was distinguished by a secret-mark, in the case of the Greek coins, the absence of a fold in the drapery of the chlamys at the right-hand side. All the Greek coins have much-exaggerated jewelling down the right-hand edge of the chlamys, as have the latest coins of Constantinople and Nicaea. Although the Greek mint was late in begining to work, it produced larger quantities of coinage than any of the other mints.

A careful check through 80 specimens for die duplication yielded 3 pairs of obverse dies, 2 pairs of reverse dies, and 2 triplets of reverse dies. One of the triplets and one of the obverse pairs, however, were among three coins in the Depentzikos hoard, and probably represent "clustering". If these are neglected, and the total reduced to 77, the estimates of the total number of dies from which the reformed gold of Alexius was struck work out at 1463 ± 1041, for the obverses, and 975 ± 559, for the reverses, treating triplets as pairs. The Depentzikos coins would lower these figures; the best estimate might be set, by inspection, at about 500 to 1500 pairs of dies, or something of the order of 10 million coins. Separate estimates for each of the mint would not be sufficiently precise to be useful: if we share out the total in proportion to the number of specimens attributed to each mint, weighting the figures slightly according to the stylistic range exhibi ted by each group, it appears likely that the Greek mint was responsible for about half the total output, say five million coins, and the

Constantinopolitan mint for about a sixth, say two million coins. These quantities are modest in relation to the population whether of Greece or of Constantinople, especially as the reformed gold was to replace, not supplement, the debased issues of the preceding decades. [2]

Among the surviving specimens of the later Greek issues occurs a preponderance of the pierced coins. The reason is doubtless to be found in the circumstances in which the coins were issued or used, but remains to be discovered. [3]

Two of the first coins from the Greek mint, closely similar to each other, were found in the course of the Corinth excavations in 1914. If the suggested date for the opening of the mint is correct, their deposit is likely to have been ca. 1106. The date of loss or concealment of another specimen of Alexius's gold from the excavations is probably even earlier: a Trapezuntine coin, struck ca. 1097 - 98, was discovered in June 1907. The centre of the obverse (which is the part of a scyphate coin most liable to wear) was exceptionally fresh, [4] so that the probable date of deposit is within two or three years of 1100. Mr R. N. Bridge [5] showed me another Trapezuntine coin, quite similar to that from Corinth, which he bought in Athens. It came from a hoard, but unfortunately no record of the stylistic varieties of the other coins is available. There was a Nicaean coin of ca. 1100 in the Corinth hoard of 1907, consisting otherwise of French silver, which is discussed below. [6]

From the rest of the Balkans there are so far only two hoards from the reign of Alexius and including his reformed gold, namely the Sofia hoard of 1897, and the Khisar hoard of 1922. [7] The circumstances of finding are not the least intriguing feature of the important Sofia hoard.

---

[2] See Metcalf, "Alexius I Comnenus", where 77 coins are catalogued. Three further coins, namely Mr Bridge's specimen referred to below, and two more from the Gurdzhaani hoard, inventory numbers 5322 and 5323, have been checked against the 77 for die-linkage.

[3] Unless it is in some way connented with the Pisan treaty of 1111 (Dölger, *Regesten*, no. 1255).

[4] I am indebted to Mrs Varoukha-Khristodhoulopoulou, who supplied me with a cast of the coin.

[5] Fellow of the Royal Numismatic Society.

[6] See Chapter XI.

[7] For the Depentzikos hoard, dated to the reign of John II, see p. 93f. The other hoards including nomismata, from the reign of Alexius I, are discussed in Chapter III.

In work on the foundations of a house, there was discovered at a depth of four and a half metres the pedestal of a marble column, very close to which there were two small earthenware vases of crude workmanship, of which one contained gold and silver coins, and the other silver coins and silver jewellery. The 35 gold coins were attributed to Romanus III, Constantine IX, Constantine X, Eudocia with her sons, Romanus IV, Nicephorus III, and Alexius I. The 171 silver coins — those of which an account is available are better described as electrum — ranged only from Michael VII through Nicephorus III to Alexius I. In exhibiting photographs of the coins at the Académie des Inscriptions et Belles Lettres Schlumberger reported that the relative number of pieces of each emperor indicated that the deposit must have been at the end of the eleventh or the beginning of the twelfth century, which may be construed to mean that there was a preponderance of the later coins. [8] The hoard awaits re-publication, but Dr Gerasimov has kindly informed me that the electrum coins of Alexius I were of the types showing a bust of the emperor holding cross and globus cruciger, with a bust of Christ as the obverse type, or holding labarum and globus cruciger, with Christ seated on a throne with back as the obverse type. [9] They are rare types, and even rarer among Balkan finds: the only parallel is the Korčula hoard. [10] There was only one of the reformed nomismata in the hoard, of the stylistic group which has been assigned to a mint at Nicaea. [11] If the date of Alexius's reform coincided, as it seems likely to have done on the numismatic evidence, with the First Crusade, the most obvious occasion of deposit of the Sofia hoard is ruled out, as it definitely is if the gold coin is Nicaean. Possibly it was hidden at the time of the Crusades of 1101. The jewellery in the hoard consisted of a massive gold ear-ring, a pair of silver ear-rings, a gold ring with a bezel-set stone of red jasper, a silver plaque set with a turquoise, and a quantity of silver-gilt pierced ornaments, namely 22 pendants, 7 rosettes, 16 triangular and 9 square little pieces, all of which had formed a necklace, having apparently been stitched onto a ribbon; there were also two little silver hooks or clasps, and some fragments of cloth. The Sofia hoard may have

---

[8] *Comptes-rendus de l'Académie des Inscriptions et Belles Lettres* 4th. series, xxv (1897), 303-04. The photographs were prepared for Dobrusky, the Director of the Sofia Museum.

[9] Cf. Ratto, *Monnaies Byzantines*, plate IL (that is, XLIX), 2061, and Sabatier, *Description Générale*, plate LII, 3. This is the same general type as Wroth, *BMC (Byz.), II* Types 4/5.

[10] See below.

[11] See Metcalf, "Alexius I Comnenus", no. 21.

been the treasure of a wealthy woman, hidden in some time of threat in the floor of an important dwelling-house.

From the Khisar hoard of 1922, 60 scyphate electrum nomismata were reported, of which one was of Michael VII, 58 of Nicephorus III, and one of Alexius I; there were also 5 gold nomismata of Alexius. Since virtually all the coins came from a three-year reign, the hoard seems to be comparable in its age-structure with that from Gyurgendzhik, and to have been concealed early in the currency of the reformed nomismata. An interesting implication is that the electrum coinages of Alexius, which are doubtless pre-reform, were struck in only trifling quantities. It was reported at the time by a reputable local person that there were another fifty coins which were not revealed, and also that there was found in the same place part of a pot, which may have been the container of the hoard. It is unfortunately possible that most of the fifty unrevealed coins were gold and that the composition of the hoard was significantly different from that of the parcel that was seen. The Sofia museum acquired the coin of Michael VII and one of the gold pieces of Alexius; it was of the group assigned to the mint of Constantinople.[12]

The silver coinages of Alexius have not so far turned up in Balkan hoards. It is a fair assumption that they were mainly the currency of Trebizond and Transcaucasia, and to a lesser extent of the western and northern coasts of the Pontus, as was true of the silver of the seventh century.[13] *BMS* LXXIII, 4-6, however, is probably Thessalonican.

The folles of Alexius have been found in enormous quantities in the excavations at Corinth and Athens. The totals include coins from the Corinth hoard of February, 1934 and the Athens "Winepress" hoard of March, 1937, and a smaller deposit found at Athens in May, 1935; in addition, there is a hoard found at Old Corinth in 1959 (not from the excavations). Sparta is the only other place in the Balkans from which a hoard of folles definitely dated to the reign of Alexius has been reported, although the little finds from Romania of Limanu, 1926 and Tulcea, 1941 are probably also from his reign. The Thasos excavations have yielded coins of Alexius, and single finds have been noted from Argos, Glyfadha, Thessaloniki, Filippaioi, the Kuruchai valley in Macedonia,

[12] Mushmov, "Nakhodki, 1921-22"; Mosser, *Byzantine Coin Hoards*, under Hissar. The gold coin of Alexius is published in Metcalf, "Alexius I Comnenus", no. 3.
[13] Metcalf, (work in progress).

and Preslav.[14] The concentration of the find - spots in the Aegean and Black Sea coastlands and especially in central Greece sets the pattern for the folles of the whole of the twelfth century. Some of the stray finds may well have been lost after the death of Alexius; the hoards, for which an earlier date of deposit is certain, suggest an even more restricted area as that within which the folles were to be found in general use during his reign.

They are of many different types. Wroth attributes to Alexius no fewer than a dozen different issues, and there are, further, two types of Rex Regnantium folles that are shown by the evidence of overstriking to be his. Several scarce types not included in the British Museum Catalogue must be added to the list.[15] Out of these various issues, five or six are in styles which associate them with the coinages of preceding emperors, while the rest are in the style that occurs, with little change, from 1118 to 1204. On this stylistic evidence, and on this alone, it has been assumed that the former issues belong to the early part and the remainder to the later part of his reign, and, therefore, that at some intermediate date Alexius reformed the bronze coinage.[16] Certainly, the issue of coinage in the "pre-reform" style was suppressed before 1118; but equally it may be taken as certain that coins in different styles were struck concurrently in different parts of the Empire. The "reformed" folles were never current in any numbers in central Greece, where the petty coinage consisted largely of the "pre-reform" issues of Alexius throughout his reign and indeed until the accession of Manuel, in 1143. The innovations in weight-standards and mint-organization, however, which characterize the "reformed" folles of later reigns and which are of more real importance than changes of style, can already be

---

[14] For the hoards, see Metcalf, (work in progress), and (for Limanu and Tulcea) Dimian, "Cîteva Descoperiri". For the stray finds; Argos, BCH lxxvii (1953), 258; Glyfadha (Basilica), BCH liv (1930), 454; Thessaloniki, BCH lviii (1934), 236; Filippaioi, BCH lxxx (1956), 230; Kuruchai valley, A. G. Bates, in correspondence in Seaby's Coin and Medal Bulletin, January 1950; Preslav, Mushmov, "Kolektivni Na khodki, 1929-30".

[15] Sabatier, Description Générale, LVIII, 16 = Bellinger, Anonymous Byzantine Bronze, Class XII; Bellinger, Class XIII = Rex Regnantium Class L; Sabatier, LIX, l; Sabatier, LVIII, 10 (possibly to be transferred to Alexius III?).

[16] Wroth, BMC (Byz.), I, pp. lx-lxiii; P. D. Whitting, "The Anonymous Byzantine Bronze", NC[6] xv (1955), 89-99. The literary records do not portray Alexius as an innovator; see G. Rouillard, "A propos d'un ouvrage récent sur l'histoire d'etat byzantin", Revue de Philologie 3rd. series, xvi (1942), 169ff., especially at pp. 175ff.

found among the "pre-reform" folles of the kinds that were most plentiful in Greece.

In the two decades before the accession of Alexius, the iconography of the Rex Regnantium series of folles, which had originally been simple and forceful, became increasingly overlaid by additional themes. The portrait of the earthly ruler was reintroduced onto the bronze coinage in the reign of Constantine X, although it did not replace the portrait of Christ, which remained the principal type. The aid of the Holy Cross for the person of the emperor was invoked in a series of initialled coins, of which the first were those of Romanus IV, while another sequence, begun under Michael VII, depicted the Cross as the Tree of Life. The coinage of Alexius made use of all these themes. The anonymous issue Class K was in the main Rex Regnantium tradition; *BMC* Type 3 and Edwards no. 126 bore the portrait of Alexius; the most plentiful issue in central Greece, *BMC* Type 9, was a Holy Cross coinage, again with the imperial portrait; Class J of the Rex Regnantium series belonged to the Tree of Life sequence. The correct arrangement and mint - attribution of the varieties even of these five types alone still presents many problems. *BMC* Type 3 and Edwards no. 126 are closely related by style. Their metrology, and their absence from the Corinth hoard of 1959 suggest that their issue in Greece began later than that of Rex Regnantium Classes J and K. The evidence of overstriking makes it quite clear that J and K were issued successively in that order; they seem both to have been struck to a weight-standard of about 6 grammes or a little less. *BMC* Type 3 and Edwards no. 126 are very much lighter, being on a standard of $3\frac{1}{2}$ grammes or a little less (possibly 96 coins to the pound). Edwards no. 126 is a scarce coin in general collections, whereas *BMC* Type 3 is very common. The totals in the site finds from Athens and Corinth (see Table 5 below) give a very different impression. They suggest that the former type is to be associated generally with central Greece, and more particularly with Corinth, where it was issued in greater quantities, relative to Type 3, than at Athens. Very probably it was struck at Corinth. In the Corinth hoard of February 1934, concealed when the Holy Cross coinage *(BMC* Type 9) was already well under way, the number of specimens of Edwards no. 126 actually exceeds that of *BMC* Type 3. The Holy Cross coins, when they are not struck on old flans, are often about $2\frac{1}{4}$ grammes in weight. This last type, however, exhibits such a wide range of style that one must ask whether it was not struck at a number of mints, possibly on more than one weight-standard. The stylistic variety that belongs to central

Greece appears to be that which dominates the Athens hoards of 1935 and 1937. [17]

The interpretation of these and the other Greek hoards from the reign of Alexius will probably become clearer when two or three more finds are available for comparison. The long, straggling age-structure of the Sparta hoard indicates that the petty currency there was not regulated by renewal; this is borne out by another hoard, deposited some decades later, at which date there had been no improvement in the situation. [18] The four hoards from Athens and Corinth have a more compact age-structure.

Five types of Alexius's folles account for virtually all those found in the excavations at Athens and Corinth. The remaining types, represented in trifling quantities, are essentially strays from other regions of the Empire. Evidence of this is that they are more plentiful at Corinth, which as a port had a somewhat larger proportion of miscellaneous pieces in its currency than Athens. *BMC* Type 7 should probab-

	Athens	Corinth
Alexius I, 1081–1118		
Class J	77	59
Class K	233	146
BMC Type 3	180	85
Edwards, no. 126	96	61
Holy Cross *(BMC* Type 9)	602	372
BMC Type 1	12	8
BMC Type 4	1	0
BMC Type 8	2	4
BMC Type 7	34	6
BMC Type 2, 5, and 6	3	1
Bellinger, Classes XII and XIII	2	4
Sabatier, LIX, 1 and LVIII, 10	0	2
John II, 1118–1143		
BMC Type 3	114	83
BMC Type 2	11	11
Types 1 and 4	4	0

Table 5. Folles of Alexius I and John II from the excavation at Athens (1931-49) and Corinth (1896-1929).

ly be re-attributed to Alexius II or III, along with Type 10. Type 8 is no doubt early. Of those that remain, Types 1 and 4 are of the greatest

---

[17] For the iconography and metrology of the folles of Alexius, and for accounts of the hoards, see Metcalf, (work in progress).

[18] See p. 110 below.

interest. The style of portraiture on them is the same, and there is a fairly close parallel with the two substantive types of Alexius's stamena:

Stamena, *BMC* Type 5, and folles, *BMC* Type 1
   Obv. Bust of Christ
   Rev. Bust of emperor with loros and labarum
Stamena, *BMC* Type 4, and folles, *BMC* Type 4
   Obv. Throned figure of Christ
   Rev. Bust of emperor with chlamys and cross

We may conjecture that this group of issues is Constantinopolitan.[19]

The scyphate coinage in bronze, which in later reigns was to dominate the currency of almost the whole of the Balkan peninsula, seems to have had only a modest beginning in the time of Alexius. It has rarely been found in hoards, and then usually only in residual quantities. The one hoard which, on the available evidence, may have been con cealed before 1118 is that which was discovered at Teshevo in 1935. Out of about six hundred scyphate coins, 21 that were examined were of Alexius I.[20] Teshevo is in the region of Gotse Delchev, on the south-western flanks of the Rhodope; in view of the date of the deposit, and the infrequent occurrence of hoards in the Rhodope, one may suspect that it is a traveller's hoard, concealed perhaps by someone making the journey between Constantinople and Thessaloniki. If scyphate bronze had been in common use in central Greece during the reign of Alexius, it would have been hoarded in preference to folles, as being more valuable: the total absence of the larger denomination from the hoards of folles argues strongly that they were absent from the currency there. However, a rather wider survey of the evidence relating to them is needed, because of their historical importance. Only two finds from south of the Danube have been properly published. There was a single piece of *BMC* Type 4 among a total of over 650 coins in the Tuzla hoard. In the Ivanovo hoard of 1955, also deposited after 1195, there were two types of scyphate bronze of Alexius, in unspecified quantities, namely *BMC* Type 5, which on stylistic grounds seems to belong close to John II *BMC* Type 6, therefore perhaps towards 1118, and another type showing the standing figure of the emperor.[21] Hoards of scyphate

---

[19] Its including the "Coronation" issue is one reason for supposing it to be Constantinopolitan.

[20] Gerasimov, "Kolektivni Nakhodki, 1934-36".

[21] For the Tuzla hoard of (?) 1914, see I. Băncilă, "Note asupra unor Tezaure de Monede Bizantine", *SCN* i (1957), 425-438, and cf. *SCN* ii (9158), 417-18. For the Ivanovo hoard, see Gerasimov, "Kolektivni Nakhodki, 1955"; Type 2 occurred in the Novo Selo (Plovdiv) hoard of 1958-Gerasimov, "Monetni Sŭkrovishta, 1958-59".

90

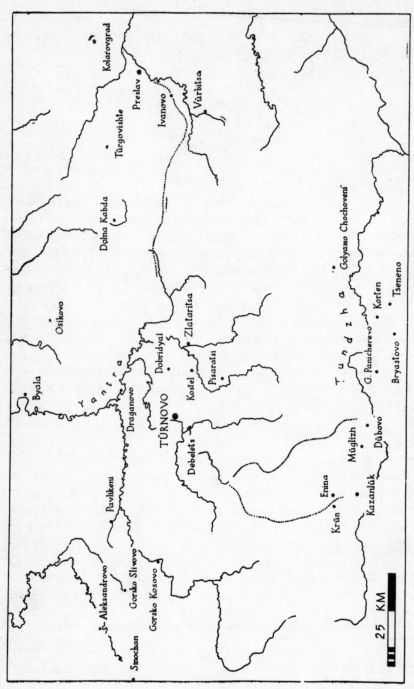

Map V. North-eastern Bulgaria, XI—XII centuries.

bronze reported to have contained coins of Alexius, of unspecified types and in unspecified quantities, have come to light in half-a-dozen localities in the peninsula. [22] From just to the north of the Danube, the Bucureşti and Copuzu hoards, and, from Transylvania, that of Făgăraş all included coins of Alexius. [23] Because relatively so few hoards of scyphate bronze have been found in Romania other than on the Black Sea coasts, the evidence of those containing coins of Alexius far outweighs the greater number of similar finds from Bulgaria, where dozens of hoards of stamena have been brought to light. In the Copuzu hoard there were no fewer than 15 coins of Type 4, and also two of the "Coronation" issue, BMC Type 7. The latter is a rare and iconographically very unusual coinage which was doubtless struck specially in 1092 for the coronation ceremonies of the young John II. The localization of these coinages on the northern frontiers of the Empire—and the Isaccea and Tuzla provenances perhaps belong to the same pattern—can hardly have been brought about as late as the reign of Manuel, when the earliest of the hoards were concealed. Possibly the explanation is to be found in the alliance between the Empire and the Cumans; the date of the "Coronation" issue fits in well enough with the date at which the alliance was terminated, 1095. [24]

It must have been obvious beforehand that the bronze nomismata would arouse hostility and criticism; and it seems unlikely that the "Coronation" issue would have been struck in bronze unless the opposition had by that time died down somewhat. If the latter conjecture is correct, the issue of BMC Type 4 must have begun in the early years

---

[22] The hoards are those from Isaccea, 1913 (see Mosser, *Byzantine Coin Hoards*); Rilo 1922 (Mushmov, "Kolektivni Nakhodki, 1921-22"); Batkun 1941 (Gerasimov, "Kolektivni Nakhodki, 1941-45"). The Lyaskovo hoard of 1949 (Gerasimov, "Kolektivni Nakhodki, 1949-50") was reported, by Tsonchev, to contain coins of Alexius I with Constantine; but these were probably pieces of Alexius III, which were incorrectly attributed in Sabatier, *Description Générale*. Three coins found in the excavations at Corinth, probably in association, and attributed to Alexius I in Bellinger, *Corinth*, 1925, seem to me to be a good deal later in date.

[23] For the Bucureşti hoard, see O. Iliescu, "Despre un Tezaur de Monede Bizantine din Vremea Comnenilor, găsit în Bucureşti", *SCN* iii (1960), 493-99. For the Copuzu hoard, see Dimian, "Cîteva Descoperiri". For the Fagaraş hoard, see I. Sabău, "Circulatia Monetara în Transilvania Secolelor XI-XIII, în Lumina Izvoarelor Numismatice", *SCN* ii (1958), 269 - 301.

[24] For the historical background and its chronology, see A. Soloviev, "La Date de la Version Russe du Digénis Akritas", *Byzantion* xxii (1952), 129-32, and M. Mathieu, "Les Faux Diogènes", *ibid.*, 133-48.

of the reign of Alexius, and almost certainly before the reform of the gold coinage. The often-quoted comment of Zonaras that Alexius exacted taxes in good gold but made payments in electrum or bronze [25] thus probably refers to the earlier part of his reign, and to a fiscal policy designed to replenish the treasury with the good gold coins of earlier emperors which had been driven out of circulation by the debased nomismata, as a prelude to Alexius's own issue of reformed gold. [26]

The requests of certain tax-collectors for rulings on the correct way in which to calculate tax-liability [27] have perhaps received disproportionate attention from historians. The work of Svoronos on the cadastral codex of Thebes has thrown clearer light on the systems of reckoning and the moneys of account involved. [28] The significant detail for the numismatist is that, in Thrace and Macedonia in 1106, there should not have been a commonly recognized exchange-rate between gold and bronze. This, and the quantities in which the reformed gold of Alexius was struck, are suggestive of a monetary economy in the provinces of limited scope.

If the pattern of the substantive issues was generally simple in each of the main provincial regions of the Empire, in the capital it was far otherwise. The requirements of protocol, ceremonial, and special imperial payments are probably the explanation for a good many of the issues which are scarce in cabinets today and which have rarely or never been reported in finds. A most instructive example from the reign of John II (1118-1143) is provided by the typicon of the monastery of the Pantocrator at Constantinople, founded by John and his wife Irene in 1136. It regulates in detail the expenses of the foundation, and specifies by name a variety of coins in which payments were to be made. A hierarchical principle is apparent, in the degree of dignity that attached to different denominations of coinage. Thus, the salaries of the highest officials of the monastery were to be paid in "gold nomismata", which were also to be used for alms on important feast-days, whereas the

---

[25] Zonaras, *Epitome Historiarum*, xviii, 22.

[26] The documentary evidence is conveniently summarized in Zakythinos, "Crise Monétaire".

[27] F. Chalandon, *Essai sur le Règne d'Alexis Ier. Comnène*", 1900, pp. 301. ff; for the date, see Dölger, *Regesten*, under no. 1245; Ostrogorsky, *Byzantine State*, p. 327.

[28] N. G. Svoronos, "Recherches sur le Cadastre Byzantin et la Fiscalité aux XIe et XIIe Siècles: le Cadastre de Thèbes", *BCH* lxxxiii (1959), 1-145, especially at pp. 89-118.

subordinate officials were paid in "new nomismata", and the upper servants in "hyperpyra". The St. George nomisma *(BMC* Type 4) was specified to be distributed at the ceremony of the procession of the icon of the Hodegetria. The "tri-cephalous" nomisma [29] was used for the payment of bonuses to the higher officials, and one was given to each of the old people whose feet were washed in the Lenten ceremonies. The "trachy"—τὸ νόμισμα τραχὺ ἄσπρον—of which there were apparently 48 to the nomisma, may have been the silver-washed scyphate billon or bronze coin *(BMC* Type 6); it was used for monthly supplements to the salaries of the clergy and subordinate officials, for gratuities distributed on various feasts, and for the purchase of wine, candles, and incense. So the instructions continue, down to the tetarteron, of which 309 were to be given as gratuities to the hospital staff at the feast of the Presentation, and 920 at the feast of the Transfiguration. [30]

The twenty-five year reign of John II has yielded few hoards in the Balkans. The find of 1927 at Mahala-Pisaratsi, in the northern approaches of the Balkan Mountains, consisted of 13 gold pieces of John II, and three to four hundred bronze coins "of the same period", contained in a pot. The locality is within the orbit of Tŭrnovo. The presence of gold and bronze in a single hoard, and the inland provenance, suggest that it may have been concealed in haste, at the time of the Patzinak incursions of 1122. The Stoeneşti hoard of 1957, from the lower Danube, was reported as containing 22 gold coins of John II. It may possibly have been concealed on the same occasion.

A small hoard from Depentzikos, near Methoni, consisting of 9 reformed nomismata of Alexius I, has been associated with the Venetian attack on Methoni in 1125.

The Gotse Delchev hoard of 1958, from the same routeway as the Teshevo hoard, is another deposit from John's reign. It contained gold of Alexius I, *BMC* Type 1, and John II, Type 2. The Novo Selo (Plovdiv) hoard, which came to light in the same year, included gold coins of the same two types, and of Isaac II, Type 1, along with stamena of Alexius I, Types 2 and 4, John II, Types 6 and 7 /i, and Isaac, Type

[29] V. Laurent, "Les Monnaies Tricéphales de Jean II Comnène", *Revue Numismatique* 5th. series, xiii (1951), 97-108.

[30] A. Frolow, "Les Noms de Monnaies dans le Typicon du Pantocrator", *Byzantinoslavica* x (1949), 241-253.

4. The number of early types of bronze, as also the absence of any coins of Manuel, are suggestive of a "double hoard" (which would be more than usually plausible for the troubled years 1185 - 87); but this uncertainty does not alter the value of the provenance. The Gotse Delchev and Novo Selo hoards together are extremely interesting because they re-open the question of the attribution between John II and John III of the coins listed by Wroth under John II, and lead to important conclusions about the striking of gold at provincial mints in the first half of the twelfth century. The primary stylistic division of *BMC*, John II, Type 2 is into the broad, elegantly engraved coins (plate LXVI, 12 and LXVII, 1) which are undoubtedly of the twelfth century and are almost certainly metropolitan, and the smaller pieces (plate LXVI, 10, 11, and LXVII, 2, 3), the attribution of which is problematic, but which seemed more likely, before the hoard-evidence of 1958 was available, to belong to John III. The coins of Type 2 from the Gotse Delchev hoard were referred to plate LXVI, 10-11, and those from Novo Selo to plate LXVII, 2. It seems quite clear that a small variety of Ty pe 2, represented by plate LXVII, 2 and 3, belongs to the reign of John II, and equally obvious that it must be assigned to a provincial mint. In light of the provenances, Thessaloniki is the strongest candidate, unless an inland centre were to be considered. [31]

The Saedinenie hoard of 1955, like that from Mahala-Pisaratsi, contained both gold and bronze, and might have been concealed at the same time. The gold was of Alexius's reformed type, and of John II, *BMC* Type 2, of the large, elegant variety. The presence of two types of stamena of John, *BMC* Types 6 and 7, may rule out a date as early

[31] For Mahala-Pisaratsi, see Mushmov, "Kolektivni Nakhodki, 1927-28". For Stoeneşti, see B. Mitrea, "Découvertes Récentes de Monnaies Antiques et Byzantines sur le Territoire de la République Populaire Roumaine", *Dacia* NS ii (1958), 493 - 98. For the Depentzikos hoard of 1927, see Metcalf, "Alexius I Comnenus". A number of hoards published as having contained coins of John II were in fact definitely of John III, and are mentioned in their appropriate place below; see Metcalf, "John Vatatzes". Others which are likely to have been of John III, although information about them is not available, are the Seltsi hoard of 1938, for which see *BCH* lxii (1938), 447, and the Athens hoard of 1928, for which see Mosser, *Byzantine Coin Hoards.* For the Gotse Delchev and Novo Selo hoards, see Gerasimov, "Monetni Sŭkrovishta, 1958 - 59". I can claim to have made it clear, in "John Vatatzes", that the smaller stylistic variety of Type 2 might belong partly to John II and partly to John III, although I opted to give it all to to John III. *BMC* 15 to 19 (plate lxvii, 2 and 3) must now be restored to John II, but it seems reasonable to continue to think that *BMC* 8 and 9 (plate LXVI, 10 and 11), with their secret - marks and with a jewelled throne, belong to John III. Most unfortunately, ths GotseDelchev hoard was dispersed.

as 1122, when the numismatic history of the reign has been further studied. In that case, one would be inclined to associate the Saedinenie hoard, and also the Stara Zagora hoard of 1935, with the disorganized passage of the Second Crusade along the Maritsa valley as far as Adrianople. The earlier discovery was represented by 18 gold nomismata, again of Alexius's reformed type and John's Type 2, in the possession of a goldsmith in Stara Zagora, and thought to be a part if not the whole of a hoard discovered somewhere in the neighbourhood of the town. [32] There are difficulties in the way of placing the Stara Zagora deposit of 1956 as early in Manuel's reign as 1147, but the date cannot be completely ruled out. [33]

The importance of the Mahala-Pisaratsi, Saedinenie, and Stara Zagora hoards, which is not greatly affected by the question of their dates of deposit, is that they show that both gold and bronze coinage was finding its way towards Bulgaria before the middle of the twelfth century.

They are also of interest as evidence of the localized circulation of different issues of nomismata in the provinces in John's reign. *BMC* Type 2 was the only issue, out of four or five attributed to John, to occur in the Saedinenie and Stara Zagora hoards; later hoards from the Balkans typically include only Types 2 and 3. The former was perhaps the earlier issue. In Asia Minor, hoards are normally dominated by Type 4. [34] The contrast with the monetary affairs of the capital is thus very sharp.

The issue and circulation of folles seems also to have been localized, although the number of different issues was much smaller. The standard type in Greece was *BMC* Type 3, which occurred in moderately large quantities in the excavations at Athens and Corinth (see Table 5). Type 2 was far less frequently found. There are only three other Balkan provenances for John's folles. The latest coin in the Drosaton hoard is a large, elegant specimen of Type 3. The Copuzu hoard, with one each of Types 2 and 3, and the Stara Zagora deposit of 1956, with one coin of Type 2, hint that Type 3 was not the dominant issue in the currency of the western coastlands of the Black Sea, as it was in Greece. Type 2

[32] Gerasimov, "Kolektivni Nakhodki, 1934-36" and "Kolektivni Nakhodki, 1955".
[33] See p. 103.
[34] See Mosser, *Byzantine Coin Hoards*, under Adana, Lindos, and Trebizond. For John II, *BMC* Type 1, in the Khadzhidimovo hoard, see below.

is perhaps Constantinopolitan. Folles of *BMC* Type 1 are so scarce in central Greece that they are most probably only strays there, carried from other regions.

The intriguing problem in the numismatic history of John's reign concerns his substantive issues of stamena, *BMC* Type 6 and variants. Type 7 is much less common, and has been recorded in only a very few Balkan hoards, of which those from Saedinenie and Pavlikeni are the most important, because they are apparently the earliest. [35] Type 7/ii (plate LXVIII, 7) is reported only as a stray find from Trebinje in the Hercegovina. [36] Type 6 itself is to be divided: there is one variety on which the jewels of the pendants are represented by pear-shaped drops, the side-ones being attached by lines; on a second variety, the pendants are represented simply by three dots, and the large cross held by the emperor has a flourish beneath it (is the iconography to be compared with the Tree of Life folles?). [37] However, neither of these quite plentiful varieties has yet been reported in Greek hoards of scyphate bronze, [38] which contain in their place a coinage of very inferior fabric and execution, smaller in module, and weighing much less than Type 6. These Greek varieties have been designated Type 6B. [39] On the simplest interpretation, they must be divided into three. The largest variety differs from Type 6 in having Christ seated on a low-backed throne as its obverse design; it was found in the Paros hoard of 1924, the "Thessaly" hoard of 1957, the Arcadian hoard of 1958, the Corinth excavations, and, apparently, in larger numbers in the Thira and Postallar hoards.[40] The intermediate variety, which was represented in the "Thessaly" hoard, has the normal Type 6 obverse, as has the smallest variety on which there are only 9, instead of the usual 12, large jewels on the

---

[35] See above, and, for the Pavlikeni hoard, also found in 1955, Gerasimov, "Kolektivni Nakhodki, 1955". Cf. also the Kostel hoard of 1938; Gerasimov. "Kolektivni Nakhodki, 1937 - 38".

[36] I am indebted to Miss Ljubinka Kojić, of the Zavičajni Museum, Trebinje, for a cast of the coin.

[37] See Metcalf, "Scyphate Bronze Coinage in Greece", 55, commenting also on the metrology. Further varieties are indicated in H. Mattingly, "The Lazania Hoard of Byzantine Coins", *Report of the Department of Antiquities, Cyprus,* 1937 - 1939, pp. 22f. and plate XVIII.

[38] With the possible exception of the Corinth hoard of 1960, for which see H. S. Robinson, "Excavations at Corinth, 1960", *Hesperia* xxxi (1962), 95-133, section, "The Coins", by R. Stroud, 130-133.

[39] See Metcalf, *op. cit.* especially at pp. 49ff.

[40] *Ibid.*

emperor's loros. Although the three varieties are restricted in their provenance to hoards from the thirteenth century or the very end of the twelfth, there seems to be no alternative but to attribute them to John II, on the evidence of the inscriptions +IѠΔ and perhaps IѠANN which can occasionally be made out on them. [41] They are to all appearances the first stamena issued by Greek mints, and they already display the variation in module which characterizes the provincial issues of Manuel. Their metrology, however, is somewhat erratic. Crucial to the whole interpretation of Type 6B is a small detail of their iconography: the three jewels of the pendants of the crown, which are normally shown thus:-$*_**$, are inverted, thus:-$_**_*$. Although there are some twenty different minor variations in the representation of the pendants in the Byzantine coinages of the ninth to thirteenth centuries, the detail was by no means haphazard. The version that appears on Type 6B is extremely unusual, and can be matched only on one other issue (which is almost as scarce), showing the emperor standing, wearing a chlamys. It is published in the Ratto catalogue, lots 2076 and 2143. If both the Ratto type and Type 6B were found only in a single style and fabric, one would bracket them as issues of the same provincial mint, not very different from each other in date, and ascribe the form of the pendants to an idiosyncrasy of the engraver at that mint. The occurrence of inverted pendants on three very different stylistic varieties of Type 6B destroys any such simple hypothesis. How and why were the engravers instructed to represent the pendants in such an unusual form? Can it have been a mistake? If, when a new type was to be issued, a drawing of it was made on a piece of paper and copied and sent out to each provincial mint, a clerical error might account for the inversion. Whatever the correct explanation, Type 6B offers an intriguing problem in the deduction of monetary organization from numismatic evidence.

Taking account of the existence of near-duplicates among the small number of specimens that has been published, it would seem likely that the issue of Type 6B in Greece began late in John's reign, at two or three mints. The distribution of the varieties among possible mint-places is, as usual, very much open to discussion and review. The larger variety might belong to a mint on one of the islands, while the

---

[41] I have wondered whether some of them could be "anachronistic" issues of John III, parallel to his gold (for which see Metcalf, "John Vatatzes"), but it really seems impossible.

intermediate and small varieties will belong to Corinth and Thessaloniki, or to both places. It is virtually certain that Ratto 2143 and 2076 must be close in date to Type 6B, for a hoard recently acquired by the Athens Museum includes specimens of the former overstruck on the latter. The same hoard contains a coin which to all appearances has Type 6B as the under-type of Manuel's Type 13/ii. [42] The fact that the emperor is bearded on Ratto 2143 and 2076 is a difficulty in the way of placing the type at the very beginning of Manuel's reign. It might be the Greek equivalent of John, *BMC* Type 7; in that case the argument that Type 6B is late in the reign loses some of its force—it might be simply that the issues were on a small scale. No. 2143 will, again, be the more southerly, while no. 2076 shows stylistic parallels with the intermediate variety of 6B. [43]

The long reign of Manuel I (1143-1180) has an exceedingly complex numismatic history, about the chronology of which hardly anything is yet known. Wroth catalogues 8 types of nomismata in the precious metals, 5 types of stamena, and 8 types of folles. In attempting to reduce this profusion of coinages to some sort of order, we may begin by noting that only one issue of nomismata, *BMC* Type 1, is normally found in Balkan hoards, that different issues of stamena are broadly localized in either the eastern part of the peninsula or Greece, and that, similarly, different issues of folles seem to belong either to Greece or Constantinople. More than three-quarters of the folles found at Athens and Corinth, for example, are of two types. A good many of Manuel's issues which are rare or absent in Balkan finds may have had a localized circulation in Asia Minor.

The only real footholds, as yet, in the numismatic chronology of Manuel's reign are that a number of deposits from Corinth can quite confidently be attributed to 1147, the year of the Norman raid, and that one issue of folles *(BMC* Type 7, the Monogram type) and one issue of stamena *(BMC* Type 9), each showing a beardless bust of the emperor, were presumably struck in his youth, at the beginning of his reign. [44] These two scraps of evidence to some extent duplicate each other. The relative chronology of the folles found in Greece can, with a degree of

---

[42] Cf. A. R. Bellinger and D. M. Metcalf, "A Hoard of Byzantine Scyphate Bronze Coins from Arcadia", *NC* 6. xix (1959), 155-164, where an attribution to Isaac II was proposed.

[43] Compare plate IV, 51 and 152 in Metcalf, "Scyphate Bronze Coinage in Greece".

uncertainty, be reconstructed from the handful of mules found among the thousands of excavation-coins of this reign from Athens.

Manuel's substantive issue of gold, *BMC* Type 1, shows a great deal of variation in style, inscriptions, and other smaller details. It has not yet been classified, but one may guess that it represents the issues of more than one mint, continuing over a considerable period; one reason for this guess is that the same sort of stylistic range is to be found among the gold coins of Isaac II. The Corinth hoard of May, 1938, which consisted of 30 coins of Manuel's Type 1, [45] contained a wide range of the known varieties, and it is therefore improbable that it was concealed in 1147. Among the 30 coins, which were of unusual interest because of the graffiti on them, there were three pairs of duplicates, a reverse die - linkage, and a reverse die-linkage to one of the pairs.[46] Although the incidence of die-duplication is thus rather high, there is no reason to think that the hoard is weighted with a group of new issues, for the die - linked coins are by no means all in similar style. The group of three coins had 5 dots at the emperor's shoulders, and an inscription beginning MA/NΘHΛ/; one pair of duplicates had 3 dots at the emperor's shoulders and the inscription MA/NOU/HΛ/, etc.; the remaining pair, and also the reverse die-link, seem to have had the same arrangement of the emperor's name, but 7 or 8 dots at the shoulders. To all appearances, therefore, the hoard is a useful sample from which to estimate the quantities of *BMC* Type 1 that were struck. The instances of die-duplication break down into 3 obverse pairs, 3 reverse pairs, and one reverse triplet. The estimates yielded by these figures are 145 ± 84 for the obverses, and 109 ± 54 for the reverses, treating the triplet as a pair. Unless the hoard is in some unrecognized way a limited sample, it must therefore seem that Type 1 was struck from no more than 100 to 150 pairs of dies, and that the issue numbered, say, one to one and a half million coins. In this case, the amount of variation in the design is hard to understand, unless the striking was sporadic. The standard issue of gold by Alexius I had been 5 or 10 times as large; here, perhaps, is a measure of the dwindling stocks of gold in the Empire. The double hoard from Lindos tells the same story for electrum. Counting multiples as pairs in order to offset the effects of "clustering" of die-

---

[44] This point is made in Bellinger, *Corinth*, 1925, p. 64, note 1.

[45] J. M. Harris, "A Gold Hoard of Corinth", *American Journal of Archaeology* xliii (1939), 268ff.

[46] The die-linked specimens stand at the head of the catalogue.

duplicates in circulation, it would seem that *BMC* Types 4 and 7, each with several type-varieties, were each struck from about 350 pairs of dies.[47]

A preliminary classification of Type 1, based on the Corinth hoard, reveals quite definitely that there are two main groupings. Coins with 5 dots at the shoulders read MA; coins with 3 and with 7 or 8 dots at
NΘHΛ

the shoulders have a three - line arrangement, $\begin{matrix} \text{MA} \\ \text{NOU} \\ \text{HΛ} \end{matrix}$ or $\begin{matrix} \text{MA} \\ \text{NΘ} \\ \text{HΛ} \end{matrix}$. The 5-dot group, which is likely to have been struck in the metropolitan region, is represented in the hoard by a dozen specimens, among which is the die-linked group of three coins. Fifteen specimens with 7 or 8 dots at the shoulders, and including a few inscriptional irregularities, are possibly local issues.

The contrast between the Corinth hoard, consisting of one type only, and the Kastoria hoard, where among 9 coins there were some of Romanus IV and John, as well as of Manuel's Type 1, [48] is perhaps of the same significance as that between the hoards of folles from Corinth and from Sparta—the currency of the more distant parts of the Empire was relatively stagnant. It may have been the family savings of some simple inhabitant of the place. Kastoria lies on the southern approach to the pass at the head of the Devoll valley, which is the easiest route between Thessaloniki and the Adriatic after the Egnatian Way, but there is nothing to associate this particular treasure with a journey that must quite often have been made; indeed, such evidence as there is points to the Kastoria find's being a local hoard rather than a traveller's hoard.

Two other small hoards were made up entirely of Manuel's gold. Three coins found in the earlier walls of the Byzantine church at Theotokou, on the peninsula which bounds the Gulf of Volos, were almost certainly associated. They were of *BMC* Type 2. At Osoitsa, in the region of Sofia, a hoard of six gold coins of Manuel was discovered in 1926. [49]

---

[47] The hoard is published in J. Balling, "A Byzantine Double Hoard from Lindos", *Nordisk Numismatisk Arsskrift* 1963, 13ff.

[48] *BCH* lxxi-lxxii (1947-48), 391-94. The types were given as Wroth,*BMC(Byz.)*, II, plate LXI, 12; LXVI, 12, LXVII, 11, LXVIII, 9; LXVIII, 14, and LXIX, 1.

[49] *ABS Athens* xiii (1906 - 07), 321. Mushmov, "Kolektivni Nakhodki, 1925-26".

The role of electrum nomismata in the currency of the Balkans is far from clear. They were presumably a denomination of lower value than the gold nomisma, and may for that reason, or simply because they were unpopular in the countryside, not often have been hoarded, although in regular use. Manuel's *BMC* Types 2 to 8 are all known in electrum; but Type 6 is to be transferred to the thirteenth century. Type 5, which perhaps belongs early in Manuel's reign, is related by style to coins of John II, *BMC* plate LXVIII, 1, with which it is recorded in a Trapezuntine hoard. Types 2 and 3, which are related by style, are problematic. Types 4 and 7, the common types, show the same kind of variation in detail as Type 11, the standard issue in bronze. The Krŭn find of 1960, from the Stara Zagora region, was reported as containing 22 electrum nomismata of Type 4, along with 10 nomismata of *BMC* Type 1 of Nicephorus III. The age-gap, and the exclusive occurrence of Nicephorus's Type 1 are very curious. The treasure is *prima facie* a savings hoard, belonging early rather than late in Manuel's reign, but without information about the dots at the emperor's shoulders on the coins of Type 4, nothing serious can be said about it. Another and larger hoard, containing bronze as well as electrum, presumably from Manuel's reign, was found at Gorsko Slivovo in 1937. [50]

The Marathon hoard of 1928, in which one Sicilian gold coin of the middle of the century was said to have been associated with 361 folles of Manuel, may reflect only the particular circumstances in which it was deposited. [51]

The scyphate bronze currency of Manuel's reign comprised different substantive issues in Bulgaria and in Greece. In Bulgaria, *BMC* Type 11 and 13/i, together with smaller quantities of Type 12, characterize the finds, while in Greece, the usual issues are BMC Type 13/ii and a variety of Type 11 with asterisks on the obverse. The style, fabric, and metrology of the coins from the two regions are quite different, and correspond, broadly speaking, with those of John II, *BMC* Types 6 and 6B. Work on the stylistic groupings among Manuel's coins is in an early stage, and the most that can be said at present is that much of the Bulgarian currency would seem likely to have been struck in the metropo-

---

[50] Gerasimov, "Kolektivni Nakhodki, 1937-38"; *ibid.*, "Monetni Sŭkrovishta, 1960-61".

[51] See Mosser, *Byzantine Coin Hoards, ad loc.*, where the Sicilian coin is dated to 1149 (which would preclude a connexion with the raid of 1147).

litan region, and that the Greek stamena are undoubtedly the work of two or more local mints. The small variety of Type 13 /ii has been provisionally attributed to Thessaloniki, and one or more of the medium - sized varieties certainly belong to central Greece. [52]

The earliest of Manuel's types of stamena is, no doubt, *BMC* Type 9, which shows a beardless bust of the emperor. This type has been identified only in the metropolitan style and fabric; many specimens are exceptionally large, deeply scyphate, and well-made. There are few provenances, and such as there are suggest a distribution concentrated in the Black Sea coastlands, which would fit in with a Constantinopolitan origin. [53] Their interest lies in the possibility that there was a radical change in the circulation-pattern of stamena in the north-eastern Balkans at some date around the middle of the century, and that they reveal the earlier pattern of a more limited circulation.

The type is not ordinarily to be found in Greece. A hoard consisting exclusively of *BMC* Type 9, which turned up in Athens in 1959, and which was said to have been found in Macedonia, is at present unparalleled. The hoard's particular importance lies in its metrology. The coins were all in very fresh condition, well made, and with clear traces of silvering on the reverses. They had an attractive green patina. All were closely similar in style; yet the weights of individual pieces varied from 6.7 gm. to 2.2 gm. The average for 28 coins was 4.1 gm. [54] Such a degree of variation certainly was not tolerated for the other issues of stamena of

---

[52] For a fuller presentation of the evidence, and for illustrations, see Metcalf, "Scyphate Bronze Coinage in Greece". The occurrence of specimens of the small variety at Tuzla and Mesembria is intriguing. The explanation is probably along the same lines as that for the occurrence of seventh century African coins in the Dobruja and in Romania; see E. J. Prawdic-Golemberski and D. M. Metcalf, "The Circulation of Byzantine Coins on the South-eastern Frontiers of the Empire", *NC*[7] iii (1963), 83 - 92. For Tuzla, see *SCN* i (1957), 425-38; for Mesembria, I am indebted to information sent by Dr. Gerasimov, Cf. T. Gerasimov, "Un Problème de Numismatique Byzantine", *XIIe Congrès International des Études Byzantines, Ochride* 1961, Belgrade - Okhrid 1961, pp. 35f., referring to the Müglish hoard. The argumentation appears to me to be insufficiently detailed.

[53] See the distribution-map in Metcalf, "Scyphate Bronze Coinage in Greece", and add Stara Zagora, 1956 and Byaga for Type 9.

[54] The weights were: 6.7, 5.4, 5.0 (5 coins), 4.8, 4.4, 4.2 (3 coins), 4.1, 4.0 (2 coins), 3.9 (2 coins), 3.7 (2 coins), 3.6, 3.5, 3.4 (2 coins), 3.3, 3.0 (2 coins), 2.3, 2.2. The balance that I used was not highly accurate, and the figures of 5.0 in particular cannot be guaranteed more closely than plus or minus 0.2 gm. I am indebted to Messrs. Bitale, of Athens, for their kindness in allowing me to record this find.

Manuel's reign, nor for John II, Type 6. The only explanation which is at all plausible is that the coins are from an early phase in the operation of a mint, therefore a provincial mint, perhaps supplied with dies from Constantinople. Is there here the trace of an unsuccessful attempt, similar to the one made in the time of Justin I, to bring the Thessaloniki mint into line with the one in the capital? [55] This is purely a guess, but the sixth-century coins, the interpretation of which is much clearer, are a reminder of the kind of incidents in mint-history, documented by very few surviving coins, that one must be prepared to look for. If there is a possibility that dies were supplied from Constantinople for the striking of stamena, one should examine the consequences for the interpretation of certain hoards of folles from Corinth for which a date of deposit of 1147 is proposed, and also for the dating of the Stara Zagora hoard of 1956.

That deposit was found near the outer wall of the Augusta Trajana, and consisted of one scyphate coin, of Manuel's Type 9, and 17 folles, which were apparently of the following varieties: [56]

John II, *BMC* Type 2	(1)
Manuel, *BMC* Type 3, large variety	(8)
Type 7, large variety	(4)
Type 7, small variety	(3)
Type 6, large variety	(1)

In the present state of our knowledge, however, and without a study of the dies of the 18 coins, it would be riding rough-shod over the evidence to seek to associate the Stara Zagora deposit with the passage of the Second Crusade.

There have been a dozen other hoards from Bulgaria in which the latest coins were bronze of Manuel. For the most part, very little detail was recorded about them, and nothing useful can be said about their date of deposit or about the stylistic groups represented in them. [57]

---

[55] See Metcalf, "East Mediterranean World".

[56] Gerasimov, "Kolektivni Nakhodki, 1956- 57".

[57] The hoards from Isaccea, 1913, Rilo, 1922, and Batkun, 1941 have been referred to above, at p. 91, note 22. There are in addition the hoards of Kostel, 1938 and Pavlikeni, 1955, the former a pot-hoard of about 200 coins of John and Manuel, the latter, consisting of about 300 coins, including Types 11 and 12 of Manuel along with coins of John, Type 7 (Gerasimov, "Kolektivni Nakhodki, 1937 - 38" and *ibid.* "1955"). The following hoards were reported as containing hoards of Manuel only: Suvatiti, 1934, 805 coins, including Types 9, 11, and 12, and Samokov, 1936, about 200 coins, including Types 11 and 12 (Gerasimov, "Kolektivni Nakhod-

Manuel's stamena of *BMC* Type 12, on which the emperor is shown standing, wearing a loros, and holding a long cross and a globus cruciger, appear to be associated with Type 9 by their general style and fabric. They are a good deal more plentiful than Type 9, having been recorded in a dozen Bulgarian hoards. Like Type 9, however, they are virtually absent from Greek hoards; the only exceptions are the Corinth site-finds and a single coin from the Olynthus excavations. The finds from that site are, generally speaking, the next-best thing to evidence from Thessaloniki, which is nearby; one coin, of course, particularly from as late as the twelfth century, is not weighty. An analysis of the Bulgarian provenances is bound to be uncertain because the quantities of the different types present in the hoards are usually unknown: there is no way of guessing which of the hoards are more significant and which less. The most definite information relates to two thirteenth-century hoards, both found in 1959, at Byaga and Logodash. A half to three-quarters of the coins, in each hoard, were of Manuel's Type 13/ii, and there were only small quantities of his Type 11, and none of Type 13/i. Byaga is in the region of Pazardzhik, and Logodash is in the region of Blagoevgrad, so that there is an obvious *prima facie* case for drawing a comparison with the Levkokhori hoard from near Kilkis, also from the early thirteenth century, and in which Type 13/ii was similarly predominant, and conjecturing that the three finds reflect a thirteenth-century trade-route from Thessaloniki by way of the Struma valley into Bulgaria. *BMC* Type 12, of which there were only 9 specimens among 479 in the Byaga hoard and 8 among a similar total at Logodash, might then be construed as having been issued in Thessaloniki under somewhat the same conditions as *BMC* Type 9 (of which there were 16 in the Byaga hoard). Such a theory would need, however, to be accommodated to the provenances of the remaining hoards. A find from much nearer the date of issue of Type 12, discovered at Tyurkmen, in the region of Plovdiv, in 1959, contained a larger proportion of the issue —37 coins, against 58 of Type 11, 18 of Andronicus, Type 3, and 3 of

---

ki, 1934 - 36"); Batkun, 1939, 18 coins, including Type 11, and Samokov, 1939, about 100 coins, including Type 13 (Gerasimov, "Kolektivni Nakhodki, 1939"); Dobridol, 1943, 70 coins, including Type 11 (Gerasimov, "Kolektivni Nakhodki, 1941-45"); Mukhovo, 1950, about 1,000 coins, including Types 11 and 12 or 13 (Gerasimov, "Kolektivni Nakhodki, 1949-50"); Dobridyal, 1957, including Type 11 (Gerasimov, "Kolektivni Nakhodki, 1956-57"). The following hoards were reported as containing coins of Manuel, but the types were not specified: Gorni Pasareli, 1935, a thousand coins, and Pazardzhik, 1935, about 700 coins (Gerasimov, "Kolektivni Nakhodki, 1934-36"); Veselinovo, 1943 (Gerasimov, "Kolektivni Nakhodki, 1941-45").

105

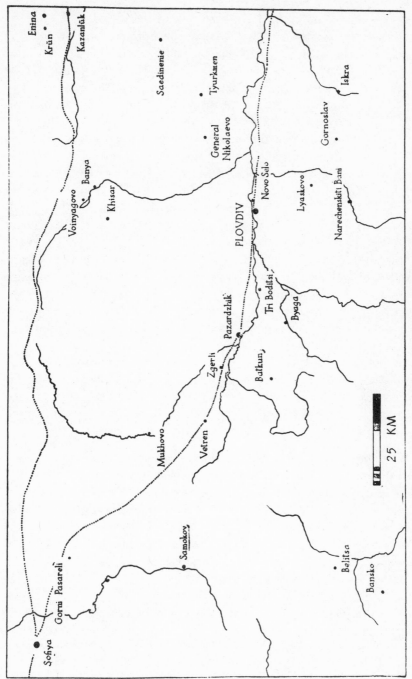

Map. VI, Central Bulgaria, XII century.

Isaac. The deposit may well have been within the period 1185-87. The Vidrare hoard, yet again of 1959, from the Sofia region, included 2 coins of Manuel's Type 12, 2 of Type 11, and 7 of Alexius III. To these south-westerly provenances should be added the Gradevo hoard of 1958 from the Blagoevgrad region, which may also belong to the 1180's; two hoards from Samokov (1936 and 1938), at the head of the Struma valley; the Draganovo, 1957 hoard from the Yantra valley and the Pavlikeni, 1955 hoard from a find-spot north-west of Tŭrnovo; the Zlata hoard from the Morava valley; the Enina hoard from near Kazanlŭk; and then, in the eastern regions of Bulgaria, the Suvatiti, 1934 hoard from the Burgas district, the Ovchartsi hoard of 1958 from the district of Sliven, and that found at Voivodo, near Kolarovgrad. The evidence points rather clearly to a localization in western Bulgaria, and only a little less clearly to some connexion between *BMC* Type 12 and the Struma valley routeway from the Aegean coasts into the upper Maritsa valley and thence to north-western and north-central Bulgaria. If the coins were issued at Thessaloniki, might they have been intended specially for the trade with Bulgaria, where the style and fabric of the coinages of the metropolitan region, not of Greece, were familiar? Alternatively, could one think of a hitherto unsuspected Byzantine mint at, say, Sofia or Plovdiv? The Corinth site-finds seem to favour the Thessalonican location. These hypotheses will need to be examined against a fuller body of evidence—as will many other hypotheses; for the history of the scyphate bronze currency in Bulgaria is still so vague and uncertain that an imaginative approach to it is required.[58]

A detailed classification of Type 11 has not yet been made, but even from a preliminary inspection, one can see that it is essential for hoard-reports to distinguish the following varieties:

A Coins in very fine style, with 3 dots at the emperor's shoulders. (Apparently a scarce variety).

B Coins in very fine style, with either 4 or 5 dots at the emperor's shoulders, and with the central panel of the loros ornamented either with an asterisk of dots and rays, or with 5 dots (:-:), of which the central one may be square.

C Coins in good style, with 3 dots at the emperor's shoulders. There

[58] D. M. Robinson, *Excavations at Olynthus: Part XIV. Terracottas, Lamps, and Coins Found in* 1934 *and* 1938 (The Johns Hopkins University Studies in Archaeology, XXXIX), 1952. For Byaga, Logodash, Tyurkmen, Vidrare, and Gradevo, see Gerasimov, "Monetni Sukrovishta, 1958-59". References for the other hoards are given on pages 103f., 112, 113, 115, and 116.

are many different minor varieties, distinguished by various com-
binations of (a) dots at the emperor's shoulders (the central dot
may be square, or may be replaced by an annulet with central
dot; or the two outer dots may be square); (b) dots on the central panel of the loros (the central one may be square, or may
be replaced by an annulet with central dot, which in turn may be
square); (c) asterisks on the obverse (most frequently with square
outer dots at the emperor's shoulders); (d) pendants of the emperor's crown (2 jewels, 3 jewels, 3 jewels of which the lowest is
larger, etc.).

D   Similar to C, but the central panel of the loros has one central
dot with 4 rays. (A scarce variety).

E   Provincial (central Greek) coins with a large number (usually
7 or more) of dots at the emperor's shoulders; poor style. Aste_
risks on the obverse of (a) 8 rays; (b) 6 rays; (c) 8 rays with cen_
tral dot (scarce); (d) 6 rays with central dot (rare).

F   Provincial (?? north Greek) coins in similar poor style to E, but
with only 3 dots at the emperor's shoulders. Small diameter.
(Scarce).

Variety C, in particular, and perhaps also E, seem to have been issued
over quite a long period. There is a close correspondence between Type
11 of Manuel and Type 4 of Isaac II, both in the range of varieties and
in the system of secret-marks.

This correspondence must be taken into account in determining
the place of *BMC* Type 13/i in the scheme. Its proportional occurrence,
relative to Type 11, is greatest in two hoards from north-central Bulgaria (among the few that have been published in detail). At Kaloyanovets, near Stara Zagora, there were 200 specimens, against 376 of Type
11; at Zlataritsa, near Tŭrnovo, there were 120, against 321. Each appears to have been concealed in the 1180's; the normal pattern of age -
structure thus suggests that Type 13/i belongs late in Manuel's reign.
Some confirmation of the order comes from a coin of Type 13/i which
is early in style (within the range displayed by the type) and which has
the blundered obverse reading IC ΘV—a hang-over from Type 11.
There are three stylistic groups, for which there is as yet no evidence of
localization. They are:

A.   7 or 8 dots at the emperor's shoulders; no fold in the inner side
of the chlamys (i.e. below the globus). The legend ΔΕCΠΟΤΗC
is normally unbroken or broken after ΔΕC (cf. Group C).

B. 3 dots at the emperor's shoulders; a fold in the inner side of the chlamys.

C. 7 to 10 dots at the emperor's shoulders; sinuous curve at lower right corner of chlamys. There are sometimes only 4 dots in the panel below the globus; normally one large round dot on the staff of the labarum (cf. Group A, which normally has nothing, occasionally one or more square dots set obliquely); legend normally Δ - ΕCΠΟΤΗC.

Several of the *BMC* Types of Manuel's folles also embrace what are undoubtedly different issues; a division into "large" and "small" varieties is only a first approximation, and does not necessarily correspond with the mint-organization behind their issue. Just as the stamena of the best styles and workmanship appear to maintain, throughout the twelfth century and into the thirteenth, a weight-standard of 84 coins to the pound (theoretical weight, 3. 9 gm.), so the evidence hints at a well-maintained standard for the best folles of 96 coins to the pound (theoretical weight, 3.4 gm.). The folles found in central Greece are typically much lighter, weighing 1½ - 2 grammes, and a stylistic variety that has been provisionally attributed to Thessaloniki weighs even less. [59] The quantities of the various *BMC* Types from the Athens and Corinth excavations are shown in Table 6.

	Athens	*Corinth*
Manuel I, 1143–80		
Type 7	1699	493
Type 6	1387	494
Type 3	307	137
Type 8	161	66
Types 2, 4, and 5	39	35
Alexius II, 1180–84		
Alexius I, *BMC* Type 10	7	2
Alexius III, *BMC* Type 2	13	0
Andronicus, 1183–85		
Types 2–3	74	19
Type 4	2	0
Isaac II, 1185–95		
Type 3	144	25
Types 1, 2, etc.	6	0

Table 6. Folles of the period 1143-1204 from the excavations at Athens (1931-49) and Corinth (1896-1929). Certain types are provisionally re-attributed to Alexius II.

---

[59] For this, and Manuel's folles generally, see Metcalf, *NC* 1964.

The specimens of Manuel's Types 2, 4, and 5, which are normally types struck on the highest weight-standard, are, once again, almost certainly issues which have strayed from the metropolitan region or from Asia Minor; the ratio between Athens and Corinth is quite different from the other ratios that can be calculated from the Table. The currency of central Greece was dominated by Type 7, the (early) "Monogram" type, and Type 6, the "St. George" type. A fuller understanding of *BMC* Type 3 is necessary before the monetary history of the early part of Manuel's reign can be written. It is found in large and small varieties; the former, which was important in the Stara Zagora deposit, and which may have made up the Sparta hoard of 1926, was perhaps struck at the beginning of Manuel's reign, although its issue in that case must have been localized, for it was certainly not to be found in central Greece. The small variety of Type 3, which occurred in the Kastri and Marathon hoards, may have been struck a good deal later in Manuel's reign.

The most recent coins in the Corinth hoard of November 1937 were 12 of John's standard issue of folles and 7 of Manuel's "Monogram" type. As Manuel's folles are many times more numerous than those of John in other deposits as well as in the site-finds, the hoard will belong not merely to the former part of Manuel's reign, but to a date very early in it. It was concealed or lost, very probably, in 1147, on the occasion of the Norman raid on Corinth. If that conjectured date of deposit is correct, a good deal of stylistic variation has to be accommodated into the series of "Monogram" folles issued in the first four years of Manuel's reign.

Another, larger hoard found at Corinth in 1937, in February, was made up predominantly of "Monogram" folles, and, in contrast with the November hoard, they were almost all of the variety struck on the small, roughly-clipped flans which are usual in the site-finds both at Corinth and Athens. The year 1147 cannot at present be ruled out as the date of deposit, especially as Corinth suffered so heavily at the time; but the comparison suggests, in any case, that if the large hoard is typical of the Corinthian currency, the hoard of November 1937 is more likely to have been brought to Corinth shortly before it was concealed, perhaps by someone who had fled in the face of the Normans, and who had come from a district where the old folles had not been called in— once again, a district with a less efficiently regulated currency than Corinth. The rather high proportion of Rex Regnantium folles of Class

B in the hoard is paralleled in the 1949 find from Sparta. Classes G and J are much over-represented in comparison with what one might have expected from the site-finds, while Classes H and I are virtually absent. These features, too, make it seem very unlikely that the November 1937 hoard was withdrawn from the local currency.

A hoard found at Sparta in 1924 or 1925 consisted of 65 folles ranging in date from Leo VI to Manuel I. It is another candidate for association with the Norman raid; unfortunately details of the coins are not available.

Two further hoards from Corinth, consisting mainly or wholly of Manuel's folles, include a larger number of varieties, and perhaps belong later in his reign. In May, 1932, a deposit of 27 coins was found. There were 4 specimens of Type 3; 2 of the large variety of the "Monogram" folles, and 7 of the smaller variety of the same type; and 14 "St. George" folles, all on small, roughly-cut flans. A hoard of 41 coins found in 1960 was very similar in its composition. Beside two earlier coins, there were 12 folles of Type 3, 9 "Monogram" folles, and 18 "St. George" folles. From Kalentzi, in Attica, there is a hoard, found in 1927, which included 1 coin of the large variety of Type 3, 11 of the smaller "Monogram" coins, and 54 of the smaller "St. George" folles. Another little hoard from Attica, dating from 1959, consisted entirely of "St. George" folles. These finds give a consistent picture of the petty currency of central Greece in Manuel's reign.

The evidence of the mules and overstrikes found among the coins from the Athens excavations should be treated with great reserve, as many of them are in the poorest state of preservation, and are certainly not of the same fabric—if indeed they are of the same designs—as the *BMC* types to which they are referred. They show sufficiently clearly that the "St. George" type succeeded the "Monogram" type, and that they are very unlikely to have been struck concurrently (otherwise mules might be expected to have been more plentiful). The critical question is whether *BMC* Type 4 should be regarded as a mule combining the obverse of Type 3 with the reverse of the "Monogram" type; if so, the large variety of Type 3 would seem to be a brief issue made at the very beginning of Manuel's reign, continuing the iconography of John's stamena, *BMC* Type 7. The majority of the coins from Athens classified as *BMC* Type 4 are not remotely like the variety illustrated by Wroth, so that the statistics of the site-finds are hardly an argument against

Type 4 being a mule. *BMC* Type 5, showing the Mother of God *orans*, is some kind of special issue, if the evidence from Athens is to be accepted.

From the rest of the Balkans, including Constantinople, there is, with the exception of the Stara Zagora deposit, virtually no evidence for the use of folles. A "St. George" follis of the large variety was found in the excavations at Olynthus, in front of the Byzantine church. [60]

Relations between the Byzantine Empire and Venice worsened in the late 1160's, until, on 12 March 1171, all the Venetians who were then in the Empire were arrested, and all their goods were confiscated. Some idea of the amount of Venetian capital involved in the "Romanian" trade may be gathered from the surviving accounts of the reparations that were made when an understanding between the two states had been restored. Andronicus, for example, sent 100 pounds of *perperi* to Venice, and partial repayments were made to merchants who applied for them, commonly at a rate specified as "per unumquemque perperum medius caratus et medius venetialis". Isaac II similarly sent to Venice 250 pounds of gold perperi. The stock of the average merchant, according to his own claims for repayment, was about 60 *perperi*. [61]

Virtually all the find-evidence confirms the view that the currency of the Balkans in the time of Manuel was made up of a small number of substantive types. All the more significance, therefore, attaches to the Sirichino find of February 1935, from Macedonia. Out of 192 bronze coins, 190 were stamena of Manuel, in good style, of a very rare type showing Christ seated on a high-backed throne on the obverse, and on the reverse the Mother of God, with her hand raised in blessing, standing beside the emperor, who wears a chlamys. Two coins were of Andronicus, of his usual type. [62] To judge from its age-structure, the hoard must have been concealed in the reign of Andronicus; it is, probably, to be

---

[60] D. M. Robinson, *op. cit.*

[61] Ostrogorsky, *Byzantine State*, pp. 345f.; A. Morozzo and A. Lombardo, *Documenti del Commercio Veneziane nei Secoli XI-XIII* (Regesta Chartarum Italiae, vol. XXVIII), 1940, nos. 360, 361, 369, 378, 380, *et alia*.

[62] M. Kokić, "Jedna Ostava Vizantiskog Novca iz XII Veka". *Glasnik Skopskog Naučnog Društva* xiv (1935), 223, where one coin of each type is illustrated; Aleksova, "Naodi". Is the Nevestino hoard of 1958, from the Kyustendil region, another provenance for this rare type?—Gerasimov, "Monetni Sŭkrovishta, 1958-59". *BMC* Type 3 in electrum, or pale electrum, is somewhat similar.

associated with the events following the invasion of the Empire by the
Hungarians and Serbians in alliance in 1183, when Belgrade, Braničevo,
Niš, and Sofia were devastated. Even on this interpretation, the coins
of Manuel in the find must be viewed as a local, and probably a special,
issue from the very end of his reign.

A few other hoards of stamena from the reigns of Andronicus I
(1183 - 85) and Isaac II (1185 - 95) can be dated quite accurately on the
evidence of the coins they contained. They give a useful retrospective
view, from the standpoint of a clearly-established date, of the composition of the currency in Manuel's reign. Hoards which terminate with
coins of Alexius III (1195 - 1203) cannot be dated with the same assurance; some of them may well have been concealed as late as the second
or third decade of the thirteenth century.

The Zlataritsa hoard of 1910, from near Tǔrnovo, contained 470
coins of which 120 were of Manuel's Type 13, 321 of Type 11, and 29 of
Andronicus's Type 3. [63] The much smaller quantity of coins of Andronicus, which is typical of the thirteenth-century hoards as well, is matched in the Enina hoard, from the region of Kazanlŭk, in which there
were 138 coins of Manuel (of Types 11, 12, and 13 /i), 16 of Andronicus,
Type 3, and 15 of Isaac II, Type 4. Here, the proportion of coins of Andronicus against the total for Manuel is 12%. [64] The Hungarian hoard
of Obuda, with 24 coins of Type 13 /i, 388 of Type 11, 57 of Andronicus
Type 3, and 6 of Isaac including a rare variety with the inscription
ICAAKIOC grouped in a column of single letters, [65] was presumably
concealed very early in Isaac's reign; but the comparable proportion
is still only 14%. The Obuda hoard appears to have a rather compact
a ge-structure, but the complex picture of the proportions of different
types in Greece, discussed below, is a warning against forming hypotheses on a very limited amount of evidence.

Most out of a score of hoards of bronze coins, incompletely recorded but apparently belonging to the 1180's, are from Bulgaria, and
may have been concealed or lost in circumstances connected with the

[63] Filov, "Novootkriti Starini", *IBAD* i (1910); but cf. B. Filov in *Jahrbuch des deutschen archäologischen Instituts* xxvii (1912), 576, reporting only 5 coins of Andronicus, and a total of 446.

[64] Gerasimov, "Kolektivni Nakhodki, 1951-54".

[65] A. Kerényi, "Egy XII. Századi Obudai Bizánci Pénzlelet", *Budapest Régiségei. A Budapesti Történeti Múzeum Évkönyve* xvi (1950), 541-47.

revolt of Peter and Asen in 1185, or the expeditions of Isaac II into Bulgaria in 1186 and 1187. [66] Whatever the exact occasion of deposit of the various hoards, they show that stamena were circulating widely in Bulgaria at that time.

Hoards of gold or electrum from the same period and region include a great treasure from Zgerli, near Pazardzhik, which was rumoured to have contained as much as 25 kilogrammes of gold coins, and which certainly included some silver dishes. It was associated by Degrand [67] with the flight of the Greek army from that of the Crusaders in 1189. Most of the hoard was melted down without having been studied. Tachella reported that he saw about four hundred gold coins, out of which there were 55 of Alexius I, 65 of John II, 62 of Manuel I, 11 of Andronicus, and 47 of Isaac II. [68] For the monetary historian, the hoard's interest lies in the high proportion of coins of John II and, particularly, Alexius I. The weighting with old coins is confirmed as a regular feature by the Khadzhidimovo hoard of 1956 and the Gornoslav hoard of 1961. The former contained 8 coins of Alexius I, BMC Type 1, 4 of John II, Types 1 and 2, 6 of Manuel, Type 1, and 2 of Isaac, Types 1 and 2. [69] Striking confirmation of the proportions of the types in

[66] Ostrogorsky, *Byzantine State*, pp. 358-60. There are the following hoards: Dolnya Boaz, 1910 (D. Tsonchev, in *Godishnik na Narodniya Arkheologicheski Muzei Plovdiv*, i [1948], 129); Momin-Brod, 1914 (Mushmov, "Kolektivni Nakhodki, 1891-1914); Toprak/Khisar, 1920 (Mushmov, "Kolektivni Nakhodki, 1919-20"); Dŭbovo, 1924, and Eremia, 1924, (Mushmov, "Kolektivni Nakhodki, 1924"); Bagarentsi, 1926 (Mushmov, "Kolektivni Nakhodki, 1925-26"); Batkun, 1937, Belitsa, 1938, Samokov, 1938, and Voivodo, 1938 (Gerasimov, "Kolektivni Nakhodki, 1937 - 38"); Tŭrgovishte, 1939 (Gerasimov, "Kolektivni Nakhodki, 1939"); Tri Boditsi 1940 (Gerasimov, "Kolektivni Nakhodki, 1940"); Okhrid, 1948-49 (Aleksova, "Nao, di"); Brestovo, 1953 (Gerasimov, "Kolektivni Nakhodki, 1951-54"); Zlata, before-1955 (Marić, "Ostave"); Veselinovo 1956/57 (Gerasimov, "Kolektivni Nakhodki, 1956 - 57"); Ovchartsi, 1958 (Gerasimov, "Monetni Sŭkrovishta, 1958-59"); General Nikolaevo, 1960, Petrich, 1960, and Dolna Kabda, 1961 (Gerasimov, Monetni Sŭkrovishta, (1960-61"); Iskra, 1938 (D. Tsonchev, "Kolektivni Nakhodki na Moneti", *Godishnik na Narodniya Arkheologicheski Muzei. Plovdiv* iv [1960], 206-14).

[67] See *Comptes-rendus de l'Académie des Inscriptions et Belles Lettres*, 1903, 390ff. Only an extremely detailed study of the coins of Isaac in this and other Balkan hoards could remove this suggestion from the level of conjecture to that of dating on internal evidence, although the provenance is, of course, in its favour.

[68] D - E. Tachella, in *RN* 1903, 380ff.; Mosser, *Byzantine Coin Hoards*, under Izgherli.

[69] Gerasimov, "Kolektivni Nakhodki, 1956 - 57". This hoard helps to confirm the correct division of coins between John II and John III. Cf. Metcalf, "John Vatatzes".

the Zgerli treasure is given by the recent Gornoslav (Palihor) hoard, where the 786 gold coins were divided as follows: Alexius I, Type 1, 239; John II, Type 1 (!), 274; Manuel I, Type 1, 264; Andronicus, Type 2 (!), 9. It and the Novo Selo hoard may well have been concealed during the troubled years 1185-87, or on the occasion of the Crusade of 1189; the provenances would fit with either theory. The age-structure of the Gornoslav hoard favours the date 1185.[70] The Kadzhidimovo hoard, from near Gotse Delchev, was incompletely recovered, but may well be connected with the events of 1186-87. The figures from the four hoards should probably be interpreted as further evidence of the serious decline in the quantities of gold coinage issued after the time of Alexius I. [71]

Incompletely recorded hoards of the same kind have come from Aleksandrovo, in the Osŭm valley, [72] and from other Bulgarian findspots. The hoard of 1926 from Banya, on the north-south route near Karlovo, was not fully recovered, but was thought to have contained about 40 gold coins of Manuel I, Andronicus I, and Isaac II, together with some 300 bronze coins of the same period. [73] Electrum of the same emperors was found at Zlataritsa (again) in 1923, in a hoard of about four hundred coins,[74] and of Manuel and Andronicus at Dolnya Boaz in the same year. [75] Also in the same year, at Granitsa, near Kyustendil, three "silver" coins of Manuel and Isaac are said to have been found along with over a thousand others of the same period. [76] Altogether, there is a remarkable amount of hoard-evidence from Bulgaria from the 1180's. Among so many finds, some, it is reasonable to assume, must have been concealed in haste; the absence of folles is therefore probably good evidence that they were little used in the region.

---

[70] Gerasimov "Monetni Sŭkrovishta, 1960-61; Kh. Djambov, "A New Gold Treasure", *Bulgaria Today*, x (1961), no. 10, pp. 36-37 (illustrating a coin of John II, Type 3, and 2 of Manuel, Type 1).

[71] See p. 62 above.

[72] The types were Alexius I, BMC Type 1; John II, Types 2 and 3; Manuel, Type 1 Andronicus; and Isaac, Type 1. Gerasimov, "Kolektivni Nakhodki, 1937-38".

[73] The accounts seem to be confused; see Mushmov, "Kolektivni Nakhodki, 1925 - 26" and the same, "1927-28".

[74] Mushmov, "Kolektivni Nakhodki, 1923".

[75] D. Tsonchev, *op. cit.*, and, for the Kaliva hoard, of scyphate gold of unspecified types, *ibid.*, p. 141.

[76] Mushmov, "Kolektivni Nakhodki, 1923".

The three north Serbian hoards of Osanica, Zlata, and Grabovac [77] are a *locus classicus* for the circulation of stamena in the Balkan hinterlands at the end of the twelfth century. Discovered at no great distance from each other, the three hoards each contained much the same *BMC* types, and yet the fabric of the coins was quite different from one hoard to another, although very consistent within each. The coins from Zlata were all of large module and good workmanship, and weighed 4 grammes or more. Those from Grabovac were somewhat smaller and in less elegant style, while the coins in the important Osanica hoard were of very poor workmanship, small size, and low weight. These hoards cannot all have been withdrawn from the local currency (if there can be said to have been one), for one cannot imagine so much variety, and such extremely sharp localization, in north Serbia. One can only conclude that merchants or travellers from further south in the Empire had carried the sums of money intact to their region of concealment. It is interesting to see that in those centres—wherever they may have been—the issues of probably at least two or three decades had remained so effectively localized. One would like to be able to take into account many other of the hoards that have been mentioned, found in the northern parts of the peninsula, but no systematic evidence about the style or fabric of the coins is yet available.

The most plentiful type in the Zlata hoard was Manuel's Type 11, making up something like half the total. The low proportion of coins of Isaac to those of Andronicus suggests a date of deposit early in Isaac's reign. The age-structure of the hoard appears, in fact, to be quite similar to that of the Obuda hoard, except for the presence of Manuel's Type 12. [78] Might the date of deposit have been later than the age-structure indicates, if new issues ceased to be carried into Bulgaria for three or four years from 1185 onwards?—The stylistic coherence of the hoard speaks against such a theory, but it ought perhaps not to be dismissed.

The Grabovac hoard was discovered during the Second World War, and was dispersed: the Belgrade museum was able to acquire 102 coins from it. The types present in large proportions were the usual ones, namely Manuel, Types 11, and 13/i, Isaac, Type 4, and Alexius III, Type

---

[77] Marić, "Ostave". Through the kindness of the late Dr Marić, I was able to examine these hoards briefly and to make short notes on their contents. The accounts that follow are only provisional.

[78] And, apparently, a specimen of John II, *BMC* Type 7.

4. In smaller numbers there were specimens of Manuel's Type 12, and Andronicus, Type 3. All the coins were of reasonably good fabric and weight; traces of silvering can still be seen on some specimens.

The Osanica find, of over 2,000 coins, was concealed beneath a stone, where the coins had perhaps lain wrapped in a piece of cloth. The Belgrade museum has acquired 682 coins from it, while about 1500 have gone to the local museum of Petrovac, in the Mlava valley. Virtually all the coins in the Belgrade parcel are of small module (20 to 25 mm. and rarely exceeding 28 mm.) and low weight (e.g. 1½ grammes) and are poorly struck. On only a few can any legend be made out. The most plentiful types were Manuel, Type 11, Alexius III, Type 4, and Isaac, Type 4, which together made up the great bulk of the hoard; there were also a few specimens of Manuel's Type 13/ii and of Andronicus's usual type, and of Theodore of Nicaea. There was a significant proportion of coins showing a bust of the emperor, of the general style and fabric of John II, Type 6B, and one or two of Ratto 2143. The hoard is, in short, obviously representative of the currency of some part of Greece or Macedonia in the early decades of the thirteenth century; but it differs from the Levkokhori hoard, in which the small variety of Type 13/ii was prominent. [79] One very scarce type, in which the emperor holds an *akakia* in his *right* hand, [80] was represented.

The more intriguing problem is to find two separate localities from which the Zlata and Grabovac hoards might have originated: if one is from the metropolitan area, where shall we place the other?

The many incompletely recorded hoards from the north Balkans in which the latest coins noted were those of Alexius III reveal the continuing importance of Bulgaria in the circulation-area of the stamena after national independence had been secured, with perhaps a slight shift in the main area of hoarding eastwards into the Black Sea hinterlands. [81] Only a few discoveries, such as those from Tuzla and Tulcea,

[79] See p. 119 below.
[80] Bellinger, "Three Hoards", Manuel, Type 6.
[81] There are the following hoards containing coins of earlier emperors as well as of Alexius III: Vŭrbitsa 1924 (Mushmov, "Kolektivni Nakhodki, 1924"); Lukovit 1933, Narechenskiti Bani, 1933/34, Osikovo, 1934 (Gerasimov, "Kolektivni Nakhodki, 1933-34"); Gradevo, 1936 (Gerasimov, "Kolektivni Nakhodki, 1934-36"); the large Osikovo hoard of 1938 (Gerasimov, "Kolektivni Nakhodki, 1937-38"); the even larger Gorsko Kosovo hoard of 1948, and the Cherkovo hoard of the same year, which apparently included coins of John II (Gerasimov, "Kolektivni Nakhodki,

have been published in detail. The Tulcea hoard included 2 specimens of Manuel's Type 13/i, 3 of Type 11, 6 of Isaac's Type 4, and 13 of Alexius's Type 4. In the Tuzla hoard there was only one coin of Andronicus in a parcel of 652, and another one in a parcel of 14 coins thought to be from the same hoard; Type 13/i was represented in the small parcel, but was absent in the larger, where there were 36 coins of Type 13/ii, of which 20 were of the small variety that is perhaps Thessalonican. [82] Type 13/ii replaces 13/i also in the Kunino hoard of 1954, a parcel from which included only one specimen of Type 13/i against 85 of the other variety; there were 29 coins of Manuel's Type 11, 13 of Andronicus, Type 3, 78 of Isaac, Type 4, and 181 of Alexius III, Type 4. [83] The high proportion of coins of Alexius III in the hoards doubtless reflects their proportions in the currency, but whether this was because the coins of Manuel were falling out of use or because such large numbers of stamena were struck in the reign of Alexius remains to be determined.

When we turn to examine the scyphate bronze coinage of Greece, we find that the coins of Andronicus played an even smaller part in the currency. There are, apparently, none in the poor styles and small fa-

1946-48"); the Stara Zagora and Mŭglish hoards of 1941 (possibly parcels from the same discovery?) both including coins of John II (Gerasimov, "Kolektivni Nakhodki, 1941-45"); Lyaskovo, 1949, including coins of John and of "Alexius I with Constantine" - probably Sabatier's mistaken attribution for the standard coins of A- lexius III (Gerasimov, "Kolektivni Nakhodki, 1949-50", and D. Tsonchev, in Godishnik na Narodniya Arkheologicheski Muzei Plovdiv, ii [1950], 274); Skopje, 1950, and Lešok, 1953 (Aleksova, "Naodi"); Chomatovski, 1953, and Chuprene, 1953 (Gerasimov, "Kolektivni Nakhodki, 1951-54"); the important Ivanovo hoard of 1955 (Gerasimov, "Kolektivni Nakhodki, 1955"); Draganovo, 1957 (Gerasimov, "Kolektivni Nakhodki, 1956-57"); Kazanlŭk, 1958, and Nevestino, 1958 (Gerasimov, "Monetni Sŭkrovishta, 1958-59"); Korten, 1960, Mŭglish, 1960 Khubavene, 1960. Golyamo Chochoveni, 1961, Kameno Pole, 1961, and Smochan, 1961 (Gerasimov, "Monenti Sŭkrovishta, 1960-61"); Plovdiv, 1950 (D. Tsonchev, "Kolektivni Na- khodki na Moneti", Godishnik na Narodniya Arkheologicheski Muzei, Plovdiv iv [1960], 206-14). Hoards apparently including coins of Alexius III only: Krini, 1934 (Gerasimov, "Kolektivni Nakhodki, 1934-36"); Kolarovgrad, 1937 (Gerasimov, "Kolektivni Nakhodki, 1937-38"); Tseneno, 1939 (Gerasimov, "Kolektivni Nakhodki, 1939"); Vetren, 1941, and Gara Levski, 1944 (Gerasimov, "Kolektivni Nakhodki, 1941-45"); Gorno Panicherevo, 1948 (Gerasimov, "Kolektivni Nakhodki, 1946-48"); Plovdiv, 1955 (Tsonchev, op. cit., 1960, 206-14).

[82] I. Băncilă, "Note asupra unor Tezaure de Monede Bizantine", SCN i (1957), 425-38; Ibid., "In Legătură cu Tezaurul de la Tuzla", SCN ii (1958), 417-18.

[83] Gerasimov, "Kolektivni Nakhodki, 1951-54", mentioning also two coins of the type of Wroth, BMC (Byz.) plate lxi, 1 (?), and describing the coins of Ale- xius III as lxiii, 1.

bric which are characteristic of Manuel's Greek issues; and there are virtually none (of whatever style) in the hoards. Andronicus, evidently, as part of the reforms he instituted, turned his attention to the currency, and put a stop to the production of stamena in local mints in Greece. To judge from the folles of his reign, he also ordered an improvement in the quality of workmanship of the petty coinage. He cut down the variety of types; the folles of *BMC* Types 2 and 3 are merely variants of each other, the design of the smaller Type 3 being a truncated version of that used for Type 2. Greek finds are normally of Type 3, and are still of low weight (ca. 1.9 gm.).

Isaac seems to have partially reversed the policies of Andronicus, for there are large quantities of stamena which are almost certainly the product of the Greek mints, even though their workmanship is of a higher standard than that of Manuel's Greek stamena. The coinage of Alexius III continued quite closely the arrangements made under Isaac.

In his reign the issue of folles in Greece dwindled, and, indeed, may have come to an end altogether. There is no hoard-evidence by which coins can be divided with assurance between Alexius II (1180-84) and Alexius III (1195-1203), with the possible exception of the Brauron hoard, discussed below; but the negative evidence, that Alexius II did-not strike stamena, is clear enough. The commonly accepted attributions of the folles—to Alexius III—are little better than conjectural. There are two arguments, both hypothetical but worth considering, for the reattributions tentatively proposed in Table 6. Firstly, there is a pattern in the ratios between different twelfth-century types of folles at Athens and Corinth. Leaving aside "strays" from other parts of the Empire, which are more numerous in the seaport of Corinth, the proportion shifts markedly in the favour of Athens after the middle of the century (probably because of the Norman raid and its consequences). This is not, admittedly, a good argument for transferring *BMC* Alexius III, Type 2 to Alexius II; its significance is as a general framework for an understanding of the Greek currency of folles. Secondly, it seems reasonable to attribute the coins of Type 2, which are "St. George" folles, to Alexius II rather than envisage the re-introduction of the design after the "St. Michael" folles of Isaac II had been in use for a decade. This theory has the advantage of simplifying the interpretation of certain mules among Isaac's coins,[84] and of presenting a pict-

---

[84] See Metcalf, (work in progress).

ure of continuity in the monetary development of the latter part of the century.

Although stamena were being carried to and fro over long distances in the north Balkans in the latter part of the twelfth century, in Greece there seem to have been regions where the currency was fairly stagnant. Certainly, hoards from the early thirteenth century reveal variations in the composition of the currency on quite a local scale in Greece. Type 6B, for example, was apparently still a significant element in the currency in the islands;[85] and the small variety of Type 13/ii had, to judge from the Levkokhori and related hoards, been supplemented by later issues only to a limited extent in some places.[86] It may have been mainly in Thessaly and the Peloponnesus that monetary affairs reflected the same kind of commercial penetration as in Bulgaria.[87]

One of the most precious Greek hoards of scyphate bronze is the tiny Corinth find of 1960. It came from the American excavations, so that its provenance and complete contents are authenticated beyond possible doubt, which is more than can usually be said. Beside a Rex Regnantium follis of Class J, there were 22 stamena, of which 2 were of the smaller variety of John, Type 6B, 2 of Ratto 2143, 14 of Manuel Type 13/ii, again of the smaller variety, 1 of Isaac, Type 4, of a small variety (probably Group H), 1 of Theodore, and 2 of a previously unpublished type.[88] The question is whether the hoard reflects the Corinthian currency or, as seems much more likely, is a traveller's hoard, brought from somewhere in northern Greece. It might be from a city that was supplied with coin, during the twelfth century, by the Thessalonican mint, but not necessarily from Thessaloniki itself.

---

[85] For the Thira and Amorgos hoards, and for a map illustrating the regional variations in Greece and the islands, see Metcalf, "Scyphate Bronze Coinage in Greece", 45, 47.

[86] For the Levkokhori hoard, ibid., 48 and 60-62.

[87] For the (?) Thessaly hoard of "about two years before the summer of 1959" and for the Arcadia hoard of "the spring of 1958", ibid., 44, and A. R. Bellinger and D. M. Metcalf, "A Hoard of Byzantine Scyphate Bronze Coins from Arcadia", NC 6. xix (1959), 155-164. It has occurred to. me that these two might in fact be parcels from the same hoard: note the near-duplication of the otherwise very scarce variety Thessaly no. 51 and Arcadia no. 204. I should be reluctant to doubt the accuracy of the report that the "1957" coins came from somewhere around Lamia or Larisa.

[88] H. S. Robinson, "Excavations at Corinth, 1960", Hesperia xxxi (1962), 95-133, section "The Coins", by R. Stroud, 130-33.

Isaac's stamena of *BMC* Type 4, the only issue that has yet been very carefully studied, fall into a number of stylistic groups, distinguished by secret-marks such as the number of dots at the emperor's shoulders, and by the arrangement of the reverse inscription, which may read

ICA		I		IC	
AKI		CAA		AA	
OC	or	KI	or	KI	and so on. Some
		OC		OC	

of the groups are almost certainly the work of Greek mints. The system of lower weight-standards in the provinces persists, the stylistic variety which is the most obvious candidate for association with central Greece (Group F) being on a standard of 96 to the pound, while a Macedonian variety (Group H) is certainly on a standard of 120 to the pound. The varieties from the metropolitan area are nominally at 72 to the pound, but many of them are on flans of lighter weight, presumably Manuel's coins restruck, at various figures around 100 to the pound. [89] The metrology of Isaac's coins represents a relaxation from the high standards which Andronicus had sought to impose, but there is nevertheless an improvement over the coins of Manuel, which should probably be interpreted as an attempt to narrow the gap in the system of weight-standards, in view of the more widespread circulation of the provincial coinages.

The stamena of Alexius III, *BMC* Type 4 show much the same stylistic range as those of Isaac. Since they are the latest issue in so many Balkan hoards, the localization of the varieties is of particular interest, the original outlines having had the shortest time in which to become blurred by the intermingling of the coins in circulation. There are half-a-dozen formal varieties that are plentiful and a few others that are scarce or very scarce. Some of the plentiful varieties may, on the basis of further study, have to be amalgamated as the work of single mints. The first requirement, however, is that hoard-reports should distinguish the following groups:

A. Large coins in very fine style with roughly 7 or 8 dots at the emperor's shoulders and a star-pattern on the loros.

B. Distinctive, well-made coins with 5 large dots at the shoulders and a star-pattern, devolving into 9 dots, on the loros.

C. 3 dots at the shoulders, sometimes with two asterisks between the standing figures.

---

[89] For Isaac's stamena, see Metcalf, (work in progress).

D. Roughly 7 or 8 dots at the shoulders; star-pattern or quincunx (: · :) on the loros. Linear cross on the globus, with two loros ends falling below it.

E. Roughly 7 or 8 dots at the shoulders; quincunx. Dotted cross on globus, with one loros-end below it.

F. Similar to D or E; quincunx sometimes with central dot ringed.

G. Quincunx on saint's loros as well as emperor's. (Scarce.)

H. Quincunx with diamond-pattern. (Scarce.)

There is as yet very little evidence of localization. Group A is no doubt metropolitan. Group B seems to be north Balkan rather than Greek. Group C probably belongs somewhere in the Aegean coastlands. Groups D and E are plentiful in both Greece and Bulgaria.

The decline in the issue of folles at the end of the century should not be taken to imply that they were falling out of use in central Greece. This was far from being the case: it was merely that the copious issues of Manuel continued in use and presumably met the region's needs adequately without further supplementation. The proportions of coins of Manuel, Andronicus, Isaac, and Alexius can therefore not be used as the basis of an argument for economic decline, especially since the chances of a petty coin's being lost are *inter alia* directly proportional to the length of time it remained in circulation.

A large hoard of folles was discovered at Kastri in 1952, among the stones of a wall, where it may have been concealed in haste. Manuel's "St. George" folles predominated; the low proportion of Isaac's coins to those of Andronicus, as compared with the same proportion in the site-finds, suggests a date of deposit in Isaac's reign. Two broken halves of the folles of John II, Type 3, and a similar broken half of the "Holy Cross" issue of Nicephorus III, had probably been broken deliberately, for use as coins of smaller value. The Arcadian hoard of Kasarelli, 1927 may have been concealed a decade or two later. One "Arabic" coin in it is matched by two Sicilian pieces (post-dating the raid of 1146-47) in the Kastri hoard.

The Brauron hoard of 1956, from the coast of Attica, consisted of a broken scyphate coin, of the small variety of Manuel's Type 13 /ii, and 205 folles, including broken halves of John, Type 3 and of Manuel, Types 7 and 8, originally of good fabric and size. Apart from the halves, there were 25 coins of the moderately good fabric and the size and weight commonly found in central Greece, and 177 coins of exceptionally poor, thin fabric and indifferent manufacture. They were mostly roughly octagonal, and weighed only half a gramme or a little over.All those that could be identified were "Monogram" folles; except that there were two unpublished types in the same poor fabric. The hoard's composition is so different from that of all other finds from Attica that it must certainly be a sum of money withdrawn from the currency of another region, although perhaps with a few coins from central Greece added after it had been carried there. Isaac's Type 2, and Manuel's Type 4 (a mule?), which were among the 25 moderately good coins, are both unusual types at Athens and Corinth. There were half-a-dozen "Monogram" folles of the Brauron variety among 51 in the Kastri hoard; this, too, suggests that it was concealed in haste. These thin, poorly-made pieces should very possibly be attributed to Thessaloniki, and provide one more instance of the issue there of a petty coinage smaller and lighter than the currency of either the metropolitan region or central Greece. They should be seen as a parallel issue to the small variety of Type 13/ii. The owner of the Brauron hoard may have left Thessaloniki in circumstances in some way connected with the Norman sack of the city in the last days of Andronicus; the tentative attribution of the two unpublished types of folles to the Thessalonican mint under Alexius II would fit in with such a theory. In general, the coins are a reminder of how ignorant it is possible to remain about the petty currency of cities from which no excavation-material is available.

In surveying the currency of the years up to 1204, it only remains to mention an estimate of the quantities in which stamena were struck. A study of die-linkage among Isaac's Type 4 suggests a total of, very roughly, 20 to 30 million coins. If the proportion of coins of Isaac in typical hoards of scyphate bronze is a reflection of the quantities in which they were issued relative to those of Manuel, Andronicus, and Alexius III—and there is no reason to doubt that this is broadly true—we may guess that very roughly a hundred million stamena were in circulation at the end of the twelfth century. There appear to have been, that is to say, two to five times as many such coins as there were folles of Theophilus or Basil; yet they are hundreds of times more plentiful today. It is striking that there should be such a vast difference in the survival rates, far beyond any possible margin of error in the calculations from which the conclusion is drawn. One main reason for the survival of so many kilogrammes of stamena is, no doubt, that they were hidden in the soil in the uncertain days after the capture of Constantinople, and, when they had in effect been demonetized, were allowed to lie there.

When Byzantine rule in the Balkans was interrupted in 1204, the monetary affairs of the region fell into confusion. The political vacuum was filled by a number of successor-states, some of them, such as that governed by Manuel Maurozomes in the Maeander valley, destined to be absorbed after only a few years in larger groupings. Trebizond, Nicaea, and Thessaloniki were the centres for those groupings, and for a struggle for hegemony. For several decades the balance of power was far from stable, until the Bulgarian, Serbian, and Frankish states made good their claims to independent rule in the new situation, and the Nicaean emperors regained the metropolis and its hinterland. The Byzantine coinage-province was replaced by a number of others, which continued the tradition of a scyphate coinage in gold and bronze. They did not, however, provide the peninsula with a plentiful new currency. Hoards of scyphate bronze may include one or two coins of Theodore of Nicaea, for example, among several hundred pieces which are otherwise typical of the currency in the time of Alexius III. The proportion of thirteenth-century coins—which, again, so far as one can see must accurately reflect their proportions in the currency—is so small that it is very possible that a number of the incompletely-recorded hoards that have been mentioned above in fact belong to the years after 1204. The Corinth find of 1960 certainly does: likewise the Osanica hoard. One should hesitate before interpreting the sudden and dramatic decline in the issue of petty coinage as evidence of economic collapse; as was certainly true of the late twelfth-century folles in central Greece, the existing stock of coin may have been found quite adequate for several decades. The volume of hoard-evidence, which is apparently meagre in comparison with that from the twelfth century, especially in Bulgaria, is a somewhat stronger argument.

In Constantinople itself, the Latin Emperors called in the scyphate bronze which they found still circulating there, clipped the flans to a size more like that of a west European denier, re-silvered them and put them back into use. It was this, very probably, which provoked the clause in a treaty between Theodore I and the doge Giacomo Tiepolo whereby both authorities agreed not to copy the other's coinage. A number of hoards from Istanbul, consisting exclusively or predominantly of these clipped coins, offer a precious glimpse into the composition of the scyphate bronze currency in Constantinople, as regards the proportions from different mints and so on, as it was on the eve of the city's capture. [90]

In the fourth and fifth decades of the thirteenth century, the Thessalonican currency was circulating into western Bulgaria, and the gold, and to some extent the bronze, of the Empire of Nicaea was in use in eastern Bulgaria and in Greece. The bronze coinage of the despotate of Epirus was in use, but probably in the smallest quantities, around the shores of the Gulf of Patras and further to the north. The scyphate bronze issues of Bulgaria and Serbia, which are very rare today, have scarcely ever been found in association with other issues, and were probably of no more than minor importance even in those areas where they were struck. [91]

The currency of central and southern Greece in the first half of the thirteenth century is discussed in a later chapter. [92]

From the north-eastern parts of the peninsula, there are half-a-dozen hoards of bronze, and several of gold. Coins of Thessaloniki (presumably: 21 specimens are described as Manuel I, *BMC* Type 6, but in bronze) occurred in a hoard of 557 coins otherwise of the twelfth century found at Kyustendil in 1960. In the Koinare hoard of 1937, issues of Manuel (1230-40) were associated with those of Alexius III. [93] Further south, at Levski, in the same year, $2\frac{1}{2}$ kilogrammes of scyphate bronze coins were discovered, in a hoard which is of particular interest because of the one coin of Ivan Asen II which it included. [94] At Dorkovo, which lies in a small enclosed plain a little to the south of the Maritsa valley, 3 kilogrammes of bronze coins were found in 1940. They were divided between Andronicus I, Alexius III, and Manuel of Thessaloniki. [95] This and the later Kamenitsa find may perhaps have been associated with the routeway from Thessaloniki which reached the Ma-

---

[90] For a fuller presentation of the evidence, which arises from the stylistic classification of Isaac's stamena, see Metcalf, (work in progress). A group of coins of this kind is illustrated in Bellinger, "Three Hoards". Ratto 2136 is possibly such a coin.

[91] For the Serbian coins, see Saria, "Altserbische Münzwesen", 22f., and Marić, *Studije*, pp. 64f. For the Bulgarian coins, see Mushmov, *Monetite* and Gerasimov, "Bŭlgarski Moneti".

[92] See below.

[93] Gerasimov, "Kolektivni Nakhodki, 1937-38".

[94] *Ibid.*

[95] Gerasimov, "Kolektivni Nakhodki, 1940".

ritsa valley at Plovdiv. To the south again, there are two hoards from
a routeway through the Rhodope from which there is otherwise virtually no evidence of monetary circulation. At Mogilitsa, in 1934, a discovery was reported from a copper-mine, consisting of bronze coins of
Theodore, Manuel, and John (ca. 1238-1244) of Thessaloniki and, uncertainly, Theodore of Nicaea (1254-58).[96] Two years later, at Ustovo, near
by, some hundreds of stamena were found; among those that were examined were pieces of Theodore and Manuel of Thessaloniki. [97] The
Ustovo hoard was the source of many of the specimens described in
a recent study by Gerasimov of the numismatic history of the Empire
of Thessaloniki. There was one coin of Theodore Lascaris in the A-
senovgrad hoard of 1960, which consisted otherwise of coins of Manuel I, Isaac II, and Alexius III. [98]

The scyphate bronze of the years after 1204 is as difficult a series
of coins as any one could name. They are for the most part of atrocious-
ly poor workmanship, and, as a result, have not received adequate publication on the occasions when they have turned up in hoards. There is
a profusion of designs, and great divergence of styles and module: the
essentially simple system of the twelfth century has given way to a rank
disorder. Even on this premise, one's ingenuity is taxed to arrange the
known specimens into order and to propose any sort of sensible synopsis
of attributions for the four or five decades to which most or all of the
types must belong. Research has not yet been carried much beyond the
level of arguments from iconography. For the monetary historian,
fortunately, the outcome of the work that remains to be done can hardly
affect the general view of the currency in the middle of the thirteenth
century; at most, a revised estimate of the importance of the coinage
of Ivan Asen II may become necessary. The primary importance of the
Mogilitsa and Ustovo finds for monetary history is that they suggest
that trade was increasingly following routes fromThessaloniki northwards
through the Rhodope. The Levkokhori hoard may have had the same
economic background, and may well have been deposited after 1204.
But no subtlety or refinement of analysis can be attempted until many
more finds have been properly published.

[96] Gerasimov, "Kolektivni Nakhodki, 1934 - 36".

[97] Ibid.

[98] Gerasimov, "Solun"; see also V. Laurent, "Bulle et monnaies inédites de
Jean Ducas Comnène, Empereur de Thessalonique", Cronica Numismatica şi Arheologica xvii (1943); T. Bertelè, "Monete di Giovanni Comneno Duca, Imperatore
di Salonico", Numismatica xvi (1950),61-79 ; and Bertelè, L'Imperatore Alato.

Two finds from Epirus itself and one from Corinth are, with the possible exception of a single coin from among 91 in the Amorgos hoard, the only Balkan provenances for coins attributed to the despotate. A stray find of a coin of Michael I (1204-ca. 1215) has been reported, and there is the important Arta hoard, which was published in detail by Mattingly. [99] More than half the coins in it were Thessalonican, and most of the rest were Epirote. The date of deposit is later than the Bulgarian hoards that have been mentioned; it gives us an isolated glimpse of monetary affairs at the time of the battle of Pelagonia (1259).

Gold was again current in the east Balkans and in Greece from some time in the reign of John III (1222-54), who struck nomismata in large quantities. Since they are hardly ever found in association with earlier gold pieces, it seems that John's coins mark the beginning of a new period of monetary affairs. One of the most interesting deposits, and perhaps one of the earliest, was brought to light at Preslav in 1953, where there were two of these gold coins, in a grave-find, along with 11 bronze coins attributed to Manuel of Thessaloniki, and 1 of Alexius III. Other finds, which await detailed publication, have come from Nesebŭr in 1933, Corinth in 1934 (in a hoard deposited after 1253), Silistra in 1936, Patrai in the 1930's, Pirgovo in 1940, Krestiltsi in 1952, Bansko in 1957, and Kovachevitsa in 1961. The Messini hoard of 1900, the Athens hoard of 1928, and the Seltsi hoard of 1938, published as containing coins of John II, may also in fact have been hoards of John III's issues. [100] Unti the coins in these finds have been illustrated, however, the only hoards that can profitably be studied are those of Corinth, 1925, [101] Drama, 1949 and Thessaly, 1949 (possibly parcels from the same hoard, and in that case more probably from Drama), and Erymantheia, 1955, and the

---

[99] Edwards, "Corinth, 1930-35"; Wroth, *BMC (Byz.)*, III, p. 226; H. Mattingly, "A Find of Thirteenth-Century Coins at Arta in Epirus", *NC* 5. iii (1923), 31 - 46. Note also the Stobi find described below. A good general survey of Epirote numismatics (but without new material for monetary history) will be found in D. M. Nicol, *The Despotate of Epiros*, Oxford, 1957, pp. 196-214.

[100] For Preslav and Krestiltsi, see Gerasimov, "Kolektivni Nakhodki, 1951-54"; for Nesebŭr, Gerasimov, "Kolektivni Nakhodki, 1933-34", and Pirgovo, "Kolektivni Nakhodki, 1940", and information kindly sent by Dr. Gerasimov that the coins were in fact of John III; for Bansko, Gerasimov, "Kolektivni Nakhodki, 1956 - 57"; for Patrai (district), *BCH* lxxx (1956), 228; for Corinth, 1934, Edwards, "Corinth, 1930 - 35"; for Messini (Ithome) and Athens, Mosser, *Byzantine Coins Hoards*; for Seltsi, *BCH* lxii (1938), 447; for Silistra, O. Iliescu, "[Cronica:] Cabinetul Numismatic", *Studii şi Cercetari de Bibliologie* iii (1960), 504-07. The Stoeneşti hoard is mentioned under John II, at p. 93 above.

[101] Bellinger, *Corinth*, 1925.

Ibrahim Pasha parcel in the British Museum. [102] Even from these few finds, it is evident that there is as great a stylistic range among the gold coins of John as there is among, say, the stamena of Manuel I, Type 11, or Isaac II, Type 4; and, in particular, there are coins in good style with three and with five dots at the emperor's shoulders, and others in indifferent style with seven or eight dots. Furthermore, it is certain that the varieties in good style were largely absent from the currency of central Greece: they presumably belong to Nicaea and north-western Asia Minor. One must, therefore, accept that there were provincial mints, but the problem is to locate them. There is the possibility that many of the coins, although they bear John's name, were struck by other rulers—for example, Ivan Asen II—but whether in imitation of a well-liked trade-coin or under some sort of agreement remains to be discovered. Some or all of the specimens on which the pendants of the emperor's crown are represented by a diamond of four dots (and on which the inscription is often blundered or carelessly drawn) may turn out to belong to the north Balkans; and some of those with seven or eight dots at the shoulders and pendants of two or three dots might be from central Greece. The problem is a difficult one, but it should yield to a detailed stylistic analysis, supported by provenances. We are left, then, with the curious conclusion, the implications of which for numismatic history are not easily grasped, that, some decades after 1204, the secret-marks and other arrangements of the Byzantine provincial mint-system were still in use in, presumably, Frankish Greece and in Bulgaria: the influence of the idea of the *imperium* was still very much alive. A correct view of the monetary history of the gold will depend to some extent on the solution of the numismatic problem. The distribution of find-spots suggests trade-routes, leading inland, north-westwards from Nesebŭr and north from Thessaloniki.

At the middle of the thirteenth century, monetary affairs had, however, on a general view, reached a low ebb in the east and south of the peninsula. The scyphate bronze coinages in the Byzantine style issued in the first half of the century had been no more than an interim currency, sustained by the momentum of an economic system which had been irrecoverably disrupted. The real successors to the Byzantine coinage-province were those of the Frankish denier tournois and of the various silver coinages deriving from the Venetian grosso. Byzantine monetary affairs had reflected the hegemony of Constantinople in the Balkans;

---

[102] Metcalf, "John Vatatzes".

when a revival came, the smaller coinage-provinces of the second half of the century were to show more clearly the influence of regional economies. The economic life of Constantinople, under the Restored Empire, sank towards provincial status; so that the formal numismatic continuity, through the coinages of the Nicaean emperors, and the re-introduction of scyphate bronze tend to conceal the fact that the Byzantine monetary system of the fourteenth century was dependent on the economy of only one small area out of a number of similar ones in the Balkans.

CHAPTER VI

MONETARY CIRCULATION IN THE MARCH-LANDS OF THE NORTH-WEST

Two right-bank tributaries of the Danube, the Drava and the Sava, run parallel to each other for more than three hundred miles, enclosing an elongated region which makes up the greater part of three historical provinces. In the west, among the foothills of the Alps, is Slovenia; in the east, at the edge of the Great Hungarian Plain, is Syrmia; in the centre is Slavonia, the largest of the three parts. During the middle ages, the province of Slavonia extended south of the Sava, as far as the watershed referred to in documents as Gvozd. [1] Slovenia also stretched beyond the Sava, and, indeed, its main town of Ljubljana was on a southern tributary of that river. Otherwise, the Drava and Sava conveniently mark off a region which formed the march-lands of the north-west of the Balkan peninsula. Thinly-settled, with many swampy valleys and forested uplands, it was a politically negative zone where Hungarian, German, south Slav, and Adriatic influences met and mingled. The name "krain" (which has roughly the same meaning as the German "Mark" and the English "march") is an indication of the region's political character. It occurs both in Slovenia and in Bosnia's Hrvatska Kraina. Similarly, Slavonia under the Hungarians was in effect a marcher-duchy; and one observes the same kind of military zone in North Serbia, where in the early fourteenth century Stefan Dragutin ruled from the fortress of Belgrade. [2] The region's character is mirrored in the pattern of its monetary affairs in various ways. First, it was, generally speaking, not able to sustain a monetary economy of its own. Instead, it was the meeting-place of the influences of a number of monetary regions: the two valleys were divided among several coinage-provinces in a way they could scarcely have been if the area had been one of close settlement and easy communications. The trend in monetary affairs

---

[1] The mountain range is now called Petrova Gora. It is at 45.16 N., 15.45 E.
[2] The area over which Stefan Dragutin "Sriemski" ruled is not known exactly, but its nuclear area was probably Mačva.

9

was inwards, towards the uplands of the peninsula; thus, the coinage in Slavonia was that of the king of Hungary, while Bosnian and Serbian pieces were rarely to be found. Secondly, more than one kind of money that was used in the lands between the Drava and the Sava seems to be associated rather with trade passing through the area than with the needs of local economic life. Thirdly, important groups of hoards have been associated with military events.

In Slovenia, the first money to be used at all regularly was brought into the area probably towards the end of the twelfth century from the Gurk valley and nearby regions, where the production of the silver-mines was minted at Friesach and St. Veit. In the early thirteenth century the Friesacher were widely imitated in Slovenia: they were struck at a number of mints, and circulated as far as Zagreb as an important element in the currency. In the latter part of the thirteenth and in the first part of the fourteenth centuries, a much larger assemblage of finds allows us to see that the influences of three monetary regions met in Slovenia. The most important coinage was that of Aquileia and the associated mints of Trieste and Gorizia. There were also the issues of Friesach; and those of Graz. The distribution of the finds shows that monetary affairs were fragmented by the terrain. They were concentrated into the few lowland basins among the hills. In the Ljubljana basin, the Aquileian coins were paramount, while in the Krka valley, a larger proportion of Friesacher is found alongside the north Italian currency. In the plains around Celje and in the Ptujskopolje the issues of the mint of Graz are the most common type of coinage in a rather varied currency. The same influences appear only just to have reached Zagreb at that period.

Stray finds of medieval coins of any kind are rare in Slovenia, and also in Slavonia until one comes to coins struck after the middle of the thirteenth century. [3] One or two Aquileian coins have been reported from Slovenia, and a few Friesacher from each province. In Slavonia, the few large hoards of Friesacher which have been discovered belong to the wider group scattered through Hungary, and are probably connected with the trade between Hungary and Germany. There seems to have been little coinage in Slavonia until the introduction of the

---

[3] Mr. A. Jeločnik, of the Narodni Muzej, Ljubljana, tells me that this is his experience. The paucity of early Slavonian finds recorded in the Zagreb accession-registers is good evidence for that region; see p. 131 below.

banovac, a small silver coin struck specially as currency for the banate, at a date not far from 1240. From then onwards, the banovci were predominant in the region. The number of stray finds suggests that by the end of the century the use of coinage was becoming more common in the west; but the eastern half of Slavonia, still sparsely populated and without important trade routes, appears to have remained virtually without coined money. In Syrmia, on the other hand, there was a regular monetary economy as early as the eleventh century in several small towns on the right bank of the Danube, which seem to have been markets for some sort of inter-regional trade with central Hungary. The Hungarian regal issues were probably always dominant in the currency, but Byzantine bronze pieces, and Friesacher, have been found in significant proportions, along with a few banovci. The circulation of the so-called saraceni [4] in Syrmia in the second half of the fourteenth century is an indication that at an earlier date also the region may have been closely linked in its monetary affairs with Hungary north of the Danube.

The hoards and stray finds from Syrmia, Slavonia, and Slovenia have so little in common that the assemblage from each province is best discussed separately. From Syrmia, there is a very large number of stray finds from the years around the turn of the century, recorded by Brunšmid in the accession-registers of the Zagreb collection. Nearly all of them come from the settlements on the right bank of the Danube. There are a dozen small places from which coins have been reported, most of them, no doubt, crossing-points of the Danube, and local markets for the rich lands at the foot of the Fruška Gora. They are strung out all along the river from Sarvaš to Zemun. Many of them are former Roman settlements. In addition, finds are recorded from Vinkovci and Ruma, Mitrovica (the old Sirmium), and from one or two settlements on the banks of the Sava. Syrmia now lies administratively in Serbia, but fifty years ago it was in Croatia. For that reason archaeological discoveries made there went to Zagreb rather than to Belgrade nearly. There are far more medieval coins with Syrmian provenances in the Zagreb collection than there are coins with provenances in the intervening regions of Slavonia. Thus, by a fortunate chance, one can feel sure that money was far more plentiful in Syrmia than in Slavonia.

[4] Coins of Nagy Lajos showing a saracen's head, which are thought to have been struck at Pecs after about 1372. See L. Huszár, *A Budai Pénzverés Története a Középkorban*, Budapest, 1958.

A phenomenal number of coins—some seven hundred for the period up to 1350—is recorded from the village of Novi Banovci. They provide a find-series of very great importance. There is nothing else from the Balkans, published so far, of comparable scope except the Corinth and Athens excavations. Nearly all the coins were sold or presented to the Zagreb museum at various dates between 1893 and 1914 by a small group of men, obviously local coin collectors. The names that occur most frequently are those of F. Manot, a mason, K. Brenner, a headmaster, F. Wenzel, an innkeeper, M. Fakundini, a teacher, K. Tomljenović, a clergyman in Zemun, L. Polutanović, a shopkeeper, W. Geisner, a ploughman, and A. Reit, a parish priest. No explanation has been recorded why there should be more stray finds from this locality than from the rest of Jugoslavia put together. It is known, however, that the Danube here has been eroding its right bank, and that at the end of the last century the remains of the Roman castle were destroyed by the encroachment of the river. Although there is no definite evidence, it seems likely that the river must also, in the decades around 1900, have been destroying the site of the medieval settlement, including, perhaps, the market-place. Coins would have been found on the river's bank, and would have attracted attention. The large numbers of coins found may well have been directly responsible for the interest in coin-collecting among local residents, which it undoubtedly fostered. [5] The presence of a ploughman and a mason among the groups of collectors suggests other ways in which coins may have been found. The several collectors whose names we know may have made a practice of walking along the riverside keeping a look-out for coins, in the same way as Mr Liska did in the fields around Osijek. [6] A spirit of competition may have stimulated their enthusiasm; no doubt they exchanged their finds among themselves, and we know that they sold or presented their duplicates to the museum at Zagreb, where the accession-registers, meticulously recording the provenance and source of each coin, add lustre to Brunšmid's reputation.

Almost all the stray finds from Corinth and Athens are of petty coinage, and many of those which are not are from hoards: the same is

---

[5] J. Brunšmid, "Arheološke Bilješke iz Dalmacije i Panonije", *VHrvat.AD* NS i (1895), 148-86. The chance excavation of a medieval site had the same result at Southampton, in England, in the middle of the nineteenth century. See the *Journal of the British Archaeological Association* v (1850), 162; xvi (1860), 334; xvii (1861), 231; xx (1864), 71f.; and C. R. Smith, *Collectanea Antiqua*, vol. IV, (1855), p. 58.

[6] See p. 161 below.

probably true of the Novi Banovci series. It is commonly supposed that in the middle part of the thirteenth century the coins of Friesach drove the debased Hungarian coinage out of circulation in its own territory,[7] but a comparison with feudal Greece, where petty coins were strikingly absent from the hoards, although plentiful in the site-finds, suggests that the hoards of Friesacher from Hungary may reveal only one element in the currency of that country, and that the official issues may have circulated widely as petty coinage without leaving any trace in the deposits.

Much of the usefulness of a long series of finds is that one can compare the quantities of different types of coins, in order to gain some idea of their relative commonness at the time when they were in circulation. The large numbers of coins from Novi Banovci, and the circumstances of their recording, allow us to suppose that the proportions of the various series reflect the proportions of petty coins, if not of the whole currency, used in the area. Hungarian coins made up over 80% of the total, and Friesacher and Byzantine coins a further 6 to 7% of the medieval coins each. The banovci account for only 3 or 4% of the total, while other series were represented in negligible proportions. One should remember, however, that Serbian and Bosnian groši, and perhaps also Friesacher, would be heavily under-represented because of their large intrinsic value. It is reasonable to assume that the money in use in the rest of Syrmia was of the same kinds; the volume of find-evidence from other sites is not great enough for one to say more than that it does not conflict with the evidence from Novi Banovci. From Sotin, for example, there are 38 Hungarian coins, 2 Slavonian, and 1 Byzantine. From Mitrovica the proportions are rather different. There are 10 Hungarian, 9 Slavonian, 5 Byzantine, 3 Friesacher, and 1 Serbian piece. Seven of the banovci, however, and one Hungarian coin, appear to be from a hoard, and three of the Byzantine coins might be from another. If one accepts the possibility of both these hoards, and "scores" each of them as a single discovery, the figures become 9 Hungarian finds, 3 Byzantine 3 Slavonian, 3 Friesacher, and 1 Serbian. These would match the Novi Banovci proportions somewhat more closely.

In detail, there are certain difficulties in drawing conclusions from the find-series from Novi Banovci. First, there is the same problem as at Mitrovica, namely that one does not know which of the coins were

---

[7] This has nothing to do with Gresham's Law, which states that good coinage will be driven out of circulation by bad *of the same legal value.*

found in parcels, and are therefore giving a false weighting to the evidence. It is additionally difficult to guess, because of the likelihood that the various collectors exchanged coins among themselves. Again, the Hungarian regal coinage from the late eleventh century onwards shows a profusion of issues, the majority of them anonymous. It is still impossible to date many of these small silver coins more closely than to within twenty or thirty years; as they were not regularly withdrawn from circulation and replaced, one cannot easily detect parcels. Secondly, although the Zagreb museum accepted a great many duplicates, one imagines that there was a limit to the number of pieces of one type that the collectors would trouble to offer, or the museum to buy. To take an example, F. Manot in 1902 sold to the museum one specimen of Réthy's no. 74,[8] one of no. 87, two of no. 88B, and two of no. 90. In 1903, he sold three more specimens of no. 74, two of no. 75, one of no. 76, one of no. 87, three of no. 88B, and four of no. 90. In all, between 1895 and 1910, the museum acquired, from various collectors, 16 specimens of Réthy's no. 90 found at Novi Banovci. Still, one ought to assume that the numbers of each type in the registers are a better guide to the quantities of the scarce pieces found, than of the very common ones. On the other hand, where a type has been recorded not only in several specimens from Novi Banovci, but also from two or three other find-spots, the indication that it was plentiful is more reliable. The types which seem to have been very common in Syrmia on this kind of evidence include the curious imitative pieces, Réthy no. 98, and also nos. 285, iii /15, and iii /18.

The Novi Banovci coins should yield more and more of interest as the Hungarian coinage is dated more precisely, and studied in detail. The finds from the twelfth century onwards are summarized in Table 7. As the Zagreb registers have been written up systematically, references to the accession-numbers have been omitted here. The descriptions of the coins have, unfortunately, had to be taken from the registers, since the collection itself was not available for study. When the Zagreb coins were stored for safety in 1939, some parts of the collection may have fallen into disorder, so that it may never be possible to recover the provenances of many of the coins. If the attempts made here to identify the pieces from the written descriptions in the registers can be superseded, then so much the better. Meanwhile, even limited information makes a useful contribution to the monetary history of the march-lands.[9]

---

[8] Réthy and Zimmermann, *CNHungariae*, part I, no. 74.   [9] *Inventar*

A. HUNGARIAN COINS

Réthy	Quantity	Réthy	Quantity	Réthy	Quantity
40	4	145	9	328	1
42	14 a	149	1	336	1
45	5	151	4	337	2
46	4 b	153	4	341, var.	2
47	9	157	1	342	1
48	9	159	1	343,vars.	2
49	6 c	162	1 k	344	2
50	1	167	1	345	5
53	5	189	1	353	1
54	11	208	2	354	1
57	5 d	210	3 l	357, var.	2 t
59	7	213	6	361	5
63	12	219	5	367	2
65	17 e	225	1	368	2
69	8 f	227	7	370	1
71	10	238,vars.	3	372	3
74	7	241	1	373	2
75	5	242	4 m	383, var.	5 u
76	7	244	1	Uncertain	2
78	1 g	245	4	Part III	
79	2	246	2	8	1 v
81	1	247	6	11	2
87	7	252	2	13	1 w
88 B	16	253,vars.	2 n	15, D R	1 x
90	16 h	261	1	17	9
92	2	262	6	18	2
96	1	264	2	18, A A	3
98	28 i	268	– o	18, B V	1 y
101–2	18 j	269	1	18, C R	1
103	1	283	1	18, S M	1
105	1	285,vars.	7 p	18, //	1
111	2	287	1	20, o–	5
118	2	288	1	21	2 z
119	2	290	4	27	2
123	3	291	1	30	1
125	1	293	– q	33, S S	4
126	1	297,vars.	5 r	34	5
127	1	298	16 s	41	3
129	1	299	1	54A óbol	1
132	1	300	3	54B	1 aa
133	3	303	1	55, B I	6
137	3	316	1	55, B L	4

Numizmatičke Zbirke Arheološkoga Odjela Narodnoga Muzeja u Zagrebu, Noviji

Notes. Other provenances for the same types, mentioned below, are:

a Srpska Mitrovica, and North
   Serbia
b Novi Slankamen
c Mitrovica
d North Serbia
e Mitrovica
f North Serbia
g North Serbia
h North Serbia
i Sarvaš, Vukovar, Sotin,
   Banoštor, Rakovac, Boljevci,
   Mitrovica, Osijek, Srpska
   Mitrovica, Zagreb.
j Sotin, and Donji Miholjac
k North Serbia
k North Serbia
l Mitrovica

m Novi Banovci, 1956-57
n Ostrovo
o Srpska Mitrovica
p Ilok, Surduk, and Vinkovci
q Mitrovica
r Sotin
s Novi Banovci, 1956–57
t Cf. Srpska Mitrovica
u Surduk
v Mitrovica, and Ruma
w Vinkovci
x Stari Slankamen, Surduk,
   Jarmina
y Bapska, Klisa Pusta, and
   Zagreb
z Hrtkovci, and North Serbia
aa Boljevci

Novci, 3 manuscript volumes, numbered consecutively, the third unbound; the same, *Bizantski Novci*, 1 manuscript volume. The registers give references to Réthy for the Hungarian coins, and drawings of the privy-marks for the Slavonian and Serbian coins. Little attempt is made to describe the Byzantine coins, except to give their metal, normally bronze, but the arrangement of the registers suggests that there may have been some folles; there were certainly stamena. There are brief descriptions of most of the Friesacher, from which I have attempted to give references to Luschin, "Friesacher Pfennige". A description of the bolder side only of the coin is given. There can be no mistake about some of them, whilst others are too vague for certainty. "Eberhard II, 2 heads and 2 stars", for example is without doubt Luschin no. 13; but what is "Indistinct type and half-moon"?..

137

Summary of the Hungarian coins

Period	Réthy	Total
Kálmán, 1095–1114	38, 40–50	52
István II, 1114–1131	39, 51–56	16
Béla II, 1131–1141	57–61	12
Géza II, 1141–1161	62–63	12
László, 1161–1162	94–97	0
Anonymous issues, 1095–1162	65–93	100
Imitative Byzantine	98–100	28
Imitative, Arabic	101–103	19
Béla III, 1173–1196	105–112	3
Imre, 1196–1204	113–114	0
Endre II, 1205–1235	115–116, 171–227	25
Anonymous issues, 1173–1235	117–170	40
Béla IV, 1235–1270	228–283	36
István V, 1270–1272	284–309, 355–356	40
László IV, 1272–1290	310–346	17
Endre III, 1290–1301	357–381	17
Venczel, Otto, 1301–1307	382–387	5
Robert Karl, 1308–1342	1–55	57
Uncertain		2

B. *SLAVONIAN BANOVCI*

Nuber	Quantity	Description and Notes
1	2	Two annulets. One reads REX, the other REGIS
2	2	Two lis. One, an obol, reads REX, the other REGIS
3	2	Two birds.
4	2	H R. Both read DUCIS, with single crosses, and an annulet above the crescent; one is apparently a contemporary forgery.
5	5	S R. One with single crosses, and annulet above the crescent; one with single crosses, and a lis above the crescent; three with 2 lis, and lis above the crescent. The first and the last three are apparently contemporary forgeries.
7b	2	R L. Both have double crosses, and a double cross above the crescent.
9	1	A to left, bird to right; 2 lis; crescent and asterisk; (?) bird above.
(?) 10	6	A, K retrograde; asterisk above crescent. Probably a parcel.

138

C. *SOUTH GERMAN COINS*

References are to Luschin, "Friesacher Pfennige", except where stated.

Type	Quantity	Description and notes
Aquileian	3	Probably twelfth–century coins of the Friesach type
Friesach	8	Twelfth–century issues
Luschin 185–188	2	St. Veit, twelfth century
Luschin 10	2	Friesach, ca. 1204–08
Luschin 13	1	Friesach, ca. 1208–12
Luschin 14	1	Friesach, ca. 1220–22
Luschin 23	5	Friesach, ca. 1222–24. Also from Progar
Luschin 26	1	Friesach?
"Carinthia: Philip; bishop above arch"	2	Friesach?
"Carinthia: indistinct type with half–moon"	1	Friesach?
Luschin 194	5	St. Veit, ca. 1212–16
Luschin 198	2	St. Veit, ca. 1216–20
Luschin 200–02	3	St. Veit, ca. 1222–24
Luschin 214	2	St. Veit, ca. 1226–30. Also at Stari Slankamen
Luschin 129 or 183	1	Slovenj Gradec or St. Veit
Luschin 132	1	Slovenj Gradec. Also from Mitrovica
Luschin 161	1	Kostanjevica
Luschin 215	1	Völkermarkt
Luschin, "Wiener Pfennige", (?) 132	1	
Luschin, "Steierische Münzfunde", 12	1	Also from Dalj

D. *BYZANTINE COINS*

Period	Quantity
Rex Regnantium folles (969–1118)	3 a
Alexius I (1081–1118)	1
John II (1118–1143)	5
Manuel I (1143–1180)	25 b
Andronicus I (1183–1185)	3 c
Isaac II (1185–1195)	1
Alexius III (1195–1203)	8 b
Thessaloniki:"John Angelus andDemetrius"	1 d
Nicaea: Theodore I (1204–1222)	1
Uncertain	4

Notes

a Two of the three are apparently of types H, I or J.
b Four of Manuel, and four of Alexius III, were given by K. Tomljeno-vić in 1894, and are almost certainly from a hoard of scyphate bron-ze. Cf. D. M. Metcalf, "The Currency of Byzantine Coins in Syrmia and Slavonia", *HBN* iv (1960), 429-444. Coins of Manuel have been found also at Sotin and Mitrovica.
c Three coins tentatively attributed to Andronicus (accession numbers 1048, 1049, 1050) were bought from K. Brenner. There is the pos-sibility that they, and half-a-dozen coins of Manuel, came from a hoard concealed ca. 1185. Mitrovica is another provenance for Andronicus.
d Possibly Wroth, *BMC (Byz.)*, III, pp. 202f.

E. *SERBIAN COINS*

Ljubić, *Opis,* Stefan Uroš I, Type III /xii, dot to left of Christ's feet, (1). Stefan Dragutin, Venetian type, (1). Stefan Dragutin, Type IIIc, nos. 33ff., (1). Stefan Dušan as king, Type Ie, (1).

F. *COINS OF SPLIT*

One spalatino, of uncertain type.

G. *GERMAN COINS*

Köln: Konrad v. Hochsteden, 1237-61, (1); Engelbert II, 1261-75, (1).

H. *ENGLISH COINS*

Short-cross: London (1)

Table 7. Coins found at Novi Banovci. From the accession-registers of the Zagreb Museum.

Four or five other coins with a Novi Banovci provenance have been recorded in other places. The find-spot of two of the coins described in Truhelka's monograph [10] was noted probably, as has often happened, be-cause they were rare or difficult to attribute. Truhelka gives the second of his "bagattini" to Endre II on the strength of the letter A on one side, and the star and crescent, the old arms of Dalmatia, on the other. The

---

[10] Truhelka, "Die slavonische Banaldenare", under the heading "Bagattini".

first coin he attributes to the same period, the beginning of the thirteenth century. Its type and denomination, however, might be appropriate to a date in the first half of the fourteenth century, and to the reign of Endre III. Recently, two small Hungarian coins and a banovac were brought into the Belgrade Museum by some people from Novi Banovci, [11] so it seems that discoveries are still being made in the village.

After Novi Banovci, it is from Sotin that the largest numbers of Syrmian finds have been recorded. This is probably fortuitous; we owe them to Robert Turmayer, the parish priest and a local numismatist. The catalogue of his collection is preserved at the Zagreb museum. [12] There are also half-a-dozen coins in the Zagreb inventories with a Sotin provenance, and where the name of the donor is recorded, it is Turmayer. The Hungarian coins which made up the medieval part of his collection are not, unfortunately, described by references to Réthy's catalogue, nor, so far as I can make out, to any other of the works on Hungarian numismatics. The fact that the first type in each of his groups is the most numerous suggests that the classification may be Turmayer's own. All that can be said is that the general composition of the Sotin finds is not dissimilar to that of the finds from Novi Banovci.

The Zagreb registers record smaller numbers of coins from various other settlements on the right bank of the Danube. These finds are set out in Table 8. They include early Hungarian coins from Šarengrad and Novi Slankamen. Two of the finds from Surduk may have been associated, in a deposit from ca. 1275, for they were acquired by the museum in the same year as each other from one Prešić, a shopkeeper, whose name does not appear in the accession-registers regularly. [13] The north Ger-

---

[11] Réthy and Zimmermann, *CNHungariae*, part I, nos. 242 and 298. Nuber, "Slavonische Münzen", type 5, S R, (?) trefoil over crescent. I am indebted to the late Dr R. Marić, who showed me these coins.

[12] *Opis u Sotinu nadjenih rimskih i drugih novaca*, manuscript. The title shows clearly that Turmayer's collection was built up from local finds. The coins are listed as follows: Anonymous, 1096-1291, 1st. type (7), 2nd. type (1), 3rd. type (1), 4th. pe (1), 5th. type (1), 6th. type (1).

Géza II, 1st. type (7), 2nd. type (1), 3rd. type (1).

Béla III, (2). Endre II, 1st. type (3), 2nd. type (1), 3rd. type (1).

Béla IV, 1st. type (2), 2nd. type (1), 3rd. type (1), 4th. type (1).

The coins from the main Zagreb registers are as follows:

Hungarian: Réthy 98 (2), 101-2 (1), 229 (1), 297 (1).

Slavonian: Nuber 1, REGIS (1). Byzantine: Manuel I, bronze (1).

[13] Nuber, "Slavonische Münzen", 5 (see Table 8) and Réthy 285, var.

man coin from Batajnica may be compared with various similar discoveries from Hungary. Two English pennies found at Rakovac, both presented to the museum in 1902, were presumably associated. They were from the mints of London and Lincoln.

Place	Description of coins
Sarvaš	Réthy 98 (1)
Dalj	An early Friesacher
Vukovar	Réthy 98 (1); Nuber 1, REGIS (1); Stefan Kotromanić, Ljubić, *Opis*, p. 192 (1).
Sotin	See p. 140
Šarengrad	Réthy 38
Bapska	Réthy III, 18
Ilok	Réthy 285
Banoštor	Réthy 98 (2); Trebizond, John II, Wroth, *BMC (Byz.)*, III, p. 267ff. (1).
Petrovaradin	Nuber 5, S R, trefoil over crescent, . . behind heads; pierced (1).
Rakovac	Nuber 7b, R L, double crosses, double cross above crescent (1); Luschin, "Friesacher Pfennige", no. 15 (1); Réthy 98 (1); English pence, Henry III, (2).
Stari Slankamen	Nuber 1, REGIS (1), 7b [var. as under Rakovac] (1); Réthy III, 15, var. (1); Luschin, "Friesacher Pfennige", (?) no. 214 (1); Ljubić, *Opis*, Stefan Dragutin, Type VI, nos. 13ff. (1).
Novi Slankamen	Réthy 46 (1); Nuber 7b [var. as under Rakovac] (1); Réthy III, 41, var. (1).
Surduk	Nuber 5, S R, annulet over crescent, contemporary forgery (1); Réthy 285, var. (1), 383, var (1), III, 15, var. (1).
Novi Banovci	See pp. 135ff
Batajnica	Aachen: Friedrich II (1).
Zemun	Ljubić, *Opis*, Stefan Dragutin, Types I–IV, cross at bottom right of staff, (1).

Table 8. Coins found at Syrmian settlements on the right bank of the Danube, from the accession-registers of the Zagreb museum. (The Bosnian coin, which was found near Vukovar, is not recorded in the registers).

South of the Fruška Gora, coins have been found at crossing-points of the Sava, and above all at Mitrovica (the old Sirmium), in the same way as those from along the Danube. They have also been discovered at places such as Ruma, Vinkovci, and Ostrovo, which lay on routeways, and where the use of coinage may have been associated particularly with the course of trade. Vinkovci, for example, is the focus of several routes crossing the Sava at Slavonski Brod and other points eastwards as far as Mitrovica; four Hungarian coins have been found there. [14]

From Vinkovci the route to the north passes through a gap in the Fruška Gora, where, at Ostrovo, an important hoard consisting mainly of Friesacher was brought to light in 1898. The bulk of the hoard was published by Brunšmid, whose detailed descriptions are still the standard source for the find. There was an interesting group of English pennies, many of them from the mints of Canterbury and Lincoln, and a smaller number of coins of Köln. About 10% of the hoard was of Hungarian coins, and its evidence for that series is of interest because they are divided among only a small number of types; Réthy's nos. 272 and 279 make up three-quarters of the total. There may be something of relevance here for the unsolved problems of the Mitrovica mint. [15] A revised account of the Friesacher in the hoard was published in summary form by Baumgartner. [16] He divided the 2255 coins that were available for study (there were perhaps 3500 originally) first between the Carinthian and the smaller Slovenian mints, thus securing useful evidence for the relative volume of coinage issued by the two groups: even as late as ca. 1255-60, when the hoard was concealed, about one-fifth of the Friesacher were from the eastern group of mints. He further divided the Carinthian coins into those issued before, and those issued after, 1200. A fifth of all the Friesacher were some sixty years old when the hoard was concealed: this shows that in their "foreign" circulation-area, the currency of the coins was not regulated by the withdrawal of old pieces, as it was in Austria. There is also the possible implication that these particular coins had been circulating in the east for much of their life.

At Jarmina, which lies between Vinkovci and Brod, a Hungarian coin has been found; [17] and at Nijemci, between Vinkovci and Mitrovica, a banovac. [18] At Ruma, which may have been a stage on the route

[14] Réthy and Zimmermann, *CNHungariae*, part I, nos. 156, 229, 285 and part III, 13. Another coin, of the type of III, 18, B V, is noted in the registers to have been found at Klisa Pusta, near Vinkovci.

[15] Brunšmid, "Našašća Novaca", VIII-XI. The Hungarian coins were as Réthy 253 (12), 263 (19), 271 (7), 272 (145), 275 (27), 279 (123), 280 (30).

[16] Baumgartner, "Die Blütezeit".

[17] Réthy and Zimmermann, *CNHungariae*, part III, no. 15, privy-mark, bird.

[18] Nuber, "Slavonische Münzen", type 7b, R L, double crosses, and double ncross above crescet.

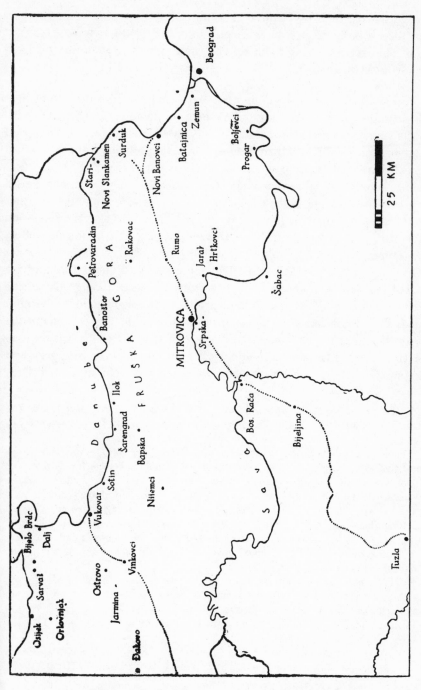

Map VII: Syrmia.

from Mitrovica to Novi Banovci, a banovac, a Hungarian coin, and per. haps also a Serbian groš have been found. [19] The discoveries from Vukovar, the river crossing-point on the route north from Vinkovci, have already been described.

From Mitrovica there is another parcel which, like that from Surduk, included both Slavonian and Hungarian coins: in 1902 a goldsmith by the name of Griesbach sold to the Zagreb museum eight coins said to have been found at Mitrovica, which very probably reflect a hoard concealed in the last quarter of the thirteenth century. [20] The only Slavonian coins from Mitrovica apart from those in the Griesbach parcel were two stray finds belonging late in the series. [21] Among the other finds, some are noted to have come from Mala or Srpska Mitrovica, on the south bank of the river. They included a coin of Kálmán as well as later Hungarian pieces. [22] The especial interest of these later coins lies in the possibility that they may yield some evidence about the mint for which there is documentary evidence from the year 1253. [23] Byzantine bronze coins from Mitrovica should probably be seen in the wider context of the circulation of scyphate bronze throughout the Balkans in the late twelfth century and in the first years of the thirteenth century, rather than as a reflection of the political relations between Hungary and Constantinople. [24] Three Friesacher and a pierced coin of Stefan Dra-

---

[19] *Ibid.*, type 7b, R L, two lis, nothing above crescent; Réthy, part III, 8. The Serbian coin is published in Ljubić, *Opis*, p. 61, and is of Stefan Dragutin, Type IV/ xvii.

[20] The man's name does not occur again in the register, and, as was said above, if the coins were stray finds, their proportions would not be typical for Syrmia. The banovci were of the following types: Nuber 1, REGIS (1); 5, S R, single crosses, lis above crescent (1); 5, S R, 2 lis, lis above crescent (2); 6, S L, lis above crescent, small cross above asterisk (1); 7b, R L, R to left, lis to right, nothing above crescent (2). The Hungarian coin was as Réthy, no. 248. The banovci are a somewhat unusual group; they might be a selection, made at the museum, from a larger number offered.

[21] Nuber 9, K S, two lis, nothing above crescent (1); Nuber 10, A K retrograde, asterisk above crescent.

[22] The coin of Kálmán was as Réthy, no. 42; there was another of his, no. 49, from the main settlement. The other Hungarian coins from Mitrovica were nos. 65, 98, 210, 293, and III/8, and, from Srpska Mitrovica, nos. 98 and 357, var. A further specimen is added to the list for Srpska Mitrovica by Zimmermann—no. II/48 (= 268A).

[23] B. Saria, article "Kovnice Novca" in *Narodna Enciklopedija Srpsko-Hrvatsko-Slovenačka*, ed. St. Stanojevic, 1927-29; and cf. B. Saria in *NLOB* ii (1963), 58-81.

[24] The accession-registers show 5 bronze coins, of which 3 are of Manuel I, 1

gutin similar to the one found at Zemun complete the small series of finds. [25] Their numbers should not be taken to imply that Mitrovica was less important as a centre of monetary affairs than Novi Banovci or Sotin, for at the latter places there were special circumstances to the discoveries. [26] Coins have been found at other crossing-places on the Sava, namely Jarak, Hrtkovci, Progar, and Boljevci. [27]

Out of the Serbian coins discovered north of the Sava, more than half are of Stefan Dragutin. This is a high proportion compared with those in the hoards of early Serbian coins, and suggests that the circulation of the groši was to a considerable extent localized. [28]

It only remains to consider the reason for the very large numbers of medieval finds from Syrmia. From the early eleventh century onwards, the region had a lively monetary economy, more so, perhaps, than any other inland district in the Balkan peninsula until the second half of the twelfth century. This is all the more remarkable because the zone of monetary activity is geographically an isolated one; in the surrounding regions the use of coinage was either fluctuating or, more usually, absent. The reason is to be found in the position of Syrmia between the plains of Hungary and the salt-mines of Tuzla. Horses and cattle must

---

of Andronicus I, and 1 of Alexius III.

[25] Luschin, "Friesacher Pfennige", nos. 185-88 (St. Veit, before 1200), 200 - 02 (St. Veit, ca. 1222-24), and 132 (Slovenj Gradec).

[26] There are also some coins at Zagreb of which the provenance is given as "North Serbia" or "Serbia". The name of Mladen Vukasinović, a labourer, is mentioned among the Mitrovica find-records, so that the north Serbian finds which were acquired from him very possibly came from the same neighbourhood. There were 9 Hungarian coins (Réthy nos. 42, 57, 69 (3), 78—these six may have been as parcel reflecting a hoard from about the middle of the twelfth century or a little earlier—90, 162, and III/21) and 2 Byzantine bronze pieces of Manuel I. Another coin of Manuel and 2 of Alexius III, which were acquired from Z. Pollak, a trader of Vinkovci, and which had been found in Serbia, may also have come from the neighbourhood of Mitrovica.

[27] Jarak; Nuber 7b, R L, double crosses, double cross above crescent. Progar: Luschin, "Friesacher Pfennige", no. 23 (Friesacher, ca. 1222-24); Nuber 7b, R L, R to left, lis to right, nothing above crescent; a Serbian groš reading STEFAN VRO-SIV'REX (either Stefan Uroš I or Stefan Uroš Milutin). Hrtkovci: Ljubić, Opis, Stefan Uroš I, Type IVc; Réthy III/21. Boljevci: Réthy 98 and III/54B.

[28] See D. M. Metcalf, "On an Unpublished Parcel of Serbian Grossi in the Slavonian Museum", HBN iv (1960), 59-64. The localized currency of Stefan Dragutin's coins in the north finds confirmation in their occurrence in Transylvania. See the finds of Obad and Săsarm in I. Sabău, "Circulatia Monetară în Transilvania Secolelor XI - XIII, în Lumina Izvoarelor Numismatice", SCN ii (1958), 269-301.

10

have salt (and indeed so must men), and salt can be obtained only in certain restricted localities in the interior of central Europe; hence trade in salt, often over long distances. Even after the Hungarians adopted a more sedentary way of life in the eleventh century, animal husbandry continued to play a major part in their economy. The distribution of coin finds in northern Bosnia indicates that the monetary economy there was linked with the salt-routes, and the same is almost certainly true of Syrmia. From Tuzla through Bijeljina salt would have been carried to Mitrovica and from there by a number of routes fanning out towards the Drava and Danube, especially, perhaps, through Ruma to Novi Banovci and through Vinkovci to Osijek and Vukovar. The use of coinage was thus associated with one specialized sector of the economy, and also, apparently, with one stage on the trade-route, namely, the river crossing-points mid-way between the salt-mines and Pannonia.[29] There is still the question why coinage was used, in place of commodity-exchange. Possibly there was an imbalance of trade, at any rate as between Tuzla and Hungary, which was made good by a transfer of silver.[30]

The unusual character of the monetary economy of Syrmia in the eleventh century is to some extent underlined by the discoveries which have been made of Hungarian coins, similar to those from Novi Banovci, used as grave-furniture at Bijelo Brdo and Svinjarevci.[31]

We turn now from Syrmia to Slavonia; the difficult questions connected with the earliest autonomous issues there will be left on one side until they can be reviewed against the background of the coinage of Béla IV (1235-70) and his successors. The efforts of Béla to reform the

[29] On the salt-monopoly from the mid-thirteenth century onwards, see Ć. Truhelka, "Das mittelalterliche Staats-und Gerichtswesen in Bosnien", *WMBH* x (1907), 71-155, at 79ff. For the Bosnian finds, see p. 215 below. For the association of coinage with a particular stage of a trade-route, cf. the earliest period of the penny in England (the late eighth and early ninth century) when the majority of the coin-finds associated with the continental trade are from the ports, and not from the important cities of Canterbury and Winchester, which are a little distance inland; D.M. Metcalf, "Offa's Pence Reconsidered", *Cunobelin, The Yearbook of the British Association of Numismatic Societies* ix (1963), 37-52.

[30] There was very possibly a similar imbalance of trade with southern England in the late eighth and early ninth centuries, made good by a flow of silver into England.

[31] J. Brunšmid, "Hrvatske Srednovječne Starine", *VHrvat.AD* NS vii (1903/4), 30-97. The latest coins from Bijelo Brdo were of Béla I (1060 - 63). Those from Svinjarevci were as Réthy nos. 26 (2), 27, and 29 (2).

Hungarian coinage were promptly extended to Slavonia. There is a documentary record that frequent *renovationes monetae* were brought to an end in 1237, and one may assume that it was from this date, or, at most, a year or two later, that there began the issue of the small silver coin which was then called "moneta banalis" or "denarius Zagrabiensis" and which numismatists usually refer to as the banovac. In *ca.* 1256 these coins were being struck at a mint at Pakrac. In 1260, and later, we read of a mint at Zagreb, which was always the real centre of Slavonian monetary affairs. The mint there continued in operation until about the middle of the fourteenth century, when the issue of banovci seems to have declined. It was officially terminated by Nagy Lajos, in 1364, in order to increase the profitability of the Hungarian regal coinage. [32]

The design of the banovci was kept substantially unchanged throughout the life of the denomination. On the obverse they show the marten, as an emblem for Slavonia, and an inscription such as MONETA B*(ela)* REGIS P*(ro)* SCLAVONIA or MONETA DVCIS P SCLAVONIA. Croatia had been united to the Hungarian crown in 1102, and was thereafter governed by either a ban or a duke. On the reverse of the coins is a double cross. In the lower angles formed by the cross are two crowned heads, and in the upper angles are a star and crescent moon. All this, again, is emblematic for Slavonia. The design is flanked by two secret-marks, which distinguish separate issues; and there are other small variations incorporated into the design which no doubt were also applied by the mint as secret-marks. There is a series of a dozen or so of the main secret-marks, and for most of them a number of minor varieties. From this it is reasonable to expect to find that the issue of the banovci was on a considerable scale.

In 1897 two scholars, C. Truhelka and C. F. Nuber, each published a systematic study of the Slavonian coinage. Integral translations of their texts into German were printed, again side by side, in the *Wissenschaftliche Mittheilungen aus Bosnien und der Hercegovina* in 1899. [33] Truhelka's monograph, which includes an admirable detailed catalogue of varieties, is the more substantial work, while Nuber's shorter contribution shows a lively intelligence. The system of numbering of the varieties in Truhelka's catalogue is outstandingly inconvenient, and the

---

[32] See I. Rengjeo, article "Banovac", in *Hrvatska Enciklopedija*, Zagreb, 1941.
[33] Truhelka, "Die slavonischen Banaldenare"; Nuber, "Slavonische Münzen".

references in the pages below are therefore generally to Nuber's types, although they are not really a sufficiently detailed system. Nuber's article is a text-book example of numismatic method. He placed the hoards that were available to him into their chronological order on the basis of the sequence of issues included in them, and suggested dates for the various issues, taking into account the secret-marks, which in some cases evidently refer to the king's name—R A, for example, is to be read Rex Andreas—and such other clues as presented themselves. The classification is reproduced, in a brief summary, in Table 9.

Nuber Type	Secret-marks	Hoards	Comments
1	O O	⎫	Zagreb, to 1270
2	two lis	A ⎬ B	Mint?, to 1270
3	two birds	⎭ C	Mint?, to 1270
4	H R		Hungariae Rex
5	S R		Istvan, 1270-72
6	S L	D	» »
7a	L R		Laszlo, 1272-90
7b	R L		» »
8	R A		Endre, 1290-1301
9	K S, K I, etc.		Robert Karl (1308-42) — with Stefan — with Ivan
10	K M, etc.	F	— with Mladen
11	K M	E	Migh Ban 1323-1342
12	M B	G	
13	B N		Ban Nicolaus, 1343-46
14	N I	J	

Table 9. Nuber's sequence of types and hoards of banovci, with his suggested attributions.

An inspection of the Table shows that the hoards available to Nuber were by no means ideal for his purpose. They throw no light on the internal arrangement of the first four groups (where, however, Nuber was able to show by a statistical analysis of certain typological details that Types 1 and 2 belong closely together).The argument for restricting Types 1, 2, and 4, the only ones that include coins reading DVCIS, to the reign of Béla IV is historical; and, prima facie, a comparison of the quantities of each type in Hoard A with the quantitites in Hoards B and C gives moderately good grounds for putting Type 4 after Types 2 and 3. This is, however, on the assumption that all four were struck at only one mint. The interpretation of R L and R A as Rex Ladislaus and Rex Andreas is convincing; but if H R stands for Hungariae Rex, S R might equally well be Sclavoniae Rex, as Stephanus Rex. Since the reign of István V was so short, the large quantities of coins of Type 5 in Hoard B and in the Rude hoard argue against Nuber's attribution. The hoard-sequence, considered in isolation, would lead one to put Type 6 after Type 7; Nuber's attribution to István and László may be treated with reserve. From Type 9 onwards the variability of the style and secret-marks of the coins suggests that their issue was less rigorously controlled than it had been in the thirteenth century, and Nuber's guesses are as good as any that could be made by means of a broad survey.

The quantities of each main type in Nuber's Hoards A to D, and in various hoards that have come to light since he wrote are shown in Table 10.[34]

Hoard	Nuber Type									
	1	2	3	4	5	6	7a	7b	8	(1)
A(Hungary, ca. 1883)	68	10	15	4	—	—	—	—	—	—
Zagreb	—	1	—	1	—	—	—	—	—	—
Bosnia	—	—	2	—	1	—	—	—	—	—
Verpelét, 1951	13	4	4	1	10	—	—	—	—	—
B (Felsö-Besnyö, 1895)	297	106	193	254	186	—	—	—	—	—
Borossebes, 1917	69	20	50	43	80	—	—	3	—	—
Margit-Sziget, 1893(?)	11	4	5	3	13	—	—	1	—	—
C (Duna-Szekcsö, 1896)	102	43	106	120	220	—	1	5	—	—
Szegvár, 1939	68	25	48	53	176	—	—	3	—	—
Vaskóh-Sziklàs, 1917	11	5	2	8	25	—	—	12	—	—
Rude, 1910	5	2	3	3	151	22	8	73	—	—
Mitrovica, 1902	1	—	—	—	3	1	—	2	—	—
D (Nemet-Csanad, 1880)	—	—	—	—	5	1	3	65	1	—
Poljančani, 1899	—	—	—	—	2	—	2	16	19	78
Zgruti, 1943	—	—	—	—	—	—	—	—	—	503

Table 10. General composition of the earlier hoards of banovci.

[34] For the additional hoards, see Homan, "Szlavon Denárok" P. Harsányi, "A Borossebesi (Arad m.) és Vaskóhsziklási (Bihar m.) Árpádkori Eremleletek", *NK* xxi-xxii (1922-32), 12-20; L. Huszár, "Éremleletek", *NK* xxxviii-xxxix (1939-40), 68; and *Ibid.*, *NK* 1-li (1951-52), 72; and below.

If one were to accept a straightforward view of the banovci in Hoard A, it would be that either the hoard was concealed early in the currency of Types 2, 3, and 4 the issue of which would have begun somewhat later than that of Type 1; or else it reflects the regional currency supplied mainly by the mint that struck Type 1 (Types 2, 3, and 4 having been struck elsewhere); or that the correct explanation combines parts of both these theories. We shall return to the hoard in a moment, to take note of the early Slavonian pence that it contained. Its date of deposit is perhaps close to the date of issue of the Hungarian pence, *CNH* 253; there is no precise evidence, but one may guess *ca.* 1245-50.

Type 5, on the evidence of the hoards later than Hoard B, is appreciably under-represented in that hoard, which is therefore *prima facie* likely to have been concealed early in the type's currency. The hoard contained one, and only one, signed issue of István; subject to revisions in our knowledge of the Hungarian anonymous varieties, its date of deposit would seem to *ca.* 1271. If so, the introduction of Type 5 very possibly antedates the beginning of István's reign. This possibility must be considered in light of the reading *Sclavoniae Rex.*

Next, there is quite a group of hoards terminating with a very few coins of Type 7b, but lacking Type 6 and, usually, Type 7a. The relative proportions of Types 1 to 5 in them show a degree of consistency which encourages one to treat them as reliable:

Hoard	Percentages					
	1	2	3	4	5	7
B	29	10	19	25	18	—
Borossebes	27	8	19	16	30	1
Margit-Sziget	30	11	13	8	35	3
C	17	7	18	20	37	1
Szegvár	18	7	13	14	47	1
Vaskóh-Sziklás	17	8	5	12	39	19

Table 10A. Proportions of the varieties in the early hoards of banovci.

All these except Vaskóh-Sziklás will presumably belong early in the currency of Type 7, but not necessarily immediately after 1272, if Type 5 was continued into the first part of the reign of László. The absence of Type 6 in so many hoards of fairly compact age-structure concealed in the currency of Type 7 is an argument against Nuber's arrangement.

When the Rude hoard was concealed, Types 1 to 4 had, at least in the Zagreb region, largely gone out of circulation. The absence of Type 8 indicates that the date of deposit is unlikely to have been more that a few months after the accession of Endre III, in 1290. Hoard D, in which there was only one coin of Type 8, is from so far afield, in Transylvania, that one hesitates to place reliance on it in detail. If its age-structure were in fact normal, its date would be *ca.* 1290-93, and the small numbers of Type 5 in it in comparison with the Rude hoard would lead one to set the date of the latter as early as possible, say, *ca.* 1280. The contrast in composition with Hoard C (at earliest *ca.* 1275) would then involve the hypothesis of a withdrawal of Types 1-4 in Slavonia itself *ca.* 1275-80, or alternatively a special character for the Rude hoard. It seems preferable to leave the attempt at analysis at this point, to await new material. Enough has been said to illustrate the uncertainty in the interpretation of even a very good hoard-series.

The Poljančani hoard consisted mainly of coins with two annulets as the secret-marks, that is, as Type 1, but with the inscription REX SCLAVONIE or variants. This variety is quite exceptional, and one need not hesitate to say, on the basis of the age-structure of the Poljančani hoard, that it belongs to the interregnum at the beginning of the fourteenth century. There are a few coins in the Rude hoard which might— although this is far from certain—be equally late in date.

The absence of Types 7, 8, and (1) in Hoards E, F, and G is suggestive of an interruption in the currency of banovci at the beginning of the reign of Robert Karl.

The question whether the banovci were struck at more than one mint concurrently must be studied in the context of the pattern of monetary circulation in Slavonia. That pattern, as in Syrmia, seems to be mainly one of towns at river crossing-points, and the routes leading to them. The coin-finds fall into half-a-dozen geographical groupings, of which the most important are those around Zagreb. Between Zagreb and the Adriatic several finds have come to light which are no doubt to be associated with the route to the coast, and others from the plains of the Kupa valley (the Pokupje) with the agriculture and commerce of that region. In the other direction from Zagreb there is a group of finds from the area around Koprivnica which are probably to be associated with crossing-points of the Drava on the route from Zagreb to Buda. These three groups from western Slavonia make up most of the total of Slavonian finds; from the eastern half of the province there is much less evidence of the use of coinage; finds from around Osijek, on the Drava, and Brod, on the Sava, really belong with the Syrmian assemblage. The only exception is the group of finds from around Suhopolje, on the Drava, which one may conjecture, from their dates of deposit, to reflect traffic between Buda and Pakrac. The framework of Slavonian monetary affairs might be thought of as a roughly equilateral triangle with Budapest at the apex and Zagreb and Mitrovica at the other angles, and not very much in the middle except for an extra line running from Budapest to Pakrac.

Just on the northern outskirts of Zagreb, at Gračansko Dolje, in 1869, a farmer ploughed up a small pot filled with Friesacher of the mint of Kostanjevica. They were bought by the Zagreb silversmith Jungmann, and the museum acquired a dozen pieces. The accession-registers show them as having been all of the same type; [35] as a Friesacher hoard the Gračansko Dolje find is thus extremely unusual. There is little with which it can be compared to decide how much of the currency of their region was supplied by the Slovenian mints; but the Celje, [36] Gračansko Dolje, and Ostrovo hoards, and the stray finds from Syrmia, suggest that it was a large proportion. The hoard from near Zagreb may, of course, have been carried there by a traveller, and may not reflect the local currency at all. From the late twelfth century, if that is the correct date for them, [37] come two finds of the Hungarian copper coins imitating Byzantine types. One was found in the Archbishop's Garden, and the other is recorded as being from the Reading Room, Zagreb. [38] Another hoard, slightly later in date than Gračansko Dolje, was discovered in the foundations of a house in Kukovićeva; it is represented in the museum by two banovci of types which indicate a date of deposit ca. 1260-ca. 1270. [39] There is a somewhat obscure record of the discovery

[35] Brunšmid, "Našašća Novaca", VIII-XI; cf. VHrvat. AD 1870, 233. Luschin, "Die Friesacher Pfennige", no. 161; the date is probably in the second quarter of the thirteenth century.

[36] See pp. 176f. below.

[37] They are attributed by Réthy to the third quarter of the twelfth century, but by Jeszensky (NK xxxiv - xxxv [1935 - 36], 35 - 47) to the fourth quarter. J. Sejbal, referring to archaeological evidence from Uh. Brod (southern Moravia) suggests the first half of the thirteenth century: Moravske Numismatické Zpravy v (June 1959), 14-17.

[38] Réthy no. 98.

[39] Nuber, Type 2, DVCIS; Nuber, Type 4, REGIS, each with crosses in the upper angles of the reverse design, and an annulet above the crescent.

of a hoard at Vukovar, near Zagreb, consisting of a large number of Aquileian coins found in or near a grave. The date of deposit, guessing from similar hoards from Slovenia, may have been in the first two or three decades of the fourteenth century.[40] Similar in date are two Hungarian coins, which were found in the Archbishop's Garden, and presented to the museum by Viktor Miljan. [41] The diversity of the coin-finds from Zagreb and its immediate region—Friesacher from the early thirteenth and banovci from the late thirteenth century, Aquileian and Hungarian coins from the fourteenth—is a good illustration of the way in which the march-land character of the north-west finds expression in monetary affairs. Zagreb came under the influence of a number of other regions in turn, and it was only in the period ca. 1220 - ca. 1300 that the town was able to sustain a really vigorous monetary system of its own.

Sisak, the old Siscia, sited where the river Kupa joins the Sava, had a long tradition of urban life. The town was eclipsed by Zagreb at about the end of the eleventh century. A Byzantine bronze coin of John II has been found there, and also a Venetian grosso of Pietro Gradenigo (1289-1311). [42] Thus, coins of two more entirely different series are added to the medley of those current in Slavonia at various times. At Ivanić a Friesacher struck in the 1220's has been found.[43] At Bjelovar a fourteenth-century banovac was discovered. [44] Two hoards of banovci complete the tally of finds from the Zagreb area. The Rude hoard of 1910 contained some 300 coins, hidden in a pot. [45] They were acquired by the Zagreb museum, where the accession-registers show 267 pieces. These are listed in Table 11.

[40] N. Maionica, Director of the archaeological museum in Aquileia, supplied the information, which was published in *Monatsblatt der numismatischen Gesellschaft in Wien* vii, 53. The provenance was given as Vukovar bei Zagreb.

[41] Réthy III/11 and III/18 B V. The copper coin was also given by Miljan.

[42] Both in the Zagreb accession-registers. For the coin of John II, see Metcalf "Syrmia and Slavonia".

[43] The register does not say whether the find-spot was Ivanić Grad or Kloster Ivanić. The coin was as Luschin, "Die Friesacher Pfennige", no. 23 (Friesach, ca. 1222-24).

[44] The secret-marks are given in the register as B M.

[45] A summary report of the hoard is given in Klemenc, "Nalazi Novaca".

Variety	Number Type	Inscription and secret-marks	Quantity	Accession-numbers, and comments
R1	I	REGIS	I	20821
R2	2	REGIS	I	21075
R3		LEGIS	I	21077; ? irregular issue
R4	3	☺	2	21015, 21024
R5		REGIS	I	21051; ? irregular
R6	4	⌣	3	21085, 21099, 21119
R7	5	☺	I	21135; ? irregular
R8		☺	4	21138-40, 21142
R9		☺, ⩗, ⌢	I	21144; ? irregular
R10		⋏⋏, ☺	I	21154; ? irregular
R11		⋏⋏, ⊕	3	21160-62
R12		⋏⋏, ✚	7	21166-72
R13		⋏⋏, ☺	53	21174, 21179-210, 21212-13, 21218-35
R14		⋏⋏, ♔	14	21238-39, 21241-52
R15		⋏⋏, ✚, • behind head	2	21255-56
R16		⋏⋏, ✚, •• behind heads	5	21258-62
R17		✦✦, ♔, • •	I	21263
R18		⋏⋏, ♔, • •	7	21264-70
R19		⋏⋏, ♔	26	21274, 276, 277, 279-82, 284-91, 299, 302-04, 306-10, 318, 320
R20		⋏⋏, ♔, v behind heads	2	21315-16
R21		⋏⋏, ♔	17	21325-26, 328-31, 335-36, 342, 349-50, 356, 359-60, 369, 372, 375
R22		✦✦, ♔	I	21377; ? irregular
R23		⋏⋏, ♔, S R	I	21378; ? irregular
R24		⋏⋏, ♔, R S	I	21382
R25		✚, ✳✳	4	21390-93
R26	6	♔, ✳✳	22	21394, 397-407, 412-21
R27	7a	♔, ✳✳	I	21422
R28		♔, ✳, ∴∴ behind heads	6	21423-28
R29		⋏⋏, ♔, ✳, •• , J R	I	21430
R30		✦✦, ♔	2	21477-78
R31		✦✦ ♔	68	21480-82, 484-86, 493-544, 546-55
R32		Ibid., without ⌒ ⌒	2	21556-57
R33		Ibid., ☺	I	21558; ? irregular
R34	(I)	○ , KEX , ⁹⁷, ☺	I	20910
R35		⊙ ⊙, DUX	I	20906
R36		⊙ ᴿ, REGIS, ⋏⋏, ☺	I	20905
R37		✚✚, REX, ⁚ ∴, ☺	I	20999. Obol, 0.519 g.m.

Table 11. The Rude hoard, 1910

Four coins that were catalogued as of the earliest type have been moved to the end of the Table. The first of them reads REX SCLA-VONIE, like the majority of the coins in the Poljančani hoard. The next, reading DVX SCLAVONIE, is of a variety not represented in that hoard. The other two are, to guess from their secret-marks, contemporary with Types 7a and 7b. Should one consider attributing the Rude hoard to the first years of the fourteenth century? In view of its age-structure (note that two varieties, R13 and R31, which are perhaps stylistically related to each other, account for more than half the coins in the list) and after a comparison with the Poljančani find, a late date of deposit seems totally unacceptable unless the hoard were a sum of money withdrawn from circulation *ca.* 1280, to which a few coins were added two or three decades later. This composite type of hoard is not unknown, but it is rare. Until fresh evidence comes to light, it seems best to suppose that the last four coins in the list either were struck ca. 1270-ca. 1280 or are intruders.

The Poljančani hoard is represented in the Zagreb museum by 117 coins. There are a further six in the museum at Pakrac. [46] The Zagreb coins are listed in Table 12.

There is no overlap between the minor varieties of Type 7b represented in the Poljančani hoard and those in the Rude hoard. Since the deposit of the Poljančani hoard was more than a decade after the issue of Type 7b had ceased, the complete absence of variety R31, for example, is certainly indicative of something about the composition of at least one of the two hoards! Even more striking is the absence from both hoards of a variety of Type 7b that is exceptionally common in Syrmia, namely the variety with double (Slavonian) crosses in the upper angles of the reverse design and a similar double cross above the crescent. This variety is recorded from Jarak, Nijemci, Novi Banovci (2), Novi Slankamen, Rakovac, and Stari Slankamen. The only other coins of Type 7b from Syrmian find-spots are those from Progar (variety P5), Ruma (variety P4), and from the Mitrovica hoard (variety P5). A stray find from Bosnia [47] is also of variety P4. The distribution-pattern reveals such a high degree of compartmentation that it is certain

[46] I am indebted to Dr. D. Narakvić for his information about the hoard, and to the good offices of Dr D. Pinterović. Four of the coins at Pakrac are of Béla IV (2), László IV (1), and Endre III (1).
[47] See below.

that different varieties of Type 7b were issued in different places. In light of the pattern of monetary affairs in Slavonia that has been suggested above (concentrations of curency in the regions of Zagreb and Mitrovica, as two angles of a triangle with Buda as its apex), the variety with double crosses is obviously a Syrmian issue. This is not necessarily to say that it was struck in Syrmia: it might in principle have been struck in Zagreb and carried to Syrmia by the mint-officials for issue there.

Variety	Nuber Type	Inscription, and secret-marks	Quantity	Accession-numbers, and comments
P1	5	⊤ ⊤, ⚓	1	21278, Cf. R19.
P2		⊤ ⊤, ⚓	1	21355, Cf. R21
P3	7a	⊤ ⊤, ⚓, ✳	2	21431-32
P4	7b	⊤ ⊤, ∪	3	21437,439,441
P5		R ⊤, ∪	6	21448-50,454,457-58. The R in R L is broken.
P6		R L , R ⊤, ∪	6	21461-62 464-65 468-69
P7		R L, ⊤ ⊤, ⚓	1	21472
P8	8	R ⊼, R ⊤, ∪	1	21588
P9		⊼ ⊤, ∪	14	21590-603
P10		⊤ ⊤ ˙˙ ∪	3	21604-06
P11		⊤ ⊤ ∴ ∪	1	21607
P12	(1)	⊙ ⊙, REX, ⸰ ⸰, ☺	2	20911, 20924
P13		⊙ ⊙, REX, ⊙ ⊙, ☺	3	20921-23
P14		⊙ ⊙, REX, ⊙ ⊙, ∪	58	20925-48, 20950-83
P15		⊙ ⊙, ERX, ⊙ ⊙, ∪	1	20949
P16		⊙ ⊙, REX, ⊙ ⊙, ∪	3	20984-86
P17		⊙ ⊙, ERX,	2	20987-88
P18		⊙ ⊙ REX, ∪ ✳	1	20989
P19		⊙ ⊙ REX, ⊙ ⊙, ∪ ✳	2	20990-91
P20		Ɛ Ɛ REX, ⊙ ⊙, ∪	4	20992-95
P21		⸰⸰ ⸰⸰ REX, ⊙ ⊙, ∪	2	20996-97

Table 12. The Poljančani hoard, 1899

However, consignment is not a very probable explanation: the reasonable working hypothesis is that, under László, banovci were struck at Mitrovica as well as at Zagreb. We know that in 1266 Béla IV gave the mint as a dowry to his wife; it may be that certain varieties of Nuber's Type 6 remain to be attributed to Syrmia. In the same year, Požega is described as an annexe of the Mitrovica mint. [48] The implications of this for the banovac series must be left on one side until some further hoards from central or eastern Slavonia have been brought to light. [49]

We may now turn back to the question of the earliest Slavonian coinages. Hóman as long ago as 1920 distinguished, mainly on grounds of stylistic affinities and iconography, 39 pence and 22 obols among those in the *Corpus Nummorum Hungariae* as being Slavonian issues minted probably in Zagreb. [50] The varieties, in the chronological order in which he arranged them, were as follows: (related pence and obols are placed together)

Endre II as duke, 1196–*ca.* 1200: 197, 198, 203, 172, 199
— , *ca.* 1200–1205:   200, 200A, 206
— , as king, 1205–11: pence: 201, 301, 307, 303, 308A
                obols: 202, 302, 308, 304, 309
Archbishop Berchthold of Kalocsa, as ban (1209-11):
                pence: Korpona hoard, 33-36; *CNH* 184, 186, 188
                obols: ibid.   37;   185, 187, —
Endre II, 1211–15, pence: 305, 204, 207
                obols: 306,   —   —
— , 1215–22,   pence: 178, 190, 282
                obols: — — 283
— , 1222–35   pence: 226, 226A, 299, 300A, 344,   —
                obols: 227,   —   — 300, 345, 346, 343
— , 1222–26   pence: 244
                obols: 243, 244A, 245, 244B
Béla IV, 1235–50, pence: 336, 360, 240, 241
                obols: 337, 361, — 242
— , 1250–54   pence: 239, 256, 248
                obols: — — —

[48] B. Saria, article "Kovnice Novca", in *Narodna Enciklopedija Srpsko-Hrvatsko-Slovenačka*, ed. S. Stanojević, 1927-29.
[49] For the later banovac series, see below, and especially the Metlika hoard, at p.
[50] Hóman, "Szlavon Denárok", where the Hungarian coins in the Slavonian hoards (cf. Table 10 *supra*) are conveniently tabulated with references to Réthy and Zimmermann, *CNHungariae*.

158

The site-finds from Buda offer a formal proof, although not an adequate one because there are so few from the first half of the thirteenth century, that these 61 varieties belong to a provincial mint.The difficulties of bringing hoards from the Budapest region into evidence are, first, that the proportion of Hóman's group in a hoard from any date after the middle of the century is not a simple index, since the "Slavonian" coinage represents a large volume of currency which continued in use for most of the period up to 1300 alongside later issues; and, secondly, that hoards from the first half of the century must be dated with confidence before the absence of the "Slavonian" varieties can be regarded as significant. Thus, Hoard A, the earliest of the hoards of banovci (Table 10) was made up predominantly of "Slavonian" pence and obols (848 specimens), and 416 out of 588 "Hungarian" pence and obols were of the one variety, CNH 253. The proportion of "Slavonian" pence to banovci, 848:97, quickly dwindles in the later hoards in which banovci bulk large. Their greater occurrence in the Borossebes and Vaskóh-Sziklás hoards presumably indicates an extra-Slavonian origin for the pence element in those hoards. Perhaps the best piece of evidence from north-central Hungary is the Gaiu Mic (formerly Kis-Gajon) hoard, from the Timişoara region, which belongs to Béla IV and probably early in his reign, and from which the "Slavonian" varieties were absent. The bracteates, CNH 272, which dominated the hoard were plentiful in the Ostrovo hoard also. There were no Slavonian pence at Ostrovo.

Such is the pattern of the evidence, excluding the Mernye hoard of 1940. No more striking testimony could have been afforded to the essential success of Hóman's analysis than was brought to light by that find. The varieties that were reported in two parcels from it were:

Pence: CNH 212 (3+1); *226 (43+31); 237 (8+1); *299 (54+45); *344 (104+89); *244 (43+35); *360 (35+19); *241 (8+4).
Obols: *227 (2+0); 238 (3+0); *245 (8+3); *300 (3+0); *345 (3+0); *346 (0+2).

The coins that Hóman listed as probably from Zagreb (marked*) amount to 531 out of 547. The find-spot is about half-way between Zagreb and Budapest, somewhat to the south of Lake Balaton. Here, we are entitled to conclude, is a traveller's hoard which is representative of the currency, most probably, of western Slavonia. The only amendment of Homan's conclusions that is called for is a possible compression of his chronology so as to set the date of the Mernye hoard before the in'roduction of the issue of banovci. [51]

---

[51] For the Buda site-finds (CNHungariae 153, 101, 224, 233, 238, 310, 324,

The considerable quantities in which the Slavonian pence occur in hoards from Hungary point to their original importance in the monetary affairs of the first decades of the thirteenth century, and one might be inclined to ask how it should be that have left no trace in the finds from the Zagreb region. But the argument *a silentio* is usually a dangerous one. How much trace have the early banovci left in western Slavonia?

The comparative scarcity of Slavonian issues in the Novi Banovci find-series emphasizes that the articulation of trade was along the routes Buda-Zagreb and Buda-Syrmia, and only to a limited extent along the third side of the triangle, Zagreb-Syrmia. That the penny in the Mitrovica parcel of 1902 should have been a Slavonian variety is another small pointer to its being a traveller's hoard.

So much for the coinages in the Hungarian style. The correct interpretation of the Croatian and Hungarian coins struck in the style of the Friesacher is more difficult, because their issue was on a far smaller scale and was less organized. Some of them are certainly to be attributed to Endre II (*CNH* 197 and 172, and some pieces recently published by Baumgartner) but they are very rare and can never have played more than an incidental part in the monetary affairs of the marchlands. Baumgartner has shown that some at least of the coins described by earlier scholars as "Hungarian Friesacher", although they were destined for Hungary, were struck in the frontier mints of Slovenia. [52]

The shortest route from Zagreb to the coast reaches the Adriatic opposite the island of Krk. A longer route crosses the Velebit Planina further south, and reaches the sea at Karlobag. At that town, and between it and Zagreb, banovci have been discovered. They suggest that the Slavonian coinage was used, for a time at any rate, in connexion with Zagreb's foreign trade. All the recorded finds from routes to the coast are late types, issued after the accession of Robert Karl: by the river Korana, near Karlovac, a piece attributed to ban Babonezić has come to light; at Kirin, near Vrginmost, and also at Čakovac, near Mun-

---

375), see L. Huszár, "A Budai Várpalota Ásatásainak Éremleletai", *Budapest Régiségai, A Budapesti Történeti Múzeum Évkönyve* xvii (1956), 197-240. For the Gaiu Mic hoard, see *NK* ii (1903), 106, and *SCN* ii (1958), 288. For the Mernye hoard, see L. Huszár in *NK* xxxviii-xxxix (1939-40), 67 and *NK* xl (1941), 90.

[52] The question of Hungarian Friesacher is succinctly reviewed in Baumgartner, "Die Blutezeit", part II)2, at pp. 57ff. On *CNHungariae* 197, which has been variously interpreted, see G. Jeszenszky, "Andreas Dux Croatiae", *NK* xxxvi - xxxvii (1937-38), 92-93.

jave, coins of Nuber's Type 9 have been found. [53] In context of the finds from the Adriatic littoral, these stray finds are useful evidence of the date at which trade developed. No earlier discoveries are reported from the Pokupje, although later ones are known.

To the north of Zagreb, from the area around Koprivnica, comes the Zgruti hoard of 1943. It contained 488 banovci and 15 halves, which were dated by Rengjeo, mainly on stylistic grounds, to 1323-25. [54] This was possibly a more precise conclusion than the evidence warranted, but the coins certainly belong to the earlier part of the fourteenth century. At Novigrad, not far away, a banovac was found at the beginning of the century, [55] and another was discovered at Kalnik at about the same time. [56]

Further down-stream on the right bank of the Drava, in the district of Suhopolje, other thirteenth-century coins have been found. The most important of the discoveries is the Gaćište hoard of 1871, which contained about six hundred Friesacher together with two gold rings with green stones, three silver rings, four fragments of a silver bracelet, and two human skeletons. According to Brunšmid, [57] the Zagreb museum aquired "14 Friesacher with gables and two towers; 56 of Eberhard II; 102 Carinthian coins of Ulrich II, Bernhard II and Philip; and 2 Styrian coins of Leopold". From the more detailed information in the accession-registers at Zagreb, [58] the date of the hoard would seem to be not earlier than ca. 1230. It is tempting to assign it to the time of the

---

[53] For the Karlobag find, see p. 191; for the Bihać and other Bosnian finds, see pp. 215 f. Karlovac: Nuber Type 8, with lion above marten. Kirin and Čakovac: the secret-marks were K I, two lis, nothing above crescent, in each case.

[54] I. Rengjeo, "Nalaz Banovaca u Zaseoku Zgruti", *NV* 5 (1955), 17, proposing 1241 as the date of deposit. Rengjeo withdrew this submission, and gave more detail about the hoard, in "Slavonski Banovci Bana Nikole (1323-1325)", *NV* 11 (1958), 2-9, The fullest description of coins from the Zgruti hoard (some of which came onto the European market) is in Rengjeo, *Corpus*, nos. 229-256, most of which were in the possession of Professor V. Radauš of Zagreb.

[55] Nuber, Type 1, REGIS.

[56] Nuber, Type 2, DVCIS.

[57] Brunšmid, "Našašća Novaca", VIII - XI.

[58] I could find only 104 coins in the Zagreb registers with a Gaćište provenance, all of them attributed to Carinthia. They were as Luschin, "Friesacher Pfennige", nos. 194 - 95 (73, including 2 Halblinge); 198 (?) (5, including one Halbling); 199 (1); 205 (?) (1); 214 (?) (13, including 6 Halblinge); 125 or 158 (1); "Carinthia, Philip, bishop above arch", (10). The proportion of halves, and the proportion of coins of St. Veit, are both somewhat unusual, and suggest a traveller's hoard.

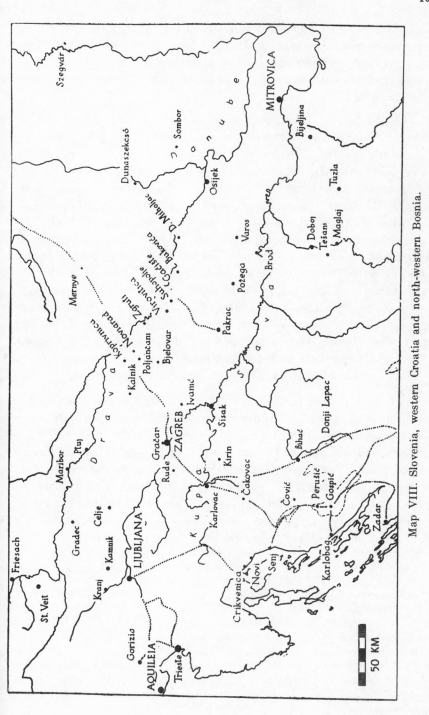

Map VIII. Slovenia, western Croatia and north-western Bosnia.

162

Mongol incursions. A stray find of a Friesacher of the same period was made at Suhopolje, where a banovac has also been found. [59] Two banovci, which very probably reflect a hoard concealed in the middle years of the thirteenth century—again, possibly in 1241-42—were found at Bukovića in 1899 or before. [60]

The situation of Osijek, on the site of the Roman Mursa, is similar to that of the Syrmian towns on the right bank of the Danube, so far as monetary circulation is concerned. From the collection formed at the town's *Gymnasium* (where Vjekoslav Celestin taught), the Zagreb museum acquired in 1909 a coin of Friesach, a Byzantine bronze piece of Alexius, and three Hungarian coppers. [61] The Slavonian Museum, at Osijek, has a rich collection of medieval coins, but there are very few recorded provenances from the district. [62] Mr Bela Liska, of Osijek, an old man and an invalid when I met him, for many years made a hobby of finding coins. After rain, he would walk in the fields and gardens of the lower town, looking closely at the ground wherever it had been freshly dug. He rarely returned without finding coins, and in the course of the years collected some 1,700 in this way. The bulk of them, as one would expect, were Roman; there were very few medieval pieces. To the best of Mr Liska's recollection, there had been about seven Serbian coins, the same number of Bosnian, and even fewer Slavonian. [63]

At Orlovnjak, not far to the south of Osijek, a hoard of Friesacher was discovered in 1887. Seventy-nine coins to which Brunšmid refers were published also in the Vienna *Monatsblatt*, where a further 37 coins were subsequently recorded. Twenty-one coins were acquired by the Zagreb museum in 1906, some at least among which are not among those listed in the *Monatsblatt*. A concordance of the coins, giving references as far as possible to Luschin, appears as Table 13. The hoard is dated, apparently, by the Hungarian coins, which Réthy attributes to Béla IV. Once again, it is tempting to envisage 1241-42 as the date of depo-

---

[59] Luschin, no. 23 (Friesach, ca. 1222-24); Nuber, Type 3, REGIS.

[60] They are both of Nuber, Type 1, REGIS. The only other find from the region was a pierced specimen of Réthy nos. 101-02, discovered in the neighbourhood of Donji Miholjac.

[61] Luschin, no. 17; Réthy, no. 98 (3).

[62] They include an important series of banovci, many of which were presented to the museum by Nuber, who was a native of Osijek.

[63] It is a misfortune that Mr Liska was obliged to sell his coins during the war. For the identification of the exact site of Mursa, see D. Pinterović, "Prilog Topografiji Murse", *Osječki Zbornik* v (1956), 55ff. It was Dr Pinterović who kindly took me to see Mr Liska.

Luschin	Quantity	Date	Source
Mint of Friesach			
1–3, 5	2– 3	before ca. 1164	B1-2; Z.
6	11	before ca. 1200	A1-9, B3-4, in- cluding one forgery
8	3	ca. 1200–04	A49-51
10, etc.	5	ca. 1204–08	A19-23
13	1	ca. 1208–12	A24
15	2	ca. 1212–16	A10, B5
19, etc.	11	ca. 1216–20	A11-18, B6-8
14 (?)	4– 6	ca. 1220–22	A72-73, B30-31; Z (2).
23, etc.	12–14	ca. 1222–24	A33-41, B17-19; Z (2).
21 /22	4– 8	ca. 1224–26	A31-32, A52, B16; Z (4).
24 (?)	6	ca. 1226–28	A43-48
25	6	ca. 1228–30	A63-67, B25
Mint of St. Veit			
183	1	before ca. 1200	A68
199	2	ca. 1204–08	A53-54
194, etc.	7	ca. 1212–16	A55-58, B20-22
198	3	ca. 1216–20	A59-60, B23
200	4	ca. 1222–24	A69-70, B26-27
190 (?)	1	ca. 1224–26	A71
207	1	ca. 1226–28	B28
214	1		Z. (Mint and da- te uncertain)
Mint of Ptuj			
17	7– 8		A28-29, B11-15; Z.
Cf. 17 /18	1		A27. (?) mint.
Cf. 18	1		A30 (?) mint.
18 /23	1		A42 (?) mint.
Mint of Brezice			
123b, etc.	4		A25-26, B9-10
Mint of Kostanjevica			
161	2		A61-62
Mint of Slovenj Gradec			
132	1		B24
Uncertain Friesacher			
	8–12		A74-76, B29, 32- 35; Z (4).

Luschin	Quantity	Date	Source
Hungary			
"3 heads in circle"	2		A77-78
bracteate	1		B36
Réthy 272	1	after 1235	Z. Cf. Ostrovo hoard
Réthy 280	5	after 1235	Z. Cf. Ostrovo hoard
Köln	1	1208–14	B37
England	1	after 1180	

Table 13. The Orlovnjak hoard, 1887. (A, B are Raimann's two lists)

sit, although this is of course speculative. On the internal evidence alone, one would have to suggest a bracket of probably 1235-ca. 1240. [64]

The sixth and last of the groupings into which the Slavonian finds have been arranged, namely finds from the area around Brod, comprises only one coin: an early Friesacher was discovered at Levanjska Varos. It may be associated with a route from Brod towards Vinkovci.

If we now review the find-assemblage from Slavonia chronologically, we see that it includes very few coins struck before 1200, and that all of them were of types that were still in use in the thirteenth century. [65] Only one coin is more likely to have been deposited or lost in the twelfth century than in the thirteenth—the Byzantine bronze piece of John II recorded from Sisak. The Friesacher which circulated in Slavonia in the third and fourth decades of the thirteenth century were the first large - scale currency that the region had had since the *Völkerwanderungszeit*, and even they may have been handled more by merchants going to Hungary than by the inhabitants. The banovci were evidently far more plenti ful than any coinage had previously been. Towards the end of the thirteenth century, however, their supply dwindled, and they virtually went out of use, except presumably in Zagreb itself; fourteenth-century banovci have been found south of the river Sava, but very rarely in Slavonia north of the Sava. There, the few finds include north Italian and Hungarian regal coins. In short, it was only in the period ca. 1220 -

---

[64] Brunšmid, "Našašća Novaca"; A. Raimann in *Monatsblatt der numismatischen Gesellschaft in Wien* ii (1892), 118 and 153.

[65] Note the frequent occurrence of Réthy no. 98, which must have been issued in large quantities. The early Friesacher commonly remained in circulation for many years.

ca. 1300 that there was a regular and plentiful coinage in Slavonia. At other times such money as there was found its way there from surrounding regions.

The find-evidence does not indicate a marked concentration of the use of money in any town except Zagreb, although Osijek, Sisak, and Suhopolje may have been small centres at river crossing-points, and Pakrac and Virovitica were perhaps centres of monetary affairs. Most of the finds are from western Slavonia, and seem to be associated, at least in general terms, with routes running from Zagreb to the north-east and south-west. There are more recorded hoards, and far fewer stray-finds, than from Syrmia; much of Slavonia was no doubt a region through which merchants passed, but in which they found only limited opportunities for commerce. Money was first carried through the country on a large scale at the time when the Hungarian economy was expanding, and in particular, when trade-relations with Germany were developed, after the fall of the Byzantine Empire. The introduction of the banovac, and its rapid rise to popularity, are undoubtedly to be associated with the economic prosperity of Zagreb, and probably also, indirectly, with the German trade. It was perhaps not until the four-teenth century that trade along the route from Zagreb to the Adriatic coast grew to importance. Thereafter Hungary's contacts with Germany were no longer through Slavonia as they had been before, and the monetary affairs of the rest of the province declined.

The hoards and other finds from Slovenia can usefully be divided into three geographical groups, based on the three main lowland areas. The Ljubljana basin is the most important of the three; eastwards, the route from Ljubljana to Zagreb passes through Trebnje to reach the Krka valley and Kostanjevica; to the north-east, Celje is the centre for another little valley, and is linked by a routeway to the Ptujskopolje, where the towns of Maribor and Ptuj lie on the river Drava. The character of the finds from each of these lowland areas is somewhat different. Slovenia had a vigorous monetary system of its own, an extension of the Carinthian one, only for two or three decades around 1220. At other times, the currency was that of the nearby regions. Italian influence was strongest in the Ljubljana basin, and that of Germany around Celje and Ptuj.

The Slovenian mints, which were active first at the beginning of the thirteenth century, had mostly declined again by the middle of the century. Their brief hey-day was based on the plentiful supplies of silver from the eastern Alps, and on the traffic between Germany and Hungary. On the broad view, some of the mint-places, in the lowlands of Slovenia, were simply small market-towns which enjoyed a coinage of their own because of the availability of bullion and because their overlords were anxious to secure the profits to be derived from minting. Others were little more than trading-posts or stages on the routes leading to Hungary, on which both towns and mints were encouraged or established from the same motive of profit to the overlord. The working-out of the richest veins of silver which had supplied Friesach and St. Veit; the accession of Béla IV to the Hungarian throne, and the different policies which he adopted; the Mongol incursions; and the unsettled political conditions in south-eastern Germany in the third quarter of the thirteenth century all checked the development of monetary affairs which the years 1200-1230 had witnessed in Slovenia.

A quantitative estimate of the coinage struck in Slovenia is not easy to make, but in forming a general impression one should remember that the series has been studied very intensively indeed, first by Luschin, above all by Baumgartner, and also by Fritsch and other scholars. Prolonged searching among the thousands of Friesacher from Hungarian hoards has yielded a great many die-duplicates and die-linked specimens, on the basis of which much of the numismatic history of the frontier coinages has been reconstructed. [66] The amount of die-duplication among the coins published by Baumgartner gives a somewhat exaggerated idea of the proportion that one might expect in a random sample; but it is obvious that the Friesacher of the first half of the thirteenth century have had an unusually high survival-rate, and that it is only for that reason that so many Slovenian coins are available for study.

Kamnik (Stein) and Ljubljana were the mints of southern Slovenia. The coins of Kamnik illustrate well the rapid changes of dynastic fortunes, and the varying balance between Austria and Italy, which were the political reflection of Slovenia's march-land character. A succession of rulers copied the issues, now of Friesach, now of St. Veit, now of the Italian cities at the head of the Adriatic. One or two types of

---

[66] Baumgartner, "Die Blütezeit", *passim;* W. Fritsch, "Anhang zu E. Baumgartner 'Die Blütezeit der friesacher Pfennige' ", *NZ* lxxix (1961), 64-71.

twelfth-century Friesacher have been attributed to Kamnik by Baumgartner: they are among the earliest evidences of monetary affairs in medieval Slovenia. Heinrich IV of Andechs-Meran struck coins on the Friesach model, first as Count, then as Margrave (1204-05; 1205-28). After his death, the Meran estates passed, by the marriage of his niece Agnes, to Duke Friedrich II of Austria-Styria. When Agnes was widowed, she struck coins in her own right. In 1248 she married again, and Kamnik passed to Duke Ulrich III of Carinthia. On his death, the town became the property of Otokar II, who struck a parallel coinage to that issued by his mint of Zeiring (1269-76). [67] At Ljubljana, as at Kamnik, there was an alternation of style which reflects the balance of Italian and Austrian influence; but at Ljubljana, a few miles further south, the Italian style predominates. Duke Bernhard II of Carinthia (1202-56) struck coins from ca. 1215 onwards. The issues in the Friesacher style from the Ljubljana mint belong to the period ca. 1225 - 40. [68]

A number of mints in the lower valley of the river Krka, which was the traditional frontier between Slovene and Slavonic territories, took advantage of its situation as an important routeway to Croatia and Hungary. The most characteristic coins of this group of mints show two facing busts, or a bust and an eagle, side by side above a wall, with a star, or a palm-tree, above and between the two figures. The bishops of Freising, who held land under the house of Andechs-Meran, set up a mint at Gutenwert. Their coins, of which there is only one scarce issue, were attributed by Luschin to Bishop Otto II (1188-1220), on the stylistic affinities of the type with certain Bavarian coins of the same date. More specifically, Luschin dates the issue to the years 1209-15 when relations between the bishop and Heinrich IV were strained. The bulk of the coins of Gutenwert are attributed to Heinrich and dated 1215-28. [69] At Kostanjevica (Landstrass), on an island in the Krka, and thus a place of refuge in time of threat, duke Bernhard of Carinthia struck coins, first in the Italian style (ca. 1210-20), and thereafter

---

[67] Baumgartner, "Die Blütezeit".

[68] E. Baumgartner, "Ljubljanska Kovnica v XIII Stoletju", *Glasnik Muzejskega Društva za Slovenijo* xv (1934), 92 - 102; translated into German as "Geschichte der Münzstätte Laibach im 13. Jahrhundert", in *Mitteilungen der numismatischen Gesellschaft in Wien* ii (xviii) (1939), 45-51 and 68-75. Note Baumgartner's subsequent reattribution of Luschin no. 148 from Kamnik to Ljubljana.

[69] See Baumgartner, "Die Blütezeit", and, on the location of the mint, a review by A. Jeločnik of D. M. Metcalf, *The Coinage of South Germany in the Thirteenh Century*, in *Argo* i (1962), 72-73

on the Friesacher model. [70] Baumgartner has identified a coin with the legend SANCTA CRVX as the issue of a mint situated in the parish of that name only two or three miles from Kostanjevica, on the south bank of the river Krka. His theory of "branch-mints" (which finds some kind of parallel in the Hungarian mint-organization discussed above) is of considerable general interest. He emphasizes how simple was the equipment required by a medieval mint. [71] Where the river Krka joined the Sava, the Brežice mint struck Friesacher of which the most plentiful issue is the series identified by Baumgartner as conventional coins of archbishop Eberhard II of Salzburg and duke Leopold VI of Austria-Styria. In a classic study of die-linkage he shows how the mint struck coins copying various other Friesacher types. He identifies Rajhenburg and Čatež as "branch-mints" of Brežice; but the latter of these has been queried. [72]

In the north of Slovenia, near the river Drava, there was a mint at the small regional centre of Slovenj Gradec. The Celje hoard, in which there was a large proportion of coins from Slovenj Gradec, suggests that the mint was very active, perhaps the most active in Slovenia, in the first half of the thirteenth century; but the confirmation of other hoards would be welcome. It was in the hands of Heinrich IV of Andechs-Meran until his death in 1228, after which it passed to his brother, the patriarch Berchtold V of Aquileia. Slovenj Gradec, by Berchtold's will, became the property of the see on his death, but the will was contested and did not become effective. [73] The market- and route-town of Ptuj had an active mint ca. 1220-30, where, it would seem, duke Leopold VI of Austria-Styria and archbishop Eberhard II of Salzburg struck jointly. [74]

In the Hungarian hoards of Abapuszta, Érszodoró, and Dorozsma, for each of which a date of deposit of 1241 has been suggested, the proportion of Slavonian coins to Austrian Friesacher struck after 1200 was 1:3, 1:2, and 1:3. [75] This gives some idea of the relative importance of the mints.

In Ljubljana itself, as in Zagreb, several foreign coinages dominated the currency in turn, and it seems that only for a brief period had the town a strong currency of its own. The date at which a monetary economy grew up in the Ljubljana basin is not exactly known, but it cannot have been long before the end of the twelfth century, and it may in fact have been a good deal later. The earliest recorded find, from

---

[70] Baumgartner, "Die Blütezeit".

[71] *Ibid.*   [72]*Ibid.* See also Fritsch, *op. cit.*   [73] *Ibid.*   [74] *Ibid.*   [75] *Ibid.*

the neighbourhood of Ljubljana, was not published in sufficient detail for the date of its deposit to be fixed. A large number of Friesacher, all of the same issue, but of three different types, was discovered. They bore "the usual inscriptions", and were said to be remarkably well struck from carefully engraved dies. [76] The most likely identification from this rather vague account is that the coins were ERIACENSIS issues of the later type, struck in the 1180's. Another two finds of Friesacher from the Ljubljana basin are both stray Halblinge. The earlier of them, from about 1220, was found in the stone-mines at Zalog, near Ljubljana,[77] while the other, a unique coin of Bernhard, of about 1240, was discovered in 1828 at Ljubljana while dredging the river. [78] In 1897, a hoard was discovered in the town during building-work on the Catholic cathedral, which lies within the bend of the river, due north of the castle. Two-thirds of the coins were from the Aquileian group of mints, and one-third were from the Tirol. The types and quantities of the "Aquileian" coins in this and other Slovenian hoards are set out in Table 14. The date of deposit of the Ljubljana hoard was after 1334. [79]

Few of the hoards of Aquileian coins are as late as that; most of them seem to fall, on the internal evidence, within the same short period ca. 1305 - ca. 1315, and one may reasonably assume that most, perhaps all, of them were hidden or lost during the fighting which took place in Slovenia between Heinrich of Carinthia and Albrecht of Habsburg in 1306-08. [80] The chronology of the Aquileian and Triestine series is not known in any detail: a hoard which contained coins of the patriarch Ottobono must have been concealed after 1302, and one with coins of Enrico II of Gorizia, after 1304. The assumption that the date of deposit of most of the group of hoards is 1306-08 rests partly on the fact that they are a chronologically isolated group. They are the best example known from the Balkans of a group of medieval hoards associated with military events. [81] When there is a number of hoards from roughly the

---

[76] *Archiv für Kunde österreichischer Geschichts-quellen* xxxiii (1865), 50.

[77] Luschin, no. 12 (Friesach, ca. 1220). I am indebted for this information to Professor A. Jeločnik. The coin is now in the Narodni Muzej, Ljubljana.

[78] Ljubljana mint, Baumgartner Typa 5a, *ca.* 1240; see Baumgartner's monograph cited at p. 167, note 68.

[79] A. Müllner, "Der Münzfund beim Baue des 'Katolški Dom' im April 1897", *Argo* v (1897), 100ff. and vi (1898), 18ff.; *Monatsblatt der numismatischen Gesellschaft in Wien* iv, 219.

[80] Jeločnik, "Dve Najdbi".

[81] Advances in our knowledge of the chronology of the Byzantine scyphate bronze may add a Bulgarian group from 1185-87.

same date, they offer a good chance of studying regional differences in the composition of the currency. It is the 1306-08 group which demonstrates most clearly the variation in the money in use within the restricted area of the several lowland basins of Slovenia.

The two small towns of Kamnik and Kranj are market-places for the northern part of the Ljubljana basin. At Kranj some time before 1851, and at Kamnik in 1856, there were discovered hoards which are both very possibly to be associated with the events of 1306-08. The varieties present in the Kranj hoard are unfortunately not known, but the rulers whose issues were represented are shown in Table 14.[82] The Kamnik hoard contained between three and four hundred coins, hidden in an earthenware pot at a depth of two feet. More than two-thirds of them were of the mint of Aquileia, while the rest were of Trieste, Gorizia, and the Tirol. The types are shown in Table 14; the number of each type was not, unfortunately, recorded.[83] Venetian grossi made up the whole of a pot-hoard of 295 coins discoverd at Kranj in 1895. It was concealed probably not long after 1310, for it contained at least three of the rare coins of Marino Giorgi; 176, or 60% of the hoard, were coins of Pietro Gradenigo, and 35 were of Raniero Zeno. The discovery of two or three more Slovenian hoards from the same decade would show whether Venetian money was challenging that of the Aquileian mints (so quickly after 1308), or whether, as is more likely, the Kranj hoard of 1895 was exceptional.[84]

---

[82] F. Schweitzer, *Abrégé de l'Histoire des Contes de Gorice et Série de leurs Monnaies*, Trieste 1851. The two bracteates from Kranj attributed by Schweitzer to Henry II are clearly fifteenth-century coins, and he must have been misled in his information that they were found associated with the early fourteenth-century coins reported by him. I am indebted to Professor A. Jeločnik, who showed me the bracteates (see *CNItalicorum* VI, p. 56, note), which are now in the Narodni Mujei, Ljubljana, and told me of a more recent hoard which puts the fifteenth-century attribution beyond doubt.

[83] A hundred and seventy of the coins went to the *Bezirksvorsteher* before dispersal, and of these 90 were sent to the imperial coin-cabinet while another part of the same parcel fell to Professor V. Konschegg. The rest of the hoard was dispersed; some coins from it are, probably, in the museum at Ljubljana, without record of provenance. See *Mitteilungen der Kentralkommission* i (1856), 185, and *Archiv für Kunde österreichischen Geschichts-quellen* xxiv (1860), 289f. The account is far from clear, but it seems to describe several types not published in *CNItalicorum*, namely, coins of Berchtold with the figure of St. Hermagorus, and of Gregor with the bust of St. Hermagorus.

[84] A. Müllner, "Fund von Venetianermünzen bei Krainburg", *Argo* iv (1896), 191. See also *Monatsblatt der numismatischen Gesellschaft in Wien* iii, 344, where the following of Papadopoli's varieties are recorded: R. Zeno, 3, 11, 12, 13, 14, 15, 17

The most usual route from Ljubljana to the head of the Adriatic was that which led to Trieste and Aquileia, but there was also a more southerly way, reaching the coast opposite the island of Krk, which was not much longer. Some evidence that it was followed by merchants is provided by the Dolenja vas hoard, from near Ribnica. It was very similar in its composition and date of deposit to the finds from Kamnik and Kranj, that is, probably 1306-08, but contained in addition some Venetian coins: out of a total of 209 coins, 184 were of the Aquileian group of mints, and 24 were grossi of various doges. There was, lastly, an extremely rare coin of Premsyl Otokar II from the mint of Kostanjevica, in the Aquileian style, which demonstrates that the mint was at work for some part of the period 1270-76. [85] An early coin of Trieste has been found at Gorenji Logatec. [86] Logatec lies on the route to the coast, and the find is possibly to be associated with trade along it, but it could well have been lost a good many years after it was struck, for the fourteenth-century hoards still include coins struck in the middle years of the thirteenth century.

The route to the east from Ljubljana, after reaching the headwaters of the river Krka, left the valley again in order to touch Trebnje. The distribution of finds in the region, and the location of the various mints, both make it exceptionally clear that monetary affairs were closely connected with trade along the route to Zagreb. The earliest of the hoards, which is of considerable importance for the monetary history of Slovenia and western Slavonia, is that found at Dečja vas in 1933, in the area of the upper Krka. It was said to consist of about fifty coins, of which Baumgartner saw seventeen or eighteen, all of the ERIACENSIS issue of ca. 1180-90. It is likely that a number of specimens from

19, 28; G. Dandolo, 4, 5, 7, 12, 16, 19; P. Gradenigo, 1, 3, 4, 5, 10, 11. The coins of Marino Giorgi are the only three in the museum at Ljubljana with a Kranj provenance recorded on the tickets. The types are *CNItalicorum* no. 6 (2) and 6, var. (1) all with trefoil secret-mark. I am indebted to Professor Jeločnik for this information. The other doges whose coins occurred in the hoard, besides those already mentioned, are Pietro Ziani (1205-29), Giacomo Tiepolo, Marino Morosini, Lorenzo Tiepolo, Giacomo Contarini, Giovanni Dandolo, and Giovanni Soranzo.

[85] Jeločnik, "Dve Najdbi". For the Aquileian issues, see Table 14. The Venetian coins were of I. Tiepolo (1), R. Zeno (2), L. Tiepolo (2), I. Contarini (1), G. Dandolo (1), and P. Gradenigo (17).

[86] Volrico, *CNItalicorum* no. 9. The coin is now in the Narodni Muzej, Ljubljana. I am indebted to Professor Jeločnik for information about it.

the Dečja vas find, formerly in Baumgartner's cabinet, are now in the museum at Ljubljana without record of provenance. [87]

Some children playing near the river Krka found a hoard of Aquileian coins at Veliko Globoko in 1936. The find passed into private hands, and has not been fully published. It included, among other types, coins from the mints of Aquileia and Trieste from the middle of the thirteenth century. If those that are recorded are typical, it must be the earliest Aquileian hoard from Slovenia, concealed in the third quarter of the thirteenth century. [88] The varieties are shown in Table 14. A similar, slightly later hoard from the same routeway was found at Lanišče. It was deposited probably in the 1280's and contained 202 coins, of which about two-thirds were of Aquileia and one-third of Trieste. There was one coin of Gorizia, one of Ljubljana in the Aquileian style, and one of Venice. The coins of the Aquileian mints are set out in Table 14. [89] In 1809, near the church of Golo, not far from Ig, a stray coin of the patriarch Raimundo was found, and a notice of the discovery, together with a drawing of the coin, were preserved in the *Liber Missarum* of the Golo church for 1808. Like the Triestine coin from Gorenji Logatec, it may have been lost a long time after it was struck. [9]

Two hoards from near Trebnje are to be added to the group from 1306-08. The Mirna find of 1884 is notable for the gros tournois of Philippe IV which it included. There were originally about five hundred coins in all, but many had been dispersed before two notes describing the rest were published. Out of 271 pieces described, all but 6 were of the Aquileian group of mints. There were said to be "two types of Bertoldus, four of Gregor, six of Arlongus..."; the types are listed, as far as the information allows, in Table 14. Two Venetian grossi, of Giacomo Tiepolo and Giovanni Dandolo, and three Serbian groši complete

---

[87] Klemenc, "Nalazi Novaca". Most of Baumgartner's collection was bought for the museum. The only coin there with a record of provenance from Dečja vas is an issue of Villach, Luschin, "Friesacher Pfennige", no. 293. Another coin from the hoard is as Luschin. no. 7; see Baumgartner, "Die Blütezeit". In 1953 Professor Jeločnik bought a third coin, of Baumgartner's Type 2 (*NZ* 1935), from a man who confirmed that the find-spot was as supposed. I am indebted to Professor Jeločnik for information about the hoard.

[88] Klemenc, "Nalazi Novaca".

[89] A. Luschin von Ebengreuth, "Der Münzfund von Lanische", *NZ* iii (1871), 516ff. The Venetian coin is given as Schweitzer no. 5, which has an annulet below the elbow as the secret-mark, but I am not sure whether it is meant that the Lanišče coin was of exactly the same variety.

[90] I am indebted to Professor A. Jeločnik for information about this find.

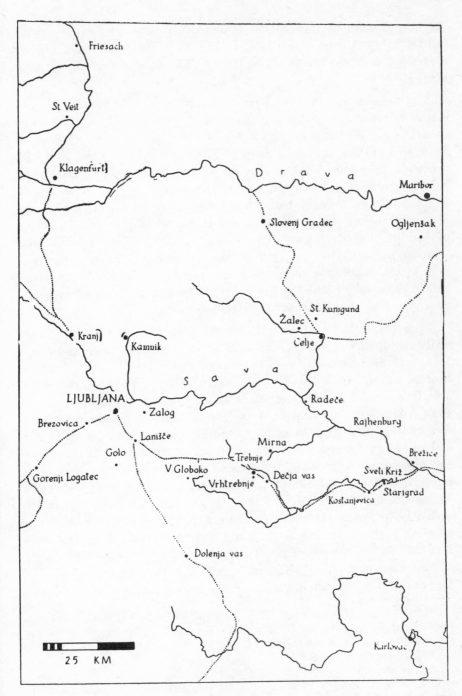

Map IX. Slovenia.

the tally. Again, the provenance is unusual; it may be compared with the Celje hoard. The surprises from the Mirna hoard include, finally, a previously unpublished coin of Trieste. The date of deposit was probably 1306-08. [91]

From near by, the Vrh Trebnje hoard of 1932 differed from the earlier discovery in that it included a large proportion of north Italian denari picoli. Out of 140 coins, 107 were published. They consisted of 32 grossi from the Aquileian group of mints (see Table 14) and 75 denari predominantly from Venice. Because of the number of Gorizian coins in the total, Jeločnik suggested that the hoard was a sum of money which had been brought from that town or its neighbourhood only a short time before its concealment, which he set in 1306-08. The coins of Mantua, Padua, Brescia, and Verona hint very strongly that the traveller to whom the money belonged had, before arriving in Gorizia, been in the middle Po valley; there is probably a parallel between the Vrh Trebnje hoard and the north Italian hoards of Venetian and Serbian grossi of about the same date. [92]

Bracteates, in the thirteenth century, were the currency of Swabia Switzerland, and Bohemia, as well as of most of north Germany. Although the Austrian coins of the second half of the thirteenth century became almost one-sided in their designs, they were not true bracteates. The small but very interesting hoard from Starigrad, in the lower Krka valley, in 1903 contained at least 33 bracteates together with 4 Aquileian coins, concealed in a pot. Some of them are now in Vienna and others in Ljubljana. A second small pot-hoard of 23 bracteate was discovered in the same place two years later. All but one of these coins, the type of which was a battlemented tower, were destroyed. No specimens of bracteates of these types from Starigrad are known with other provenances, and it has been suggested that they were struck by Otokar II, who ruled in Carinthia and the Krain during the years 1269/70-76, for the use of his Bohemian troops, who were accustomed to that kind of money. [93] The Starigrad finds are another example of deposits in the Balkan march-lands associated with military events.

[91] See *VHrvat.AL* vi (1884), 122-23 and vii (1885), 24; A. Puschi, "Eine unedierte Münze der Bischöfe von Triest", *NZ* xxvi (1894), 37ff. The legends of the Serbian coins were given, I imagine by error, as STEFAN VROSIUS S M VENETI.

[92] Jeločnik, "Dve Najdbi".

[93] The hoard-reports and photographs of the types may conveniently be studed in Luschin, "Friesacher Pfennige". See also W. Kubitschek, in *Mitteilungen der Zentralkommission für Kunst und historische Denkmale* iii, series ii, 400. Professor Jeločnik was kind enough to discuss the coins with me.

CNItalicorum plate Description	KRANJ, 1851	KAMNIK, 1856	LANIŠČE, 1870	MIRNA, 1884	ST. KUNIGUND, 1891	LJUBLJANA, 1897	STARIGRAD, 1903	VRH TREBJE, 1932	VEL.GLOBOKO, 1936	DOLENJA VAS, 1945
MINT OF AQUILEIA										
Bertoldo, 1218–51		2?		x					x	
I, 27 Friesacher										
I, 26 3-turretted castle										
I, 25 Eagle										
I, 24 Bust of Virgin			2							
Gregorio, 1251–69	x	2?		x					x	
II, 1 St. Hermagorus		x	9			x				4
II, 2 Lily, Standing patriarch			2			x		1	1	5
II, 3 Lily, seated patriarch		2	12			x				8
II, 5 Cross with trefoils		x	15			x				3
II, 4 Eagle		3	33			x	2			10
Raimondo, 1273–98	x									
II, 13 Eagle		x	8	x		x				3
II, 14 Tower		4	38	x		x			1	12
II, 12 Crossed batons		x	8	x		x			2	7
II, 11 Heraldic arms		4		x		x			1	24
Pietro Gerra, 1299–1301										
II, 17 Eagle, heraldic arms		15		74		25			1	31
Ottobono, 1302–15		16?								
II, 18 Arms		x				46				35
Pagano, 1319–32										
II, 20 Crossed batons						44				
Bertrando, 1334–50										
III, 3 Eagle						x				
III, 4 St. Hermagorus						x				
MINT OF TRIESTE										
Volrico, 1234–54				x					x	
XXII, 17 St. Giusto										
XXII, 18 Altar, lance		1	5							3
XXII, 16 Battlemented walls			2							
Anonymous, 1254										
XXII, 15 View of city		3	8	x		1				2
Givardo II, 1255–60										
XXII, 20 Paschal Lamb										
Arlongo, 1260–82	x			x						
XXII, 21 Paschal Lamb		1	7			x				
XXII, 22 Dove			12			x			1	13
XXIII, 3 Temple						x				2
XXII, 15 Rose			1			x			1	
XXII, 25 Star and crescent		4	34			x	1		1	19

CN Italicorum plate Description	KR	K	L	M	S	LJ	ST	T	G	D
XXIII, 1 Crossed sceptres										
XXIII, 2 Star			3							
Volvino, 1282–86										
— Star				1						
Rodolfo, 1303–04										
XXIII, 4 Unicorn		1								
MINT OF GORIZIA										
Mainardo III, 1232–58										
V, 3 Lion / Rose										
Mainardo IV, 1258–71										
V, 4 Lion / Rose										
V, 5 Shield / Cross										
Alberto II, 1271–1304	x			x						
V, 6–10 Lion / Rose			1			35		22		3
V, 8 Lion / Cross						4				
Enrico II, 1304–23	x									
V, 13 Shield / Rose		x				7				
V, 14 Shield / Cross										
Alberto IV, 1338–74										
V, 17 Shield / Rose										
V, 18 Shield / Cross						?		(1)		

Table 14. Slovenian hoards of coins of the Aquileian group of mints.

North-eastern Slovenia (as it is today), has in the past been linked more closely with Styria. In the hoards from the area of Celje, Maribor, and Ptuj from the first quarter of the fourteenth century, Aquileian coins are almost entirely absent. In the first half of the thirteenth century Friesacher made up the currency, as they did in southern Slovenia, but a little later there seems to have been a sharply-defined boundary in monetary circulation which cut across Slovenia. The fourteenth-century coins of Friesach and Graz can be dated with even less assurance than those of the Aquileian group of mints, and the association of Friesacher hoards with the events of 1306-08 is therefore too conjectural to be of much value.

The earliest of the hoards from the region is of great importance for our knowledge of monetary circulation in Slovenia, since no other similar find has yet come to light. The Celje hoard of 1897 consisted of about four hundred Friesacher; details are available about only half of them. [94] The date of deposit, ca. 1250, is after the hey-day of the Slovenian mints, and yet only a quarter of the parcel is from the mints of Friesach and St. Veit. One can scarcely generalize from this and the Gračansko Dolje hoard, [95] but if they are representative, the local mints were providing most of the currency of Slovenia in the first part of the thirteenth century, and certainly a far larger proportion than obtained in the Hungarian hoards.

A Serbian coin has been found at Celje, near the railway-station. It may have been from an unrecorded hoard similar in composition to the Mirna hoard of 1884; if it was simply a stray find, the same hoard suggests the most likely route by which it reached Slovenia. [96] Also at Celje a stray Friesacher has come to light. [97]

Eight kilometres away, at St. Kunigund, a hoard of about three thousand coins was found in 1891. Luschin was able to examine 1,856 pieces from it, most of which were issued by Rudolf of Habsburg and his successors at Graz and, probably, Zeiring. There were Viennese and a few Aquileian coins. Four specimens attributed to Rudolf and Ludwig of Bavaria (1294-1317) were perhaps the latest in the hoard, and if so it is a candidate for inclusion in the 1306-08 group. The find also shows the northern limit of influence of the Italian money. [98] Another find from near Celje, discovered at Petričeva Pristava in 1936 or earlier, contained about a hundred fourteenth-century Pfennige of Vienna, Friesach, Graz, and Bavaria. [99]

Von Renner, in his study of the Virštajn hoard, listed the very varied types, predominantly from the mints of Graz and Zeiring, in that and also in several other similar finds. The Žalec and Ogljenšak hoards from north-eastern Slovenia, are candidates for inclusion in the 1306-08 group, as are the Radeče and Virštajn finds, from the Sava valley, which suggest that the money of northern Slovenia was carried along the routeway which led towards Zagreb.[100]

[94] Baumgartner, "Die Blütezeit". The mints from which the coins came were as follows: Slovenj Gradec (85), Friesach (44), Kamnik (41), Völkermarkt (18), St. Veit (5), Ljubljana (2), Ptuj (1), Zeiring (1), Uncertain (3).
[95] See p.   above.
[96] Ljubić, Opis, Stefan Uroš I, Type III/xii (plate IV, 13).
[97] Luschin, "Steierische Münzfunde", no. 143.
[98] See Monatsblatt der numismatischen Gesellschaft in Wien iii, 17 and 28, where a list of the types is given.
[99] Klemenc, "Nalazi Novaca".
[100] V. von Renner, "Der Münzenfund von Wierstein" Mitteilungen der öster-

Finally, there is the Maribor hoard of 1931, which is among the earliest deposits of west European gold coinage from any country, dating from 1329 or shortly thereafter. The coins, consisting of about a hundred gold pieces and half-a-dozen Pfennige, were found among the burnt remains of bones. They come from the site of a ghetto, and were very possibly the stock-in-trade of a money-changer or merchant, lost apparently during a fire, which even melted some of them. Out of 52 coins published by Baumgartner, 45 were Florentine gold florins, mostly struck between 1312 and 1329; there was a Venetian gold piece and a Goldgulden of Prague. Of the silver coins, 4 were of Graz and one was of Vienna. There are two further fiorini in the museum at Ljubljana which are doubtless from the hoard. [101] At Brezovica, which, like Gorenji Logatec, is on the route from Ljubljana to Trieste, a fiorino d'oro was discovered in 1854. It was not in fresh condition, but was possibly concealed or lost a little before the middle of the fourteenth century. [102]

Town and route were very much the framework of monetary affairs in the march-lands of the north-west. Of the towns at river crossing-points, some, such as Mitrovica and Sisak, were old-established centres of urban life, while others, such as Zagreb and Kamnik, were more recent foundations. The main routes with which the use of money was associated ran obliquely through the march-lands, from Tuzla into Hungary, from Buda to Zagreb and from there through Ljubljana to Austria. In the fourteenth century the western approaches shifted from Austria to the head of the Adriatic: north Italian coins were carried into the march-lands, and banovci were carried along the route from Zagreb to Senj and other ports. The Slavonian coins were also car-

---

reichischen Gesellschaft für Münz- und Medaillenkunde xi, 81-83, 89-94, 101-105, 113-118. See also Monatsblatt der numismatischen Gesellschaft in Wien ii, 274. There were about 300 coins in the Zalec hoard, 276 from Ogljenšak (Kohlberg), about 2,000 from Virštajn, and about 200 in the Radeče hoard, which Jeločnik hopes to publish.

[101] E. Baumgartner, "Važna numismatička najdba v Mariboru", Časopis za Zgodovino in Narodopisije xxvii (1932), 34ff. gives a list of the segni on the florins, and their disposition. Dr P. Berghaus has kindly informed me that certain coins unidentified by Baumgartner can be found in Joseph's publication of the Bretzenheim hoard: B24 is J100, B25 is J103, B26 is J56, B28 is J96, B 29 is J81, and B31 is J22.2 The segni of the two further coins at Ljubljana are a pair of scissors, and a crossbow (J70).

[102] The coin is in private hands. I am indebted for the information about it to Professor A. Jeločnik, who has himself examined it.

ried into Bosnia, thus once again suggesting a trade-route linking different regions.

When the impetus given to monetary affairs by the circulation of Austrian silver towards Hungary was exhausted,—after the *Blütezeit der friesacher Pfennige*, in Baumgartner's suggestive phrase—Slovenia was able to maintain a monetary economy; and Syrmia still had the traffic between Bosnia and Pannonia. Slavonia, however, fell back to an economy in which coinage seems to have played little part. The most intriguing question which a survey of the numismatic evidence sets for the historian is how Slavonia was able to profit so much from its geographical situation in the thirteenth century.

CHAPTER VII

THE ADRIATIC COAST AS A MEETING-PLACE
IN MONETARY AFFAIRS

Two conflicting tendencies may be discerned in the monetary history of the Balkan peninsula's western seaboard. First, the fragmented geographical character of the littoral was reflected in the region's fragmented pattern of monetary affairs. Several coastal towns were each the focus of a circulation-area limited to the narrow plains in which they lay, together with the trade-route leading inland. Secondly, the sea-lane of the Adriatic united these little territories, and was the means by which the same kinds of coinage were often carried from one to another of them. It is the petty coinages which reflect the fragmentation of the coasts, since they were not used far away from their place of issue; the trade-coinages, on the other hand, show the unity of the seaboard, and its economic links with the hinterland, because they met the needs of the widely-travelling merchant.

The interesting local coinages of Split, Dubrovnik, Kotor, and (similarly, but after 1355) of Shkodër, Bar, Ulcinj, Drivasto, and Šas [1] were mainly municipal currencies, used in the market-place and at the quay-side. [2] In the thirteenth century, the more valuable coins of Carinthia, and subsequently those of Slavonia, were carried to the coast

---

[1] See Rešetar, *Dubrovačka Numizmatika*; Stockert, *Spalato*; K. Stockert, "Die Munzen der Städte Nordalbaniens", *NZ* xliii (1910), 67-128; *Ibid.*, "Die vorvenezianischen Munzen der Gemeinde von Cattaro", *NZ* xliv (1911), 202-36, xlv (1912) 113-48.

[2] Cf. J. G. Milne, in *Transactions of the International Numismatic Congress*, London, 1936, p. 94. "A few years ago I was enquiring for coins at Dubrovnik, and was told by a local collector that he had formerly got examples...from Ragusa Vecchia but the supply had ceased after the erection of some buildings along the shore... At Split... I saw market-boats from the islands lying at the water's edge, and the occupants handing out goods and receiving payment over the bulwarks...there would be ample opportunity for dropping coins into the water, especially if arguments arose and were carried out with as much spirit as they are today".

by traders, and circulated there. Indeed, some of the early Friesacher appear to have been issued specially for this trade.[3] At the end of the thirteenth and in the first part of the fourteenth century, the grossi of Venice were being used in parts of the littoral, and those of Serbia were being carried down from the interior and were circulating along the coast, whilst groši of Dubrovnik, a little later, were, conversely, being carried inland. At various times, coinage was carried to and from Dalmatia by half-a-dozen routes which led to the hinterland, as well as by sea from Venice and Constantinople. At the head of the gulf, the Aquileian coinage went through the Pear Tree Pass to Slovenia; Friesacher reached the coast probably at Aquileia, and were carried south from there; routes from both Ljubljana and Zagreb came to the Adriatic near the modern Rijeka, and other routes from Zagreb ended further south at Senj and, probably, at Karlobag, if we may judge by the banovci which have been found along them. The Una valley from Knin to Bihać was followed by merchants who carried money from Slavonia towards the coast, while the early Serbian groši were carried to the A-driatic by various routes, but particularly, it would seem, by those which led down to Kotor. Dalmatia was, in short, a meeting-place for the currencies of many regions, for it lay mid-way athwart the trade-routes which linked the industrial markets of Venice and other commercial towns with their complementary economic regions in the west Balkan hinterland.

There are a good many references to money in the documentary records that have survived, particularly from the late twelfth century onwards. On examination, however, it frequently turns out that they are of little help as a guide to the currency of the coast, because they are not specific enough as regards the coins. Also, the moneys mentioned in the merchants' agreements and in legal undertakings are probably, in many cases, moneys of account. One of the most interesting records, which is also one of the most specific as regards coinage, concerns a misadventure on the Dalmatian coast in 1177. Some pirates from the neighbourhood of Šibenik attacked a ship which was sailing down the Adriatic and overreached themselves so far as to rob an apostolic legate, a cardinal. They called down on the heads of theArchbishop of Split and the Bishop of Trogir the displeasure of Alexander III, who threatened the whole district of Šibenik with a general interdict, excluding only penance and infant baptism, if the cardinal's belongings were not re-

---

[3] Cf. I. Rengjeo, *Prvi Hrvatski Novci*, Sarajevo, 1936.

turned. A clerk drew up a list of the missing goods, among which various kinds of coins were named: *sterlingi, tarreni,* and *masmutini,* as well as the more usual *perperi* were among them.[4] The presence of north European, Sicilian, and Arabic coins in central Dalmatia, however, may have been quite exceptional, and the record is of value mainly as a reminder of the complexities of monetary circulation.

We read of Archbishop Gaudius of Split, in 1150, trying to secure the money necessary for a visit to Rome; by custom his churches were not required to make a contribution, but they provided 50 nomismata on this occasion: "... partem nostram decimarum civitatis cum oblatione nummorum a praedecessoribus nostris... nihil de Curia nostra ...habuimus, nisi quartam partem decimarum, videlicet restaurationis, qua potiebamur, cum oblatione nummorum, quousque ipsi 1. Bysantii cum usuris extorqueri possent, eis tenere concessimus".[5]

The commonest document is the merchants' agreement, or colleganza; it is of interest to the monetary historian mainly because it shows the routes along which the merchants worked their way. Here is a typical one: Petrus Michael makes an agreement with Petrus Faletro, at Venice in 1191, "pro libris denariorum venecialium centum, quas de me in collegancia recepisti et tu posuisti...alias libras venecialium quinquaginta... de hinc usque Dyrachium sive per totum districtu Curfum et ubicumque compagnia eiusdem navis concordasset atque cum suprascripto habere negociari et procertare debebas per suprascriptas partes per mare et per terram et usque Saloniky...".[6] Men such as these ranged widely in their search for profit; a similar agreement of 1161 specifies the route "per terram de Constantinopoli usque Dyrachium et de inde per mare... in Venetia",[7] but that was an unusually long journey. Merchants setting out from Constantinople would generally not go further than the Peloponnese, and those setting out from Venice would generally keep to the Adriatic coasts and islands.

---

[4] G. Wenzel, *Codex Diplomaticus Arpadianus Continuatus,* vol. VI, *(*890-1235*)* (Monumenta Hungariae Historica, Ser. Diplomataria, vol. XI), Budapest, 1867, nos. 77-8. The list mentions 100 *masmutine,* 9 *oboli masmutini,* 4 marks of sterlings and other silver coins including *megulienses, igeunos, provinos, puglios,* and *oboli megulienses,* and *tarreni* of the king of Sicily.

[5] *Ibid.,* no. 43.

[6] A. Morozzo and A. Lombardo, *Documenti del Commercio Veneziane nei Secoli XI - XIII* (Regesta Chartarum Italiae, vol. XXVIII), 1940, no. 400.

[7] *Ibid.,* no. 150.

The peace treaty of 1186 between the Ragusans and the Grand Župan illustrates the economic contacts between the coastal cities, with their mixed population, and the Slavs of the immediate hinterland: "... et quod secure Ragusei per totam terram illorum, nominatim portum Narente, mercando, laborando, pascendo, et sua reposita recipiendo, et ligna incidendo, pergant sine ullo contrario secundum antiquam consuetudinem... et... denarios tollatur, per quos antea acceptum fuit. et quod solidos nullo unquam tempore super Raguscis...accipiant, sicut prius retro tempore acceperunt, pro nulla culpa quorumlibet hominum... et Sclavi Chelmunia, ut per civitatem, ubi voluerint, emant".[8] A more localized monetary circulation, of the kind that we may envisage from this extract, may in fact have dominated the monetary affairs of the coastlands.

In any case, the impression that different kinds of coins might have mingled freely on the littoral is, on balance, almost certainly mistaken. Rather, one currency may have succeeded another, and Venetian coins may have been used sometimes widely and at others only in certain areas, and so on. If this view is correct—and a hoard containing a mixture of different coins has never been recorded from Dalmatia—the pattern of monetary affairs must have been very varied. Any attempt to describe it would obviously have to rest on a large quantity of find-evidence. Until this is available, any discussion of the relative importance of unifying and separative tendencies is bound to be conjectural. Unfortunately the number of coin-finds which have been recorded is only enough to prove that far more are needed.[9] From Albania, little is available except the general impressions about finds noted down by Valentini. Without a detailed find-assemblage, the monetary historian can say nothing about the importance of the route from Dyrrachium to Thessaloniki, which figures so often in the military and political history of the times. When more finds have been published, one will probably be able to sharpen considerably the outlines of the picture that can now be given, and to add new sections to a particularly interesting chapter of monetary history.

---

[8] Wenzel, *op. cit.*, no. 105; and cf. S. Ljubić, *Listine o Odnošajih izmedju Južnoga Slavenstva i Mletačke Republika*, vol. I, 1868, no. XVII.

[9] F. Bulić for many years maintained a numismatic accession-register in the Split Archaeological Museum. Until recently, it was, unfortunately, not available for study.

Some small but valuable fragments of evidence from the tenth century come from central Dalmatia. At Solin, the ancient Salona, a follis of Constantine VII was found in 1914, of the type issued during the regency of his mother Zoe (913-19). Two more such pieces were the earliest from the second hey-day of Byzantine currency represented in the Kalodjera collection: there is a strong presumption that they were found on the island of Korčula. In the same collection there was one further coin of Constantine, from a later date in his reign. [10] The bronze of Constantine and Zoe is not particularly plentiful; at Athens and Corinth, for example, it makes up only 2 or 3 per cent. of the folles from the years 913-59. Together, the four finds are probably indicative of the phase of renewed Byzantine interest and effort in Dalmatia which began with Zoe's global policies against Bulgaria in the years 917-18 (compare the little Yakimovo hoard, from the region of Mikhailovgrad), and was continued under Romanus I, who invested the Croatian king, Tomislav, with the government of the Dalmatian cities and islands.

The next coins in the Kalodjera collection, in order of date, are two of Romanus (*BMC* 14ff.), and a Rex Regnantium follis, Class A, of variety 29/41 (see Table 3). There are three more specimens of the same variant, in a parcel of only 7, now in the Split Archaeological Museum without record of provenance. A gold coin of Constantine VII with Romanus II (*BMC* 60ff.)—if that is its correct attribution—has been found at Nadin, near Zadar. [11]

From the eleventh century there are numerous gold coins of Romanus III, for which a special explanation has been proposed. Further provenances await publication from the Split museum. A hoard of at least 23 such coins was found at Klobuk, near Ljubuški, in 1930; single pieces have come from the site of Narona or its vicinity (in 1933) and from Zagvozd, Balijin Dolac, more recently. Otherwise, the only find is a nomisma of Theodora, discovered at Bobovišće on Brač in 1915; [12] four coins with a presumed Korčula provenance are nomismata of Romanus IV and Michael VII, and silver (or electrum) of Michael VII and Alexius I. [13] The last coin in particular is an interesting one, for there

---

[10] *BMC* 45ff.
[11] Split museum, no 878.
[12] *Ibid.*, nos. 257-79, 869, 2311, and 354.
[13] *BMC* Type 1; 4. 35 gm. *BMC* Type 2; 4. 13 gm. *BMC* Type 2; 2. 17 gm. *BMC* cf. Type 5; 4. 33 gm. Split Archaeological Museum, Numismatic accession-register nos. 2615-8. The date of accession was apparently 1956 or not long before. I am much indebted to the authorities of the museum for making this information available.

is little else from the Balkans which is comparable with it except the Sofia hoard of 1897. [14]

Of about the same date as the group of four coins from Korčula, the Lepuri hoard of 1878 shows Hungarian influence in northern Dalmatia. One small silver coin of Kálmán was acquired by the Split Museum in that year, and another five were added later. They were said on the authority of S. Barbieri, an administrative officer in Benkovac, to have come from a hoard of at least two thousand coins. [15] All those which went to the Split Museum were in extremely fine condition. Kálmán conducted military campaigns in Dalmatia in 1102-1105; one may suspect very strongly that the Lepuri coins were concealed in those years. They may have been part of the military treasure chest. No other Hungarian silver of the period has been recorded from Dalmatia or from Slavonia, with the exception of a single coin from Donji Lapac. [16]

A third deposit from the same time or a little later, which again is entirely different in character, was discovered at Novi Vinodol, on the coast opposite Krk. Six obols of Champagne were presented to the Zagreb Museum by Dr. Dragutin Smokvina, parish priest of Novi. Although the coins of Champagne were carried far and wide, the fact that the parcel was made up of coins of only one region, and a distant one, suggests that they represent a sum of money brought to the Balkans by a traveller. [17] Like the Lepuri find, the coins from Novi are almost certainly exceptional, and therefore do not throw light on the regular currency of northern Dalmatia at the time.

By the late twelfth century, the usual coinage seems to have been the Friesacher. A hoard of some hundreds of such coins was discovered

---

[14] See pp. 83ff. above. Note that a "silver coin of Alexius I" was included in a hoard of Stefan Dušan and Stefan Uroš V found near Durrës before 1901, and published by Ipen in *Monatsblatt der Numism. Gesellsch. in Wien* v, 242.

[15] *BASDalmat.* i (1878), 126, and ii (1879), 176. Cf. Stockert, *Spalato*, p. 10, note 3, where he records that the Zadar Museum had various small coins of Kálmán (Réthy, plate 4, 42; 43; 49) found near the town. One may reasonably assume that they were from the Lepuri hoard.

[16] Stockert, *loc. cit.*, mentions that he had noticed, in a private collection, some similar coins [of Kálmán, cf. those at Zadar] which, according to the statement of their owner, came from deposit brought to light in Dalmatia. Whether or not these coins were from the Lepuri hoard can hardly be determined now; but in any case one may assume a connexion with the same events. For Donji Lapac, see p. 161 above.

[17] See below.

at Rogoznica, a little port on the headland between Trogir and Šibenik. They may have been carried there by sea from Aquileia or Trieste. [18] A stray find of a Friesacher of the same period has been reported from Lika. [19]

The Kalodjera collection included a follis of Manuel I of the "St. George" type, and a group of scyphate bronze coins, of Andronicus and Alexius III. One cannot feel as sure as with the earlier coins from the collection that they were found on Korčula, but if they were they are of considerable interest, for they show how far north, in the Adriatic coastlands, Byzantine coinage could circulate.

At Crikvenica, on the coast opposite Krk (a few miles north of Novi), a hoard of Italian denari piccoli was discovered in 1892. Their deposit may have been at about the same date as the Rogoznica treasure, or possibly up to two or three decades later. Most of the coins, it appears, were Veronese issues; but the Venetian issues are more useful as a guide to the date of concealment. There was one coin of Orio Malipiero (1178 - 1192), and two of Enrico Dandolo (1192-1205). Unfortunately, one cannot be sure that coins of later doges would have been present if the hoard had been withdrawn from circulation in, say, 1220. [20] A little to the south, once again in Lika, a similar hoard, also dated by a coin of Enrico Dandolo, was found at Perušić at some date before 1903. Denari of Bologna, Verona, and Padua, as well as Venice, occurred in it. [21]

Further south again, between Knin and Benkovac, a hoard of petty coinage struck at Split, in the same style as the coinage of Hungary, was found in 1896. [22] From the middle of the thirteenth century comes a coin of Ancona, which was found at Senj. [23]

---

[18] Brunšmid, "Našašća Novaca", VIII-XI, reports the accession of two coins to the Zagreb collection. I was able to notice only one recorded in the register, apparently of the type of Luschin, "Friesacher Pfennige", no. 184. From Brunšmid's description, the other was probably *ibid.*, no. 6. One wonders whether the museum acquired only. two specimens from the hoard because it was largely made up of these two types The date of discovery was 1899, and the date of deposit must be set at *ca.* 1200, or possibly later.

[19] Brunšmid, *loc. cit.*

[20] Cf. the Slatine hoard; see p. 190.

[21] The registers of the Zagreb museum record only one coin from each of the four towns.

[22] A. Luschin von Ebengreuth, "Der Fund von Zažvić", *NZ* xxxiii (1901), 16588.

[23] F. Kenner, "Beiträge zu einer Chronik der archäologischen Funde in der öster-

So far, a sequence of a dozen finds has been set out, illustrating six or seven apparently separate aspects of the monetary history of the Adriatic coast. Each aspect will need to be documented by several coin-finds before it will be possible to define the extent of Hungarian, Byzantine, and Venetian influence and the regions of circulation of the various currencies. The distribution of the few finds that are so far recorded suggests that by the end of the twelfth century the coast opposite Krk, the region of Lika, and the Krka valley from Knin to Šibenik may already have been areas with a more developed monetary economy than some other parts of the Adriatic coastlands.

For the local coinage of Split, the most valuable source of information is the Žažvić treasure of 1896. Some seven hundred coins, which had been wrapped up in dozens, in a bundle of linen cloth, were brought to light in the foundations of an eighth-or ninth-century basilica. The coins were tiny pieces of base silver (about one-third fine) similar in their general appearance and value to the Italian denari piccoli, which, indeed, they may have been intended to replace in the currency of central Dalmatia, although the Žažvić coins were Hungarian, not Italian, in style. The hoard would be precious if the only information it had yielded had been that the petty currency passed from hand to hand in packets of a dozen; there was, however, a great deal more to be learned from it. Luschin was able to study 641 coins from the hoard, out of which 629 were of a Hungarian model and 12 were inscribed SPA LATI NO. He had reason to suspect that there were originally more of the latter variety. He divided the 629 into eleven stylistic groups, of which the first eight accounted for 95 coins, while Groups IX to XI included 534 coins; there were 455 coins in Group X alone, with no essential variation in the dies. Here, then, was a hoard of an easily-recognized age-structure, drawn, it would seem, from a currency that had been maintained by a series of large issues during a preceding period of at least several decades. There is no way to judge the quantities of coins struck in any given period of years, but one may confidently assume a coinage on a large scale.

The origins of the Spalatine petty currency are referred to the reign

---

reichischen Monarchie. VII Fortsetzung", *Archiv für Kunde österreichische Geschichtsquellen* xxix (1863), at p. 336, where the coin is described as a denaro. Cf. *CNI* vol. XIII, plate i, nos. 2-3, but with rosette on either side of the initial-cross.

of king Imre of Hungary (1196-1204), whose HENRICVS monogram became the "type immobilisé" of the coinage, and, in a degenerated form, was continued for a period of roughly a century. It was replaced by a new type, with the legend SPA LATI NO or variants, possibly during the period between the extinction of the Arpád dynasty and the accession of Robert Karl to the Hungarian throne. Stockert discussed the possibility that the monogrammatic coins and those with the name of the town might, at least for a short time, have been issued concurrently. However that may be, the Slatine hoard, discussed below, shows that the SPALATINO series eventually replaced the earlier coinage completely in the currency. If there had been a simple change from one type to the other, and if the Žažvić hoard had been concealed very shortly after the introduction of the new type, one would expect all the SPALATINO coins in it to be very alike; but they were not. The relative dating of the hoard, and the place in the scheme of the scarce variety inscribed SPALATINVS, therefore remain to some extent problematic. Stockert's view that the elegantly-produced SPALATINVS variety is the introductory one raises difficulties in the interpretation of the Žažvić hoard, and his suggestion that the two types were issued concurrently, the signed type for use in the city and the unsigned type for use in the surrounding countryside, presupposes a pattern of monetary affairs that is hard to envisage. It is unsupported by such hoard-evidence as there is, and the stylistic similarities upon which it was based are not compelling. The economic dependence on Split of the immediately neighbouring islands is sharply pointed by a Venetian document of 1354 which Stockert quotes: "...homines insule de Braza faciebant sua mercimonia pro maiori parte tam in vendendo quam emendo cum illis de Spalato ...". We may suppose, provisionally, that the Žažvić hoard.belongs to the first or perhaps the second decade of the fourteenth century. [24]

There are traces of the existence of a little hoard deposited at a much earlier date, in the holdings of the Zadar museum. Stockert's *corpus* included only two Spalatine coins from Zadar, and he was surely correct in placing them both together at the very beginning of the Spalatine series. They are among the few examples of which the revers preserves something resembling a legend; on most of the coins, there are not even degenerate letters, but only a pattern of lines. Part of one specimen was submitted to chemical analysis, which was well worth while,

[24] Stockert, *Spalato*.

for it was found to contain, besides 38 parts per thousand of silver, 31
parts of gold. This suggests an origin for the metal in some Byzantine
electrum coinage. The cross-and-crosslets reverse type is, on the evidence of the coins at Zadar, doubtless the earliest variant, and Luschin's
Groups II, IV, V, and VI would thus appear to stand at the beginning
of the sequence. His Groups A and B are certainly not the earliest.

The hoard of Slatine, from the island of Čiovo, very near to Split,
was brought to light in 1897. Among 690 coins with the name of the city,
one showed the reading SPALATINVS, while all the rest had SPALATI-
NO. The hoard was completed by two Venetian piccoli, one of Enrico Dandolo, and the other, according to Bulić, of Giovanni Dandolo.
Stockert stated that he had examined both and that both were in fact
of Enrico Dandolo. [25] There can in any case be little doubt that the Slatine hoard is from the fourteenth century; it shows how long the Venetian coins could remain in use, and how unreliable they might be as evidence for a date of deposit.

The Muć hoard, [26] from which 110 coins passed into the hands of
D. Savo, of Split, was published in detail by Stockert, who included the
coins in his *corpus*. They are all of the varieties signed SPALATINO.
Another hoard, found in the environs of Split in about 1800, is not properly recorded, although it is likely to have been similar; sixteen coins from
it were divided among three stylistic groups. [27]

The dates of deposit of the Slatine, Muć, and Split hoards cannot
be guessed even to within a decade or two. None of the three is likely
to be much before 1350, and indeed all might be later. Another Spalatine
coinage, showing the head of St Domnius or Doimus, is apparently mentioned in a document of 1352 under name of *Basciolini;* but whatever
its date, this coinage did not play an important part in the currency of
Dalmatia, if one may judge from the small number and the restricted
stylistic range of the known specimens.

The circulation of the Spalatine coins was mostly in the immediate
locality of the town. The same is probably true of the bronze folari of
Dubrovnik, which are even more difficult to date. A deposit of Ragusan

---

[25] *BASDalmat.* xx (1897), 125. The Venetian coins are carefully described (Papadopoli, p. 86, plate V, 7 and p. 138, plate VIII, 4); but cf. Stockert, *Spalato*, p.
15, note 1.
[26] *BASDalmat.* xxiii (1900), 192.
[27] *BASDalmat.* xxxiv (1911), *Supplemento*, p. 12.

bronze was found, at some date before 1899, at Trpanj, on the coast nearby. [28]

Yet another kind of coinage it added to the list of those represented among finds from the Adriatic coasts by a Slavonian banovac, found at Karlobag, which probably served as the port for the Lika region. It was a coin of Nuber's Type 9, from the reign of Robert Karl.[29] Either directly or originally it must have come from Zagreb. From about the same time there is a late Friesacher from Križpolje, in the hinterland of Senj, [30] and two Viennese Pfennige found at Starigrad on the island of Hvar. [31]

Venetian grossi lost or hidden in Dalmatia before the middle of the fourteenth century are probably not so commonly found as might have been imagined; this is a very curious commentary on the monetary affairs of the Adriatic coastlands. One such coin of Lorenzo Tiepolo (1268 - 1274) was found at Čović, near Otočac, and another, not far away, at Čanak, near Gospić: the second was of Giovanni Soranzo (1310-1327). [32] Both add to the picture of Lika as a region with a rather lively monetary economy. Two Serbian groši, similar in appearance and value to the Venetian coins, are catalogued by Ljubić as having been found on the northern Adriatic shores, one from Senj, [33] and the other from an uncertain find-spot in Dalmatia. [34] A similar unspecified Dalmatian provenance was given for one of the rare early Bosnian coins copying the Venetian grosso, in Truhelka's catalogue. It may have come from a hoard consisting mainly of Serbian coins, like that found at Dobrište, or mainly of Venetian coins, but in any case the provenance, suggesting that the coin had once been in ordinary use, is of interest for the origins of monetary history among the Bosnians. [35]

---

[28] The Zagreb museum acquired one coin of the "first type" (1.85 gm.) and two of the "ninth type" (3,02 gm, and 1.50 gm.).

[29] Initial-marks, K S; privy-marks, fleurs-de-lis.

[30] In the Zagreb museum register; the type is as Luschin, "Steierische Münzfunde", no. 196.

[31] Kenner, op. cit., part VIII, in Archiv xxxiii (1865), at p. 144, where the type is described as the "Bindenschild".

[32] Both are recorded in the Zagreb accession-registers.

[33] Ljubić, Opis, Stefan Uroš I, Type III/xvii, no. 1.

[34] Ibid., Stefan Uroš I, Type III /xxvi, no. 42. This and the preceding coins may perhaps have come to the notice of Ljubić while he was curator at Split, 1858-1863.

[35] Truhelka, "Verzeichnis"; and see p. 198.

The question of connexions between the Adriatic coast and its hinterland further to the south focuses on Dubrovnik. Merchants from that city were trading in Bosnia by the end of the twelfth century, and were to maintain special links there for many years. The Ragusan groši are first mentioned in 1301; the date of their introduction may have been somewhat earlier, but it almost certainly falls between 1301 and 1284, since their obverse design would seem to derive from that of the Venetian zecchini first struck in that year. Already in 1282, however Serbian groši were of sufficient importance in Dubrovnik for the citizens to have a vested interest in them: the first Venetian embargo on the circulation of Serbian coins specifically excluded Dubrovnik. Before that, various coins and moneys of account are mentioned in documents referring to Dubrovnik. One quite clear reference to a coinage which seems not to have survived to find its way into the cabinets of modern collections speaks of "folaros qui dicuntur capuciae, et generaliter omnes folaros factos et facturos in formam veteram." The caputiae were prescrib, ed in 1294, in which year measure were also taken against false grossi. These legal decisions are perhaps an echo from the date of introduction of the groši of St. Blasius. Rešetar's outstandingly fine catalogue of the series of groši was not able to overcome the uncertainly which still surrounds the chronology of the coins before 1350. It seems that they wernot carried inland very much in that period, for they have not been recorded in the hoards from Serbia and Bosnia. Nevertheless, it is doubtless correct that the group of coins without secret-marks below the saint's right hand is the earliest. Their weight-standard, *ca.* 1.84 gm., corresponds convincingly with the reduced Serbian weight-standard that Saria would date to 1282. Rešetar catalogues 151 specimens that he considers to be before 1356 in date, and among them there are 13 instances of obverse die-linkage, of which one is uncertain, and one uncertain instance of duplication. This clearly implies that more than one reverse die was used with each obverse die. A first estimation of the number of obverse dies involved gives a figure of about 800; $\frac{y}{x}$ is rather too large to be tolerable, and no precise conclusion should be drawn from the application of Brown's formula. One could say that the volume of the Ragusan coinage in the period represented by Rešetar's Types 1 - 6 would seem to have been of the order of 5 to 10 million coins, and that this is probably a very small figure in comparison with the output of the Serbian mints in the same period. [36]

---

[36] On the early monetary history of Ragusa and its links with the hinterland, see Rešetar, *Dubrovačka Numizmatika;* J. Nagy, "Prva Utanačenja izmedju Bosans-

Kotor is another locality in the coastlands where in all probability the early Serbian coins found their way into the current of Adriatic trade. Coins from the cabinet of Žulić, a local collector, were possibly found in the district. Ljubić published a dozen early Serbian coins which either were or had been in Žulić's possession. [37]

The coins of Andreas Dandolo (1343-54), the latest with which we are concerned, were issued in great numbers, and were a common currency in central Dalmatia. Finds of ducats, grossi, and soldini have been recorded. At Gala, near Sinj, in 1911, a hoard of 34 Venetian gold and silver coins was discovered. [38] A comparison with the recorded find-spots of fifteenth-century Spalatine and Bosnian coins suggests that the hoard was concealed on the route-way leading through the Sinjsko-polje to Livno and the Vrbas valley, and that they may have been in some way associated with trade from Split into the interior. [39] A ducat of Andreas Dandolo turned up shortly before 1939 at Nin, near Zadar; [40] and silver of the same ruler has been published from Bribir, Bilišane, and Dolovi. [41]

In summary, the find-evidence from what is today Jugoslavia shows that in Lika and on the north Dalmatian coast, north Italian pic, cioli were circulating at the beginning, and Venetian grossi by the end of the thirteenth century; that the local coinage of Split must have been extremely plentiful in central Dalmatia, including the islands, in the thirteenth and fourteenth centuries; that Serbian silver was brought to the coast in the south in the late thirteenth and early fourteenth cen-

---

kih Banovca i Dubrovnika", *Zbornik iz Dubrovačke Prošlosti, Milanu Rešetaru o 70 oj Godišnjici Zivota Prijatelji i Učenici (*=Dubrovnik, II), Dubrovnik, 1931, pp. 25-32; B. Saria, "O Težini Najstarijih Dubrovačkih Dinara", *loc. cit.*, pp. 39-42; M. Rešetar, "Najstarije Dubrovačke Mince", *Numizmatika* ii-iv (1934-36), 65-69; *Ibid.*, "Početak Kovanja Dubrovačkoga Novca", *Rad Jugoslavenske Akademije, Znanosti i Umjetnosti*, CCLXVI, Zagreb, 1939, pp. 149-70.

[37] See Ljubić, *Opis*, pp. 37, 40, 45, 50, etc. For a discussion of the catalogue from this point of view, se D. M. Metcalf, "Ljubić's *Jugoslavenski Novci* as a Source - book", *NC* 6. xx (1960), 201-08.

[38] See *BASDalmat.* xxxv (1912), 80. There were 6 ducats of A. Dandolo, and 28 grossi, of M. Morosini (1), R. Zeno (?2), L. Tiepolo (1), J. Contarini (1), G. Dandolo (1), P. Gradenigo (3), G. Soranzo (9), F. Dandolo (6), and A. Dandolo (4). The proportions suggest a date of deposit not too long after 1350.

[39] See D. M. Metcalf, *op. cit.*

[40] Split Archaeological Museum. The coin was bought at Nin, and may be presumed to have been found in the neighbourhood.

[41] *BASDalmat.* iv (1881), cover; *ibid.* ii (1879), 160; *ibid.* ii, 176.

194

turies; and that Venetian gold and silver was common in central Dalmatia in the middle of the fourteenth century. A fuller definition of these episodes in the monetary history of the Adriatic coast will probably become possible when more finds are available for study.

One or two Serbian coins which have been found in Slovenia, at Trebnje and Celje, [42] may have been carried there by way of Dalmatia, rather than through Bosnia or Slavonia, for they belong to the limited period during which Serbian issues were common on the coast. The find from Senj is evidence that they reached the seaward end of the routes to Ljubljana and Zagreb. These few coins, together with the Austrian ones from Rogoznica and Hvar, suggest that different currencies "wandered" along the littoral sometimes, away from their general area of circulation.

The run of Albanian finds was described by Valentini, [43] who reported that Venetian grossi of the thirteenth and fourteenth centuries were found in enormous numbers, and that there were fair quantities of early Serbian groši. Byzantine scyphate gold was not often to be seen, even though it was valued for use as jewellery; Byzantine bronze coins were more common. A few Bulgarian coins had turned up, [44] and one of the rare pieces of Manfred was definitely found in Albania. [45] Valentini was in charge of the Museo Albandogico del Collegio Saveriano in Shkodër, so that his experience related to northern Albania. Even there, as he noted, coin-finds were not at all common as compared with other countries; further south on the Adriatic coast, coinage may have been even more scarce.

This account finds some confirmation in the small find-series of Byzantine coins from archaeological excavations in Albania, published by Cesano, in which coins of the second hey-day are absent apart from three or four twelfth-century stamena from Feniki. [46]

---

[42] See p. 177 above.

[43] G. Valentini, "La Numismatica in Albania (Esperienze di un Collezionista)", *Numismatica* v (1939), 122ff.

[44] They should be considered along with the Sarajevo provenance of a coin of Aleksandŭr attributed to Asen II in Truhelka, *Verzeichnis*. See p. 235.

[45] G. Valentini, "Vestigia di Manfredi di Hohenstaufen re di Sicilia e 'Signore di Romania' in Albania", *Numismatica* v (1939), 63ff.

[46] S. L. Cesano, "Monetazione e Circolazione sul Suolo dell'Antica Albania", *Atti e Memorie* (Istituto Italiano di Numismatica) vii (1932), 47-98, lists coins from archaeological expeditions, mainly at Feniki in 1926-27 and Butrinto in 1928-31.

From Epirus, there is an early and important hoard of Venetian grossi, which came from Ioánnina in 1821 or thereabouts. It terminates with the issues of R. Zeno, and, since it includes almost all the secret-marks known from his dogate, is perhaps not earlier than 1265. It may reflect a Venetian trade-route to Trikkala and Lárisa. [47]

Cf. L. M. Ugolini, "L'Acropoli di Fenice", *Albania Antica* ii (1932), 167, and *Ibid.*, *Butrinto, il Mito d'Enea gli Scavi*, Rome 1937, p. 175 for "a gold coin in a tomb by the Byzantine church".

[47] O. Iliescu and others, "Cabinetul Numismatic, Achizitii din anii 1959-1960" *Caiet Selectiv de Informare* vi (1962), 251-370, at p. 320.

CHAPTER VIII

SILVER-MINING AND THE RISE OF THE SOUTH SLAV MONETARY SYSTEMS

Between the Sava river to the north, the limestone plateaux which rise steeply only a few miles from the Adriatic to the west, the complex of mountain ranges which links the Iron Gate with the Balkan Mountains to the east, and the Šar Planina to the south, lies a region of uplands and mountains which became the territory of the thirteenth-century states of Serbia and Bosnia. The forests which covered it were largely unbroken except above the tree-line and in the more fertile valleys and *polja;* because of the obstacles of forest and hills, routeways had to keep to a few valleys. In this folk-fortress of the Balkan peninsula, the south Slavs, living mainly by pastoralism, grew in numbers and strength until they were able to assert their independance finally. The political pressure, and the example, of neighbouring countries helped to unify the several small early states, such as Zeta, Usora, and Raška into two larger states. The rulers of Serbia and Bosnia, owing to the fortunate accident that rich silver deposits lay within their territories, and that the Saxon miners of Transylvania were driven by the Mongol incursions of 1241 to find a fresh outlet for their technological skills, were enabled to issue a very plentiful coinage. The early Serbian coins travelled far beyond their official circulation-area; the three regions where they are characteristically found—Serbia, the Adriatic coast, north Italy—illustrate one of the routes followed by Balkan and south European trade. We may conjecture that the export of bullion in the form of coin made possible an increased trade with the industrial markets of Italy, particularly Venice, while the circulation of good coinage initiated and stimulated the monetary economy of a region largely given over to primary production, which would otherwise not have been able to sustain its own monetary system, and helped in the economic and political development of the state. Along with the coinages of the two south Slav countries must be mentioned a third: the groši of Dubrovnik (Ragusa) were trade-coins, with a considerable purchasing power, similar to the Serbian and Bosnian in their fabric and types, and, so far as the evidence goes, in the character of their circulation-area and the circumstances of the necessary supply of silver; but the extension of importance of the Ragusan coinage into the hinterland came after the middle of the fourteenth century, and so falls outside the scope of this study. The history of the Bosnian currency, too, belongs mainly to the second half of the fourteenth and to the fifteenth century, so it is the Serbian coinage that is primarily under consideration. Serbian and Bosnian groši, and perhaps those of Venice which were the prototype, provided the currency of the west Balkan hinterland from some date in the third quarter of the thirteenth century. The earliest documentary reference to Serbian groši is to their use in 1276, [1] but the number of years for which the coins were struck without attracting a written record destined to survive is a matter which must remain uncertain. The issue of the coins of Dubrovnik cannot have begun earlier than 1284, but was probably within about a decade from that date. The Bosnian coinage began in 1302/04, a fact which is of less interest to the monetary historian than to the numismatist, since only a dozen specimens from the first two decades are known. [2] Bosnian coinage of the first three or four decades seems to have been used mainly along the routes in the Tuzla area, most probably in connexion with the salt trade.

The earliest hoards of Serbian groši contain virtually no Venetian or Bosnian coins, and there is thus no evidence that the circulation of the different types was originally intermixed to any significant extent, or that the Venetian grossi were ever important in the currency of the hinterland. There may conceivably have been a period of a decade or two (say 1250-1270) during which they were important, and this might explain why the "denarii de Brescoa" copied the Venetian pieces so closely; but it is more probable that the typological parallel was intended to facilitate the export of bullion.

---

[1] On the question of the silver mines, see art. "Sasi" in S. Stanojević, *Narodna Enciklopedija Srpsko - Hrvatsko - Slovenačka*, Zagreb, 1929, and more recently, B. Saria, "Die Erforschung des altserbisches Münzwesens", *NLOB* ii (1963), 58-81, especially at 76ff. See also p. 77, note 22 above, and p. 203 below.

[2] I. Rengjeo, "Novci bana Pavla Subića", *Numizmatika* ii-iv (1934-36), 94ff. for a corpus, which is supplemented by Rengjeo, *Corpus*, pp. 64-5. Four coins of these types turned up in the Dobrište hoard. Note that the issue was on the Venetian weight-standard.

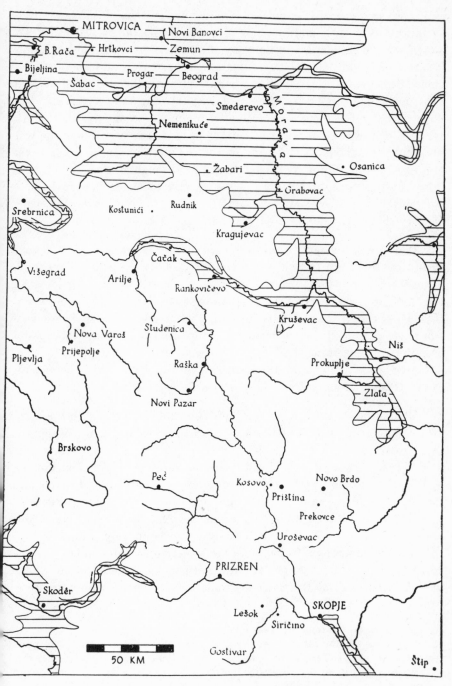

Map X. Serbia and eastern Bosnia.
(Land *under* 300 metres shaded.)

The rapid rise of the south Slav monetary systems in the last quarter of the thirteenth and the first quarter of the fourteenth centuries, which was made possible initially by the exploitation of mineral resources, reflected and aided the growing political strength of Serbia and Bosnia, and, equally, their trading connexions with the west. Before that time, not much coinage had found its way into the area, which seems to have been for the most part without a monetary economy. In the latter part of the twelfth century, Byzantine scyphate bronze coinage was plentiful throughout south Serbia and also along the routes of the lower Morava and the Krain, as it was so widely throughout the Balkan peninsula at the same time. There was some Slavonian coinage in Bosnia, particularly north-western Bosnia, in the middle of the thirteenth century; but with these exceptions, there seems to have been little else.

If all the provenances from the area are plotted on a map, it is very clear that there are concentrations in three or four of the valleys, and, in between, wide tracts from which scarcely a coin is recorded. Most of the finds are from north Serbia—the lower basin of the Morava—or old Serbia—especially the regions around Skopje and Prizren. There is a third, geographically quite separate group from the Bosna valley, and one or two finds from the Tuzla area between there and north Serbia. A fourth group comes from the basin of the river Una, well to the northwest. Outside these valleys, there is singularly little.

The earliest coins, after those of Theophilus, [3] are Byzantine gold pieces. There are traces of a small hoard of such coins of Nicephorus III, discovered at Mitrovica in 1898 or earlier. [4] A pierced nomisma of John II was reported from Bosnia, and a nomisma of Alexius I from Trebinje.[5] Pees, in a commentary on the coin-finds from Prizren and its neighbourhood, wrote, "Although one would think from the general talk of the town here in the metropolis of Old Serbia that numerous coin-finds were made, I have actually set eyes on only a few pieces... the only common types to be found are Venetian zecchini and Byzantine scyphate gold coins". [6] In the twelfth century, gold coins may have been valued in Serbia and Bosnia for reasons not connected with commerce.

---

[3] See p. 27 above.

[4] See Metcalf, "Syrmia and Slavonia", at p. 439.

[5] Both are in the registers of the Zagreb museum. Trebinje is on the route through Nikšić to the Tara valley, but the coin of Alexius may be unconnected with the routeway. The coin of John was bought from J. Ličanin, a retired district administrator.

[6] *Monatsblatt der numismatischen Gesellschaft in Wien* i, 400.

Byzantine scyphate bronze hoards of the late twelfth and early thirteenth centuries are quite commonly found in Macedonia, although Pees does not mention such finds. The important Siričino hoard of 1935 has been discussed above; [7] hoards of more normal composition have come to light at Lešok, nearby, and also at Skopje, Ohrid, and Bitola. [8] The Skopje hoard would seem to have been concealed early in the reign of Alexius III. Three coins of Manuel I found at Skopje, which were acquired by the Zagreb museum in 1901 from T. Slišković, a teacher, may perhaps have been from another hoard similar to those mentioned already. Two coins from an uncertain find-spot in Macedonia, probably in the neighbourhood of Štip, were acquired by the same museum in 1907 and 1908 from a captain stationed there; the first was silver, and the second was of bronze, pierced and gilt. Both were attributed to Theodore of Thessaloniki. [9] There are two coins in the Slavonian Museum, Osijek which were found at Stobi. They were the gift of Milojčić, a native of Osijek and an archaeologist of some distinction, so that it seems possible that they are excavation-coins. One, which is gilt and pierced, is of Isaac II, *BMC* Type 5, a scarce type; the other appears to be an unpublished issue of the thirteenth century. [10] Finally, there is a hoard of silver coins, again of Theodore of Thessaloniki, discovered in the neighbourhood of Niš in 1935 or thereabouts. [11] It will be interesting to see whether a larger find-assemblage shows the same high proportion of the coins of the successor-states, and whether any more

---

[7] See pp. 111f.

[8] Aleksova, "Naodi". The Ohrid hoard of 1948-49 included coins of Manuel and Isaac; that from Bitola 60 coins of unspecified types; that from Skopje, 1950, 112 coins, divided as follows: Manuel, 20, Isaac, 70, Alexius III, 20, unattributed, 5, for which (?) read 2; the hoard from Lešok, 1953 contained about 300 coins, of which 270 were divided as follows: Manuel, 92, Andronicus, 3, Isaac, 76, Alexius III, 79, unattributed, 20.

[9] Information from the accession-registers.

[10] I am indebted to Mr E. Spajić, Director of the Slavonian Museum, for the information about Milojčić. The obverse of the second coin showed Christ seated on a backless throne, the right hand raised in blessing. IC XC. Double struck, and difficult. Reverse: the emperor standing facing, holding in his right hand a long cross or sceptre; beside him, a winged figure in a long dress (St. Michael), holding a long

$$\frac{X}{M}$$

(?)cross, at the bottom of which, —. Double struck. 30 mm. 4.41 gm.

[11] J. Petrović, "Numizmatičke Novosti. 5. Theodorus Angelus Comnenus Ducas, 1222-30", *Numizmatičar* No. 2 (May, 1935), 30; R. Marić, "Iz Numizmatičke Zbirke Narodnog Muzeja", *Starinar NS* v-vi (1954-55), 349-55 describes and illustrates two coins in very fine condition. Cf. Gerasimov, "Solun".

Thessalonican silver is reported from Jugoslavia. If the few scattered find-records known at present are typical (they include coins from Novi Banovci, described above),[12] they suggest that trade from Thessaloniki into Macedonia and northwards towards Hungary may have been quite important in those regions in the decades after 1204.

Hoards of Byzantine scyphate bronze from north Serbia from the last decades of the twelfth century and the beginning of the thirteenth are important because they indicate that merchants were coming there from more than one part of the Byzantine Empire; the fabric and style is generally consistent within each of the Zlata, Grabovac, and Osanica hoards, yet quite different as between them.[13] Little detail is available about two other hoards of scyphate bronze. One came from Rankovičevo, where the river Ibar joins the West Morava; two kilogrammes of coins "of the period of Manuel I" were discovered in the course of road-works. The hoard passed into the Belgrade museum, but alas has been lost. From Srbovo, near Negotin, there came another hoard of the same period. The coins were in very poor condition. The date of deposit of these two hoards must remain uncertain.[14]

Srbovo and Osanica lie in the Krain, through which ran convenient routeways leading north to Belgrade. Copper was mined in the area, so that it is possible that the use of coinage there was associated with the industry and the trade that flowed from it. Zlata and Grabovac are both in the Morava valley. Rankovičevo is the most interesting of the provenances; even if it is a route-hoard, it would seem to indicate that scyphate bronze was to be found in the west Balkan hinterland.

An agreement of the early thirteenth century between the Grand Župan Stefan (Prvovjenčani) and the Ragusans shows what the economic background to the use of such coinage is likely to have been: "ut veniant vestri homines per meam terram cum mercimoniis sine ullo timore... ut vendant et comparent libere, et illud quod est mercatorum consuetudo in terra mea, ut dent mihi".[15]

---

[12] See p. 138 above.

[13] See p. 115 above.

[14] See Mosser, *Byzantine Coin Hoards* under Kraljevo-Raschka; B. Saria, "Numismatischer Bericht aus Jugoslawien", *NZ* lx (1927), 10ff.; Klemenc, "Nalazi Novaca". There might be some reason to associate the hoards with the period of Byzantine power in Croatia.

[15] S. Ljubić, *Listine o Odnošajih izmedju Južnoga Slavenstva i Mletačke Republika*, vol. I, 1868, no. XXXIX.

After the decline of the Byzantine monetary system, and before Serbian groši began to be struck, there can have been little coinage in Bosnia and Serbia. One hoard, now in the Belgrade museum, shows that Friesacher were carried into north Serbia as well as into Syrmia and central Hungary in the decades around the middle of the thirteenth century: the Nemenikuče find, represented by 105 coins, includes Friesacher of the classic period of eastwards expansion, and apparently quite a high proportion of the issues of the Slovenian mints. [16]

The numismatic history of the Serbian coinage for the first fifty years during which groši were struck—Serbian scyphate bronze is extremely rare, and cannot have played an important role in monetary affairs [17]—has attracted a great deal of scholarly attention, and there have been conflicting views about even the broadest outlines of the interpretation. The difficulties of dating the coins exactly stem from the lack of thirteenth-century hoards, and they are aggravated by the repetition of the names STEFAN and VROSIVS on the coins of Stefan Uroš I (1243-76), Stefan Dragutin (1276-82; 1284-1316 in north Serbia), Stefan Uroš II Milutin (1282-1321), and Stefan Uroš III Dečanski (1321-31). The coins with the name of the anti-king Vladislav (1321 - 24) provide a foothold in the early fourteenth century; but it is from the last three decades of the thirteenth century that evidence is most wanted. There are five items from those decades that are extremely interesting to the monetary historian as well as to the numismatist. First, there is the document of 1281 referred to above, which indicates that Serbian coinage was being struck already in 1276: "Obratus Longus, gener Johannis de Baysclava, quod Leonardus de Cocote mihi dedit et solvit, iam sunt transacti quinque anni, solidos denariorum de Brescoa viginti quinque, quos ipse Leonardus pro me et nomine meo recepit...". [18] Brskovo, in the Tara valley, behind Dubrovnik, was the mint which coined the metal from the local silver mines. Secondly, there are the documents recording the measures taken by Venice against the Serbian

---

[16] Marić, "Ostave". The late Dr. Marić kindly allowed me to examine the hoard, at Belgrade. It included, for example, Luschin, "Friesacher Pfennige", no. 194 (St. Veit), and examples of Luschin 124 or 154, 125, and 161 (Kostanjevica, Brezice, Gutenwert).

[17] Marić, *Studije*, pp. 64f. and. for a silver scyphate coin, R. Marić, "Iz Numizmatičke Zbirke", *Zbornik Radova Narodnog Muzeja* iii (1962), 17-30, an article which includes an obituary bibliography.

[18] See G. Čremošnik, "Prilozi dubrovačkoj i srpskoj numizmatici", *Slavia, Časopis pro Slovanskou Filologii* vii (1928-29), 564-584.

groši in 1282. A promulgation of 3 May of that year requires officials of the exchange, and those who receive money on behalf of the commune to check carefully for "coins of the king of Raš copied from our large Venetian coins". Fines are laid down, and the Serbian coins are proscribed throughout the Dalmatian territories except in Dubrovnik. On 29 October the embargo is applied more rigorously, and is to have effect in Zadar, Dubrovnik, Kotor, and Dyrrachium.[19] Thirdly, there is the Verona hoard of 1929, which is securely dated to ca. 1284. It contained 3,477 coins, nearly all Venetian grossi, but with 37 Serbian pieces among them.[20] Fourthly, there is a document of 1283 referring to "denarii de Brescoa de bandera"; and finally, a most important reference, in 1281, to "soldos denariorum grossorum de Brescoa de quibus fuerunt soldi denariorum grossorum centum septuaginta de denariis de cruce et de lilio et residui triginta soldi fuerunt de denariis de macia".[21] Among the earlier Serbian coins there are those which copy the Venetian prototype closely, showing a bare-headed king holding a banner—these are the "denarii de bandera"; on others the banner is replaced by a double cross —these are "denarii de cruce"; a quite different type showing the bare-headed king seated on a throne and holding a sword across his knees is the "denarius de macia"; and another version of that, where the king wears a crown and holds a sceptre with fleur-de-lis and a globus with a single or double cross must be the "denarius de cruce et de lilio". As there was a "denarius de cruce" in the Verona hoard, all four types go back to the early 1280's. "Denarii de cruce" and another variety of the "Seated King" type were still being issued[22] in the time of Stefan Dušan (1331-46 as king), so that *prima facie* the organization and patterns of circulation which the monetary historian has to disentangle involve, for fifty years at least, the issue of quite different types concurrently. Several of the varieties seem to be *Konventionsmünzen*,[23] struck for Stefan Uroš II and Stefan Dragutin, but this does not necessarily prove their localization. There are in fact clear signs that coins of Dragutin were localized in the north, and that the "Seated King" varieties

---

[19] S. Ljubić, *op. cit.*, nos. CLXXXIX and CXCVIII.

[20] G. Gerola, "Numismatica Serbo-Veneta. I "Grossi di Brescova" di un Ripostiglio Veronese", *Rassegna Numismatica* xxvii (1930), 177ff.; G. Čremošnik, *Razboj Srpskog Novčarstva do Kralja Milutina*, Belgrade, 1933, where 19 coins are illustrated, but unfortunately by means of blocks of indifferent quality; Dimitrijević, "Problemi", 81, etc.

[21] Dimitrijević, "Problemi", 73.

[22] *Ibid.*

[23] Cf. the South German *Konventionsmünzen* mentioned above, p. 168.

are also northern. The "denarii de cruce" seem to be more numerous in finds from the south. These are, however, very tentative attributions, and the most curious fact is the predominance, in the finds, of the "denarii de bandera".

The detailed chronology and arrangement of the coins is only gradually becoming clear, although there is good reason to hope that, with a few more fixed points provided by the detailed publication of some early hoards, stylistic sequences could be constructed and the dating of particular groups of die-varieties established. Certain coins with a youthful, beardless portrait of the king, for example, can be attributed to the early part of Dragutin's reign with some confidence, as there was one in the Verona hoard. [24] The element of hypothesis will not, however, be removed from the monetary history associated with the early Serbian coinage until the year-by-year work of the mints has been reconstructed from the empirical evidence of die-similarity; and the whole numismatic approach may continue to be governed by the fact of a low survival-rate from the first two or three decades.

The coins copying the Venetian model most closely, the "denarii de bandera", include some specimens in fine style which even have the secret-marks that are characteristic of the Venetian issues. These are almost certainly the earlier. Saria, without setting out any evidence, observes that the marks on the Serbian coins definitely correspond with those on the Venetian coins of the years around 1275, and that research on the chronology of the latter series might bring results also for the former. [25] It is the work of a moment to dispose of this seductive hypothesis: the secret-marks on the heavy Serbian coins are predominantly marks unrecorded by Papadopoli for the Venetian issues of L. Tiepolo (1268-75), J. Contarini (1275-80), or even G. Dandolo (1280-89). Papadopoli's lists for these reigns (see Table 15) are not comprehensive, but the additions that can be made do not change the character of the lists—triangles or diamonds are usual on the coins of L. Tiepolo, dots and annulets on those of J. Contarini, and dots, annulets, pyramids of three dots, or (??) whips, on those of G. Dandolo. The marks that are usual on the Serbian coins, by contrast, are trefoils, crosses, asterisks of 5 rays, asterisks of 6 rays, and less frequently dots and annulets. The

---

[24] Dimitrijević, "Problemi", 80. See Ljubić, *Opis*, plate V, 16 (and cf. V, 6). Note that one of the coins of Dragutin in the Delphi hoard of 1929 (Table 20, no. 4) has a secret-mark of the Venetian kind.

[25] Saria, "Altserbische Münzwesen", 33.

206

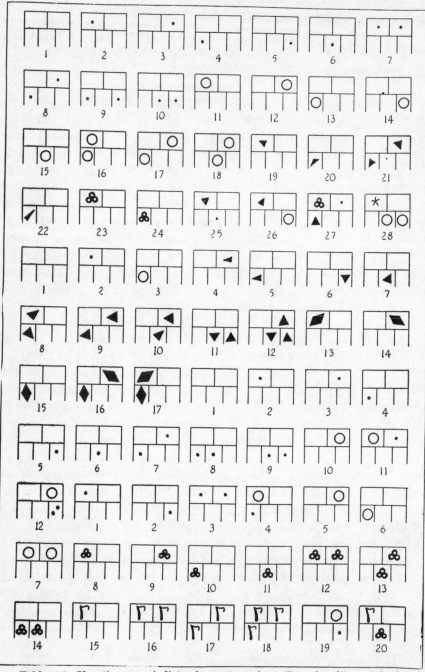

Table 15. Venetian grossi: list of secret-marks. (Papadopoli's numbering is given for each reign, namely, R. Zeno, 1252-68, 1-28: L. Tiepolo, 1268-75, 1-17: J. Contarini, 1275-80, 1-12; G. Dandolo, 1280-89, 1-20).

particular arrangements of dots and annulets on the Serbian coins are, by and large, not paralleled on the Venetian coins (compare Tables 15 and 16).

A small clue to the interpretation of the Serbian secret-marks—for which die-similarities are the only method of study that will be fully satisfactory—is that the range of marks in the Dobrište hoard is restricted, trefoils and 5-rayed asterisks accounting for 12 of the 16 specimens catalogued by Marić. There were many more varieties in the Carribollo hoard. Those represented in the parcel acquired by the Zagreb museum are shown in Table 16. Some of the varieties in the Table have irregular numbers of dots (2, 3, or 5, instead of the usual diamond of 4) on the saint's shoulders, on the reverse.

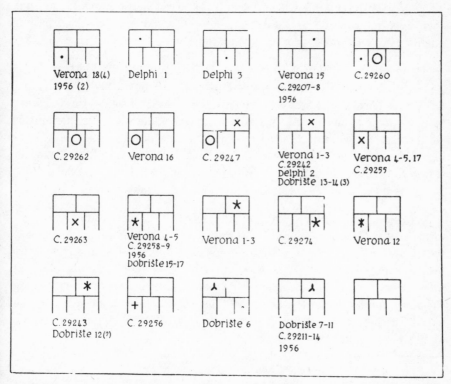

Table 16. Serbian groši: secret-marks in the Verona and Carribollo hoards. (The references are to Perini and accession-numbers of the Zagreb Museum).

The very early Serbian coins are of about the same weight as the Venetian (Saria records that those in the Verona hoard had an average weight of 2.12 gm., and the 16 coins mentioned from the Dobrište hoard have an average weight of 2.14 gm.); later coins are apprecially lighter, and were exchanged against the Venetian ones, according to records of 1294, 1302, and 1303, at various ratios such as 8:7, 9:8, or 10:9.[26] It seems reasonable to suppose that the Venetian embargo of 1282 was in response to a reduction in the weight-standard of the Serbian groši early that year or in 1281. There is, as one might expect, variation in weight from one coin to another, and the argument which seeks to attribute the coins with little secret-marks (which are generally of good weight) to the period before 1282[27] is therefore not clear-cut—perhaps not sufficiently clear-cut to assign the coins of that group reading VROSIVS definitely to Stefan Uroš I instead of Stefan Uroš II, although the evidence of style might confirm such an attribution. Saria weighed 120 "stempelgleiche und stempelfrische Stücke" from the Studenica hoard, of the later kind without the little secret marks, and found that their average weight was 1,807 gm.; but out of 60 coins weighed individually, 10 were over 2 grammes, and the heaviest weighed 2,38 gm.[28]

One of the earliest Serbian hoards was brought to light at Novi Pazar in about 1955. Out of some 740 coins, all but a few are "denarii de bandera", and the rest are "denarii de cruce". Twenty-three coins, or about 3% of the hoard, are struck in the name of Stefan Dragutin. Of the rest, 19 were attributed by Dr. Marić according to his classification to Uroš I, and the rest to Stefan Uroš II Milutin.[29] Novi Pazar is a fairly isolated find-spot, in relation to the whole find-assemblage. It seems possible, therefore, that the hoard is a route-hoard.

A somewhat similar hoard of about 590 coins was found at Studenica in 1908. It was acquired by the Belgrade museum in 1910, but was regrettably dispersed at the time of the First World War, and was never properly published. If there were in fact 120 die-duplicates in it, it must have been a sum of money that had been kept intact since leaving the mint, perhaps shortly before.[30] The most interesting aspect of the hoard, in the present state of information, is that it was found near one of the royal monasteries.

---

[26] *Ibid.*, 38; Dimitrijević, "Problemi", 73.

[27] Saria, "Altserbische Münzwesen", 32-33.

[28] *Ibid.*

[29] The late Dr. Marić kindly showed me the hoard, while it was on deposit in the Belgrade museum, and discussed it with me. It was acquired by the Novi Pazar museum.

[30] B. Saria, "Numismatischer Bericht aus Jugoslawien", *NZ* lx (1927), 10ff. Saria, "Altserbische Münzwesen"; see above.

Hoard	Thessaly, 1949	Verona, 1929	Delphi, 1933	Dobrište	Carribollo	Delphi, 1929	Lurate Abbate (Como)	Thessaloniki, 1934	«1956»
Date of Deposit	ca, 1255	ca. 1284	1301-ca.1305	1305-ca.1309	ca.1295-ca. 1300	1311?	ca. 1320	ca. 1315-25	ca. 1340?
P. Ziani, 1205-29	9	64	—	1	7	—	9	—	1
I. Tiepolo, 1229-49	17+1	225	1	1	12	—	10	—	7
M. Morosini, 1249-52	4	69	1	—	3	—	6	—	—
R. Zeno, 1253-68	7+2	1225	3	2	63	2	90	—	7
L. Tiepolo, 1268-75	—	710	2	7	31	6	39	2	12
J. Contarini, 1275-80	—	706	2	6	44	6	35	5	31
G. Dandolo, 1280-89	—	441	8	4	67	10	64	2	25
P.Gradenigo1289-311	—	—	1	5	108	58	317	17	131
I. Supantio, 1312-28	—	—	—	—	—	—	—	10	2
F. Dandolo, 1328-39	—	—	—	—	—	—	—	—	4
B. Gradenigo,1339-43	—	—	—	—	—	—	—	—	1

Table 17. Proportions of Venetian grossi in certain hoards. (I am indebted to Mrs Varoukha-Khristodhoulopoulou for making the Thessaloniki and «1956» hoards available for study).

From southern Serbia, the Dobrište hoard of 1935 can be dated to after 1305, perhaps not more than three or four years after that date. An Albanian peasant of the village discovered a copper vase containing a large number of silver coins. They were heavily discoloured, so that he thought they were copper. His hopes of having found a valuable treasure being dashed, he threw the coins into the ditch in disgust. They remained there for several months, until they were eventually noticed by some passers-by, who gathered them up. The coins came into the hands

14

of the numismatist Celekijana in Skopje. Although in poor condition, they included some rare pieces, and in particular 4 Bosnian coins of Pavao and Mladen II Subić, by which the deposit is at present dated. There were 6 silver Bulgarian coins, and 42 Venetian coins. The remainder out of a total of 782 were of Stefan Uroš I, Stefan Dragutin, and Stefan Uroš II. The evidence of the Dobrište hoard is valuable because it shows that Bosnian and Bulgarian coins might find their way—albeit in trifling proportions—into the currency of south Serbia. Dimitrijević states that the hoard published in detail by Marić as being from an unknown findspot in southern Jugoslavia, discovered in or before 1935 and acquired at Skopje, is in fact part of the Dobrište hoard. The 312 coins now in the Belgrade museum are divided as follows: Stefan Uroš I, 23: Stefan Dragutin, 4; Stefan Uroš II Milutin, 252; Venice, 28; various forgeries, 5. All the Serbian coins except 13 of those attributed to Milutin were "denarii de bandera". The 13 were "denarii de cruce". The Venetian coins make a contribution, if an uncertain one, to the problem of the Serbian currency in the 1270s. If their proportions are compared with those in other hoards concealed at roughly the same time, it appears that the issues of L. Tiepolo and J. Contarini are over-represented (see Table 17.) One possible interpretation of the statistics is that, although Venetian coins were being carried into Serbia, obviously, after the Serbian issues had begun, there was an element in the currency of the early fourteenth century consisting of coinage that had been brought into the region in the time of L. Tiepolo and J. Contarini, and had remained there.

The extremely limited proportion of coins of Stefan Dragutin in the Novi Pazar and Dobrište hoards is in contrast to their occurrence in the north. From the Transylvanian hoards of Német-Csanád (deposited after 1290), Obad, and Săsarm, and from an unpublished parcel of groši acquired by the Slavonian Museum in 1927, doubtless from a hoard, it is evident that in the years when Dragutin was ruling in Mačva and the north, the coins with his name played a large, perhaps a predominant, part in the currency there. Even the Kragujevac hoard of 1928, which was deposited not less than five years after Dragutin's death, contained 44 of his coins out of a total of 88 Serbian pieces. Thus, there were two remarkably separate circulation-areas in the Serbian coinage-province. [32]

---

[31] H. Lederer, "Dva Nalaza Staroga Novca", *Numizmatičke Vijesti* Year 1, vii - viii (No. 4) (1939), 7-8; Marić, *Studije*, pp. 169-233; Dimitrijević, "Problemi",126.

[32] See D. M. Metcalf, "On an Unpublished Parcel of Serbian Grossi in the Slavonian Museum", *HBN* iv (1960), 59-64. If the Venetian coin in the parcel was in

Of even more interest than the proportions of coins reading STEFAN and VROSIVS in the Transylvanian hoards is the fact that Serbian groši should heve been carried there at all. They seem to mark out another of the south-west to north-east trends in monetary circulation that are characteristic of the Balkan march-lands. [33]

A little parcel of coins of Stefan Dragutin, dating back to the middle of the nineteenth century or earlier, belonged to a Mr Avram Petronievié of Belgrade; the hoard that it represents may well have come from the locality. The coins are "denarii de cruce", each with a letter S at the base of the cross, and with related secret-marks on the obverse also. [34]

The Serbian coins in the hoards from central Greece, which are mostly "denarii de bandera" with a few "denarii de cruce", are discussed below. [35]

Stray finds of the same two types have occasionally been reported from Syrmia and from Serbia. Coins from Novi Banovci, Hrtkovci, Progar, Stari Slankamen, Mitrovica, Zemun, and Ruma have been mentioned above. [36] Two further coins, from Belgrade and from an uncertain Syrmian find-spot, may be added to the list; [37] and there is a coin of Dragutin, originally published by Šafařik (as was the Petronievié parcel), which was at that time in the possession of an architect in Belgrade, a Mr Nenandović. Quite possibly it was found locally, and came into his hands from a building-site. [38]

The Kragujevac hoard of 1928 contained coins of a type that has not yet been mentioned. It shows, on the reverse, a standing, facing figure of the king, and was struck by Vladislav II (1321-24) as well as Stefan Dragutin, most probably at the mint of Rudnik, in north Ser-

---

fact of G. Contarini (1275-80), the hoard may turn out to have been one of the earliest of its kind. See also I. Sabău, "Circulatia Monetară în Transilvania Secolelor XI-XIII, în Lumina Izvoarelor Numismatice", *SCN* ii (1958), 269-301.

[33] See p. 67 above.

[34] See D. M. Metcalf, *op. cit.*, p. 61; Ljubić, *Opis*, Stefan Dragutin, Type IIIc (nos. 2, 7, and 8 on p. 55).

[35] See pp. 232-4 below.

[36] See pp. 139-45 above.

[37] Ljubić, *Opis*, Stefan Dragutin, Type IV/xxi (p. 61), and Copper, Type 1 (p. 68).

[38] *Ibid.* Type IV/xxi, no. 5.

bia. The Kragujevac hoard (which contained only one coin of Vladislav) has been published in full detail by Marić. [39]

A deposit of roughly the same date, found at Gostivar in south Serbia in 1925, was only very imperfectly recorded. It was said to contain 116 Serbian, Venetian, and Bulgarian coins. The Serbian coins were "denarii de cruce" and of types with Serbian inscriptions. The single Bulgarian piece, by which the date of deposit is shown to be after ca. 1322, was of Georg II Terter. [40]

Marić's catalogue of the Žabari hoard reveals, perhaps more clearly than any other part of his monograph, *Studije iz Srpske Numizmatike*, certain basic inabilities to grasp the force—or the limitations—of numismatic evidence. His book was very sharply criticized by Dimitrijević, in a lengthy review-article, and I have not attempted to rehearse the arguments on either side; but it must be said that Dimitrijević's comments were exceptionally damaging. The 48 surviving coins from Žabari, which are of the type with the seated figure of the king holding a sword across his knees, but in this case wearing a crown, constitute a small hoard of compact structure, within which there are certain obvious stylistic groupings. To divide a single stylistic group between two mints (as for example nos. 12 and 14 in the catalogue, which are divided between (?) Brskovo and (?) Novi Grad;—and nos. 1 and 2 must surely be from a single mint) is to demonstrate a profound lack of understanding of medieval numismatics. Let the reader study the catalogue, and illustrations, for himself. Dimitrijević attributes more than half the coins in the Žabari hoard to Stefan Dušan, and all of them to the Rudnik mint, not far from which they were found. [41]

The Sent-Andrej hoard contained an even larger proportion of the issues that Dimitrijević gives to Dušan. Out of 31 coins, 3 were in the name of Stefan Uroš III, 17 bore the inscription СТЕФАNb КРАЛb, and 11 read STEFAN REX. All the 17 coins with the Cyrillic inscription, apparently, had the letters A Ф to the left and right of the

[39] Marić, *Studije*, pp. 151-167; Dimitrijević, "Problemi", 77-78, 80-81; the hoard was said by Saria originally to have contained about 180 coins and to have been concealed in a pot. It was found at Pajsijevic, at the Čukar mine.

[40] Saria, "Altserbische Münzwesen", 22ff.

[41] Marić, *Studije*, pp. 235-48 and plates XL-XLI; Dimitrijević, "Problemi", 92, 93. I have felt obliged to comment frankly on the late Dr. Marić's book; but I should add that he was very correct towards me, and received me kindly in the Belgrade museum, some years ago.

throne on the obverse;[42] the Žabari coins, on the other hand, were almost all marked N B. The hoards amply confirm the evidence from Ljubić's catalogue that the A Ф and N B coins were on different weight-standards. The interpretation of both of them will probably have to remain tentative until it can be considered in the context of a much larger find-assemblage; but it is because there can occur hoards with so little overlap, in the particular varieties of a single type they contain, that there is such a good prospect of reconstructing Serbian monetary history from the coins.

A similar hoard, perhaps a little earlier in date, is to be traced in three coins which Šafařik recorded as being in the possession of Professor Konstantin Branković, of Belgrade. There were similar specimens in the collection of Lolio, in Zemun, and in the Belgrade museum, also recorded by Šafařik. [43] The existence of this hoard strengthens the case for the localization of the "Seated King" type in the extreme north of Serbia.

Finally, there is a hoard of the "Helmet" type, which was struck by Stefan Dušan as king; again, it is recorded by Šafařik, and can be traced in a parcel that was in the possession of Petronievič, of Belgrade. Dimitrijević attributes the type given by Ljubić to Stefan Uroš IV *(Opis,* plate IX, 9), of which there was one specimen in the parcel, to the earliest period of Dušan's imperial rule. [44]

A hoard of a hundred groshi of Ivan Aleksandůr with Mikhail was found near Skopje in 1921. [45] This, and similar finds from Pljevlja and Albania [46] show that the Bulgarian coins were being carried into Serbia, and far beyond their official circulation-area, in the middle of the fourteenth century.

In forming an estimate of the patterns of circulation within the Serbian coinage-province, we may take into account the find-spots

---

[42] S. Dušanić and G. Orlov, "Nalaz Srpskog Srednjovekovnog Novca iz Sent - Andreje: Prilog Klasifikaciji Srpskog Srednjovekovnog Novca", *Rad Vojvodjanskih Muzeja* ix (1960), 51-61.

[43] D. M. Metcalf, "Ljubić's *Jugislavenski Novci* as a Source-book", *NC* 6. xx (1960), 201-08.

[44] *Ibid.;* Ljubić, *Opis,* p. 76, Type Ia, 7, 8, 9, and (?) 10, Type Ib, (?) 2, 5,13, 15, 21, 36, and 40 are all candidates for inclusion in the parcel, and there may well be other coins in Ljubić's catalogue from the same source.

[45] Mushmov, "Kolektivni Nakhodki, 1921-22".

[46] See p. 194 above.

of a number of recently-discovered hoards, which await publication, as well as others of which the dates of deposit fall outside the period under review. These hoards, from Novi Banovci, Belovo, Stobi, Kičevo, Malo Bonjince, Prokuplje, Priština, Kostunići, Prekovce, Uroševac, Nova Varoš, Bosanska Rača, Demir Kapija, Selce, Skopje, and Prilep, make even clearer the importance of the routeways and the main centres, in Serbian monetary affairs. [47]

In contrast with the find-assemblage from Serbia, there are few hoards or stray finds from southern Bosnia. Truhelka gives a Sarajevo provenance for fifteen of the coins in the museum there; but the fact that so many of them are pierced somewhat reduces their value as evidence. Nevertheless, taken as a whole, they are the best that is available as an indication of the currency of Vrhbosna and its surrounding area. [48] Five early coins, of Stepan Kotromanić II, may have come from a hoard. There were seven Serbian "denarii de bandera", one coin of Vladislav and one attributed to Stefan Uroš III. From Pljevlja, on the route between Nikšić and Raška, the same source records two more early Serbian coins, as well as the Bulgarian coin mentioned above. The currency of southern Bosnia was probably supplied by Serbian coins before the autonomous issues began to be struck.

The rivers of northern Bosnia flow down to the Sava, and the region's contacts were with the provinces which lay to the north. The outlying north-western part of Bosnia, where a route ran through Bihać and the Una valley towards the coast, has yielded a varied group of finds. At Donji Lapac a coin of Kálmán was found. It may have been lost at much the same time as the Lepuri hoard was deposited. [49] An early Friesacher, struck about a century after the Hungarian coin, was discovered in 1845 or earlier (it is one of the first recorded finds of medieval coins from the Balkans) in the Sasina valley, at the old mines, and gives another small hint that the use of coinage was associated with mining industries. [50] Another hundred years separate that and a third

---

[47] See Marić, *Studije;* Saria, "Altserbische Münzwesen"; Ljubić, *Opis* for coins from the Kosovo hoard; Dimitrijević, "Problemi", 128; Dimitrijević, "Hronologija"; Aleksova, "Naodi".

[48] Truhelka, "Verzeichnis".

[49] From the Zagreb accession-registers; Réthy and Zimmermann, *CNHungariae*, part I, no. 48. See p. 161 above.

[50] See Brunšmid, "Našašća Novaca, VIII-XI". The date of discovery is given in the Zagreb registers.

find, from the Una basin: at Kalata, in 1928, a hoard of 28 banovci was discovered. The later pieces, of Nuber's Type 9, were in outstandingly good condition, and this fact led Klemenc to set the date of deposit not far from the end of the rule of Ban Stefan Babonezić. [51] Three other find-records where the provenance is given simply as "Bosnia" will be mentioned at this point. They seem more likely to have come from the Bihać area than from further east, although of course one can only guess. Truhelka gives a Bosnian provenance twice in his catalogue of Slavonian coins; [52] the Zagreb museum acquired a pierced banovac, of Nuber's Type 7b, found in Bosnia, from a Mr Pavlinović, and a second coin, with the same vague provenance, of which the secret-marks were recorded as. R (retrograde) M.[53] Yet another Slavonian coin was acquired by the museum from a Mr. J. Irković of Bihać; it may have been found locally. [54] From these records, uncertain as they are, it can be seen that banovci were current in north-western Bosnia in the first decades of the fourteenth century. From the middle of the same century, there is a single find of a Bosnian coin of Stefan Kotromanić II from Bihać, [55] which adds a fourth kind of coinage to the list of those used successively in the Bihać area and along the routeway which passed through the town.

The region of Soli took its name from the salt-mines of Tuzla, which were the source of a commodity of permanent importance in the trade of inland regions where animal husbandry was important.[56] In Truhelka's lists there are very few find-spots from the outlying parts of Bosnia, but Dolnja Tuzla is one of them, and Bijeljina is another. In fact, apart from Sarajevo, the only Bosnian provenances for the period before 1350 are Bijeljina, Bihać, Vitina, Dolnja Tuzla, and Pljevlje.[57] As in the case

---

[51] Klemenc, "Nalazi Novaca". The coins were of Nuber's Type 5 (3) and Type 9, K I, etc. (15) and K S etc., (10).

[52] Truhelka, "Die slavonische Banaldenare", Béla IV, Type a, II, 2 specimens, and Stefan V, Type I, 1 specimen. The occurrence of trefoil-marks in the inscriptions of all three, when they are so unusual in the types concerned, indicates rather clearly that these coins are from a hoard.

[53] The coin of Type 7b was of the variety with fleurs-de-lis, and nothing above the crescent, for which an eastern localization has been argued above. The second coin was of a kind well represented in the Brdari hoard.

[54] Nuber Type 9, K I.

[55] Cf. Ljubić, *Opis*, Type III, no. 8.

[56] See p. 145 above.

[57] Truhelka, "Verzeichnis". There are a couple more coins from Tuzla, of Stefan Dušan as emperor.

of Syrmian finds recorded at Zagreb, the absence of provenances from the intervening area between Soli and the *Landesmuseum* is of value as evidence. [58] While it seems fairly clear, then, that most parts of Bosnia were without a lively monetary economy, quite a few hoards and stray-finds have been recorded from the routeways converging on Tuzla. It is not as obvious as it is for Syrmia that these finds are to be associated with a salt-trade; the use of coinage may already have been associated with other mining industries in northern Bosnia. [59] However, there can be little doubt about the regular use of coinage, for whatever purposes, in that region. The issues of Stepan Kotromanić II are to be associated especially with northern and north-eastern Bosnia, and—witness the Lisopolje hoard—most probably with the economic development fostered by the Ragusans. [60]

From Dolnja Tuzla came two pierced Serbian groši. From Bijeljina—probably on the route to Mitrovica—there were two more, and also a coin of Stepan Kotromanić II. [61] From Tešanj, two banovci in Truhelka's catalogue are probably separate finds. [62] From an unknown find-spot in' Bosnia, the Zagreb museum has a Serbian groš of the scarce variety of "denarius de cruce" with fleurs-de-lis on the obverse, which is very probably early and is certainly connected, on stylistic grounds, with the "Seated King" variety identified as the "denarius de cruce et de lilio". [63] One notes that the extremely rare coin of Robert Karl of the Venetian type also bears fleurs-de-lis in the same place. [64]

Having disposed of the few stray finds, we turn to a group of particularly important hoards. They were discovered at Lisopolje, and at two find-spots in the lower Bosna valley, Maglaj and Klopče. Along with them should be mentioned the Zvečaj hoard of early Ragusan groši, from the same valley, although its date of deposit may lie outside the

[58] Cf. p. 130f. above.

[59] See D. Kovačević, "Prilog Proučavanju Zanatstva u Srednjevjekovnoj Bosni", *Godišnjak Istoriskog Društva Bosne i Hercegovine* x (1959), 279-296.

[60] Note the bearing of this on D. Kovačević, "Gdje je bila kovnica Novca Bosanskih Vladava", *Ibid.*, iv (1952), 269-76.

[61] Ljubić, *Opis*, Type III.

[62] Truhelka, "Die slavonische Banaldenare", Béla IV, Type a, III and Ban Stefan Babonezić. The coins are too far apart in date for there to be any likelihood of their having been associated.

[63] Cf. Ljubić, *Opis*, Stefan Uroš I, Type VI, no. 44.

[64] See Ljubić, *Opis*, pp. 51-2 and plate V, 5.

period under consideration. [65] Only the first out of the four has been published fully. The Lisopolje find of 1883 contained over 100 Bosnian coins of a previously unknown type, combining the Ragusan obverse of the standing figure of St. Blasius in a mandorla with a reverse showing the Bosnian version of the "Seated King" type. This design, which also occurs in combination with the more usual obverse design of the throned figure of Christ both in the Lisopolje hoard and in that from Bosanska Rača, is, in light of the Bijeljina and Lisopolje finds, a valuable further piece of evidence for the localization of the Serbian "Seated King" type to the northern borders of the country. The hoard was published in admirable detail by Valtrović; Stockert discussed the iconography; Rengjeo examined the relative chronology of the type in his survey of Bosnian numismatic history. [66] Specimens of the same type, in the Slavonian Museum, Osijek, published by Celestin, probably include stray finds, for two of them are pierced; here is yet another shred of evidence for the northern localization. [67]

The Maglaj hoard, discovered in or shortly before 1898, is represented by a parcel in the Zagreb museum. There are a dozen pieces on which the Ban is shown standing, in a mandorla, holding a sword:

1, 2.	BANVS STEFAN	P M	(Osijek)
3.	STAEFAN STAEFAN	two birds	
4, 5.	STEPAN BANVS	two birds	
6.	» »	Ā B	
7, 8.	» »	IB Ā	
9—11	» »	I M	
12.	» »	N I	
13.	» »	N I	

Table 18. Bosnian groši: secret-marks in the Maglaj hoard.

In light of the range of secret-marks represented (see Table 18), it is clear that the few varieties known to Ljubić in 1875 are from another hoard, characterized by the mark N S. The Osijek coin, which has been

[65] The Zagreb registers list "Groš, I A", two specimens, and "Groš, II A", four specimens.

[66] See *Starinar* i (1884), 32ff.; and *NZ* NS xvi (1923), 10ff.

[67] V. Celestin, "Beschreibung einiger bosnischen Münzen des städtischen Museums in Essegg", *WMBH* vii (1900), 221-230.

included in the list as probably from the Maglaj hoard, was published by Celestin two years after the date of discovery given above. [68]

The Klopče hoard of 1950 is one of the most valuable that has come to light, from the point of view of the composition and circulation of the currency in the west Balkan hinterland. It contained about sixty coins, mostly of Stefan Kotromanić, which were hidden in a metal box. There were also 2 Venetian grossi, of which the more recent was of Giovanni Soranzo (1312-28) and the other probably of P. Gradenigo. There was one Serbian coin, of the "Seated King" type, with the inscription CTEΦANЬ KPAΛЬ, which Dimitrijević gives to Stefan Dušan. The Bosnian coins were all of the type with the standing figure of the ban, and bore various secret-marks, among which the letters A, I, and K were commonest. There was one coin showing the ban without a sceptre. [69] The Maglaj, Klopče, and Lisopolje hoards show that by the time of Stepan Kotromanić II, the currency of northern Bosnia was being supplied predominantly by the country's own issues. The Lisopolje hoard may have been associated with the route from Tuzla towards Belgrade; Vukovar is another find-spot for the Bosnian series east of Tuzla. [70]

The route from southern Bosnia to the coast followed the Neretva valley. The only coin recorded from the area is a stray find of a Serbian coin from Vitina, in the Trebizat valley. [71]

The total of about sixty find-records from Serbia and Bosnia is already sufficient to reveal the general outlines of the region's monetary affairs. Progress in understanding the details will probably have to come from a comparative analysis of hoards. The next decade could witness extremely fruitful advances, but it will only be on the basis of very careful hoard-reports. Photographic illustration of a sufficiently high quality to permit die-identification may seem an extravagance; but the Serbian coinage is of such complexity, and so problematic, that to publish a hoard in less detail than, for example, Marić gave would be regrettable.

---

[68] D. M. Metcalf, "Ljubić's *Jugoslavenski Novci* as a Source-book", *NC* 6.xx (1960), 201-08; V. Celestin, *op. cit.*

[69] M. Vego, "Nalaz Bosanskog Novca u Selu Klopču kod Zenice", *Glasnik Zemaljskog Muzeju u Sarajevu* NS vi (1951), 324ff.; I. Rengjeo, "Nalaz u Klopču", *Numizmatika* v (1953), 27ff.

[70] See p. 143 above.

[71] Truhelka, "Verzeichnis".

CHAPTER IX

THE PETTY CURRENCY OF FEUDAL GREECE

The occupation of Greece by the Latins after 1204 was from two directions. Boniface de Montferrat, after securing Thessaloniki, advanced south to take Thessaly and central Greece. His progress was halted at Corinth, which remained in Greek hands; before returning north, he gave Athens and Thebes as a fief to Othon de la Roche. Secondly, Guillaume de Champlitte undertook the conquest of southern Greece beginning from Patras and establishing himself most firmly in the northern and western parts of the Peloponnese; his successor as Prince of Achaia, Geoffroi I, gained the keys to the Aegean seabord, Argos, Navplion, and, most important, Corinth (1210 and 1212). Methoni and Koroni, at the south-western extremity of the Peloponnese, remained in the hands of Venice, along with the principal islands of the Aegean. The fortress of Monemvasia, at the south-eastern tip of the peninsula, was held by the Greeks until 1248. Thessaloniki and Macedonia were re-captured by Theodore, despot of Epirus, in 1224. In the years immediately following, the Latin Empire lost territory to those of Nicaea and Epirus until it was reduced to little more than Constantinople and its environs. From about 1228, therefore, central and southern Greece was a geographically isolated group of Frankish states which was necessarily self-reliant. There was a contrast between the northern Peloponnese, where the Frankish political and economic structure was based very largely on feudal tenure, and Hellas (as it had been before 1204) together with Corinth and the other Aegean ports, where manufacture and trade appear to have continued in some importance, even if they declined from the position in the twelfth century. After strengthening his hold on the southern Peloponnese ca. 1250, Guillaume de Villehardouin (1245 -78) brought the central Greek territories of Athens, Negripont (Euboea), Salona, and Bodonitza into submission to himself (1258). This work of rationalization had scarcely been completed when it was undermined by Guillaume's military defeat at the hands of Michael Palaeologus and by the cession, as ransom, of the four fortresses that controlled the southern Peloponnese. Mistra thereafter became an important centre of Byzantine political and cultural life. In 1267 Guillaume placed himself under the protection of Charles of Anjou, and from that time onwards, Achaia became more and more a dependency of Naples. From the late thirteenth century, Negripont came under Venetian control. Athens grew in prestige and power at Achaia's expense. In 1260 Guy de la Roche (1225-1263) emerged from the War of the Terzieri of Euboea with the considerable political advantage of French backing against Guillaume's attempt to place the duchy under his own control. Guy's successors Jean (1263-1280), Guillaume (1280-1287), and Guy II (1287-1308) maintained an influence which extended over the Greek despotate of Great Wallachia (Thessaly). In 1311, however, all that the Franks had built in the Duchy of Athens was destroyed by the Catalan victory at the battle of the river Kifissos; from 1311 to 1387 the duchy was held by the Grand Calatan Company, and was organized as a sort of military republic. Through the many political changes of the thirteenth century, the balance of power in the Mediterranean world was moving away from Byzantium and towards Italy. Greece suffered particularly from these changes. In the process of transfer from the Aegean orbit to that of the Italian cities, political fragmentation, insecurity, and exploitation destroyed much of the country's prosperity.

The coinage that circulated in feudal Greece was of various kinds. In the first years after 1204, the Byzantine folles and stamena of the twelfth century probably continued in use, and were supplemented, although only on a trivial scale, by similar coinages issued in Asia Minor. Nicaean gold, which was used widely throughout the eastern Balkans in the first half of the century, found a place in the Greek monetary economy. Another trade coinage, which was used in the late thirteenth and early fourteenth centuries, was the Venetian grosso and the Serbian coinage that was closely modelled on it. Perhaps from ca. 1240, the Megaskyr of Athens struck his own petty currency, on a Genoese model. From a similar date, possibly 1250, the prince of Achaia began to strike his own copper coinage, at Corinth; and from an uncertain date, which is unlikely to have been earlier than 1270 and may have been *ca.* 1276, he struck *deniers tournois,* modelled on the French coins of the same type, at Clarentzia. Rather later, the Theban mint also began to strike tournois; and from 1294 or a little thereafter Philip of Taranto, who ruled over Epirus and Corfu, struck tournois at Lepanto. In the early fourteenth century, the rulers of a number of small territories struck their own coinages, of the tournois type; but the quantities issued were minute in comparison with the output of the three main mints of Thebes, Clarentzia, and Lepanto. There had, also, been some minor coinages in the thirteenth century. The insignificance of all but the three main mints is especially interesting in light of the political fragmentation of Greece and of the number of rulers who might have issued coinage on a large scale if there had been a sufficient need for it in their territories. One may conclude without hesitation that a monetary economy was largely restricted to the cities of Thebes and Corinth and the area which lay between them, and the shores of the Gulf of Corinth. The Gulf may have been used to some extent as a trading-route between the East and Italy, but we may conjecture that the use of petty coinage was closely associated with a more localized economy, in which the Duchy of Athens and the coastlands of the Gulf of Corinth were complementary regions, and of which the coasts of Epirus, and Corfu, were the further limit. The distribution of coin-finds recalls that of the twelfth-century folles, so much so that it is certain that the two series reflect a similar pattern of monetary affairs. The hoards in both cases are concentrated in central Greece, with one or two in Euboea. The tournois series, however, includes in addition some hoards from the north-western Peloponnese, and from Delphi, which would seem to have been on the route that was followed in the fourteenth century from Boeotia to the Gulf of Corinth. One may be confident that this difference in the geographical pattern of the finds that have been recorded reflects a genuine shift in the pattern of monetary circulation in central Greece between the twelfth and the late thirteenth centuries.

The years between 1204 and 1300, which witnessed so many political developments and changes in Greece, are of much greater interest to the monetary historian than the fourteenth century. Unfortunately, the number of hoards from each century is inversely proportional to the interest. For the fourteenth century there is a long and quite satisfactory find-series. For the thirteenth century there are several very difficult problems and, as yet, scarcely any hoards to throw light on them. These problems have to do with the bronze and gold coinages of Nicaea, with the circulation of French tournois in Greece, and with the chronology of the earliest Frankish issues. They concern the period 1204-*ca.* 1270: only one large deposit of Frankish coppers has been recorded, and the earliest hoard of Frankish tournois to have been published (that discovered at Xirokhori in 1957) was concealed 1285-*ca.* 1287.

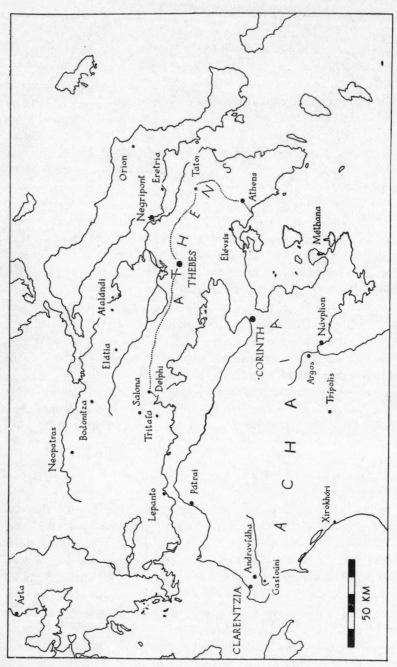

Map XI· Central Greece.

A small parcel of scyphate bronze coins including some of Theodore of Nicaea (1204-1222) was obtained in the Piraeus in 1926. [1] Its provenance is uncertain, but it may have formed part or the whole of a small hoard from central Greece or from one of the islands. A similar, larger hoard, apparently with a lower proportion of Theodore's coins, came to light in Athens in 1933. [2] Again, the provenance is a matter for speculation; but the twelfth-century coins in the hoard hint at a Macedonian origin. Thus, neither of these finds shows with any certainty that Nicaean coins were circulating in central Greece. Their occurrence in the islands is well established by the Thira and Paros hoards; [3] but for central Greece the site-finds provide better evidence. Nine of Theodore's stamena were found at Corinth in the period 1896-1929, 7 more in the years 1930-35, and a further 5 duriug 1936-39; while only one was found in the Athenian Agora. The dates at which Athens and Corinth were occupied—1205 and 1210 respectively—might be a sufficient explanation for the different quantities. The most intriguing question about the scyphate bronze of Theodore is the mint or mints at which it was struck. The style and fabric of the specimens found in north Greek hoards such as the Thessaly hoard of 1957 and that from Levkokhori, 1959 are generally so similar to the twelfth-century Greek issues that one would like to attribute them, also, to Greek mints. Many of them may have been struck at Corinth in the period 1204-1210, but this is only a guess. Sgouros, who made himself master of Corinth, claimed St. Theodore the Warrior as his patron, so the type would have been appropriate. There are, moreover, several varieties with different ornaments on the emperor's loros. The number and arrangement of the dots at the shoulders, on the emperor's chest, and on the central panel of the loros may well constitute some kind of mint-mark. The rows of dots on the saint's cuirass are usually horizontal, but occasionally vertical. These small variations hint at the operation of more than one mint. [4] Apart from Corinth, Monemvasia and the islands would be worth considering as possible mint-places.

The only deposit published so far which brings forward specific evidence that twelfth-century folles continued in use after 1204 is that from the Areopagus at Athens, discussed below, but one may reasonably conjecture that they were current in large numbers, since it is hard

[1] Bellinger, "Three Hoards".
[2] Ibid.
[3] Metcalf, "Scyphate Bronze Coinage in Greece".
[4] Ibid.

to imagine a complete breakdown in the monetary economy of places such as Thebes.

The Chronicle of the Morea contains a garbled reference which has been construed as possibly implying that the emperor Robert, in 1218, conferred on Geoffroi of Achaia the right of striking coinage. Since it conflicted with Sanudo's statement that coinage was first struck in A-chaia in 1250 or thereabouts, it has been the conventional view that, if there were in fact autonomous issues in the first half of the thirteenth century, they are to be identified among the copper coins of the principality, and that the tournois are not to be dated before 1250. Bellinger, in presenting evidence from the excavations on Acrocorinth, suggested that petty coinage might well be attributed to the reign of Geoffroi (1218-45). [5] The excavations yielded 24 specimesn of the type with a gateway, somewhat similar to that on Genose coins of the period (which however are in silver), and with the inscription CORINTI, [6] but only one specimen of the issue depicting a fortess, perhaps intended to be the fortifications of Acrocorinth itself, and the inscription CORINTUM. [7] The relative proportions are strikingly different in the main Corinth excavations, where, during the period 1896-1929, 136 specimens of the CORINTI type (Schl. XII, 10) and 192 of the CORINTUM type (Schl. XII, 7) were found. Bellinger noted that it was Guillaume (1245-78) who was mentioned by a chronicler as having carried on the building and repairs on Acrocorinth, and he suggested that the two types could not be contemporary, and that Schl. XII, 10 should be assigned to the early part of Guillaume's reign, before the Achaian mint was transferred to Clarentzia, and that XII, 7 might be assigned to Geoffroi.

A study of the site-finds from Athens (where work began some years after the excavations on Acrocorinth were completed) and of the large deposit recently discovered on the slopes of the Areopagus at Athens suggests substantial alterations to the chronological scheme. A comparison, first, of the deniers tournois (see Table 19, where the statistics refer to the period *ca.* 1280-*ca.* 1308) shows that, at Athens, the issues from the mint of Thebes were twice as plentiful as those from Clarentzia; at Corinth, the proportions were equal. In fourteenth-century hoards. the ratio is normally intermediate, Achaian tournois being about three-

---

[5] A. R. Bellinger, "The Coins", in C. W. Blegen and other, *Acrocorinth, Excavations in* 1926 (Corinth, vol. III, part 1), Cambridge, Mass., 1930, pp. 61-68.

[6] Schlumberger, *L'Orient Latin*, plate XII, 10.

[7] *Ibid.*, plate XII, 7.

quarters as numerous as those of Athens. The figures show that the Achaian and Athenian tournois were accepted indiscriminately in both fiefs, and they are at the same time a measure of the extent to which the coins were localized in their circulation.

			At Athens	At Corinth
(a)	Deniers tournois			
	Athenian issues		89	33
	Achaian issues		45	33
(b)	Petty coinages			
	Athenian: Schl.	XII, 31	32	2
		XII, 30	20	0
		XII, 32	61	1
		XIII, 1	20	2
		XIII, 6, 8, and 12	123	0
	Achaian:	XII, 6	94	1
		XII, 7 and 8 (obol)	276	192+2
		XII, 10 and 9 (obol)	49	136+1

Table 19. Quantities of Frankish coins in the site-finds from Athens and from Corinth (1896-1929). The Achaian tournois are of the period 1278-1307 only, and the Athenian tournois are of the period 1280-1308 only, for purposes of equal comparison.

The petty coinages virtually never occur in the hoards, and yet they are far more plentiful than the tournois among the site-finds. This can only be because, on the one hand, the most valuable of the available coins were hoarded, and, on the other, the least valuable denomination was handled a little more carelessly or was not always searched for with persistence if a piece was accidentally lost. Since the deniers tournois were themselves of comparatively small value, the different occurrence of the two denominations in hoards and site-finds is a good illustration of the importance to be attached to the purchasing-power of a coinage in interpreting find-records. Another point is that the many examples of very large hoards containing no, or few, coins of higher face value than tournois is a strong argument that more valuable coins were at the time not readily available in central Greece. At the other extreme, one may argue from the paucity of the little Corinthian obols (Schl. XII, 8 and 9) among the site-finds that they were never issued in quantities.

The substantive issues of coppers from the excavations show a much greater contrast between Athens and Corinth than do the tournois. The Athenian issues scarcely ever found their way to Corinth, whereas the Corinthian issues outnumber the local coinages among the Athens finds. Taking the evidence at face value, the only likely explanations would be either that the output of petty coinage from the Corinth mint was vastly greater than that from Thebes, or that there was a period when the Athenian currency was, for some reason, supplied from Corinth.

The Areopagus deposit of 1963 [8] consisted of 200 Athenian coppers, all of a single type, 2 Negripontine coins of Guillaume of Achaia, a follis of Manuel I, and 9 French and one Provençal tournois. The Athenian coins are those with the "Genoese" gateway as their principal design (Schl. XII, 31). The complete absence of Corinthian coins proves as clearly as negative evidence ever could that they were unimportant in the currency of Athens, if not entirely absent from it, at that date. It seems likely, therefore, that they came flooding into the city after Guillaume's victory over Guy at the battle of Karydhi, in 1258, and before Guy's vindication in 1260, and that the hoard is to be dated to a little earlier, say 1255-50. This rather surprising chronological scheme finds support in the localization of the finds within the Agora area at Athens. The Athenian coppers show a clear concentration in one small part of the lower Agora, and the Corinthian coins are plentiful there, too. But the latter are even more plentiful in another small, and quite separate, area on the north-eastern flank of the Areopagus (not far from where the deposit was found in 1963); and Athenian coins do not occur in any concentration there. Some special explanation is required for this differential localization of coinages that must have been virtually contemporary issues on the time-scale of urban development. It seems possible that the pattern of finds results from Corinthian troops, or other personnel in the service of the prince of Achaia, having been quartered on or near the Areopagus.

One of the issues classified by Schlumberger as Achaian (XII, 6) stands out in Table 19 as an irregularity. It is the one type which is without a mint-signature, and is doubtless an Athenian issue attributable to the same period, 1258-59, in which so many specimens of XII, 7. and XII, 10 were put into circulation in the city.

---

[8] The account of the Areopagus deposit, and the arguments about it, are condensed from D. M. Metcalf, "Frankish Petty Currency from the Areopagus at Athens", *Hesperia* (in press).

If these revisions allow one to suppose that the petty currency of Corinth, as well as Athens, was ordinarily very localized, it will not be possible to argue from the absence of Corinthian coppers in Athens up to the date of the Areopagus deposit that their issue did not begin until almost that time. Nevertheless, if Corinthian issues had begun as early as 1218, a few specimens might have been expected to turn up in a deposit of 200 coins, especially when it included two Negripontine pieces. The relative proportions of XII, 7 and XII, 10 are quite different at Athens and Corinth; on the hypothesis outlined above, the straightforward explanation of them is that XII, 10 is earlier, while XII, 7 (and XII, 6) were in issue during the Corinthian ascendancy over Athens. This reverses Bellinger's order, although XII, 10 could still very well belong to the earlier part of the reign of Guillaume.

Guy de la Roche made important trading concessions, in 1240, to the Genose residing in Thebes, and the issue of his first coinage, which was modelled so closely on the coinage of Genoa, although obviously not for reasons of monetary circulation, may have begun not long afterwards. Athenian coppers are firmly attributed to the minority of Guy II, 1287-94; various types inscribed G. DUX may belong to Guy I, Guillaume I, Guy II, or may even be as late as the reign of Gauthier (1308-11). In any case, the series was issued in quantities over several decades. The Corinthian coppers, on the other hand, are apparently all earlier than 1278, and such little evidence as there is suggests that they might all belong in the second half of the century. The propaganda-coinage that Guillaume struck for (and probably at) Negripont ca. 1256, and the even scarcer copper coinage of Clarentzia (Schl. XX, 28) seem to stand together.

One must suspect, although proof can not yet be found, that it was principally in the lordship or duchy of Athens, and only to a limited extent in Achaia, that there was an insistent demand for petty currency throughout the thirteenth century. The city where, above all, there was an industrial community, likely to have had to buy their everyday requirements of food, and so on, in the market-place, and to pay in coinage of an appropriate denomination, was Thebes. Benjamin of Tudela records that, in the 1160's, there were 2,000 Jews in Thebes, and that they were workers in silk and purple. The community compared in size with that at Constantinople, and was very much larger than any other which Benjamin visited. At Corinth, for example, there were said to be 300, and at Negripont 200 Jews, while at Athens, there were apparently none. [9]

Even though the centre of gravity of Frankish monetary affairs seems to have been in Thebes, the account of the origins of the local coinage in Achaia, given by Marin Sanudo, may be substantially correct. His *Istoria del Regno di Romania,* written some sixty or seventy years after the event, records that Guillaume de Villehardouin sought and obtained permission, from king Louis IX while he was in Cyprus, to issue coinage. "Signor Sir", he is reported as saying, "tu sei maggior Signor di me, e poi condur gente dove vuoi e quanta vuoi senza denari: io non posso far cosi". [10] Guillaume's request, that is to say, was based on his desire to be able to pay his military forces. The incident should be considered in the context of Guillaume's Negripontine coinage, of his political ambitions generally, and of the interpretation that has been suggested for the finds from the Athenian Agora.

The first Achaian tournois are undoubtedly earlier than 1278, and the first Athenian tournois are undoubtedly later than 1280, but only by a year or two: the composition and close age-structure of the Xirokhori hoard, which establishes these facts, [11] suggest that the date of origin of the Achaian tournois was not more than a few years before 1278. The absence of Frankish issues among the tournois from the Areopagus deposit, concealed 1255-*ca.* 1258, implies strongly that their issue had not begun at that date. The deposit virtually destroys the traditional dating of the first Achaian tournois to 1250.

More exact evidence can only come from other hoards from the sixth, seventh, and eighth decades of the thirteenth century. Regrettably few are known. The Corinth hoard of 1934, deposited after 1253, consisted mainly of deniers tournois, none of which were Frankish: it was interpreted originally as a traveller's hoard, but may in fact reflect the local currency. The same uncertainly applies to a recently-discovered hoard of French deniers said to have come from Eretria (near Khalkis), [12] the date of deposit of which (perhaps 1250-70?) can be determined only after a detailed study of the die-varieties has been completed. One can

---

[9] See A. Andreades, "The Jews in the Byzantine Empire", *Economic History* iii (1934), 1-23.

[10] See Schlumberger, *L'Orient Latin*, pp. 308-12.

[11] Metcalf, *"Deniers Tournois* in Frankish Greece".

[12] Varoukha-Khristodhoulopoulou, "Aquisitions, 1962".

be much more confident, on the other hand, that the French and Provençal tournois in the Areopagus deposit were withdrawn from circulation locally in the ordinary way. In the Thessaly hoard of 1949, deposited *ca.* 1255, the silver coins were all grossi, and in any case the find-spot is too far north for the lack of tournois to be significant. The Patrai and Erymantheia hoards of gold of John III (1222-54), although they are very much from the area where the earliest Achaian tournois might be expected to have been current, cannot be shown to belong to the second half of the century. [13] Also, gold might well have been hoarded to the exclusion of billon. This objection applies equally to the Corinth hoard of 1925, dated by a nomisma of Theodore II (1254-58). A little hoard of three coins, it is of interest for the mint-attributions of the "Nicaean" gold. The two with John's name have seven or eight dots at the emperor's shoulders, and the secret-mark on the obverse is, apparently, on each piece a dot to left and right of the throne, although only that to the right is very distinct. A number of similarities can be found with the dies represented in the Erymantheia hoard. [14] It seems probable that many of these gold coins, like the bronze pieces in provinvial style of Theodore of Nicaea, were struck at Balkan mints. Pegolotti's reference to "lo pipero di Chiarenza" as a money of account in the middle of the fourteenth century may have as its distant origin the Greek τριχεφαλα of the time of John III.

The Corinth find of 1934 contained 369 tournois, 10 English pennies, 7 Venetian coins, one denier of Champagne, and a gold nomisma of John III. The Venetian coins were 3 of I. Tiepolo (1228-49), 1 of M. Morosini (1249-53), and 3 of R. Zeno (1253-68), which give the earlier *terminus* for the date of deposit. Early Venetian grossi, particularly of I. Tiepolo, have turned up in small quantities as stray finds at Corinth, but there have been none of M. Morosini or R. Zeno. English pennies also have been found in the excavations, regularly if in small quantities, so that the presence of such coins in the hoard certainly does not prove that it belonged to a traveller.

A comparison of the Corinth hoard of 1934 with the Thessaly hoard,

---

[13] See Metcalf, "John Vatatzes" for references and for illustrations of 9 coins from the Erymantheia hoard. The Patrai hoard was dispersed.

[14] For die-similarities between the Corinth and Erymantheia hoards, cf. Bellinger, *Corinth*, 1925, plate II, 4 and 5 with Metcalf, "John Vatatzes", plate 10, especially, nos.10-12. Cf. p. 223 for the bronze of Theodore, and p. 126 for the Nicaean gold. For Pegolotti, see Schlumberger, *L'Orient Latin*, p. 311.

described below, and with the stray finds from Corinth, suggests a date fairly early in the reign of R. Zeno for the deposit of the Corinth coins, although of course the number of Venetian pieces is too small for any firm conclusion. The proportions of French coins rest on larger numbers, and they, too, speak in favour of an early date. If therefore, as seems more likely, the hoard is a sample of the Corinthian currency, it shows, like the Areopagus deposit, that 1250 is too early a date to be tenable for the introduction of the Frankish deniers tournois, and it has the added force of coming from the territory of Achaia.

A hoard of English "short-cross" pennies, appreciably earlier in date than most of the site-finds of English coins, must be mentioned as one of the very earliest discoveries of the Frankish period. It came from Methana, just across the Gulf of Aegina, and was represented by five specimens in Finlay's collection, of which two were from the London mint, two from Canterbury, and one, unexpectedly, from Exeter. This last coin indicates a date of deposit after 1215. The later *terminus* might be put at *ca.* 1224. The Methana hoard may well have been concealed by an English traveller. [15]

Thus, there are as yet no hoards that can be considered as good evidence for the question of deniers tournois in Greece in the 1260's and 1270's. There is, however, one argument which is almost as conclusive as hoards would be. French tournois occur in only very small proportions in Frankish tournois hoards of the end of the thirteenth and the beginning of the fourteenth centuries, yet they have turned up as stray finds in the Corinth excavations in very much larger proportions. Over the years 1896-1939, 141 stray finds of French regal and feudal issues were discovered, while the Frankish tournois amounted to twice as many. This implies that the French coins were at some date far more plentiful in the Corinthian currency than might have been thought from the composition of the hoards.

The unexpectedly high proportion of Provencal coins in both the hoards and site-finds suggests that some quite specific connexion between Provence and Greece may have played a part in Frankish monetary history. Charles I of Anjou, count of Provence, was also prince of

---

[15] G. Finlay, MS "List of Antiquities", S. 9. 3 (b) in the library of the British School at Athens. The legends of the coins are BENEI. ON. LVND; PIER. EIS. M. ON. LVN; GOLDWINE.ON.C; ROGER.ON.CANT; IOHAN.ON.ECCE. A sixth coin, also found in Greece, is a "Long-cross" penny of Class III or a copy of one.

Achaia, from 1278 to 1285. He struck deniers tournois both in Provence and Achaia, although perhaps not concurrently. The administrative links between the two territories, which no doubt occasioned various official journeys and may have stimulated trade, might explain the occurence of Provençal coinage in Greece: some such theory seems to be necessary, for example, to explain the particular numbers of coins attributed to Raimond VII, as marquis of Provence, in the Xirokhori hoard, and also the exceptionally high proportion of coins of ·Charles as count of Provence in the Corinth site-finds. On the other hand, the Provençal tournois might to some extent have been exported to Greece because their circulation in France had been forbidden by Louis IX. That this cannot be a complete explanation is shown by the Provençal coin in the Areopagus deposit, which certainly antedates Louis's legislation of 1263. By the treaty of Viterbo in 1267 Guillaume de Villehardouin willingly accepted Angevin everlordship of Achaia. Might the Achaian tournois which bear his name have been issued from that date? The Corinth hoard of 1934 and the Areopagus deposit, however, in the context of the site-finds, put it beyond question that Provençal and other French coins were finding their way to Greece before 1267; and the age-structure of the Xirokhori hoard favours a later date, as has already been said, for the introduction of the Frankish issues.

The currency must indeed have been rather mixed in the period before the autonomous issues of tournois began. The occurrence of so many different types, and, even more, such a wide range of denominations—folles, stamena, deniers, pennies, grossi, and nomismata—leads one to think that the economy of central Greece was both resilient to political changes and complex in its monetary requirements, throughout the first half of the century.

Venetian grossi, which, because of their purchasing power, should be viewed as trade-coins, may well have been in use at Corinth in some quantities in the 1240's, and perhaps the 1230's, for there is a concentration in the reign of I. Tiepolo (1228-49) in the site-finds. The numbers are trifling, but in assessing them one must remember that the rate of loss of coins as valuable as grossi was very many times smaller than the rate of loss for petty coins. The use of grossi at Corinth may have been a rather isolated case; the widespread circulation of the Venetian, and also Serbian, coins in the Aegean hinterlands forms a chapter of monetary history belonging essentially to the last quarter of the thirteenth and the first quarter of the fourteenth century. The numismatist, in considering the Corinth finds (and likewise the Tsrŭncha hoard from near Pazardzhik, reported to contain 21 coins of I Tiepolo) will wish to bear in mind how easy it is to mistake them and the issues of L. Tiepolo, 1268-75. A hoard said to have been discovered in Thessaly in 1949 is unusually early. It consisted of one nomisma of John III, 46 Venetian coins, and 7 fragments of grossi. Another find acquired in 1949 by the Greek cabinet consisted of 2 nomismata of John III said to have come from Drama. No other hoard of John's gold has been recorded from Greece north of Attica, so it is worth asking whether the two parcels of 1949 are likely to have come from a single discovery; but the style of the nomisma from Thessaly is by no means the same as that of the two from Drama, which are quite similar to each other, and which belong with those that have been very tentatively given to the north Balkans. [16] The Venetian grossi are listed in Table 17. They are somewhat corroded. There is no reason to think that the unidentified specimens, of which there were 9 and 4 fragments, are other than similar to the rest. The date of deposit is after 1253. An estimate of the later terminus must take into account the proportions of coins of R. Zeno to those of I. Tiepolo and of M. Morosini. In the Verona and Carribollo hoards the coins of R. Zeno are four times more numerous than those of the previous two doges together. Allowing for the uncertain coins one may place the terminus at *ca*. 1260, and guess at a date a year or two earlier.

Serbian as well as Venetian grossi appear in the Delphi hoard of 1933, concealed 1301-*ca*. 1305. The proportion of coins of G. Dandolo to P. Gradenigo, 8:1, is surprisingly low for a date of deposit in the fourteenth century, and suggests that either the sample in the hoard is not typical or that the currency of grossi in Greece was weighted with old coins. The latter theory is difficult to reconcile with the evidence of the Delphi hoard of 1929, deposited very possibly in 1311, and containing only 10 coins of G. Dandolo to 58 of P. Gradenigo (again, see Table 17). The proportion of Serbian coins is much higher, too: there are 18 against 82, whereas there was only one against 18 in the 1933 hoard. The question whether the Serbian coins reached central Greece by an Aegean route or in a more roundabout way from the currency of the A-

---

[16] The three gold coins are described and illustrated in Metcalf, "John Vatatzes". Each has 9 dots at the emperor's shoulders; the two from the Drama hoard have pendants to the crown of 4 dots arranged in a diamond pattern; the Thessaly coin is important for the secret-mark II. I am indebted to Mrs Varoukha-Khristodhoulopoulou for permitting me to study the hoard.

driatic coastlands seems very difficult to answer until one or two more hoards are available. A hoard of uncertain provenance acquired by the

1. Denarius de bandera, S STEFAN VROSIVS REX. Dot by Our Lord's right elbow (or annulet?), and smaller dot by his left elbow. Rev. Small cross on staff of cross, and small, fat cross at its foot. 1.6 gm. PLATE XIII, 1.

2. Similar, but in a linear style. Note particularly the treatment of the beards. Secret-mark x by Our Lord's left elbow. 2.16 gm. Die-axis ca. 165°. PLATE XIII, 2.

3. Denarius de cruce, S STEFAN STEFAN R E X. Cross in middle of king's breast, x on saint's left shoulder. 2.18 gm. PLATE XIII, 3.

4. Very similar, but with dot between Our Lord's feet. 2.15 gm.

5. Denarius de bandera, uncertain inscription to left, but perhaps CTE..., crude linear style. Cross to right of throne on obverse. Base silver? 1.82 gm. PLATE XIV, 5.

6–18. Denarii de bandera, S STEFAN VROSIVS REX.

6. Secret-mark x on Saint's left shoulder. 2.13 gm. PLATE XIV, 6.

7. The same, similar style.

8. Secret-mark x x on Saint's shoulders; thick 6-rayed asterisk by bottom right of staff.

9. Nothing on Saint's shoulders? Top edges of throne slope as on no. 2, but without dot at corners.

10. Secret-marks, crosses on Saint's shoulders.

11. Secret-marks apparently: ·:· on Saint's shoulders.

12. Secret-mark ·:· on Saint's right shoulder. 1.95 gm. PLATE XIV, 12.

13–14. Very similar to no. 12.

15–16. Similar to no. 12. Average weight of nos. 12-16 is 1.96 gm.

17–18. Indistinct but apparently similar to no. 12.

Table 20. Serbian coins in the Delphi hoard of 1929.

Athens museum in 1956 can be assumed to be relevant for a consideration of the currency in the western Aegean: the Venetian coins in it are
summarily listed in Table 17. The date of deposit is after 1339; and yet
it is quite clear that many of the 26 Serbian coins are thirteenth-century issues. Twenty-four read VROSIVS, and one has STEFAN: these
are all "denarii de bandera"; there is one "denarius de cruce" of Stefan
Dragutin, showing the king crowned, and with the secret-marks M L
on the obverse and T R at the foot of the cross on the reverse, but it is
pierced, if that affects the consideration of it. At least five specimens
have the little secret-marks of the Venetian system on the obverse.

The 18 Serbian coins in the Delphi hoard of 1929 are, however, more
important, because their provenance is known. The composition of the
little group reinforces the suspicion that the grossi from this deposit are
not typical. The varieties are listed in Table 20.

The publication by Mrs. Oikonomidhes of a series of stray finds from
archaeological excavation at Trikkala settles beyond reasonable doubt
that the curious coins with a wing in the field, tetatively attributed by
Bertelè to Thessaloniki, are after all issues of the sebastocrator of Great
Wallachia, John Ducas (1271-96). [17].

It is worth bearing in mind the possibility that further Thessalian,
and other north-central Greek issues of the fourteenth century remain
to be identified. In 1349 Stefan Dušan became "Despot of Arta and
Count of Vlachia", and thereafter placed Epirus and Acarnania under
the command of his half-brother, Symeon Uroš, with the title of despot.
In 1356 Symeon proclaimed himself "Emperor of the Serbs and Greeks"
at Kastoria; and in 1359 he was ruling over Thessaly as Serbian emperor
at Trikkala.

To return central Greece: a dozen hoards of Frankish deniers tournois from the first half of the thirteenth century provide the material
for a comparative analysis, from which the main outlines of the mint-

---

[17] M. Καραμεσίνη - Οἰκονομίδου, Νομίσματα ᾿Ανασκαφῶν Θεσσαλίας, Θεσσαλικά,
᾿Αρχαιολογικὸν Περιοδιὸκν Δημοσίευμα, iv (1962), 3-15. Of three thirteenth-century
coins from the site, one was of John's "Standing Figure" type, one was of his "Seated Figure" type, and the other was as H. Mattingly, "A Find of Thirteenth-century Coins at Arta in Epirus", NC⁵ iii (1923), 31-46, Class X. See further Bertelè,
L' Imperatore Alato, p. 28 and plate iii (nos. 35-37); Wroth, BMC (Byz.) III, lxxiv,
227-8, and plate xxxi, 12 and 13; Schlumberger, L'Orient Latin, pp. 376-78. The
coins may first have been issued on the occasion of the ecclesiastical council at Neopatras in 1279.

history and also the circulation can be made out. For the period of Charles I and Charles II d'Anjou, the Xirokhori hoard, from the west coast of the Peloponnese, shows that large quantities of Athenian coins had very quickly found their way to distant parts of Achaia, even if, as one might expect, they were outnumbered by the local issues from Clarentzia. The reign of Charles II saw a good deal of fighting between the Franks and Byzantines in the Peloponnese, particularly in Arcadia, during which the advantage often lay with the Byzantine forces. The Xirokhori hoard may have been concealed *ca.* 1285-87 because of these disturbances.

After Xirokhori, the next hoards by date of deposit are those discovered at Delphi in 1933 and 1929, concealed 1301-ca. 1305 and (?) 1311. They are of interest because they indicate the use of the routeway from the Duchy of Athens to the Gulf of Corinth. The Elevsis hoard of 1862, which may also have been concealed in 1311, contained 175 French gros tournois and 100 grossi of Federico of Sicily. Lenormant suggested that the Sicilian coins had been brought to Greece by members of the Catalan Company, and that the French coins had been brought on the occasion of the visit of the French admiral Cépoy; but it is more likely that both the Elevsis hoard and the fourth Delphi hoard of 1894 [18] were travellers' hoards, illustrating only the general connexions between Sicily and Greece at this period: note the round numbers of coins in the Elevsis hoard. Otherwise, one might have expected at least a few strays of similar large silver coins among a whole series of hoards from the first half of the fourteenth century, which consist exclusively of tournois, or, from *ca.* 1330, of tournois and soldini. [19]

---

[18] One may draw attention to Ljubić, *Opis*, plate viii, 7, which, together with not a few of the varieties represented in the Durrës hoard, are possible candidates for a southerly attribution: Arta, Kastoria, and Trikkala are three possibilities as mint-towns, the last, perhaps, for some of the "Coronation" and "Horseman" coins. See D. M. Nicol, "Thessaly in the Middle Ages", Chapter III in *Meteora, The Rock Monasteries of Thessaly*, London, 1963, pp. 46-69. In similar vein, note the possible connexion between finds of Bulgarian coins in Albania and the fact that John Comnenus Asen, the brother-in-law whom Stefan Dušan made governor of his acquisitions in Albania, was the brother of Ivan Aleksandŭr.

[19] See E. Caron, "Trouvailles de Monnaies du Moyen Age à Delphes", *BCH* 1897, 26ff. The hoard comprised 26 grossi, principally Sicilian, and was dated by Caron after 1316. For a catalogue of the hoards of Elevsis, Tatoi 1860, Attica 1951, Attica 1950, Orion 1959, Tritaia 1933, Atalandhi 1940, Delphi 1894 B, Elatia 1885, Delphi 1894 Γ, and Patras 1955, see Metcalf, *"Deniers Tournois" in Frankish Greece*.

When Guillaume de la Roche became duke of Athens he began to put out tournois from the mint of Thebes. During his reign (1280-87) about three times as much coinage was struck there as at Clarentzia. After his death, however, the position was apparently reversed, as the Athenian mint almost ceased production, under Guy de la Roche (1287-1308)—unless some of the coins attributed by Schlumberger to the later part of his reign [20] in fact belong to the years of his minority (1287-94). There is as yet no hoard to settle this point.

The hey-day of the Frankish tournois coinage was in the period 1294-1311. However the coins of Guy II are attributed, it is clear that the total output of the mints rose greatly *ca.* 1295, and fell again almost as sharply after the defeat of Athens in 1311. There were three major mints at work, since Philip of Taranto issued tournois at Lepanto before becoming prince of Achaia, and kept both that and the Clarentzia mint in operation afterwards. On his accession as prince, however, the output of the Lepanto mint was cut to about one-third of what it had been. At this level it was striking 10-20% as much coinage as the Clarentzia mint, which was very active under Philip. An estimate of the output of the mint of Thebes will depend on the question of dating Guy's coins, but if those reading GVI DVX belong after 1294, Thebes was from then on striking rather more coinage than Clarentzia. In Thessaly the minor mint of Neopatras struck perhaps 5% as much coinage *per annum* as Thebes, if not more. The uncertainty is because the product of this and the other minor mints may not have been fully intermingled in the currency of the areas from which the hoards have come. The mint of Tinos seems, with this reservation, not to have been important, while those of Corfu and Salona were even less so. The monetary historian will find a special interest in the large scale of Philip's coinage in Epirus.

During the reign of Jean de Hainault (with Maud de Hainault, 1318-21; alone, 1321-33), Clarentzia was the only mint of any importance still striking tournois; the output was far less than it had been in the hey-day. After 1333 few tournois were struck, but the Clarentzia mint may have been responsible for a large quantity of imitations of Venetian soldini. [21] Tournois struck in the latter part of the thirteenth

---

[20] Schlumberger, *L'Orient Latin*, plate XIII, 9.

[21] For a criticism of the arguments of D. H. Cox, *The Caparelli Hoard*, New York, 1930, see Metcalf, "*Deniers Tournois* in Frankish Greece", p. 57. On the irregular issues of tournois of the fourteenth century, on which much remains to be done, and where a more detailed numismatic method is required, see Metcalf, *op. cit.*, p.

century were still circulating at the middle of the fourteenth, although their proportion in the currency were beginning to dwindle. In the 1320's, small quantities of tournois were struck at Arta and Chios. The Epirote coins (DE ARTA CASTRU) occur in hoards from central Greece in trifling qantities. Even at Patrai there were only 2 among 160. It is interesting to note, therefore, that Lambros was able to publish 14 die-varieties.[22]

It remains to mention a few discoveries that have been published only summarily. At Athens in 1938, 20 grossi of the thirteenth century were found.[23] Over five hundred stray finds were brought to light at Delphi in the German excavations; a proportion of them was medieval. The excavations of the British School at Sparta produced some hundreds of medieval coins in 1924-25, and some more in 1927.[24] Among a dozen stray finds from Haliartos in 1926, one Frankish coin was noted.[25] Finally, there is a recent hoard of billon from Gastouni Elis, in the Peloponnese.[26]

59, and A. J. Seltman, "Two Deniers of Medieval Athens", *Numismatic Circular,* lxix (1961), 186. On the physical setting of the mint, see G. A. Soteriou, "Le Château Fort de Chloumoutzi et son Atelier Monétaire de Tournois de Clarencia", *JIAN* xix (1918-19), 273-79.

[22] P. Lambros, in *NZ* iii (1871), 485-500.

[23] *BCH* lxii (1938), 447.

[24] *Mitteilungen des Deutsches Archaeologisches Institut in Athen* xx (1895), 232. *ABSAthens* xxvi (1925), 157f. and xxviii (1926-27), 14.

[25] *ABSAthens* xxviii (1926-27), 139.

[26] Varoukha-Khristodhoulopoulou, "Aquisitions, 1962".

CHAPTER X

COINAGE IN THE RESTORED EMPIRE AND IN BULGARIA

The eastern part of the Balkan peninsula in the second half of the thirteenth and in the first half of the fourteenth century was a weather-vane for all the winds of political change in the east Mediterranean world. Control and political influence over the region swung to and fro between the restored Empire, Bulgaria, and Serbia, combined and re-combined in various alliances involving Epirus, Sicily, Hungary, Rome, and the Turkish tribes of Anatolia and the Steppes, and was complicated by the presence of the Tartars of the Golden Horde, the devastations of the Grand Catalan Company, and civil strife between Andronicus II and Andronicus III.

The numismatic history of the period is still obscure at many points, although Palaeologan numismatics is now a field in which rapid progress is being made.[1] The chief *desideratum* is a very detailed study of the groshi of Ivan Aleksandŭr (1331-71); enough hoards of such coins have been found for a comparative analysis that should reveal much about Bulgarian monetary history. Byzantine gold and Venetian silver, the Bulgarian silver of Todor Svetoslav (1300-1321), and bronze of the Palaeologi, of the twelfth-century emperors, and, again, of Todor Svetoslav were the other common currencies in the period under review. Coins of the earlier Bulgarian rulers are for the most part scarce, and by implication did not play an important part in monetary affairs. A gold coin of Ivan Asen II, and limited numbers of silver and bronze pieces are of great numismatic interest, and have received attention from that point of view.[2]

---

[1] See, for example, Gerasimov, "Neizdadeni Moneti"; Gerasimov, "Andronic II et Andronic III"; Longuet, "Une Trouvaille"; Bertelè, "L'Iperpero". Among other recent papers note T. Bertelè, "Autocratori dei Romani, di Constantinopoli, e della Macedonia", *Numismatica* NS ii (1961), 75-82; and A. Veglery and G. Zacos, "Silver Coins of Andronikos II and Andronikos III", *Numismatic Circular* lxx (1962), 76-80; and, for an important hoard of late silver, E. Varoukha-Khristodhoulo-poulou, in *BCH* lxxxi (1957), 498.

[2] T. D. Gerasimov, "Pŭrvata Zlatna Moneta na Tsar Ivan Asen II", *IBAI* viii

The finds show that the east Balkans fell into two broad regions, open to different monetary influences. To the north and east of Plovdiv, roughly speaking, the currency seems to have been carried into the country from the Black Sea coasts and from Constantinople, while to the south and west of Plovdiv, it came from Macedonia and the region of Thessaloniki. A similar division of the territory in the first half of the thirteenth century is documented by the scyphate bronze of Thessaloniki, in the south-west, and by the gold of Nicaea, in the north-east. Again, at the middle of the fourteenth century, the distinction is that the groshi of Ivan Aleksandŭr were hoarded in conjunction with Venetian and Serbian silver in the south-west, but alone in the north-east. At Vidin and in the Krain, where there was as autonomous coinage in the second half of the fourteenth century, the finds from the period 1250-1350 hint at a rather separate currency.

After the Tsrŭncha hoard, [3] the next in date of deposit is, perhaps, that from Postallar, near Edirne. More than half of the 374 bronze coins it contained were of Manuel I, Type 13/ii, while others were of Thessaloniki and Nicaea. The hoard is dated by a coin of Michael VIII (1261-82) [4]. It seems to represent a petty currency that had been stagnant for a century, and contrasts sharply with the Arta hoard in that respect. It is presumably a traveller's hoard, brought from further west.

Three hundred silver grossi of Venice, deposited after 1280, were discovered at Kamenitsa in 1926, [5] in the same valley-routeway as two earlier hoards which may have been carried from Thessaloniki. [6] The find was incompletely recorded, but on the evidence available, its date of deposit seems likely to have been in the 1280's and unlikely to have been later than, say, 1295. An early Serbian coin has been found at Kazichene, near Sofia; a similar specimen in the Zagreb museum is recorded to have been found somewhere in Bulgaria.

(1934), 361-68; Mushmov, *Monetite;* Mushmov, "Neizdadeni Moneti"; Gerasimov, "Bŭlgarski Moneti"; and a very balanced contribution by I. Băncilă, "Eléments d' Art Monétaire Bulgare au XIIIe. Siècle", *IAI* xxv (1962), 65-69. There are several other brief notes, particularly in *IBAI* and *IAI*.

[3] Reported as containing 21 coins of I. Tiepolo (1229-49), and thus unusually early. Gerasimov, "Monetni Sŭkrovishta, 1960-61".

[4] See the note by Regling in Mosser, *Byzantine Coin Hoards*.

[5] Mushmov, "Kolektivni Nakhodki, 1925-26".

[6] See above.

[7] Filov, "Novootkriti Starini", *IBAD* iii.

[8] Mushmov, "Kolektivni Nakhodki, 1891-1914"; Gerasimov, "Kolektivni Nakhodki, 1941-45".

In contrast with the rather large Kamenitsa hoard, a hoard of the silver of Todor Svetoslav discovered at Tŭrnovo in 1914 contained only 14 pieces; the Kŭntina hoard of silver of the same ruler contained only 6 pieces; and the Kilifarevo hoard of 1943 contained 9 of his bronze coins There were 80 silver coins of Todor Svetoslav in the Dŭbene hoard of 1958, deposited after 1325, and one in the Byala Cherkva (Tŭrnovo) hoard, which was probably equally late in its date of deposit. [9]

A hoard which turned up in an antique shop in Sofia in 1934, and which was said to have been found at Kyustendil, consisted of 162 groši of Stefan Uroš III, 7 grossi of G. Dandolo and 4 of P. Gradenigo, and 3 imitations of Serbian groši "de bandera". [10] It is tempting to associate this deposit with the battle of Velbuzhd, fought nearby between Serbia and Bulgaria in 1330.

An early hoard of Palaeologan bronze was found at Ŭglen in 1912. There was about a kilogramme of coins, which were attributed to Michael VIII and Andronicus II. [11]

Stray finds of bronze of a similar thirteenth-century date have been recorded from the Dobruja; along with dirhems of the same date, they are issues of the khans of the Golden Horde, mostly of Toctai (1290-1312). Iliescu has suggested that they are essentially strays from a currency-area further to the north, in Moldavia and Transylvania. The find-spots are similar to those from which eleventh- and twelfth century coins have come—Mangalia, Tulcea, Isaccea, and Cernavoda. [12]

One of the earliest, apparently, of the hoards of gold from the period under review came from Karlovo, in the passes of the Balkan mountains, in 1899. It contained 6 coins of Andronicus II. [13] The date of deposit should, however, be considered doubtful, for the two gold coins in the German hoard of 1914, concealed after 1331, were likewise of Andronicus II. The gold currency in south-western Bulgaria may have been rather stagnant compared with that in north-eastern Bulgaria, and the Karlovo hoard may be characteristic of the south-western

---

[9] Gerasimov, "Andronic II et Andronic III", 322-23.
[10] Gerasimov, "Kolektivni Nakhodki, 1934-36".
[11] Filov, "Novootkriti Starini", *IBAD* iii.
[12] O. Iliescu, "Monede Tătăreşti din Secolele XIII-XV, găsite pe Teritoriul Republicii Populare Romîne—Notă Preliminară", *SCN* iii (1960), 263-77.
[13] Mushmov, "Kolektivni Nakhodki, 1891-1914".

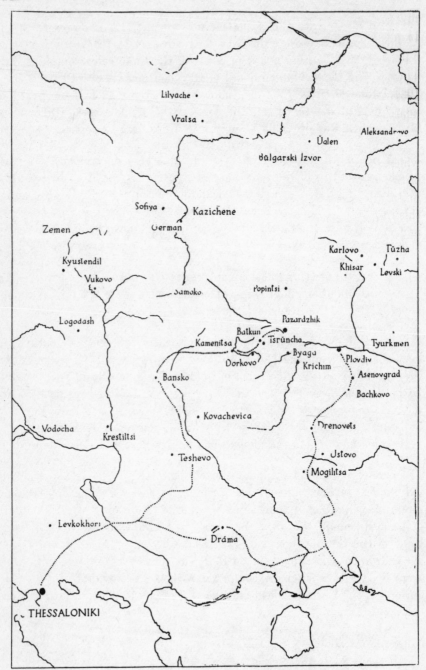

Map XII. Bulgaria and near by territories

The routeways from Thessaloniki towards the north-east of Bulgaria and from

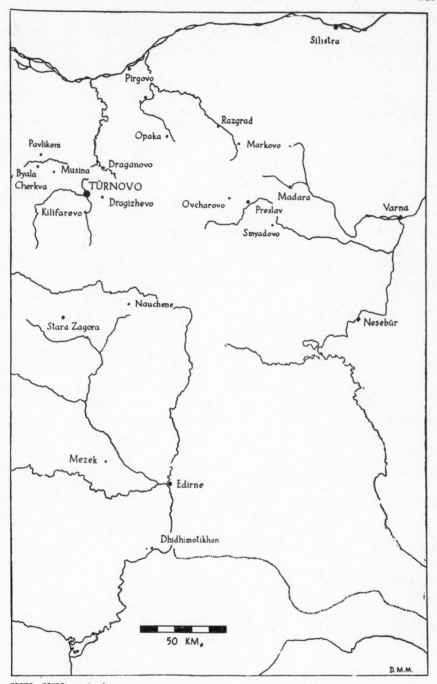

XIII - XIV centuries.

Dhidhimotikon towards Constantinople, are shown by dotted lines.

group. The Draganovo hoard, from the Yantra valley, deposited after 1295, apparently included twelfth-century gold along with that of the Palaeologi; and a second hoard, of 1925, from the same locality, consisted of 9 kilogrammes of scyphate bronze coins of Manuel I, Andronicus, and Andronicus II with Michael IX.[14] It may be that one should allow for these being hoards of an unusual character.

A hoard which is more certainly early than that from Karlovo came to light at Smyadovo in 1946. Smyadovo lies in the Golŭma Kamchiya valley, which is the routeway leading from the Black Sea coast to Preslav, and, beyond it, towards Tŭrnovo or the middle reaches of the Danube. Many other of the hoards of Palaeologan gold come from the same routeway or from the region between Tŭrnovo and the Danube, and Gerasimov, noting that they are often from villages rather than from the main towns, has argued that they reflect an inter-regional trade in grain, the purpose of which was the provisioning of Constantinople. He draws attention to a reference by George Pachymeres to such a trade in the time of Todor Svetoslav, and to the clause in the treaty of 1324 which permitted Venetian merchants to import agricultural products into Constantinople from the Black Sea coastlands.[15] The Smyadovo hoard contained 12 nomismata of John III Vatatzes (the localization of which in this region has already been noted[16]), 3 of Michael VIII, and 4 of Andronicus II with Michael IX.[17] It is the only hoard in this series which is a link between the Nicaean and the Palaeologan gold. The date of deposit may have been before 1300.

The majority of the hoards of gold, Gerasimov has recently argued in a valuable study,[18] include specimens which are correctly to be attributed to the joint reign of Andronicus II and Andronicus III, and their deposit therefore falls in the second quarter of the fourteenth century, and not, as had been supposed, merely after 1295. There is another find from Smyadovo, brought to light in 1937, and consisting of about a hundred coins.[19] A hoard that came from Dragizhevo, in the

[14] Mushmov, "Kolektivni Nakhodki, 1925-26".

[15] Gerasimov, "Andronic II et Andronic III", 225. For a coin of Andronicus II, *BMC* 13, weight 2,90 gm., found at Galita on the lower Danube, see B. Mitrea, "Découvertes Récentes et Plus Anciennes de Monnaies Antiques et Byzantines en Roumanie", *Dacia* NS v (1961), 583-93.

[16] See p. 126 above.

[17] Gerasimov, "Kolektivni Nakhodki, 1946-48".

[18] Gerasimov, "Andronic II et Andronic III".

[19] *Ibid.*, p. 223.

Tŭrnovo region, in 1912, contained 10 gold coins, originally published as being of Andronicus II with Michael IX, but incorrectly so. The date of deposit of the Dragizhevo hoard was however given by the 3 bronze coins of Mikhail Shishman which, together with two silver bracelets and a silver ring, completed it. [20] The large Byala Cherkva hoard of 1934, also from the Tŭrnovo region, was dispersed, but it is very possible that it included coins of Andronicus II with Andronicus III. There were at least 22 coins of Isaac II in the hoard, as well as the grosh of Todor Svetoslav that has been mentioned. [21] From further to the north, the Opaka hoard of 1929 contained 13 gold coins, of which at least one, apparently, was of Andronicus II with Andronicus III. [22] The Aleksandrovo (Lovech) hoard of 1948 contained 3 coins of the two emperors, 13 groshi of Ivan Aleksandŭr, and a silver ring. [23] At Dŭbene, in 1958, 5 coins of Andronicus II with Michael IX and with Andronicus III were found along with 80 groshi of Todor Svetoslav. [24] At Lom, on the Danube, another hoard of Palaeologan gold was found in the same year. [25]

An analysis of these hoards shows that it is hardly possible to attribute all the hyperpera reading ANΔPONIKOC / ANΔPONIKOC to the brief joint reign of Andronicus II with Andronicus III (1325-28), as Gerasimov proposed to do. Apart from the considerable range of stylistic variation among the coins (e. g. columnar or circular inscriptions), the secret-marks in any one hoard are usually very restricted. Thus, the Dŭbene hoard, which is almost certainly early in the series, is characterized by the marks B Ⴈ and K̈ N̈; the Lom hoard by K̈ N̈; the Dragizhevo hoard by Γ M; the Markovo hoard (mentioned below) by K A or (fleur-de-lis) A; and the Aleksandrovo hoard, which is evidently late, by K̈ Ẍ and N X. Since ANΔPONIKOC / ANΔPONIKOC coins were the last substantive issue of Byzantine gold, it seems reasonable to conclude that they became a *type immobilisé*. Much work remains to be done before the mint-organization and chronological order of the hyperpera is fully elucidated.

---

[20] *Ibid.*, pp. 222 and 223, where the two accounts and the footnote are quite exceptionally confused; Filov, "Novootkriti Starini", *IBAD* iii.

[21] Gerasimov, "Kolektivni Nakhodki, 1934-36", and Gerasimov, "Andronic II et Andronic III", 222.

[22] *Ibid.*, 222 and 224. Here again the text is not clear.

[23] *Ibid.*, 223.

[24] *Ibid.*, 223.

[25] *Ibid.*, 223.

246

From the lower Maritsa valley, there are the hoards of Mezek, 1937, [26] and Dhidhimotikon, 1951, [27] the latter being of bronze coins.

Hoards including coins of Andronicus III, Anne of Savoie, and John V have been found at Plovdiv in 1938, [28] and at Markovo, in the Kolarovgrad region, in 1926. [29] Others among the incompletely-recorded hoards that have been mentioned may also have contained coins of the same issue, but even allowing for the uncertainty, and for the scarcity of the type, it seems that there is a special concentration of hoards in the decades after 1325. Certainly, there is a contrast with the half-century before 1325, even if the hoards terminating with coins of Andronicus II with Andronicus III are to be spread out over some decades. In fact, it appears likely that many or most of them ante-date the Bulgarian groshi of Ivan Aleksandŭr (1331-71). The number of hoards may be largely a reflection of the troubled times, and they may exaggerate the extent of the coinage: nevertheless, there are, as Gerasimov notes, no instances of die-duplication in his catalogue of 53 specimens of the hyperpera of Andronicus II with Andronicus III; he says, quite rightly, that this implies a large volume of coinage. The full explanation of the numismatic evidence must almost certainly take account of the gold - silver ratio and the attempts at manipulation by Byzantium and by Venice, above all in the second quarter of the fourteenth century. [30]

Brunetti has recently worked out the quantity of silver coinage struck during the reign of Anne of Savoie. His estimate is that some five million pieces were issued by the Constantinople mint in the five-year period *ca.* 1341-46. Bertelè has commented on the extreme interest attaching to this result as revealing an unexpectedly large coinage. The total was, however, derived by multiplying the central estimate for obverse dies (2,830) by an output figure of 1,800. There is no justification for choosing so small a figure; an average of 8-10,000 for each reverse die (estimated at 5,330) is probably very much nearer the truth, and the total issue will appear to have been in the range 20 to 75 million coins. But the whole attempt at estimation is placed under reserve by the evidence that the hoard on which it is based is not a fully random

[26] *Ibid.*, 224.
[27] *BCH* lxxvi (1952), 206.
[28] Gerasimov, *op. cit.*, 224.
[29] *Ibid.*, 223.
[30] See Bertelè, "L'Iperpero", especially pp. 73-77.

sample. All the instances of duplication occur in only one of the six types into which Bertelè divided the coinage of Anne of Savoie with John V. The absence of duplicates among the 40 specimens of Types II-VI might, however, be held to imply an original total of at least 260 dies (let p=3) and an original coinage of two-and-a-half million, to which may be added, on a conservative estimate, a further 2½ million represented by the 166 specimens of Type I. [31]

The German hoard consisted of two gold coins and 230 silver grossi, of which 136 were Serbian, 22 Venetian, and the remainder of Ivan Aleksandŭr. The Serbian coins were of Stefan Dušan (120) or earlier rulers (16). [31] The Drŭnovets hoard, among 78 coins, mostly groshi of Ivan Aleksandŭr, included one of G. Dandolo, 2 of P. Gradenigo, and one attributed to Stefan Uroš Milutin. [32] There was one coin of G. Dandolo in the Krichima find, [33] and at least 2 in that from Bachkovo. [34] The three hoards last named are all from the central Maritsa valley, while the German find, like that of Kyustendil, is from the upper Struma basin. It is interesting that none of the other hoards of Ivan's groshi, listed in Table 21, should contain any other kinds of coinage.

Three finds from the Krain conclude the survey. One, which was discovered at Vidin in 1933, contained bronze of Isaac II, Alexius III, Andronicus II and Andronicus III, together with one copper coin of Bela IV and one silver grosso of Dubrovnik. [35] A second hoard from Vidin, discovered in 1936, consisted of 9 bronze coins of Michael VIII and one of John V. [36] A hoard from Yasen, nearby, in 1956 consisted of bronze of Andronicus II and III. [37]

---

[31] L. Brunetti (with T. Bertelè), "Sulla Quantità di Monete d'Argento Emesse Sotto Anna di Savoia Imperatrice di Bisancio Bisanzio (1341-47)", *Rivista Itali ana di Numismatica*[5] xi (1963), 143-68; T. Bertelè, *Monete e Sigilli di Anna di Savoia Imperatrice di Bisanzio*, Rome, 1937; note also T. Bertelè, "Monete dell'Imperatore Giovanni VI Cantacuzeno", *Zbornik Radova Vizantoloshkog Instituta* viii/1 (1963), 43-59.

[32] Gerasimov, "Kolektivni Nakhodki, 1939".

[33] *Ibid.*, 1937-38.

[34] *Ibid.*, 1941-45.

[35] *Ibid.*, 1933-34.

[36] *Ibid.*, 1934-36.

[37] *Ibid.*, 1956-57.

Provenance	Date	Quantity	Reference
A. *Groshi of Ivan Aleksandŭr with Mikhail, alone*			
Ovcharovo	1906	40–50	"Kolektivni Nakhodki 1891–1914"
Pirgos	1907	68	*Ibid.*
Vodocha	1913	13	*Ibid.*
Skopje	1921–22	100	1921–22
Batkun	1922	300	*Ibid.*
Miyatev	1933	15–20	1933–34
Popintsi	1933 /34	200	*Ibid.*
Lilyache	1935	238	1934–36
Bŭlgarski Izvor	1935	60, with earring	*Ibid.*
Musina	1945	5	1941–45
Vratsa	1948	ca. 10	1946–48
Sofia	1953	10	1951–54
Razgrad	1954		*Ibid.*
Nesebŭr	1955	127	1955
Zemen	1955	54	*Ibid.*
Tŭrnovo	1956	950	1956–57
Archar	1957	310	*Ibid.*
Tŭzha	1959	47 or more	"Monetni Sukrovishta, 1958–59"
Nauchene	1960	12 or more	1960–61
Belogradchik	1961	13 or more	1960–61
B. *Groshi of Ivan Aleksandŭr with Mikhail, along with other coinages*			
German	1914	230	p. 247
Vukovo	1925	ca. 400, with Venetian coins	"Kolektivni Nakhodki, 1925–26"
Drŭnovets	1934	78	p. 247
Krichima	1938	56	p. 247
Bachkovo	1942	206	p. 247
Aleksandrovo	1948	16	p. 245

Table 21. Hoards of groshi of Ivan Aleksandŭr with Mikhail. (References are to Mushmov, "Kolektivni Nakhodki", Gerasimov, "Kolektivni Nakhodhi", or Gerasimov, "Monetni Sŭkrovishta").

CHAPTER XI

TRAVELLERS' HOARDS

Among the hundreds of hoards of medieval coins discovered in the Balkans, half-a-dozen stand apart from the rest in that they consisted of coins of kinds that were not in general circulation in the area. The classic example is the deposit of Franconian and Bavarian half-bracteates found somewhere in the Maritsa valley between Plovdiv and Edirne. The coins of Conrad III of the Nürnberg mint which were included in it suggest that the owner may have been a Franconian participant in the Crusade of 1147. This hoard, and others of a similar character, each consist evidently of a sum of money withdrawn from the currency of a distant locality, supplemented perhaps by coinage obtained during the journey from that place to the Balkans, and concealed for the night or in an emergency and never recovered. It is tempting to assume that some of these deposits—such as that from the Maritsa valley—were concealed by Crusaders, but this is no more than speculation unless the hoard can be very exactly dated on internal evidence, and even then, of course, it is not certain. What is certain is that the hoards are travellers' hoards.

Some of them antedate the First Crusade. A hoard found in the north of Jugoslavia fifty or more years ago, and consisting of 70 French feudal issues of three types, namely of Limoges, Albi, and Le Puy, is from the middle of the eleventh century. None of the coins can yet be dated more closely than to within two or three decades, but there is a good chance that it will eventually be possible to determine the age-structure of the hoard quite exactly, through detailed stylistic studies using French hoards that contain the same types. The same holds good for most of the other hoards of west European coins from the Balkans. The very fresh condition of the coins of Albi, and the occurrence of die-duplicates and die-linked specimens in such a high proportion hint at a tight age-structure. [1]

---

[1] D. M. Metcalf, "The Money of a Medieval French Traveller in the Balkans", *NC* 7.i (1961), 145-49; J. Duplessy and D. M. Metcalf, "Le Trésor de Samos et la Circulation Monétaire en Orient Latin aux XIIe et XIIIe Siècles", *Revue Belge de Numismatique* cviii (1962), 173-207, at p. 202.

Another deposit of roughly the same date has come from the environs of Niš. A grave-find, discovered during restorations, consisted of 56 coins from north-eastern France, mostly from the mints of Amiens and Beauvais. A provisional list is given in Table 22.[2]

1–2.	Amiens, deniers, Poey d'Avant, plate CXLIX, 4.
3–20.	— ,— , with wedge.
21.	Beauvais, denier, P. d'A. plate CL, 17; with dots in the first and fourth quarters.
22–29.	— , — , dots in second and third quarters.
30–31.	— , —, oboles.
32–34.	St. Martin-de-Tours. (One is uncertain; these, and nos. 35 - 40, are almost uniface).
35–40.	— , — , with crescent in one angle. (One is uncertain).
41–43.	— , — , oboles.
44–49.	Mint? Oboles, weakly struck; obv., cross, degenerate inscription; rev., KAROLVS monogram?
50.	Chartres, denier, cf. P. d'A. plate XXXIV, 5 and 6.
51.	Rouen, denier, bracteate fabric, cf. P. d'A. plate V, 8, which is perhaps rather later.
52.	Mint? Obole, with design of interwoven curves, somewhat similar to P. d'A. plate CLVIII, 18.
53–56.	Various types, uncertain.

Table 22. The Niš hoard of French coins.

The Istanbul hoard of 1875 was also from northern France; coins of Melle, Brittany, Chartres, and Rouen predominated. A date after 1084 has been suggested. The hoard may well have belonged to a member of the First Crusade.[3]

A particularly good example of a traveller's hoard came to light in the Corinth excavations in 1907. In all 121 coins were found together, with traces of the cloth in which they had been contained, in the foundations of a Byzantine house. All but two of them were of the mint of Clermont (where the First Crusade was preached), and included 7 oboles. A coin of Le Puy, and a nomisma of Alexius I made up the total: the leadership of the Crusade was in the hands of the bishop of Le Puy. The hoard is dated, for the present, by the gold coin of Alexius, for

[2] Marić, "Ostave". The late Dr. Marić permitted me to examine the coins when they were in the Belgrade museum.They await publication. Six representative coins were acquired by the Belgrade museum, and the other 50 are in the Niš museum Cf. Duplessy and Metcalf, op. cit., note 29.

[3] Duplessy and Metcalf, op. cit., p. 203 and references cited there.

which an attribution to the mint of Nicaea, *ca.* 1100, has been proposed. [4]

Two years previously, in the Corinth excavations, there was found a traveller's hoard consisting of 9 coins of Valence and 5 of Lucca. They were found together in dug earth, again with traces of cloth adhering to them. The date of deposit may be very much the same as that of the hoard of 1907. [5]

A third hoard from Corinth consisted of 4 Byzantine coins, the latest of which was a Rex Regnantium follis of Class I (1078-81), and 69 rare oriental coins. [6]

From Novi Vinodol, on the north Adriatic coast, there are traces of a small hoard of obols of Champagne, from the mints of Provins and Troyes. The coins are not at present available for study, but written descriptions of them suggest that they were deposited around 1130. [7]

Finally, there is the Maritsa valley hoard of 77, or perhaps 79, half-bracteates, already referred to, which may be tentatively associated with the Second Crusade. [8]

These deposits of coins of types not ordinarily current in the Balkans are obviously travellers' hoards. There are several other finds which consisted of Balkan coinages but which, for one reason or another, were evidently travellers' hoards too. Thus, for example, the Corinth hoard of November 1937, of twelfth-century folles, seems not to be typical

[4] *Ibid.;* Metcalf, "Alexius I"; p. 83 above. One other coin of Le Puy has been excavated at Corinth, in the period 1930 - 35.

[5] Duplessy and Metcalf, *op. cit.* and references cited there.

[6] *American Journal of Archaeology* xxxii (1928), 481f.; R. L. Scranton, *Mediaeval Architecture in the Central Area of Corinth* (Corinth Reports, XVI), p. 50.

[7] Duplessy and Metcalf, *op. cit.*, pp. 203f.

[8] *Ibid.*, 204; also for the Sombor and Samos hoards, which fall just outside the scope of the survey; for Sombor add the reference, L. von Bürkel, "Süddeutsche Halbbrakteaten, III. Der Fund von Zombor bei Essegg (Ungarn)", *Mitteilungen der Bayerischen Numismatischen Gesellschaft* [xxi (1902), 56ff.; for a re-publication of the Gran hoard, see F. Király, "XII Századi Pénzek Magyarországon", *Folia Archaeologica* vii (1955), 127 ff. The "Crusader's hoard" of 1934 from Corinth is discussed at p. 228 above. At Vratsa (on the route from Belgrade to Plovdiv?) in 1950, 804 unspecified west European silver coins of the fourteenth century were found in an old church (Gerasimov, "Kolektivni Nakhodki, 1949-51"); and at Kalavryta in 1934 various unspecified west European medieval coins were found (*BCH* lix [1935], 244).

of the local currency; [9] the Brauron hoard, from later in the century, is certainly not typical of the currency of Attica; [10] the Gaćište hoard of Friesacher contained so large a proportion of the issues of St. Veit that it is likely to have been brought to Slavonia only shortly before its concealment; [11] the same is true of the Gračansko Dolje hoard of Friesacher of the Kostanjevica mint. [12] The Vrh Trebnje hoard of Italian coins, and possibly others from the Krka valley routeway, are traveller's hoards; [13] the Zlata, Grabovac and Osanica hoards of Byzantine stamena, although they were all found in north Serbia, were so different in the style of the coins that they must have been traveller's hoards; [14] there may be an untypical element in the Delphi hoard of 1929; [15] and so on. There are scores of finds which might, if one had any means of knowing, be put into the same category. The whole question of travellers' hoards needs to be borne in mind when one is considering the theory of coinage-provinces. No very systematic conclusions can be drawn, except that an unusually large proportion of the hoards from the marchlands of the north-west seem to have belonged to travellers, and that many of the other deposits that have been mentioned are either from obvious valley-routes, or from coastal sites.

[9] See p. 109.
[10] See p. 121.
[11] See p. 160.
[12] See p. 152.
[13] See p. 175.
[14] See p. 115.
[15] See p. 234.

CHAPTER XII

CODA: THE EMPIRE OF STEFAN DUŠAN

The deposition of Stefan Uroš III in 1331 gave the Serbian throne to his son Stefan Dušan, whose reign marks the high point in the lines of political and economic development of the Balkan peninsula that have been traced from the ninth century onwards in the pages above. By 1334, the Serbian expansionist drive into Macedonia was threatening the main strategic centres of Ohrid, Prilep, Strumica, Kastoria, and Vodena. A decade later, Stefan Dušan had consolidated his hold over Macedonia (profiting from the internal struggles in the Byzantine Empire) and in September 1345 he captured the key fortress of Seres. Before the end of 1345 he began to style himself, "Emperor of the Serbs and the Greeks", thus making explicit his claim to hegemony in the Balkans. On Easter Day 1346 his coronation as emperor, by the newly-created Serbian patriarch, took place in Skopje; in May 1349 he promulgated the first version of his new legal code. In these years he extended the boundaries of his rule to include Albania, Epirus, Acarnania, Aetolia, and Thessaly. Thessaloniki, and the duchy of Athens, remained beyond his grasp. His son, king Stefan Uroš V, ruled in the Serbian territories in the north, while he himself kept control of the southern half of his Empire, which was predominantly Greek, and which extended as far as the Gulf of Patrai. His great constructive effort was nullified even more quickly than it had been accomplished, for after his untimely death in December 1355, the young Stefan Uroš was unable to secure his authority over the new Empire. From 1359 the Ottoman conquest went forward rapidly, until, at Kosovo Polje, on 15 June 1389, and at Tŭrnovo, on 17 July 1393, came the turning-points at which the fate of nationalism and Christianity in the Balkans for the next four to five centuries was determined. [1]

The richly varied coinage of Stefan Dušan begins with his issues as king of Serbia (1331-46). Dimitrijević attributes to him the "denarii

---

[1] Ostrogorsky, *Byzantine State*, pp. 450 f. and 466-68.

de cruce" with the inscription STEFAN S STEFAN REX, and on which the king is shown crowned. (Ljubić, *Opis*, plate V, 8-14) He distinguishes between the "denarii de cruce" of Stefan Dečanski and Stefan Dušan by the inscriptions—the earlier coins read VROSIVS, as may be argued on the grounds of provenance (the hoards of Novi Banovci, Stobi, and Kičevo) and metrology. [2] Secondly, there are the "denarii de maçia", from Rudnik, on which the king's crown, instead of being prominently fleur-de-lisé, is more or less flat-topped: varieties reading STEFAN REX (*Opis*, plate V 23-24) and СТЕФАНЬ КРАЉЬ (*Opis*, plate VI, 1-3) are both to be attributed to Dušan. [3] Thirdly, there are coins of the "Helmet" type signed STEFANVS DEI GRA REX or MONITA REX STEFA.

The "Helmet" type inscribed STEFANVS INPERATOR or MONITA INPER SEFAN will, on the evidence of the Ruzhdavitsa hoard, belong in the first years after Dušan became emperor.

The earliest imperial coins, however, may be those on which Stefan Dušan retains the title of King of Rasia, or of the Rasians, while styling himself Emperor of Romania, or of the Romans. There are three varieties, all "denarii de maçia", but with the handle of the sword at the emperor's right hand instead of at his left, as in earlier varieties. The first (very scarce) variety, which is placed early on the basis of its design, has a semi-circular top to the back of the heavenly throne, a detail that is otherwise found only on some regal coins of the "Helmet" type. The inscription is RX RASIE ST IP ROMA (Rex Rasiae Stefan Imperator Romaniae). The second variety, with the same inscription, is shown by the age-structure of the Novi Banovci hoard to be earlier than the third, which is represented in a very limited way in the hoard, with REX RIA ST IP ROIOM (Rex Rasianorum Stefan Imperator Romaiorum) as its inscription. On all three varieties Stefan wears a domed imperial crown, with pendants.

Dimitrijević gives these coins to the first period of imperial rule, after the capture of Seres, but before Stefan's coronation. He divides the remaining varieties among three further periods. To the second period he gives the "Coronation" issue, on which Stefan is shown standing in imperial Byzantine dress, with angels crowning him; also the type with a four-line inscription; and five varieties showing the standing

---

[2] Dimitrijević, "Problemi", 87.
[3] *Ibid.*, 91ff.

figures of the emperor and empress (i, with sceptres; ii, without sceptres, and holding a double cross; iii, without sceptres, and holding a triple cross; iv, without sceptres, and holding a single cross; v, with sceptres, but without an inscription. Only i and ii were substantive issues). To a third period he gives the "Horseman" issue, on the grounds that it is absent from the Belovo hoard but present in those from Uroševac, Nova Varoš, and Bosanska Rača. To the fourth period are assigned the third-groši (not half-groši), which have come to light very largely in the Kosovo Polje hoard, and of which there are varieties showing the emperor and empress standing, or seated, or looking at each other, or the emperor alone, seated; and also large groši on which Christ is shown standing, and (uncertainly) one further "two standing figures" type with a problematic inscription. Dimitrijević's classification, together with the hoard evidence and the weight-standards on which it rests, are summarized in Table 23.[4]

A hoard that was found at Ruzhdavitsa, near Kyustendil in western Bulgaria, in 1937 or 1938 has been interpreted by Dimitrijević, no doubt correctly, as a traveller's deposit. Out of 81 coins from the hoard that are now his collection, 71 are countermarked. The degree to which this is unusual is sufficiently described by saying that among the thousands of Serbian coins that have survived to the present day there are only 22 others bearing countermarks of the same kind. Sixty-three of the 71, and also the other 10 coins, are Serbian; 3 are Bosnian; and 5 are perhaps irregular issues. There are in all 45 "Helmet" coins, including a unique type of Stefan Kotromanić, and 13 of the scarce varieties of Stefan Dušan with Christ standing in a mandoria as the obverse design. Because of this echo of the standard Ragusan design (which was used also in Bosnia), because so many of the coins had Latin rather than Cyrillic inscriptions, and for a number of other reasons, Dimitrijević inclines to see the hoard as a sum of money withdrawn from currency in some part of the Adriatic hinterland, possibly Zachlumia not long after its re-annexation to Bosnia in 1351, or on the accession of Tvrtko in 1353. The Ruzhdavitsa coins, many of which were clipped or worn, raise a number of extremely interesting, and perhaps inter-connected, questions for the monetary historian, particularly those of a local shortage of currency (for which there is confirmation in documents from Dubrovnik from 1347 onwards for a decade), of the effects of the Black Death on Balkan monetary affairs, and of the local issue of varieties

---

[4] See Dimitrijević, "Hronologija".

	Weight-standard	(?) Belgrade	Novi Banovci	Ruzhdavitsa (part)	Belovo	Uroševac	Nova Varoš	Bosanska Rača	Kosovo Polje	Durrës
Denarii de cruce, *Stefan S Stefan Rex*	1.60	—	13	1	—				—	
Denarii de maçia, *Stefan Rex*		—	1	—	—				—	
—, Стєфанв Кѻалв		—	—	—	—				—	
"Helmet" type, *Stefanus Dei Gra Rex*	1.65	11	46	7+1	—				9	
—, *Monita Rex Stefa*	1.41	5	117	21	7				12	
"Seated king" type, *Rx Rasie St Ip Roma*		—	—	—	—	—	—	—	—	—
—, *Rx Rasie St Ip Roma*	1.41	—	35	6	—	—	—	7	—	1
—. *Rex Ria St Ip Roiom*	1.37	—	2	10	1	—	—	4	—	
"Helmet" type, *Monita Inper Sefan*		—	—	3	—	—	—	1	—	
—, *Stefanus Inperator*		—	—	11	—	—	—	—	—	
Seated king, Christ in mandorla		—	—	2+1	—	—	—	—	—	
Two standing figures, Christ in mandorla (several varieties)		—	—	11	—	—	—	—	—	
Coronation	1.37	—	—	—	112	x	3	—	153	3
4–line inscription	1.41	—	—	—	7	x	15	5	13	2
2 Standing Figures, with sceptres	1.0	—	—	—	49	x	2	—	70	3
—, without; double cross	1.00	—	—	—	93	x	2	—	258	—
—, without; triple cross		—	—	—	2	—	—	—	2	—
—, without; single cross		—	—	—	1	x	—	—	6	—
—, without sceptres; no inscription		—	—	—	1	x	—	—	7	—
Horseman	1.34	—	—	—	—	x	2	13	144	7
2 Standing Figures, with sceptres	0.58	—	—	—	—	—	—	—	479	—
Emperor seated	0.58	—	—	—	—	—	—	—	273	—
2 Seated Figures	0.46	—	—	—	—	—	—	—	674	—
2 Figures, looking at each other	0.46	—	—	—	—	—	—	—	60	—
2 FihuresChrist standing		—	—	—	—	—	—	—	—	—
Uncertain type	1.07	—	—	—	—	—	—	—	—	—

Table 23. The coinage of Stefan Dušan. (From Dimitrijević, «Hronologija», 130 and 131 and "Kontramarke", 94-95, columns 1-2, and 129; and Marić, *Studije*, 249-320 and 339-46).

with Latin inscriptions in the south-west at a time when the main Serbian currency was inscribed in Cyrillic. [5] The general context in which the hoard should be viewed is probably that of the penetration of the Balkan hinterland by Ragusan trade, along an axis running north-eastwards into Bosnia and thence to Syrmia [6] and the Krain.

It may well be that the last word on the chronology of Stefan Dušan's coinages has not yet been said. When figures are available for three or four more hoards, it may be possible to analyse out further factors of localization, and to arrange the issues of different mints into a more complicated chronological sequence, instead of into the present unitary series. The stylistic range of the "Helmet" type, for example, is sufficient to leave open the possibility that it should be divided up between two or three mints. The "Horseman" and "Christ standing" design as well as the "Helmet", are continued under the emperor Uroš, and while the typological argument is not by itself a conclusive one, it does suggest a multiple pattern. Dimitrijević's conclusion that the "Horseman" issue belongs to a later period than the "Coronation" issue is inadequately supported by the hoard-evidence. On grounds of metrology and, especially, style there seems to be a case for putting the introduction of the "Horseman" type earlier in the sequence and very close to the "Coronation" type. It might, for example, originally have been struck at the same as the "Coronation" type and immediately following it. This is only a conjecture, but it is the kind of conjecture that will need to be tried out against the new facts as they become available. It would lead one to regard the Serbian component of the Bosanska Rača hoard as having been of compact age-structure, and the Nova Varoš hoard as being only a little less compact. The Durrës hoard of 1901, which has been added to the Table, apparently belongs after 1355, although it will not be much later. The coins were found in a little stone box in the form of a sarcophagus, along with an episcopal ring. [7] It might

---

[5] See Dimitrijević, "Kontramarke".

[6] Note that Ljubić, *Opis*, pl. *VII*, 22 came from Sabac.

[7] T. Ipen, "Arheološke Bilješke iz Albanije", *GZMBH* xv (1903), 181-83, where the find-spot "between Drača (Durrës) and Kavaja" is described, and is associated with the Via Egnatia. Ipen (Ippen) describes the coins in *Monastblatt der numismatischen Gesellschaft in Wien* v, 242. They passed into private hands. There were twenty or more Serbian coins, and one silver piece of Alexius I. The Serbian coins were listed according to Ljubić, *Opis*, as follows: Plate VII, 17 (1); VIII, 3 (3), 16 (2), 19 (1), 22 (4), 22, var. (1); IX, 1 (2), 5 (2) 19 (1), 19, var (1), 27 (1);X, 10 (1).

be a traveller's hoard (it was found close to the *Via Egnatia*) more typical of the currency of the westerly parts of Serbia than of Macedonia or north-east Serbia. In any case, the Bosanska Rača, Nova Varoš, and Durrës hoards appear to be a group. Another potential group in the analysis of locazation that should eventually be possible is the Rex/Imperator group which, not surprisingly, seems to be concentrated in north Serbia. One wonders whether their issue might not have been continued at Rudnik beyond the brief period that Dimitrijević allows them.

The rich variety of Stefan Dušan's coinage is evident, but an assessment of the patterns of monetary history in Serbia at the middle of the fourteenth century will be open to much uncertainty until some estimates of the volume of the main varieties have been made.

KEY TO THE PLATES

FRONTISPIECE

This handsome specimen of a very scarce coinage of Manuel Angelus Comnenus Ducas, despot of Epirus and Thessaloniki, 1230– *ca.* 1238, shows Manuel and St. Demetrius seated side by side on a double throne. Manuel is holding a model of the city of Thessaloniki, with three turrets. Between the two seated figures is the inscription

Π Ο Λ Ι C Θ
Ε C C Α
Λ Ο Ν
Ι Κ Η

Around the edge are traces (not fully struck up) of the inscription

Μ Α Ν Ŏ Η Λ Δ Ε C Π Ο Ο Α Γ Ι Ο C Δ Η Μ Η Τ Ρ Ι Ο C

The obverse shows St. Michael, winged, standing facing. *BMC* (*Byz*) III, p. 198. 2.27 gm. Oxford, Sir Arthur Evans bequest, ex Lord Grantley collection, obtained in Istanbul. Direct photography by R. L. Wilkins, Institute of Archaeology, Oxford. Enlarged x 4.

THE STYLISTIC VARIETIES AMONG THE FOLLES
OF THEOPHILUS

(Plates I-II)

Group
A   There is an unusually large number of jewelled panels on the part of the loros falling from the emperor's left shoulder to his right hip. Note the dotted forefinger. 7.08 gm., 27 mm. Ashmolean Museum, Oxford.

B   Note the vertical outline of the figure, and the almost flat bottom to the tufa head-dress. 5.55 gm., 27 mm. Bundessammlung von Medaillen, Münzen, and Geldzeichen, Vienna.

Δ   The very wide E and narrow V of the reverse inscription are characteristic, as are also the row of three dots in the tufa and the triangular end of the loros. Note the high, rather square shoulders. 4.29 gm., 24 mm. Bibliothèque Nationale, from the Schlumberger collection, 3030.

E   A rare variety. Note the crude style, especially of the broad face and "gloomy" mouth; and the wide band of parallel lines indicating drapery, at the lower right. 5.13 gm., 25 mm. Kungl. Myntkabinettet, Stockholm.

S   Struck in central Greece. Note the eyes, and the nostrils; and the style of seriffing on the reverse. 5.31 gm., 28 mm. Paris, 825.

Z   Struck in central Greece. This stylistic group is distinguished from the poorer specimens of S by the b of bASIL, which is always backwards-sloping. 6.66 gm., 27 mm. Stockholm.

SOME GREEK VARIETES AMONG THE FOLLES OF
BASIL I

(Plates III and IV)

The numbering of the varieties refers to Table 1 in the text.

9   "First Three Busts, II". 7.92 gm., 27 mm. Paris, ex Schlumberger, 3084.

10   "Second Three Busts, II". 5.7 gm., 26 mm. Koninklijk Kabinet van Munten, Penningen en Gesneden Stenen, 's - Gravenhage, 13,741.

12   "Two Seated Figures, III". 4.75 gm. 27mm. (Restruck on a coin of Theophilus, of uncertain variety, but probably S). Vienna.

13   "First Three Busts, III". 6.02 gm. 27 mm. (Restruck on a coin of Theophilus) Fitzwilliam Museum, Cambridge, 3412 - 1950.

14   "Second Three Busts, III". 28 mm. Museo Civico di Taranto (from the Taranto hoard).

15   "Two Busts, small". 6.74 gm., 27 mm. Cambridge, 3414 - 1950.

REX REGNANTIUM FOLLES, CLASS A
(Plates V and VI)

The coins are from the excavation of the Athenian Agora. For the list of varieties see Table 3.

1. Class A1. The portrait is characteristic of this variety. On the reverse, at right-angles to the inscription, can be seen traces of an earlier type—a follis of Nicephorus II, with the four-line legend beginning NICHF. The corresponding obverse under-type can be seen at 3 o'clock on the obverse—the spade-shaped pattern on the emperor's vestment, corresponding with *BMC* Type 2. At 8 o'clock on the reverse can be seen traces of what must be yet another undertype—an arm and part of the imperial vestment, and the cross at the beginning of the obverse legend. It probably belongs to a coin of Romanus I. Found near the south end of the Stoa of Attalus (Section Π, March 22, 1935, no. 16).

2. Variety 3? This rather pitted but otherwise well-preserved specimen belongs to all apearances to variety 3, with a dot below the reverse inscription and nothing above. When it is compared with the following coin, however, there are so many similarities to be seen that one must wonder whether it is not in fact of variety 5, but lacking the dot above the reverse inscription. It might simply not have been struck up: this quite often happens, especially on re-used flans. On the obverse, the folds of the drapery at the throat and on the arm are very similar to no. 3, as are the Book and the letters IC XC. Found in the wall of a Byzantine house on June 15, 1950. in Section P of the excavations (near the present-day entrance to the Agora Park).

3. Variety 5. Cf. the comments on no. 2 above. The fabric is partly flaked away on the obverse. but is in good condition on the reverse, perhaps because of the position in which the coin lay in the soil. Excavated on March 5, 1937 (no. 2), on the lower slopes of the Areopagus (Section Y).

4. Variety 24. In excellent preservation; 8.55 gm. Note the treatment of the beard, the deep loop of drapery at the throat, and the large C of XC. On the reverse, note the long letters L and E. Found to the east of the Panathensic Way, on the lower slopes of the Acropolis (Section HH, March 26, 1936, no. 14).

5. Variety 39. In splendid condition. The ornament on the Book is clear on this specimen, which is of the same general style and fabric as variety 40; Bellinger distinguished varieties 24 and 40 as "intermediate". Compare the lettering of the reverse with no. 4 above. On the obverse, the drapery is similarly stiff and linear, but the modelling of the right shoulder (i.e. to the observer's left) is better. Note that the inscription is blundered. reading IC XI. Found on June 10, 1937, near the Church of the Holy Apostles, not very far from no. 4. (Section T).

6. Variety 45. The ornament is perhaps a lis, an emblem connected with Nicaea. On the obverse there are two detached curls of hair on the shoulder, which are characteristic of this variety: cf no. 5 above, where the same two curls are more closely attached. The reverse is mis-struck, the coin having "jumped" in the dies during striking. Found near the Stoa of Attalus (Section Σ, May 19, 1937, no. 16).

STAMENA OF ALEXIUS III
(Plates VII and VIII)

The coins are from a hoard found in southern Serbia. For the classification of varieties, see the text, p. 120.

1. Group A. This handsome specimen, with a carefully-engraved cross on the globus, and two loros-ends, may be an early coin in the same mint-sequence as Group D. The outline of the cross in the nimbus, on the obverse, is double.

2. Group B. Note the nine dots on the central panel of the emperor's loros, and the uncompartmented panel on the saint's loros. The extremities of the loros-ends are characteristic.

3. Group C. The reverse is obscure through double-striking, as is so often the case. There is, however, apparently no loros-end between the figures. This specimen is of especial scientific value because of the detail of the nimbus cruciger on the obverse. In the left-hand arm there is only one dot, whereas in the right-hand arm there is the usual quincunx. This detail is confined to Group C, and is thus a useful criterion of classification.

4. Group E. The single loros-end between the figures is clearly struck. The pendants of the crowns each have three dots, of which the bottom one is larger.

5. Group F. The standing figures have unusual long beards. The portrait of Christ on the obverse is somewhat unusual in style, too, in that the eyebrows are heavily marked; but this may be a variation of no significance.

6. Group G. This coin is recognizably in the style of Group G, although the detail is not too clear. The five dots in the saint's loros are irregularly spaced.

7. Group H. The globus is shown at shoulder-height, unsupported. There are three (very faint) dots above it to represent the cross.

GOLD COINAGE OF JOHN III
(Plates IX and X)

1. A coin in the best style, with three dots at the emperor's shoulders. The lettering is small and neat. There are only 4 dots on the emperor's chest; and 9 on the central panel of the loros. The face is rather narrow and the beard is pointed. The diamond of four dots is high on the right shoulder (i.e. to the left) of the Mother of God. The coin is representative of nos. 1-3 in the Ibrahim Pasha parcel (Metcalf, "John Vatatzes"), and similar also to no. 4, which has 7 dots at the shoulders. The secret-mark on all four is a cross on each side of the throne on the obverse. 3.73 gm. *BMC*[3], no. 3.

2. Not very different from no. 1 in general style, this coin has 5 dots at the shoulders, and no sign of an inscription other than MP ΘV. There are 6 dots on the emperor's chest and 12 on the central panel of the loros. The diamond of 4 dots is larger, and lower on the figure of the Mother of God. There is a large pellet on the staff of the cross. The thumb of the hand holding the akakia is exaggerated. The emperor's neck and shoulders are very well modelled. The secret-mark on the obverse is a dot to left and right of the throne. 4.28 gm. (pierced). From the Ibrahim Pasha parcel. *BMC*[3], no. 11.

3. The style of this and all the succeeding coins contrasts with that of nos. 1 and 2. It is distinctly inferior. There are 8 dots on the shoulders, and pendants of

3 small dots. There are 4 dots on the chest, but an additional line to the left of them, not found on nos. 1-2. The lettering is large and straggling. There are 3 small dots on the staff of the labarum. The diamond of 4 dots on the shoulderers of theMother of God is interrupted by a diagonal line. The emperor's face is fatter. The obverse is mis-struck, but even so one can see that it is unusual both in having a strongly radiate cross in the nimbus and in that the nimbus is linear rather than dotted. The inscription is blundered, reading II for IC; the letters are large and the strokes terminate in heavy dots, like those on the reverse. The secret-mark is a dot to the right of the throne. The hand raised in blessing, and the drapery over the right knee, are coarsely drawn. There is no jewelled panel horizontally below the cushion of the throne, but there is a line above the cushion to left and right. From the Erymantheia (Patrai) hoard. 4.61 gm.

4. The style is appreciably different from that of no. 3. There are 7 dots at the shoulders, but pendants of 4 dots. The engraving of the figure of the emperor is more squat and bold; the face is spade-shaped. The akakia is fat, with rounded ends. On the obverse, the dots in the jewelled panels of the throne are very large. The secret-mark is a large dot to the left, and 4 small (faint) dots, arranged in a rectangle, to the right. From the Erymantheia hoard. 4.40 gm.

5. Similar in style to no. 3, but with pendants of 4 dots, and with two dots close together on the staff of the labarum. There are 9 dots at the emperor's shoulders. The modelling of the obverse is rather better than that of no. 3, and the nimbus cruciger is normal. No secret-mark. From the Drama hoard. 4.52 gm.

6. The style of this obverse is perhaps rather closer to no. 5 than to no. 3. Note the alignment of the strokes representing the cushion, to left and right of the throne and also the way that the Book fits into the left shoulder. The secret-mark is a dot to the left. From the Drama hoard. 4.25 gm.

7. The stylistic affinities here are with no. 4. The cross in the nimbus cruciger is double (as it seems partly to be on no. 4); the dots in the jewelled panels are large; and the shading of the cushion in is the same direction. (The pendants, on the reverse, are not a pair).From the Thessaly hoard. 4.49 gm. A whiter alloy than usual.

8. In cutting the dies for this very remarkable coin, the engraver seems not to have understood the drapery of the loros fully. The diamond of 4 dots has changed into a large group of 5 dots on the Mother of God, and the modelling of the hand is naturalistic. On the obverse, the secret-marks are prominent. There is a quincunx in each arm of the cross in the nimbus. The shading of the cushion is in two quite different directions to left and right. The lines of the drapery over the right knee are in pairs. The Book is misunderstood or possibly omitted. The long line of drapery ending on Christ's right shoulder divides into two: this detail exemplifies the very careful workmanship of the die. From the Erymantheia hoard. 4.24 gm.

COINAGES FROM HUNGARY AND FROM THE ADRIATIC COAST
(Plate XI)

All five coins are in the Ashmolean Museum, University of Oxford.

1. Stefan I, 997-1038, obol. Obv. STEPHANVS REX Rev. REGIA CIVITAS. The obols of the Bavarian mint of Regensburg have been identified as the model for the first Hungarian coinage, of which the theoretical weight is one-sixtieth of

the "solidus" of 45 gm. The mint-place is uncertain, but probably Gran. *CNHungariae* 1. 0.57 gm.

2. Salomon, 1063-74, obol. The use of a stylized portrait is probably, again, in imitation of German coins of the period. Obv. SALOM ONI REX Rev. PANNONEIA. *CNHungariae* 19. 0.42 gm.

3. Venice, denaro piccolo of Sebastiano Ziani, 1172-78. Obv. SEB DVX Rev. S. MARCVS. *CNItalicorum* 11. 0.38 gm.

4. Split, autonomous coinage, fourteenth century. SPALATINVS. Stockert, *Spalato*, no. 84. 0.30 gm.

5. Hungarian copper coin of the later XII (or perhaps early XIII) century This curious imitative piece has been connected with the Ismaelites in the time of the pretender Stefan IV, 1162-63. The inscriptions are intended to read SANCTA MARIA and REX STS REX BELA. *CNHungariae* 98. 3.18 gm.

COINAGES FROM THE MARCHLANDS
(Plate XII)

All four coins are in the Ashmolean Museum, University of Oxford.

1. A Balkan Friesacher. Obv. DVX LIVPOLDVS. Standing bare-headed figure holding sceptre and orb. Rev. Copy of the Friesach issue L. 15. EPI S ACH. Head and wings of angel; large cross above. L. 301. The division of varieties in the name of duke Leopold of Austria-Styria between Ptuj and Brezice is difficult or impossible. This variety is given to Ptuj because the reverse of a specimen in the Gschiess hoard is from the same die as is associated with a Ptuj obverse (L. 119). 1.77 gm.

2. A banovac. MONETA REGIS P SCLAVONIA. Nuber 1. 0.91 gm.

3. A grosso of Aquileia, of patriarch Berchtold of Meran, 1218-51. *CNItalicorum* 1-10. 1.18 gm.

4. A coin of Ljubljana in the same style as no. 3; struck by Bernardus II, duke of Carinthia, 1202-56. 1.19 gm.

SERBIAN GROSI
(Plates XIII and XIV)

For a description of the coins, see Table 20 (p. 233).

BULGARIAN GROSHI
(Plate XV)

All four coins are in the British Museum.

1. Mikhail Asen, 1246-57. Grosh, copying the Venetian grosso. The reverse inscription, completed vertically beside the staff of the labarum, has IP (*Imperator*) where the Venetian coin reads DVX and the Serbian version REX. Cf. Mushmov, *Monetite*, nos. 9 and 20. 2.08 gm. (pierced).

2. Todor Svetoslav, 1300-22. Grosh, in rough style and high relief. The inscription reads SVATSLYAV TSR BLGRM, with the letters AT, YAV, TSR, RM ligate. Cf. Mushmov 40, 41, 1.59 gm. From the Hasluck bequest.

3. Mikhail Shishman, 1323-30. Grosh, showing the emperor on horseback on the reverse. Both the obverse and reverse dies are similar to Mushmov 53. 1.57 gm.

4. Similar, but from dies of rougher workmanship. The obverse is closely similar, but from dies of rougher workmanship. The obverse is closely similar to Mushmov, "Neizdadeni Moneti", no. 6 (fig. 161). 1.61 gm.

ADDENDA

The continuing flow of publications which relate to the numismatic history of the medieval Balkans has brought forward much valuable new material, even since the lines above were in page-proof. It is noted here; and, at the same time, the opportunity is taken to mention some items that were omitted from the text by oversight.

The beginnings of the second hey-day in Greece. The most important additional evidence comes from Kenchreai, the Aegean port for Corinth, where excavations in 1963 yielded, among other medieval coins, 5 miliaresia of Basil II[1]. On the evidence previously available, Corinth seemed to have less silver in circulation in the ninth and tenth centuries than Athens. This needs to be confirmed by the more detailed publication of the Corinth finds of 1930 onwards, and the Kenchreai series, but if it should show Corinth-Kenchreai as an urban complex in which Kenchreai had a lively monetary circulation at an early date, it would be another pointer to the maritime character of the economy of Greece at the time.

Medieval coins from the excavations of the sanctuary of Artemis Orthia at Sparta provide a further series to illustrate the gradual recovery of monetary affairs in the provinces[2]. The earliest coin of the second hey-day is, interestingly enough, a pre-reform follis of Theophilus (*BMC* 15). It is the only coin from the ninth century. There is one coin of Leo VI, 3 of the period of Constantine VII, 3 of Nicephorus II. and 58 from the late tenth and eleventh centuries. Thus, the recovery in the south of the Peloponnese seems to have come, effectively, towards the end of the tenth century.

The Rex Regnantium series. Out of 11 coins of Class A at Sparta, 8 were of Bellinger's variety 16. One cannot now be certain whether they reflect a hoard, or are in fact stray finds, but in either case the concentration on a single scarce variety is remarkable. The proportions of the later Rex Regnantium classes were as follows: B, 8; C, 2; D, 6; E, (?)1; G, 1; H, 6; I, 6; K, 2.

Coins of Zoe and Constantine (913-919). The Yakimovo (Progorelec) hoard, from the region of Mikhailovgrad in north-eastern Bulgaria, consisted of 3 "bust" folles of Leo VI and 2 folles of Zoe and Constantine[3]. The provenance stands so much in isolation that it is tempting to see some connexion with Zoe's efforts against Bulgaria. This is not quite the only find from the area: Lishev notes a bronze coin of Theodosius III (716-17), from Mikhailovgrad[4].

Gold hoards connected with military events of 965-66? Excavations at the fortress of Iatrum, near Ruse, on the Danube, have brought to light a group of 9 gold coins, of Constantine VII with Romanus II and of Nicephorus II with Basil II[5]. The Iatrum find is paralleled by the Edhessa hoard of 1936, in which there were 16 gold coins of Constantine VII with Romanus II and 3 of Nicephorus II with Basil II. Although distant from each other, the two find-spots have something in common: they lie at the frontiers of the Bulgarian Empire, as they were at the time. In the autumn of 965 a Bulgarian mission demanded the resumption of the tribute that had been paid by earlier Byzantine governments. Their representations were rejected, and Nicephorus demolished a number of frontier forts. Thus, it seems plausible that both the hoards, and perhaps also that from Voden, are as late in date as 965-66.

Finds from Pernik (Dimitrovo). From this site, a little to the south-west of Sofia, a series of 17 Byzantine coins of the second hey-day begins with a Rex Regnantium follis of Class A, of the larger variant of Bellinger, variety 39 or 40. Its main interest is that it includes 3 silver coins of Michael VII, *BMC* Type 2 (emperor in military dress).

An incompletely-recorded hoard of gold coins from the same place included Type 1 of Alexius I, Type 2 of John II (in metropolitan style), and Type 1 of Manuel I.[6]

Nicephorus Bryennius (?). Of the very rare folles tentatively attributed to Nicephorus Bryennius (see p. 54), one of the 4 specimens noted by Grierson, and the only one with a provenance, came from Sparta in 1949. A fifth specimen is among the finds from the Sanctuary of Artemis Orthia at Sparta[7] Although this does not bring the problem of attribution much nearer solution, it makes a very strong case for supposing that the variety was a Peloponnesian issue.

Grave-find from Khisarluk. Excavations at the fortress of Khisarlŭk, in the region of Plovdiv, yielded a grave-find of 7 gold coins, of which 3 were of Nicephorus III and 3 were of Alexius I, apparently post-reform issues[8].

Localization of Manuel's BMC Types 12 and 13/i. A splendid series of new hoards adds substantially to the evidence of localization of various issues of stamena. Their discussion still involves the difficulty of recognizing travellers' hoards. Two finds with an early date of deposit are particularly welcome. That from Yagoda, 1962, in the region of Stara Zagora, deposited *ca.* 1185, included coins of Type 11 (108), Type 12 (1), and Andronicus (39). From a little further to the east, the Krushare hoard of 1962 included coins of Type 11 (84), Type 12 (3), Type 13/i (111), and Andronicus (59).[9] Thus, Type 12 was virtually absent from both finds, but the Krushare hoard (in which the coins of Type 11 had asterisks on the obverse: this is, on stylistic grounds, certainly a separate variety) was rich in Type 13/i. In this, it was similar to the Kaloyanovets hoard, from just south of Stara Zagora, which was also quite early in date (1185 - *ca.* 1190?), and which contained coins of Type 11 (376), Type 13/i (200), Andronicus (73), and Isaac (240). By comparison, it appears likely that the Tyurkmen hoard of 1959, in which there were so many specimens of Type 12, was a traveller's hoard from somewhere further to the west. This is borne out by the Tsrŭncha hoards I and II of 1963, from near Pazardzhik. There were important similarities in their composition; thus there is a *prima facie* case to conjecture that they reflect the local currency.

	Type 11	Type 12	Andronicus	Isaac	Alexius III
Tsrŭncha 1	149	23	10	480	590
Tsrŭncha II	109	13	8	865	427

Type 12 is only about one-seventh as plentiful as Type 11, and Type 13/i is again completely absent.

The final confirmation of the area to which Type 12 belongs is provided by two thirteenth-century hoards from the region of Blagoevgrad, in the Struma valley—Zheleznitsa and Pokrovnik, both discovered in1962, and very similar to each other.[10] In spite of the late date of desposit, attested by the coins of Theodore, the proportion of Type 12 reaches nearly half of that of Type 11. Type 13/i is completely absent, and (in contrast with the Byaga and Logodash hoards) so is Type 13/ii:

	Type 11	Type 12	Isaac	Alexius III	Theodore
Zheleznitsa	107	49	78	140	4
Pokrovnik	123	53	123	186	3

Some further definition of the Struma-Maritsa route as the zone for Type 12 is provided by the hoard from Kyustendil, 1960, which lies aside from it, and from which the type was absent. The Kyustendil find contained coins of Type 11 (92), Type 13/i (11), Andronicus (2), Isaac (200), Alexius III (242), and 21 specimens of a coinage of Manuel with St. Theodore (? Ratto 2125). This may, of course, be a traveller's hoard. One notes the absence of Type 13/ii.

A discovery which surely is a traveller's hoard, consisting of the small variety of Type 13/ii, was made at Kamenets, near Pleven in north-central Bulgaria, in 1963[11]. This may turn out to be one of the earliest hoards of stamena from the Balkans, and might be of importance for the internal chronology of the Thessalonican variety of Type 13/ii.

Other recent hoards of stamena contribute less. In the thirteenth-century Lom hoard I of 1962 there were still some specimens of Manuel's Type 9, possibly an indication of a stagnant currency in the north-east. The Lebed hoard of 1962, from the Rhodope, is dated to the thirteenth century by coins of Theodore, and, with the Mogilitsa, Ustovo, and Asenovgrad hoards, gives further evidence of the shifting pattern of monetary circulation after 1204. There are also hoards from Vŭrbitsa, and Lom II, 1962, Asenovitsa (Pleven), Tŭrnovo, and Stara Zagora, 1963[12],

With this more precise information, it is worth-while to look more closely at the distribution pattern of Type 13/i. The number of hoards from which it is completely absent gives additional sugnificance to the Krushare find, where it was actually more plentiful than Type 11. If this were all, it might be enough to argue that the Krushare, Kaloyanovets, and (probably) Zlataritsa hoards, all from the 1180's, were heavily weighted with recent coins—as indeed they were—and that Type 13/i was a quite small issue from late in Manuel's reign. It is, however, almost as numerous as Type 11 in the Istanbul hoard A of 1946, and even more plentiful in the small Istanbul parcel of 1933. Type 12, it may be remarked, was absent from both those hoards. It will be argued below that the Istanbul hoards were typical of the currency of Constantinople itself in 1204. Type 13/i cannot, at that rate, have been such a small issue. Why then, one must ask, did it find its way into the provinces so much less than Type 11? This is a *crux*, but a great deal more detailed evidence will be needed before it can be handled properly. It may be that the confiscations of 1171 resulted in a serious disruption of entrepreneurial effort in the north Balkans in the 1170's. If so, we have a commentary on the large share that the Venetian merchants had been taking in the trade.

The metropolitan coinage of the Latin Empire of Constantinople. Two newly-published hoards from Istanbul are precious evidence from the Byzantine capital, about the currency of which we know in general so little; and at the same time, the interpretation that has been put on one of them would, if it were accepted, reduce much of the analysis in Chapter V to a shambles. The Istanbul hoard A of 1946, of which there is good reason to believe that it was found actually in the city, consists of 1088 coins of small module, many with traces of silvering. Bellinger suggests that they are perhaps a different denomination from the coins of the same types published in *BMC*, and in any case that they are a group in terms of mint-organization. He claims that the dies are smaller—*ca.* 16 mm. as against *ca.* 18 mm. for the regular coins—and he observes that there is no sign of their having been cut down after striking. [13] The Istanbul hoard of 1933 [14] together with this new one make a very strong case for supposing that the coins of this "style" belong to the city, i.e. that they were issued there. Measurement of "normal" coins from extremely similar or near-duplicate dies to those illustrated on plate XXXII of Bellinger's article has assured me that the Istanbul specimens are not from "smaller dies specially prepared". As indicated above (p. 123), I believe they are ordinary twelfth-century issues which have been cut down and re-silvered, for re-issue in Constantinople under the Latin emperors. The stamena of Isaac with an asterisk or quincunx on each side of the back of the throne are part of a stylistic group, within *BMC* Type 4, with the characteristic that the top of the throne is marked by a dotted line. This same detail can be seen on the "small" coins on plate XXXI, and can, I submit, be explained only on some such hypothesis as that put forward here. The coins of Alexius III illustrated on plate XXXII are of especial interest, since they help to localize the varieties into which *BMC* Type 4 has been divided (see p. 120 above) and to confirm the classification. Plate XXXII, 3 is an early coin of Group B; no. 4 is almost certainly of Group D1, although the double linear cross cannot be seen; no. 5 is of Group B, showing the degenerated pattern of 9 dots; no. 6 (with elaborate pendants) is of Group A; no. 7 is a good early coin of Group B; no. 8 is a characteristic example of Group A (note the pendants, and 4 dots on the chest of both emperor and saint); no. 9 is of Group B, rather like no. 3; nos. 10 and 11, to all appearances from the same die, are of Group A, and not unlike no. 6; 12 is another early coin of Group A, again with 4 dots on the chests; no. 13 is a scarce variant, for which, however, a close stylistic parallel can be found; and no. 17 is of Group A. These identifications rest on die-similarities with coins in a hoard from southern Serbia, which is to be published shortly. Thus, out of 13 coins chosen for illustration—not necessarily a representative selection, one must add—no fewer than 12 are of Groups A and B. The omission of the obverse inscription KERO HΘEI can be illustrated from coins of normal size.

The main part of the Istanbul hoard B of 1946 seems to be a traveller's hoard, in any case illustrative of the currency of north-western Asia Minor, and thus outside the scope of the present survey, except that the type showing Manuel holding a sword, which was prominent in the treasure, occurred in quantity at Corinth. The Istanbul and Troad hoards make its Asian localization clear; but what is its date? Gerasimov's attribution to Manuel of Thessaloniki of "Solun", nos. 33-34 seems to be contradicted by the Istanbul and Troad hoards. Should one, however, recognize two varieties of different module?—Ratto 2147 (wrongly described: it shows Christ on the obverse) corresponds with "Solun", nos. 35-39, of which there were 4 in the Logodash hoard. The whole question remains puzzling.

Cut coins. Condurachi mentions the discovery of cut stamena near Silistra,[15] and similar finds were made at Nesebŭr in 1952: halves and quarters were associatted with 7 whole coins of Manuel and Alexius.[16] A further provenance, also from north-eastern Bulgaria, is Sushina, near Kolarovgrad, where, in 1963, there were found 10 halves and 2 quarters, with one whole coin attributed to Alexius I.[17] It seems possible that these cut coins reflect a need for petty currency in the Black Sea coastlands in the middle years of the thirteeth century.

Frankish petty coins at Sparta. The early excavations at Sparta[18] produced 6 specimens of Schl. XII, 7, the CORINTUM type. The date proposed for them above. (p. 227) fits in satisfactorily, for what it is worth, with the return of Mistra toByzantine rule (pp. 219f.).

Palaeologan gold. Laurent has made the very interesting submission that the financial effort by Michael VIII to help the Sicilian rising against Charles of Anjou led to a new debasement of the hyperperon, which, having already lost a carat on a similar occasion in 1269-70, was only 14 carats fine at the accession of Andronicus II (1282). The two devaluations brought an imbalance in the Byzantine currency, and drove Venice to create, in 1284, the ducat, "less to compete with the coins of Genoa and Florence than to provide for the Veneto-Byzantine commerce, which was still active, a stable value of estimation".[19]

The secret-marks of 5 coins of Andronicus II with Michael IX from a hoard found in the region of Varna are published by Gerasimov: two specimens with $\overset{*}{K} \overset{*}{N}$, and one each with B ꝗ, M Γ, and $\frac{C\ \Pi}{K\ N}$ A hoard with coins of the same rulers came to light at Taya in 1962.[20]

Frankish petty coinage in Bulgaria. A curious new chapter of monetary history is revealed by the discovery of Frankish deniers tournois in Bulgaria. Excavations of a medieval church at Kŭrdzhali, in the eastern Rhodope, produced coins of Athens of Guillaume I and Guy II (14 specimens), of Achaia, mostly fourteenth-century issues (14), and of Chios, *ca.* 1320-29 (1).[21] Chiote coins were so scarce in the currency of the mainland[22] that the presence of one among thirty here is enough to raise the question whether the Kŭrdzhali finds are not a sample of the currency of Phocaea and Chios rather than of Greece. They may be connected in some way with the diplomatic or commercial enterprises of the Zaccaria.[23]

The petty coinage of John II of Epirus (1323-35) has been found at Tŭrnovo and other Bulgarian centres. Gerasimov has published a study of the finds, with a map showing their distribution.[24]

Countermarked groši of Stefan Dušan. Coins from a find at Dobrogled, near Varna, in 1927 are published by Kuzev. They probably constitute another traveller's hoard.[25]

Notes

1 R. L. Scranton and E. S. Ramage, "Investigations at Kenchreai, 1963", *Hesperia* xxxiii (1964), 134-45.

2 A. M. Woodward, "The Coins", in R. M. Dawkins (editor), *The Sanctuary of Artemis Orthia at Sparta*, London, 1929, pp. 393-98.

3 Gerasimov, "Monetni Sŭkrovishta, 1960-61".

4 Lishev, *Paritsa*, p. 82.

5 T. Ivanov, "Razkopki v kastela Jatrum prez 1962 g.", *Arkheologiya* v /4 (1963), 9-18.

6 I. Yurukova, "Moneti i pechati ot Pernishkata krepost", *Arkheologiya* iv /4 (1962), 39-45; Gerasimov, "Monetni Sŭkrovishta, 1962-63".

7 Woodward, *op. cit.*

8 Kh. Dzhambov, "Krepostta 'Khisarlŭka' krai Zlatovrŭk", *Godishnik na Narod. Arkh. Muzey Plovdiv*, iv (1960), 188-90.

9 Gerasimov, "Monetni Sŭkrovishta, 1962-63", *IAI* xxvii (1964), 237-48.

10 *Ibid.*

11 *Ibid.*

12 *Ibid.*There are a few more incompletely-recorded hoards omitted from the text, among which should perhaps have been mentioned Tyurkmen 1952, 24 stamena of which "11 were of Manuel" (Tsonchev in *Godishnik na Narod. Arkh. Muzey Plovdiv* iv) and Preslav (Gospodinov in *IBAI*)

13 A. R. Bellinger, "Three more hoards of Byzantine copper coins", *Museum Notes* xi (1964), 207-26.

14 Bellinger, "Three Hoards".

15 E. Condurachi, "Monnaies Byzantines coupées", *Cronica Numismatica si Arheologica* Year 15, nos. 117-18 (1940), 227-29, at note 4. Condurachi mentions also a hoard from the Argolid which I have not been able to locate. The coins he describes from the Balş hoard appear to be of Alexius III rather than Alexius I or John II.

16 Gerasimov, "Kolektivni Nakhodki, 1951-54".

17 Gerasimov, "Monetni Sŭkrovishta, 1962-63".

18 Woodward, op. *cit.*

19 V. Laurent, "Les Vêpres siciliennes et la dévaluation de l'hyperpère", Χαριστήριον εἰς 'Αναστάσιον Κ. 'Ορλάνδον I, Athens, 1964, 36-45.

20 Gerasimov, "Monetni Sŭkrovishta, 1962-63".

21 *Ibid.*

22 See Metcalf, *"Deniers Tournois* in Frankish Greece" (and note Hoard M).

23 See W. Miller, *Essays on the Latin Orient*, Cambridge, 1921, pp. 287ff.

24 T. D. Gerasimov, "Moneti na frankskiya vladetel Ioan II Orsini, namereni v Tŭrnovo", in the *Izvestiya* of the Tŭrnovo museum (not accessible to me at the time of writing).

25 A. Kuzev, "Groshove na Stefan Dushan s kontramarki", *Arkheologiya* iii /2 (1961), 14-17.

INDEX I

COIN FINDS FROM THE BALKANS SOUTH OF THE RIVERS DANUBE AND DRAVA

Orthography. The modern local forms of place-names have been used, with the exception of a few names that have a well-established form in the English language, e.g. Corinth. Bulgarian names have been revised in accordance with the orthographic reform of 1945.

Transliteration. Serbian place-names have been transliterated into the official Croatian form. Greek and Bulgarian names have been transliterated as recommended by the Permanent Committee on Geographical Names for British Official Use.

Alphabetization. The transliterated names have been arranged in accordance with the English alphabet, all diacritical marks being ignored for the purpose of the arrangement.

Entries. Each entry is a hoard or conjectured hoard except where stated other-wise. Coin finds outside the scope of the index are listed under "Hoards" or «Site-finds»in Index II.

Belene, 56
Belgrade, *see* Beograd
Belitsa, 105, 113
Belogradchik, 248
Belovo, 214, 255-56
Beograd (Dragutin), 211
Beograd (Seated King), 213
Beograd (Helmet), 213, 256
Beograd, stray find, 211
Bihać, stray finds, 159, 161, 215
Bijeljina, stray finds, 143, 161, 199, 215-17
Bijelo Brdo, grave-finds, 143, 146
Bilišane, 193
Biševo, 48f.
Bitola, 201
Bjelovar, stray find, 153, 161
Black Sea coasts, stray finds, 25
Blato, 49
Bobovišće (Brač), 49, 185
Boljevci, stray finds, 143, 145
Bosanska Rača, 143, 199, 214, 217, 255-58
Bosnia, stray finds, 149, 155, 159, 200, 215
Brač, *see* Bobovišće
Bratimir, 35
Brauron, 118, 121f., 252
Brestovo, 113
Brezovica, 178
Bribir, 193
Bua, *see* Čiovo
Bukovića, 161, 162
Bulgaria, stray find?, 29
Bŭlgarski Izvor, 242, 248
Butrinto, site-finds, 194
Byaga, 102, 104, 105, 242, 267
Byala, 90
Byala Cherkva, 241, 243, 245

Čačak, 199
Čakovac, stray find, 159, 161
Čanak, stray find, 191
Canlia, stray find, 46
Caparelli, *see* Kasarelli
Celje, 152, 161, 176f.
Celje, stray find, 177, 194
Cernavoda, stray finds, 241
Cherkovo, 116

Chomatovski, 117
Chuprene, 117
Čiovo, see Slatine
Comuna 23 August, 53
Constanta, 22f., 46
Constanta, stray finds, 53
Copuzu, 95
Corinth 1905, 251
Corinth 1907 (Alexius I), 83
Corinth 1907 (Traveller's), 83, 250
Corinth 1914, 83
Corinth 1925 (gold), 126, 229
Corinth 1925 (scyphate bronze), 91
Corinth 1928 (oriental), 251
Corinth 1929 (Rex Regnantium D), 51
Corinth May 1932, 98, 103, 110
Corinth February 1934, 85, 87
Corinth May 1934 ("Crusader's"), 126, 228-31
Corinth 1934 (Romanus I), 37f.
Corinth February 1937, 98, 103, 109f.
Corinth November 1937, 33, 35, 98, 103, 109f.
Corinth May 1938, 99ff.
Corinth 1959, 53-54, 85
Corinth 1960, 110
Corinth 1960 (scyphate bronze), 96, 119, 123
Corinth (Romanus I), 38
Corinth, site finds from the American excavations, 5, 18, 20, 25, 27, 29-30, 33, 35, 36f., 40, 41ff., 54, 83, 85, 87-88, 96, 98, 104, 108f., 185, 223-25, 230, 231
Corinth (at or near), stray find, 21
Čović, stray find, 191
Crikvenica, 187
Crikvenica, stray find, 161

Dalj, stray find, 141, 143
Dalmatia, stray finds, 191
Dalmatia, central, *see* Imoski
Debelets, 90
Dečja vas, 171f.
Delos, stray find, 26
Delphi 1894 B, 222, 235
Delphi 1894 Γ, 222, 235
Delphi 1894 Δ, 222, 235

GENERAL INDEX

Chronological indications follow V. Grumel, *La Chronologie* (Bibliothèque Byzantine: Traités d'Etudes Byzantines, vol. I), Paris, 1958.

A

B

Δ

THEOPHILUS

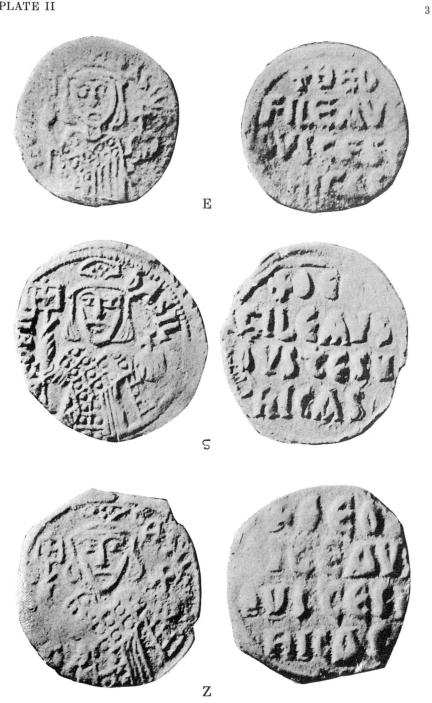

PLATE II

3

E

Ϛ

Z

THEOPHILUS

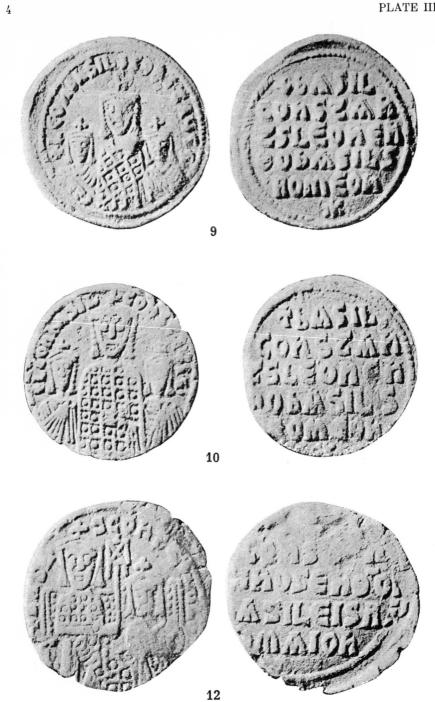

9

10

12

BASIL I

PLATE IV

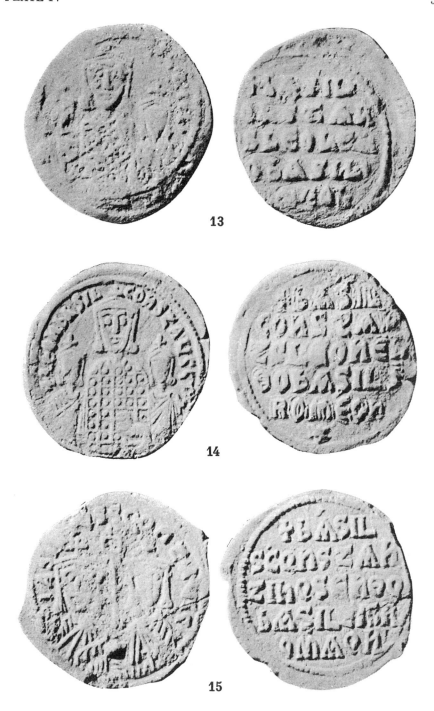

13

14

15

BASIL I

1

2

3

PLATE VI 7

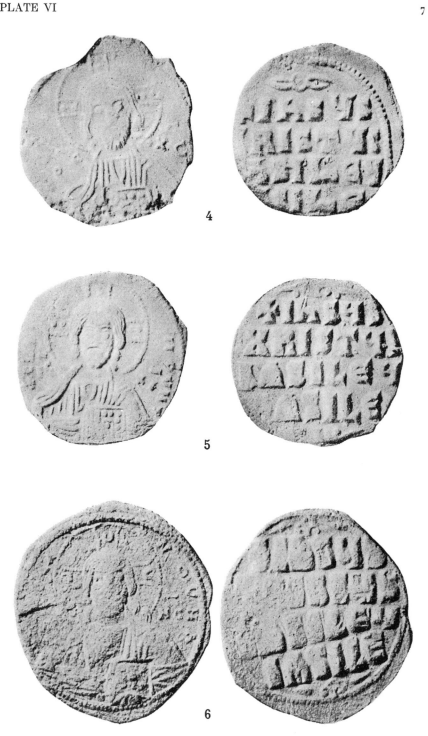

4

5

6

PLATE VII

1

2

3

PLATE VIII

9

4

5

6

7

1

2

3

4

PLATE X

5

6

7

8

1   2   3

4

5

PLATE XII
13

1

2

3

PLATE XIV   15

5

6

12

PLATE XV

1

2

3

4